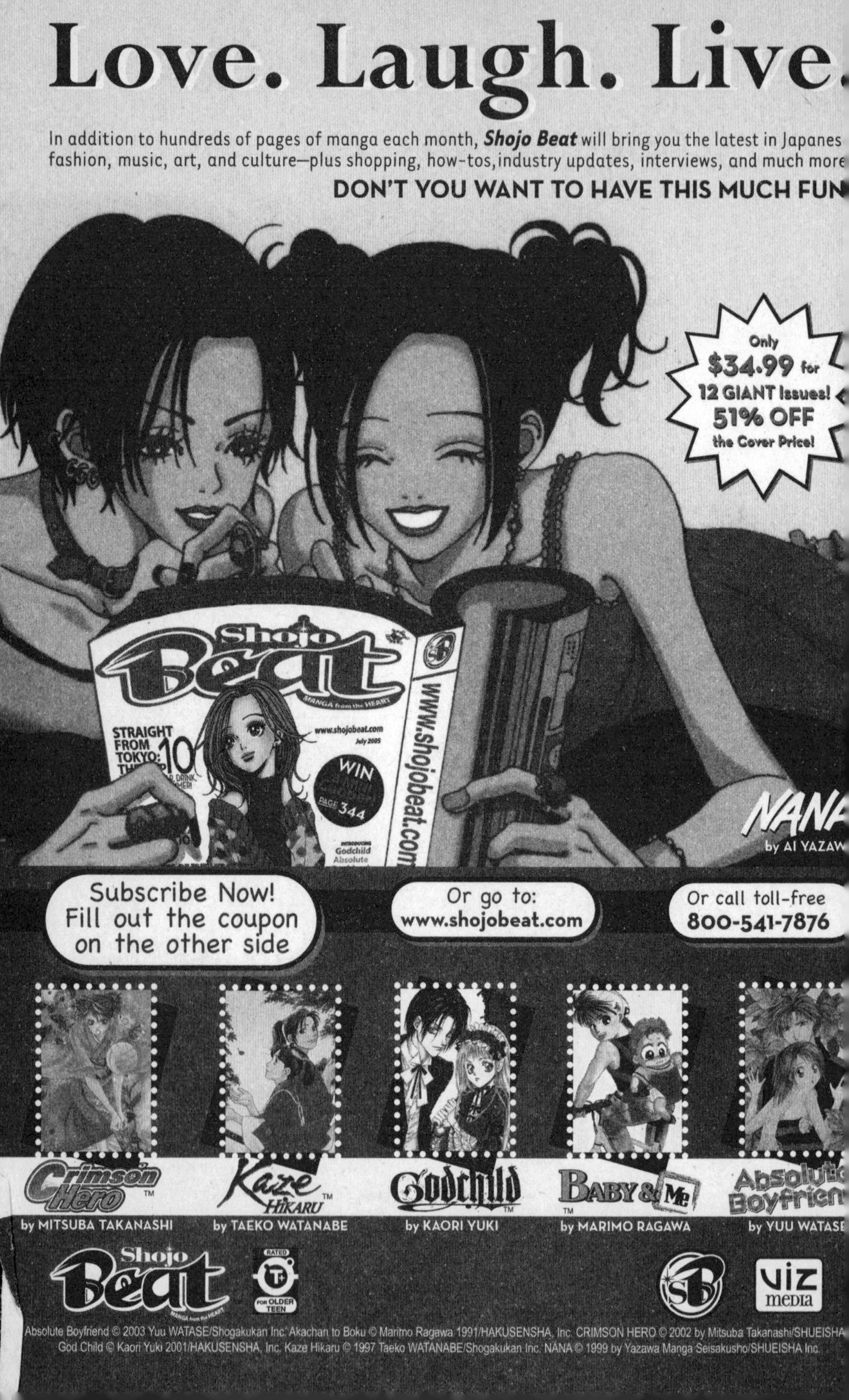
Love. Laugh. Live.
In addition to hundreds of pages of manga each month, Shojo Beat will bring you the latest in Japanes
fashion, music, art, and culture—plus shopping, how-tos, industry updates, interviews, and much more
DON'T YOU WANT TO HAVE THIS MUCH FUN
Only $34.99 for 12 GIANT Issues! 51% OFF the Cover Price!
Shojo Beat
MANGA from the HEART
www.shojobeat.com
July 2005
STRAIGHT FROM TOKYO: 10
WIN
PAGE 344
Godchild
Absolute
www.shojobeat.com
NANA
by AI YAZAW
Subscribe Now! Fill out the coupon on the other side
Or go to: www.shojobeat.com
Or call toll-free 800-541-7876
Crimson Hero
by MITSUBA TAKANASHI
Kaze Hikaru
by TAEKO WATANABE
Godchild
by KAORI YUKI
Baby & Me
by MARIMO RAGAWA
Absolute Boyfrien
by YUU WATASE
Shojo Beat
MANGA from the HEART
RATED T+ FOR OLDER TEEN
viz media
Absolute Boyfriend © 2003 Yuu WATASE/Shogakukan Inc. Akachan to Boku © Marimo Ragawa 1991/HAKUSENSHA, Inc. CRIMSON HERO © 2002 by Mitsuba Takanashi/SHUEISHA
God Child © Kaori Yuki 2001/HAKUSENSHA, Inc. Kaze Hikaru © 1997 Taeko WATANABE/Shogakukan Inc. NANA © 1999 by Yazawa Manga Seisakusho/SHUEISHA Inc.

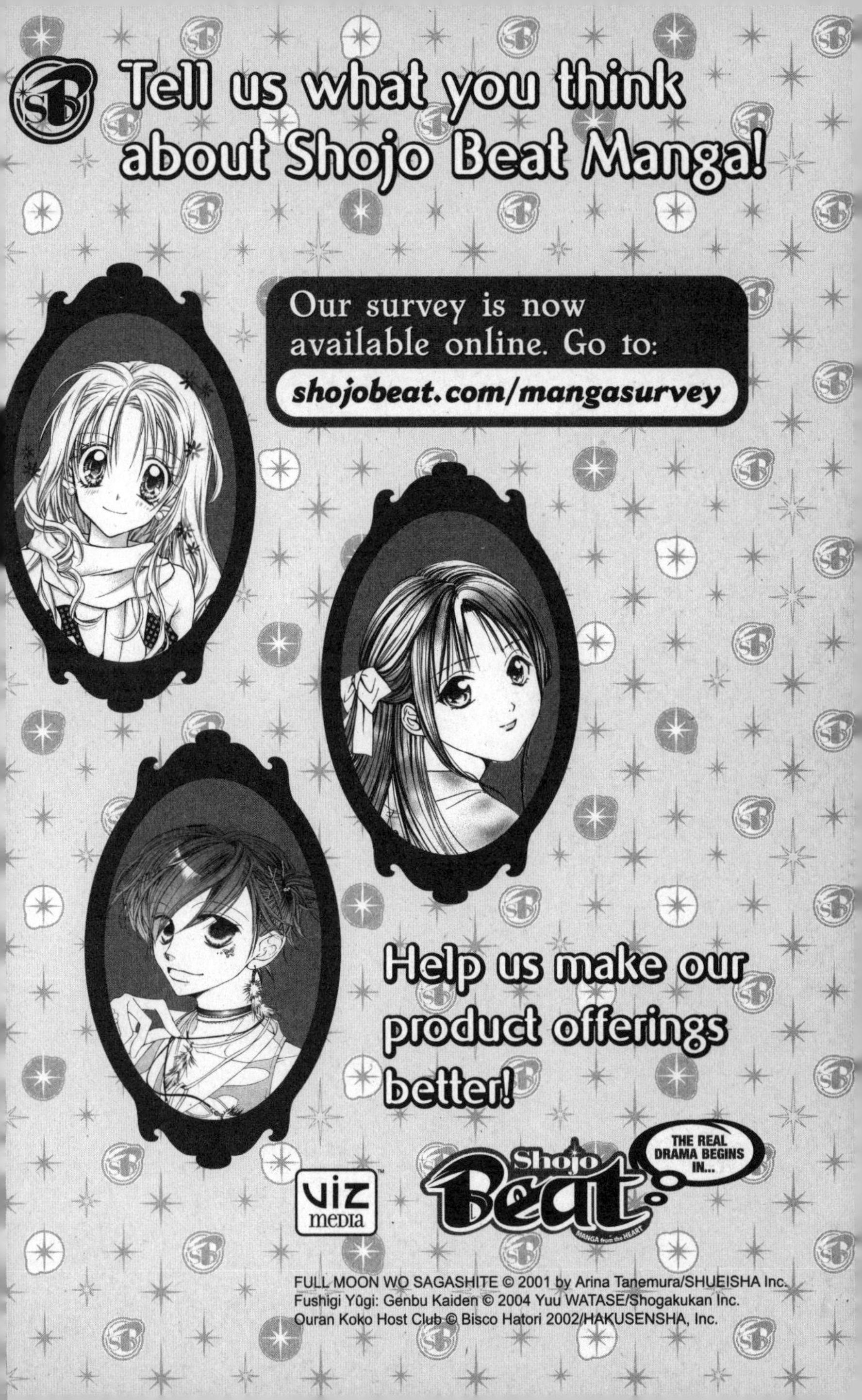
Tell us what you think about Shojo Beat Manga!
Our survey is now available online. Go to:
shojobeat.com/mangasurvey
Help us make our product offerings better!
viz media
THE REAL DRAMA BEGINS IN...
Shojo Beat
MANGA from the HEART
FULL MOON WO SAGASHITE © 2001 by Arina Tanemura/SHUEISHA Inc.
Fushigi Yûgi: Genbu Kaiden © 2004 Yuu WATASE/Shogakukan Inc.
Ouran Koko Host Club © Bisco Hatori 2002/HAKUSENSHA, Inc.

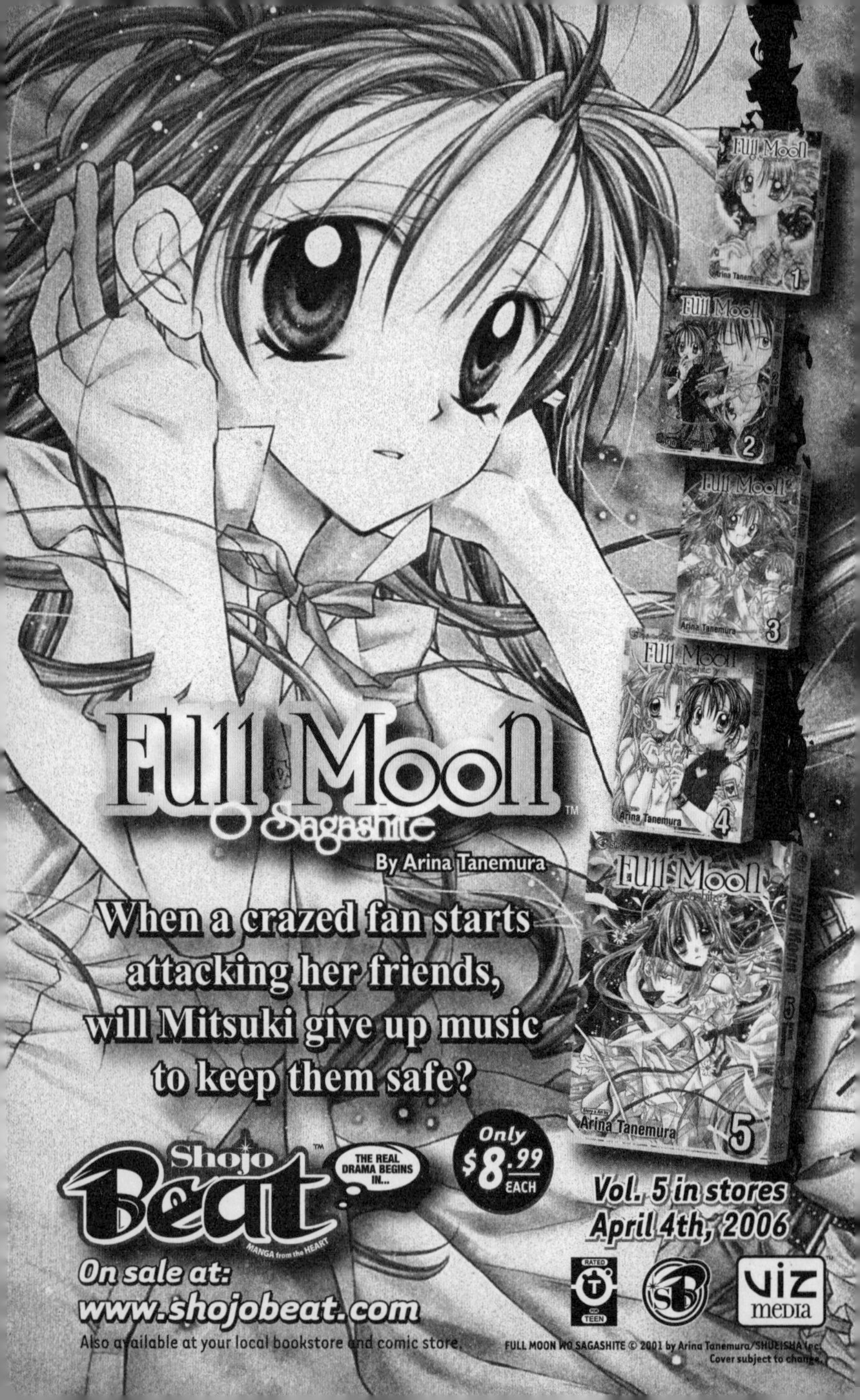

CRIMSON HERO

VOL. 2
The Shojo Beat Manga Edition

This manga volume contains material that was originally published in English in
Shojo Beat magazine, #5–8.

STORY AND ART BY
MITSUBA TAKANASHI

Translation & English Adaptation/Naoko Amemiya
Touch-up Art & Lettering/Mark Griffin
Design/Courtney Utt
Editor/Nancy Thistlethwaite

Managing Editor/Megan Bates
Director of Production/Noboru Watanabe
Vice President of Publishing/Alvin Lu
Vice President & Editor in Chief/Yumi Hoashi
Sr. Director of Acquisitions/Rika Inouye
Vice President of Sales & Marketing/Liza Coppola
Publisher/Hyoe Narita

CRIMSON HERO © 2002 by Mitsuba Takanashi
All rights reserved. First published in Japan in 2002 by SHUEISHA Inc., Tokyo. English
translation rights in the United States of America and Canada arranged by SHUEISHA Inc.
Some scenes have been modified from the original Japanese edition. The stories,
characters and incidents mentioned in this publication are entirely fictional.

The ASICS word and logo are trademarks owned by ASICS America Corporation.

Printed in Canada

Published by VIZ Media, LLC
P.O. Box 77010
San Francisco, CA 94107

Shojo Beat Manga Edition
10 9 8 7 6 5 4 3 2 1
First printing, April 2006

www.viz.com   store.viz.com

♥This manga has lots of nameless side characters. Some of them have personalities that spring forth the moment I first draw them. Take the manager-type guy with glasses in the boys' volleyball club. He's only in a few panels, yet he seems irresponsible, like he never thinks about anything. And then there are those girls who just pass by. I amuse myself thinking about how this girl here is the "ko-gal" type, and that one there has her own individual style, all the while telling myself that nobody's really going to look anyway.

—Mitsuba Takanashi, 2003

Mitsuba Takanashi debuted her first short story, *Mou Koi Nante Shinai* (Never Fall in Love Again), in 1992 in *Bessatsu Margaret* magazine and now has several major titles under her belt.

Born in the Shimane Prefecture of Japan, Takanashi now lives in Tokyo, where she enjoys taking walks, watching videos, shopping, and going to the hair salon. Takanashi has a soft spot for the Japanese pop acts Yellow Monkey and Hide, and is good at playing ping-pong.

Shojo Beat

Story & Art by
MITSUBA TAKANASHI

CONTENTS

STORY THUS FAR

Nobara Sumiyoshi is a first-year high school student who lives and breathes for her one fierce passion, volleyball. She's the eldest daughter and successor to Seiryu, the high-class ryotei restaurant that her family runs, but she enrolled in Crimson Fields High School because she wanted to play volleyball. Little did she know that her own mother had quietly pulled some strings to get rid of the girls' volleyball club...!

After a fight with her mother, Nobara ran away from home and ended up at Crimson Field Dorm, the dorm reserved for volleyball scholarship students. She became the live-in dorm mother, cooking and cleaning for Haibuki and the other boys—each with his own idiosyncrasies. With no experience doing housework, clumsy Nobara kept botching up things, injuring Yushin in the process!

At school, Nobara set out to gather members for the girls' volleyball club, but no one was interested. Why? It turns out that the boys' club has a long history of clashing with the girls' club. Someone even vandalized Nobara's flyer, writing "losers" on it. Furious, Nobara approached the boys' volleyball captain with a challenge...!

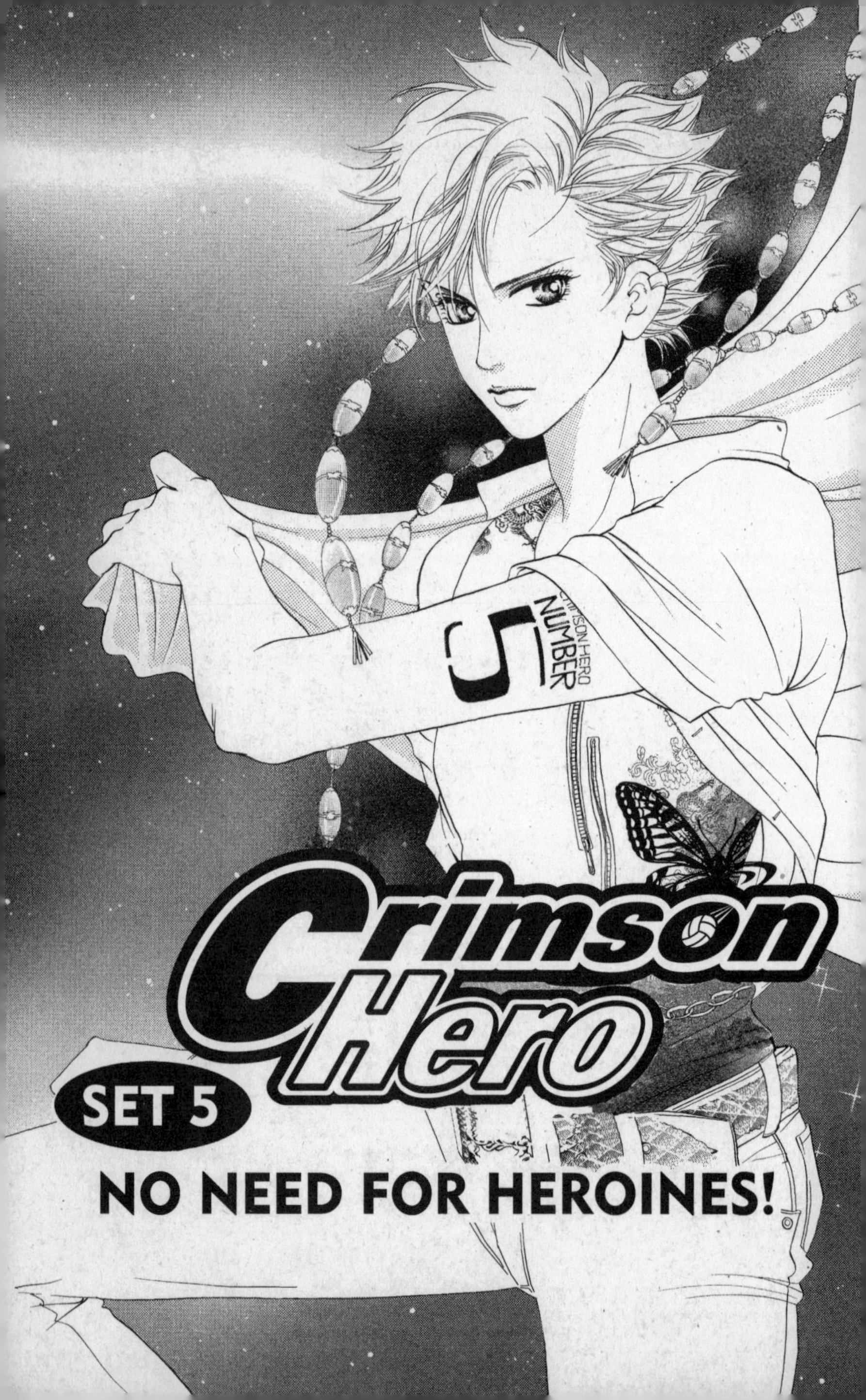
5
CRIMSON HERO
NUMBER
Crimson Hero
SET 5
NO NEED FOR HEROINES!

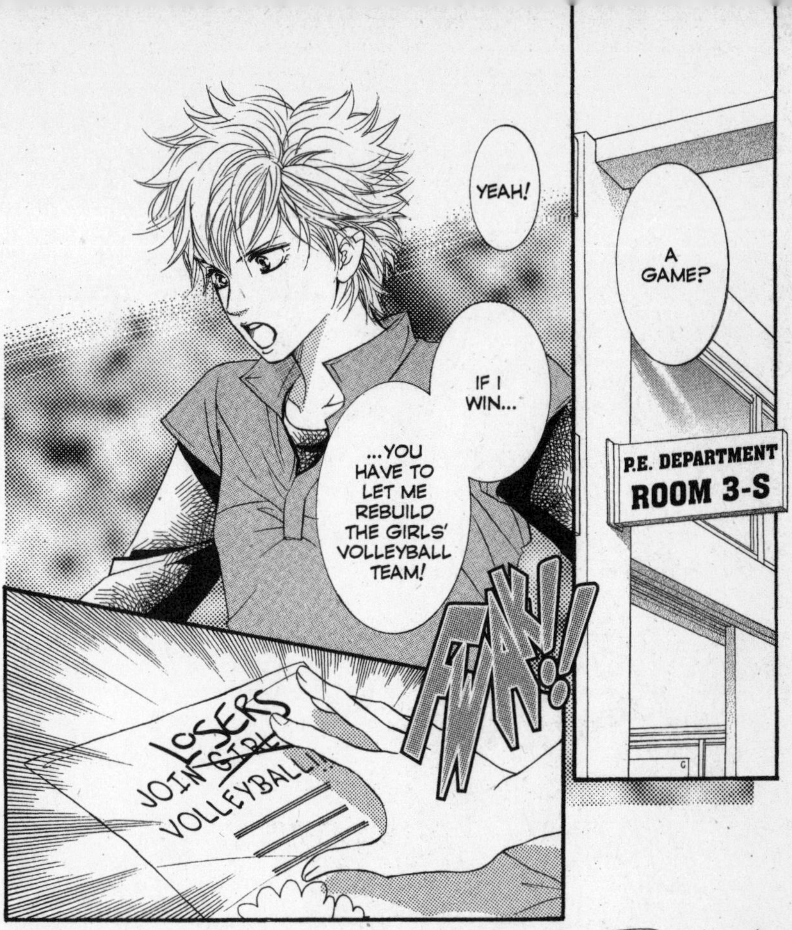
A GAME?
P.E. DEPARTMENT
ROOM 3-S
YEAH!
IF I WIN...
...YOU HAVE TO LET ME REBUILD THE GIRLS' VOLLEYBALL TEAM!
FWAK!!
LOSERS
JOIN ~~GIRL~~ VOLLEYBALL!!

THE MAKING OF CRIMSON HERO

Vol. 1

HELLO. THIS IS TAKANASHI, HERE IN VOLUME TWO. IT'S ALREADY BEEN 10 MONTHS SINCE THIS MANGA STARTED. THAT SEEMS BOTH LONG AND SHORT. I FEEL LIKE I'VE BEEN RUNNING THE WHOLE TIME, BUT IN TERMS OF THE STORY, IT'S ONLY JUST BEGUN. I ALWAYS WANT TO PUSH THE STORY FORWARD, BUT EACH TIME I RUN OUT OF ROOM SO QUICKLY!

NOW THEN, THE THING THAT'S STRIKINGLY DIFFERENT ABOUT THIS MANGA IS THE AMOUNT OF RESEARCH I DO. THIS WAS A WHILE BACK NOW, BUT I WENT TO RESEARCH SPRING HIGH SCHOOL VOLLEYBALL AND EVEN WENT TO YOYOGI STADIUM. I THOUGHT I'D GIVE YOU A LITTLE REPORT ABOUT THAT.

THURSDAY, MARCH 20TH, 2003. UNTIL THE DAY BEFORE, I'D BEEN PULLING ALL-NIGHTERS TO GET MY STORYBOARD IN. IN THE TAXI ON MY WAY THERE I GOT CARSICK. I ENDED UP WALKING THE REST OF THE WAY, INCONVENIENCING MY EDITOR RIGHT FROM THE GET-GO. BUT THE MOMENT I ENTERED THE ARENA I WAS MOVED BY THE ENTHUSIASM OF THE FANS AND THE PRESS FILLING THE STADIUM. IT WAS TOTALLY LIKE COKE'S SLOGAN IN JAPAN AT THE TIME, "MOVED BEYOND REASON."

AND I EVEN GOT A STAFF PASS FROM THE FOLKS AT FUJI TV SO I GOT TO WATCH FROM THE PRESS SEATS RIGHT NEXT TO THE COURTS!!!

WORKING ON STORYBOARD

GONNA RUN OUT OF ROOM AGAIN

WHAT ?!

STOP THE CAR. I'M DYING.

PALE-FACED

BY THE WAY, THE SPRING HIGH SCHOOL VOLLEYBALL TOURNAMENT IS, SIMPLY PUT, THE KOSHIEN OF VOLLEYBALL, KOSHIEN BEING THE POPULAR NATIONAL HIGH SCHOOL BASEBALL CHAMPIONSHIPS. HIGH SCHOOLERS FANTASIZE ABOUT THE ORANGE COURTS AT YOYOGI.

WOW! AMAZ-ING! ← SIMPLE BEYOND REASON!

BY THE WAY, THE GAMES HADN'T STARTED YET, LET ALONE THE OPENING CEREMONY.

WHAT A MAGICAL PIECE OF PAPER!

STAFF PASS MITSUBA TAKANASHI

WOW

TO BE CONTINUED...

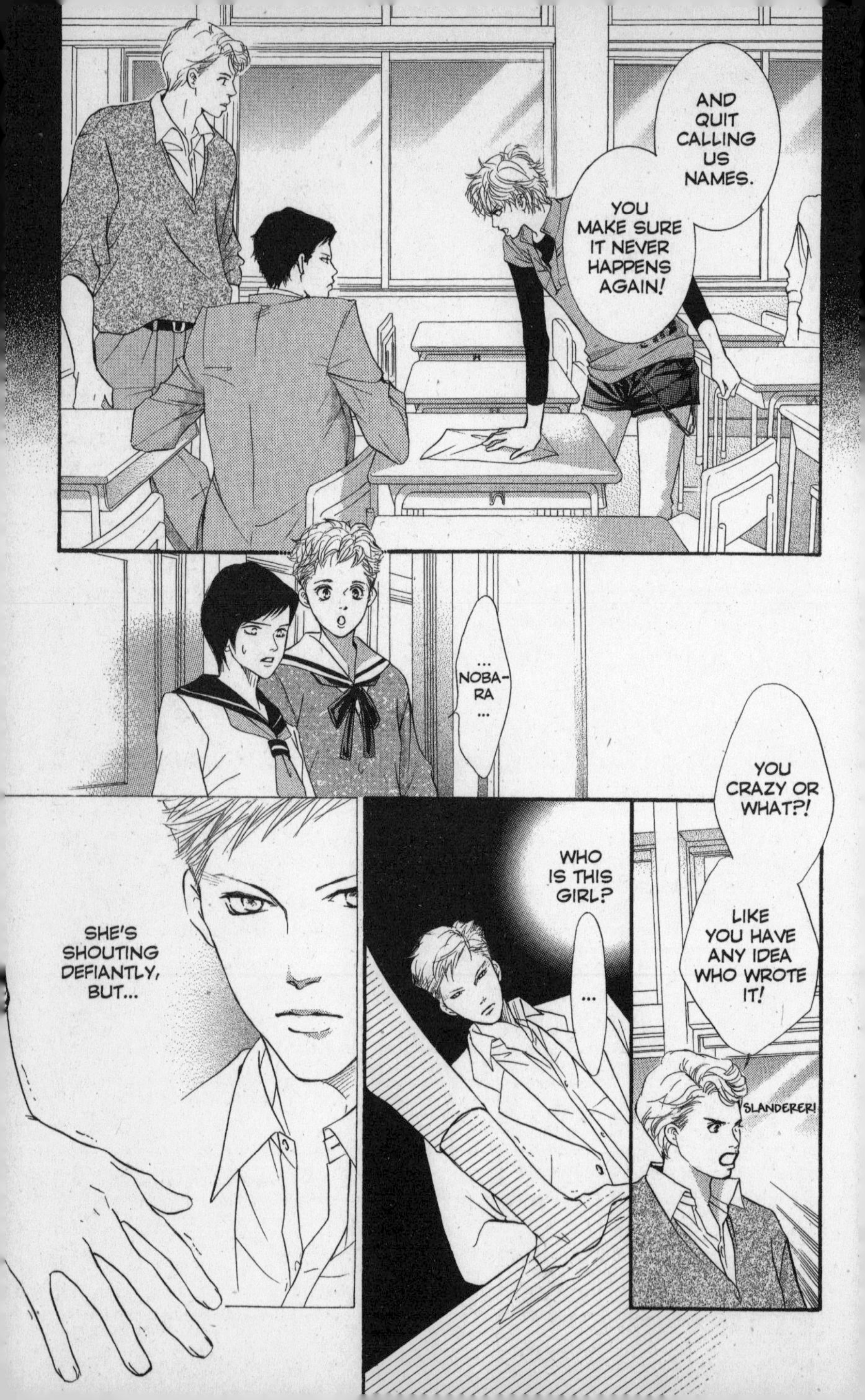
AND QUIT CALLING US NAMES.
YOU MAKE SURE IT NEVER HAPPENS AGAIN!
...NOBA-RA...
YOU CRAZY OR WHAT?!
LIKE YOU HAVE ANY IDEA WHO WROTE IT!
SLANDERER!
WHO IS THIS GIRL?
...
SHE'S SHOUTING DEFIANTLY, BUT...

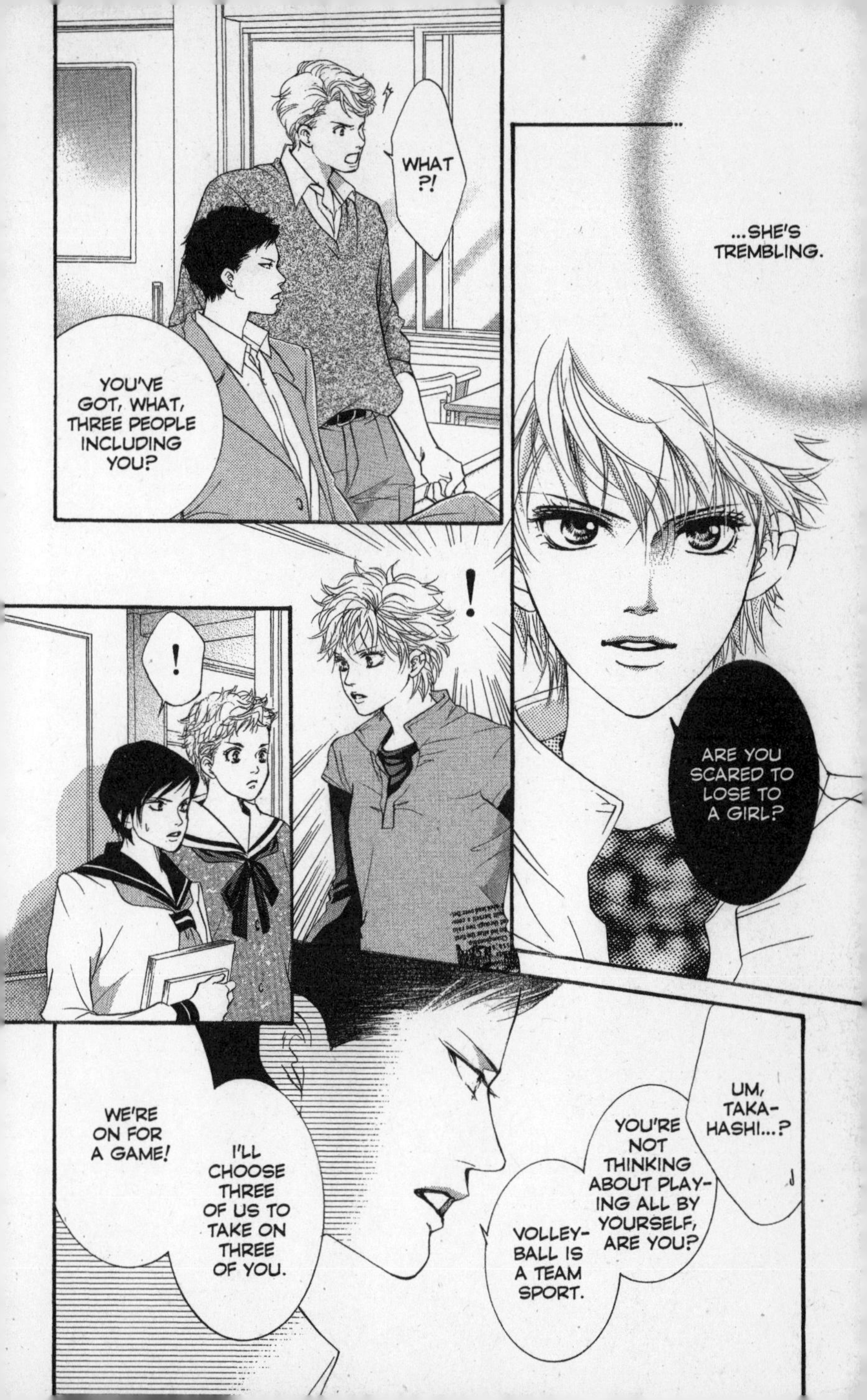
...SHE'S TREMBLING.
ARE YOU SCARED TO LOSE TO A GIRL?
WHAT ?!
YOU'VE GOT, WHAT, THREE PEOPLE INCLUDING YOU?
!
!
UM, TAKA-HASHI...?
YOU'RE NOT THINKING ABOUT PLAY-ING ALL BY YOURSELF, ARE YOU?
VOLLEY-BALL IS A TEAM SPORT.
WE'RE ON FOR A GAME!
I'LL CHOOSE THREE OF US TO TAKE ON THREE OF YOU.

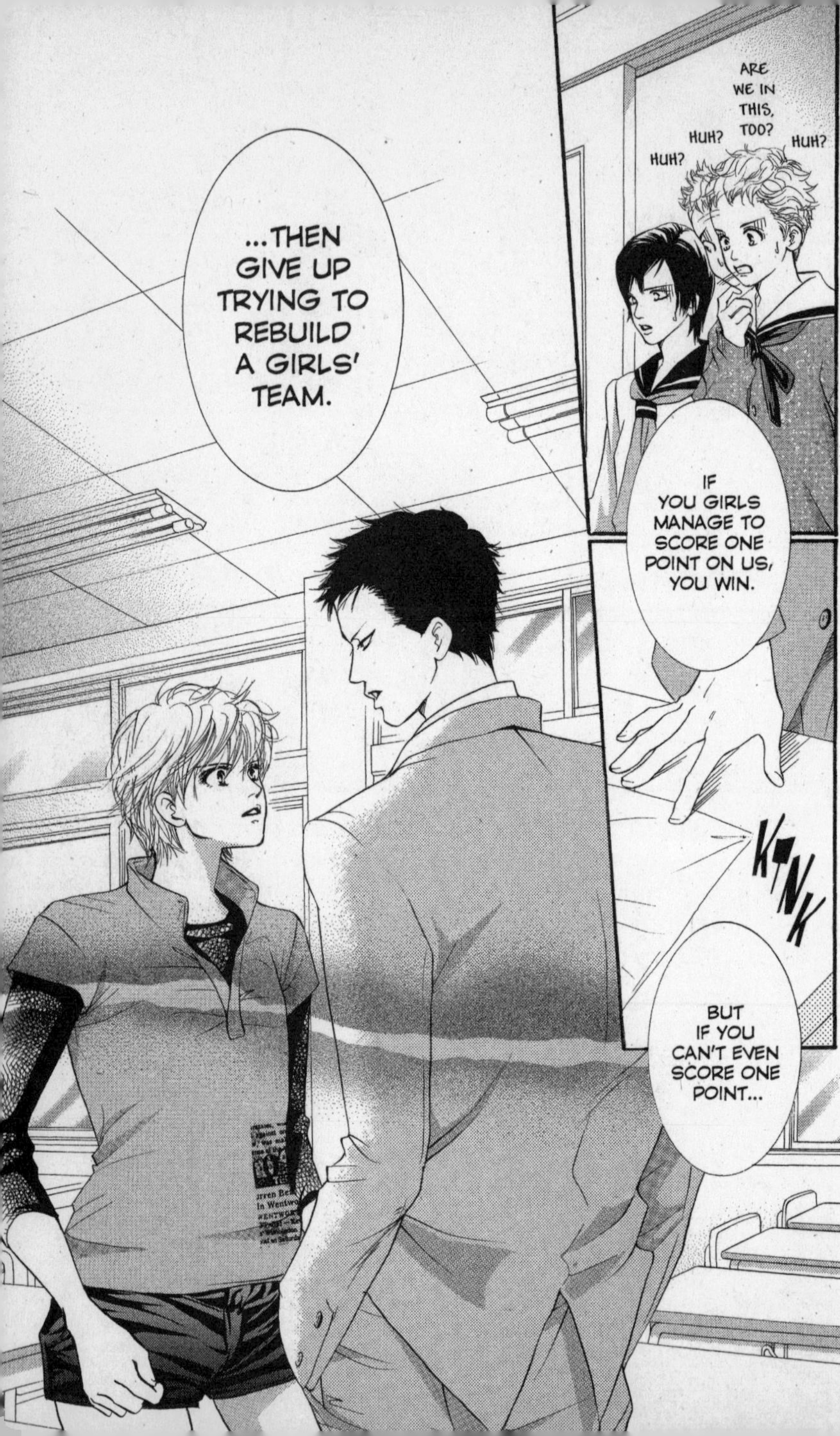
HUH?
ARE WE IN THIS, TOO?
HUH?
HUH?
IF YOU GIRLS MANAGE TO SCORE ONE POINT ON US, YOU WIN.
KINK
BUT IF YOU CAN'T EVEN SCORE ONE POINT...
...THEN GIVE UP TRYING TO REBUILD A GIRLS' TEAM.

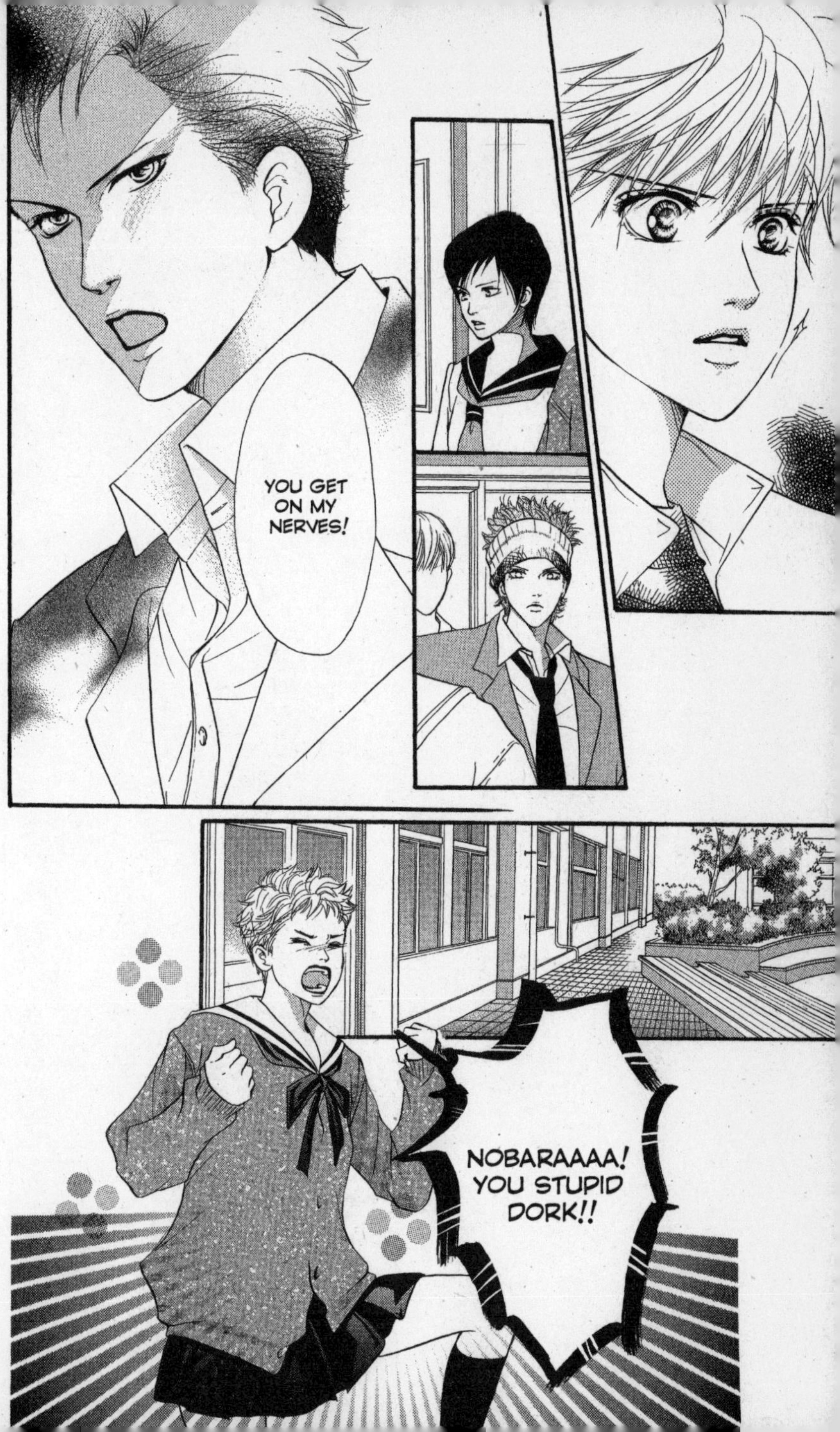
YOU GET ON MY NERVES!
NOBARAAAA! YOU STUPID DORK!!

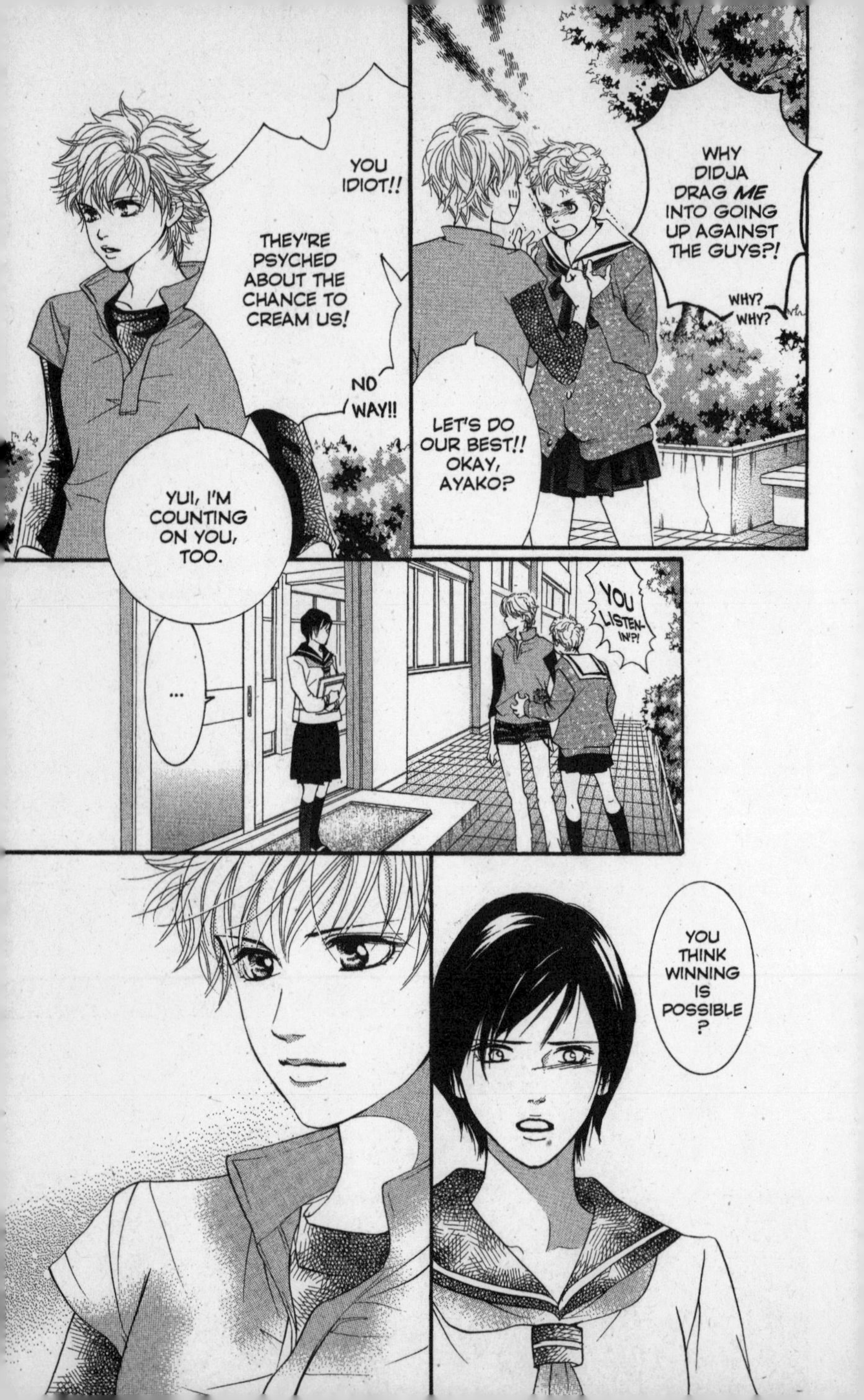
WHY DIDJA DRAG ME INTO GOING UP AGAINST THE GUYS?!
WHY? WHY?
LET'S DO OUR BEST!! OKAY, AYAKO?
YOU IDIOT!!
THEY'RE PSYCHED ABOUT THE CHANCE TO CREAM US!
NO WAY!!
YUI, I'M COUNTING ON YOU, TOO.
YOU LISTEN-IN?!
...
YOU THINK WINNING IS POSSIBLE?

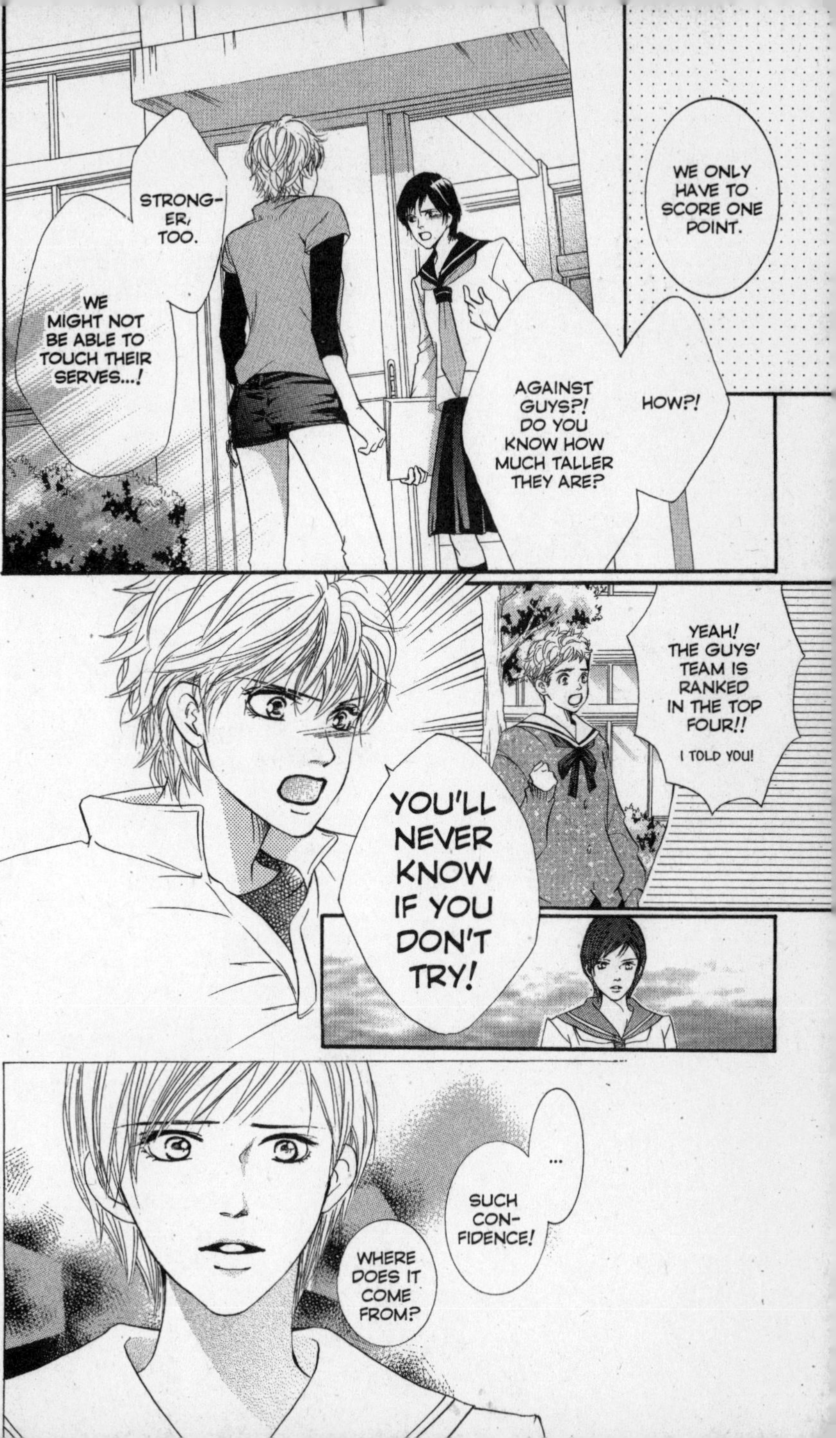
WE ONLY HAVE TO SCORE ONE POINT.
HOW?!
AGAINST GUYS?! DO YOU KNOW HOW MUCH TALLER THEY ARE?
STRONGER, TOO.
WE MIGHT NOT BE ABLE TO TOUCH THEIR SERVES...!
YEAH! THE GUYS' TEAM IS RANKED IN THE TOP FOUR!!
I TOLD YOU!
YOU'LL NEVER KNOW IF YOU DON'T TRY!
...
SUCH CONFIDENCE!
WHERE DOES IT COME FROM?

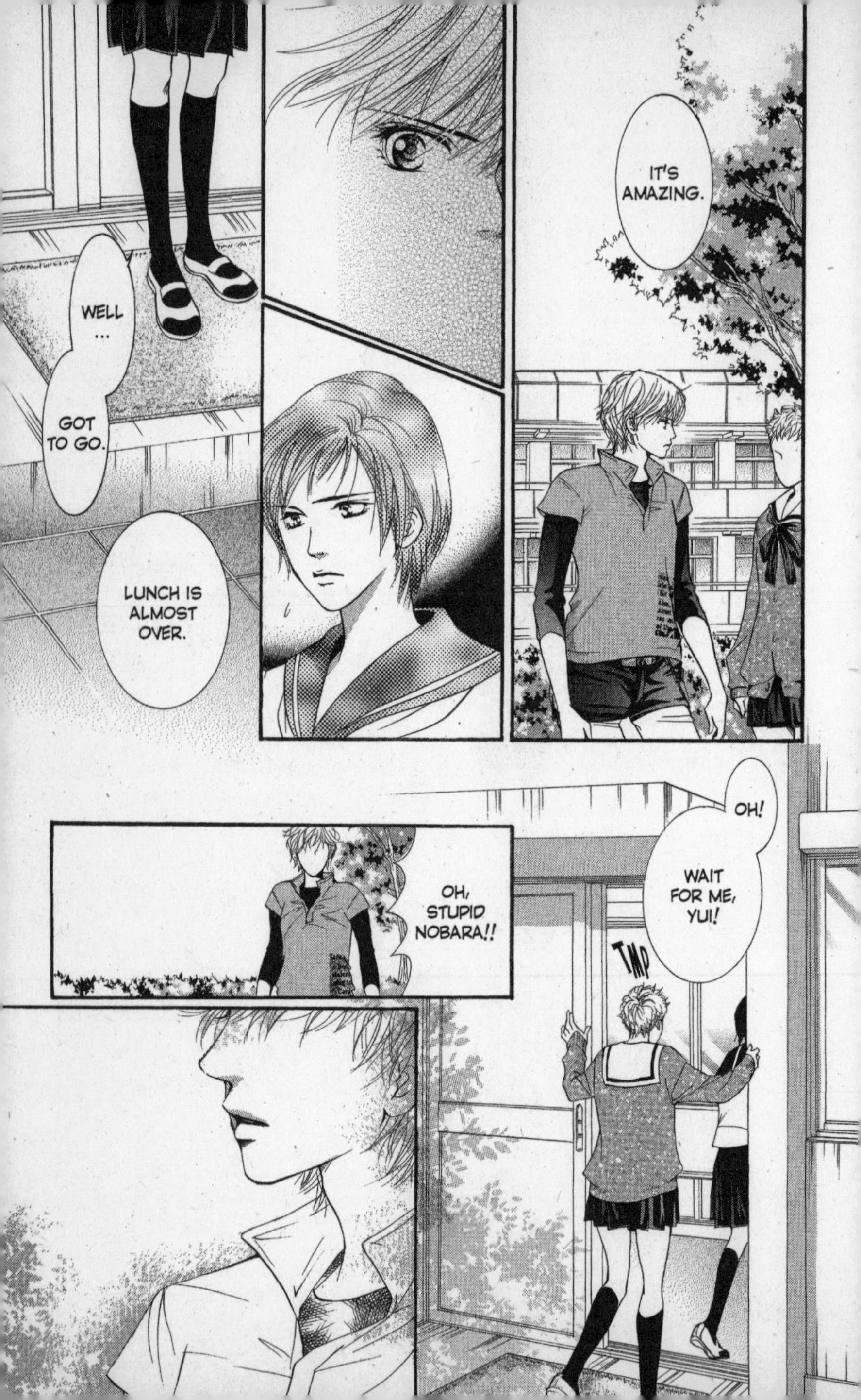
IT'S AMAZING.
WELL ...
GOT TO GO.
LUNCH IS ALMOST OVER.
OH!
WAIT FOR ME, YUI!
TMP
OH, STUPID NOBARA!!

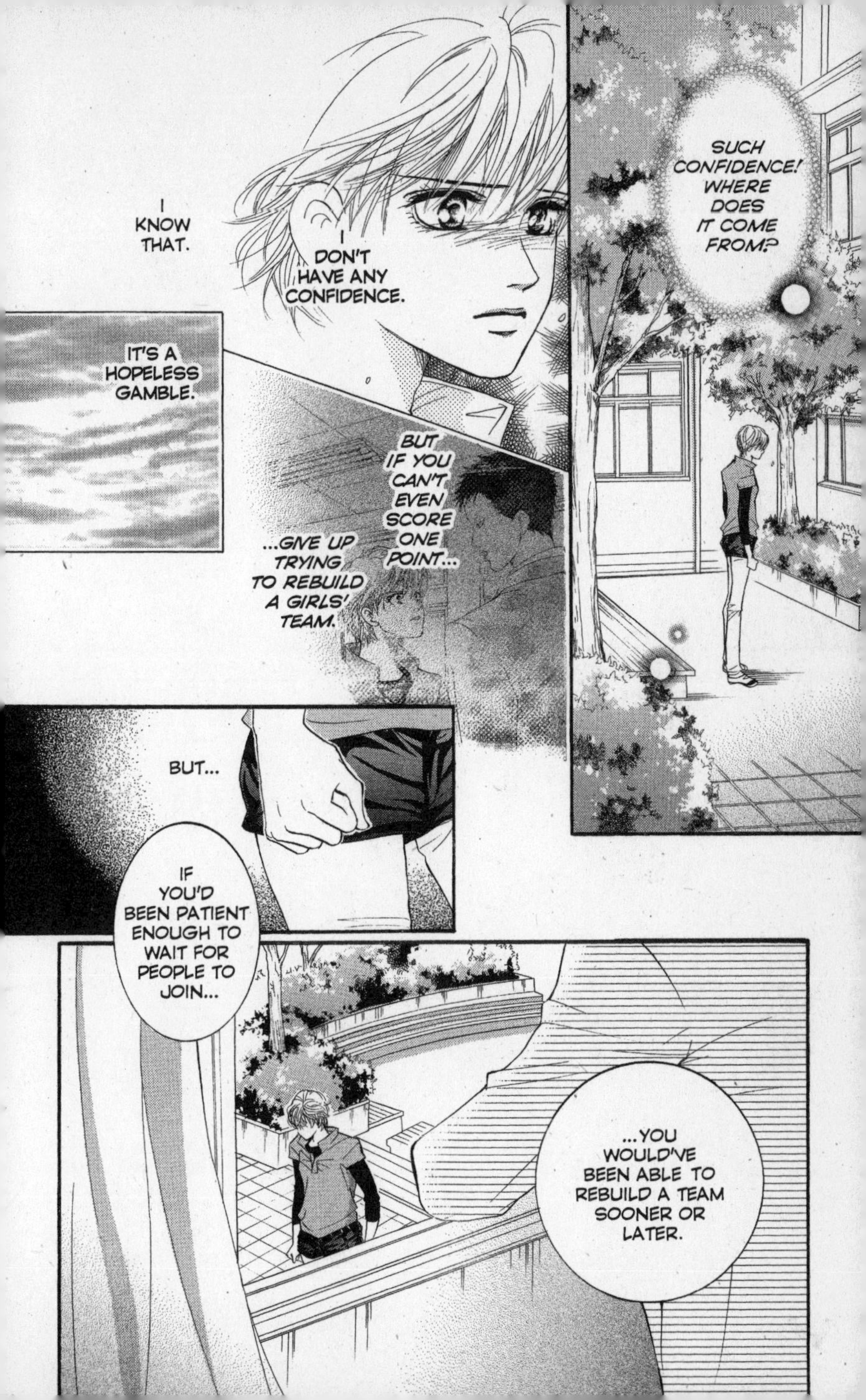
SUCH CONFIDENCE! WHERE DOES IT COME FROM?
I DON'T HAVE ANY CONFIDENCE.
I KNOW THAT.
IT'S A HOPELESS GAMBLE.
BUT IF YOU CAN'T EVEN SCORE ONE POINT...
...GIVE UP TRYING TO REBUILD A GIRLS' TEAM.
BUT...
IF YOU'D BEEN PATIENT ENOUGH TO WAIT FOR PEOPLE TO JOIN...
...YOU WOULD'VE BEEN ABLE TO REBUILD A TEAM SOONER OR LATER.

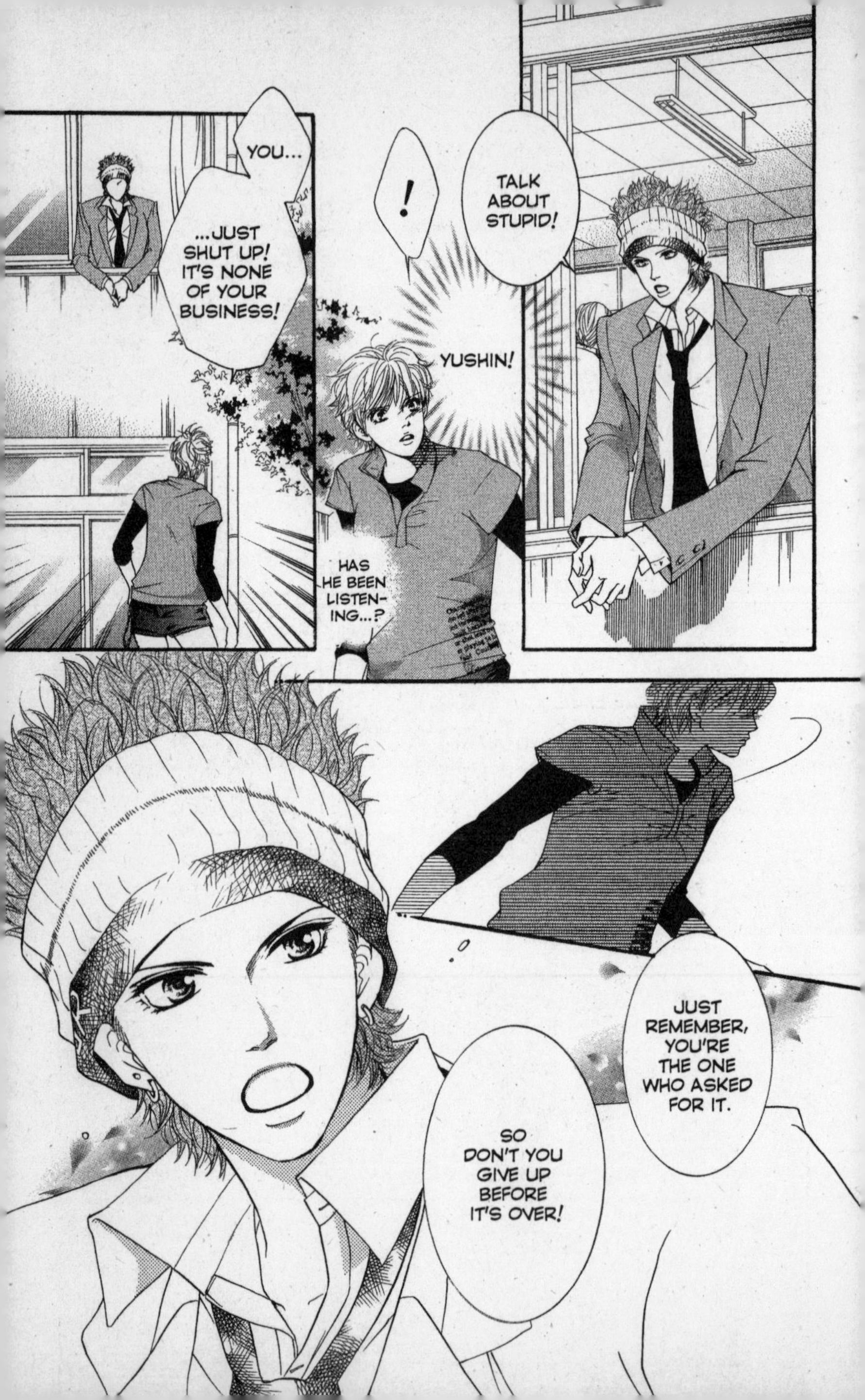
TALK ABOUT STUPID!
!
YUSHIN!
HAS HE BEEN LISTENING...?
YOU...
...JUST SHUT UP! IT'S NONE OF YOUR BUSINESS!
JUST REMEMBER, YOU'RE THE ONE WHO ASKED FOR IT.
SO DON'T YOU GIVE UP BEFORE IT'S OVER!

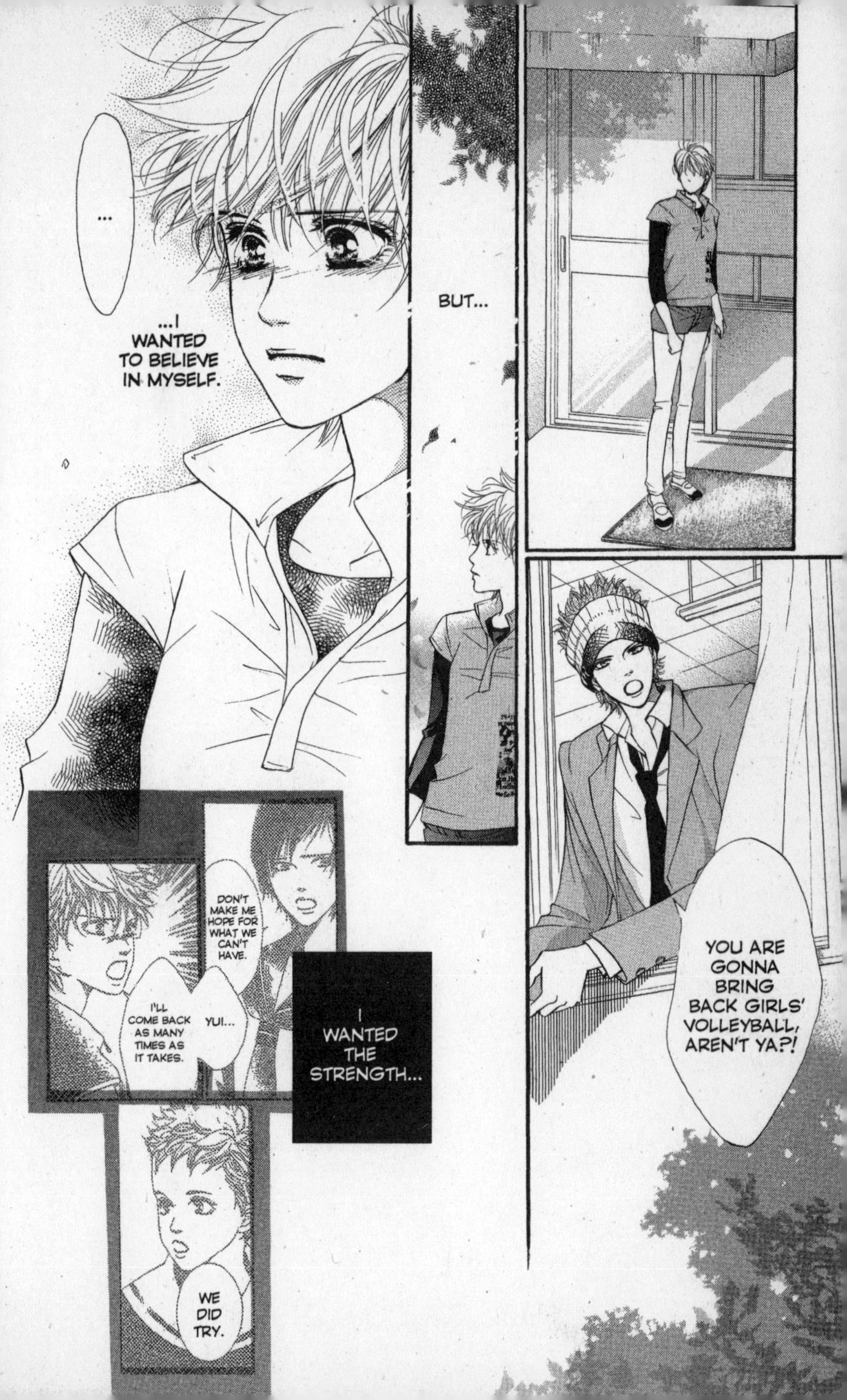
YOU ARE GONNA BRING BACK GIRLS' VOLLEYBALL, AREN'T YA?!
BUT...
...
...I WANTED TO BELIEVE IN MYSELF.
I WANTED THE STRENGTH...
DON'T MAKE ME HOPE FOR WHAT WE CAN'T HAVE.
YUI...
I'LL COME BACK AS MANY TIMES AS IT TAKES.
WE DID TRY.

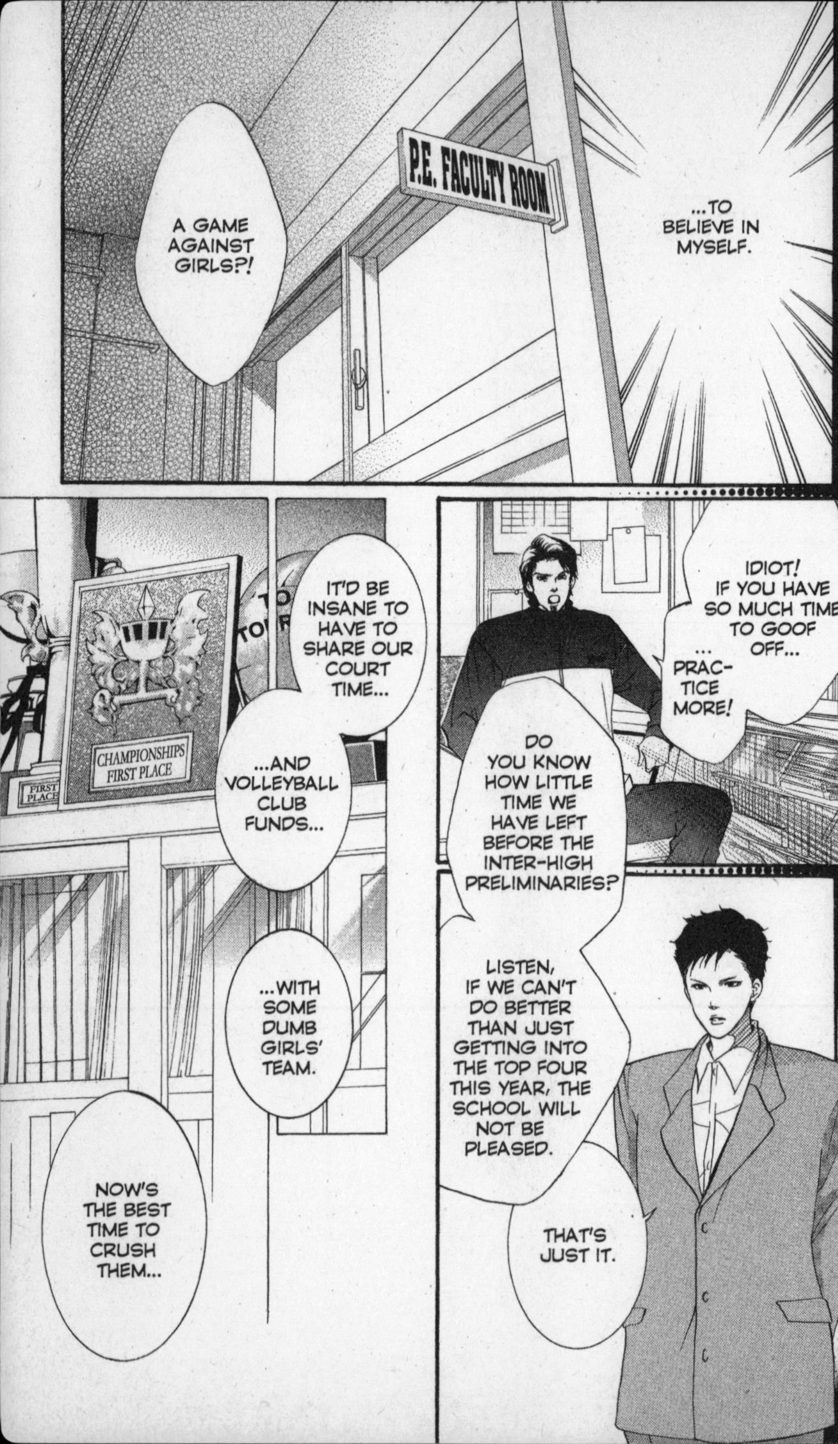
...TO BELIEVE IN MYSELF.
P.E. FACULTY ROOM
A GAME AGAINST GIRLS?!
IDIOT! IF YOU HAVE SO MUCH TIME TO GOOF OFF... ...PRACTICE MORE!
DO YOU KNOW HOW LITTLE TIME WE HAVE LEFT BEFORE THE INTER-HIGH PRELIMINARIES?
LISTEN, IF WE CAN'T DO BETTER THAN JUST GETTING INTO THE TOP FOUR THIS YEAR, THE SCHOOL WILL NOT BE PLEASED.
THAT'S JUST IT.
IT'D BE INSANE TO HAVE TO SHARE OUR COURT TIME...
CHAMPIONSHIPS FIRST PLACE
FIRST PLACE
...AND VOLLEYBALL CLUB FUNDS...
...WITH SOME DUMB GIRLS' TEAM.
NOW'S THE BEST TIME TO CRUSH THEM...

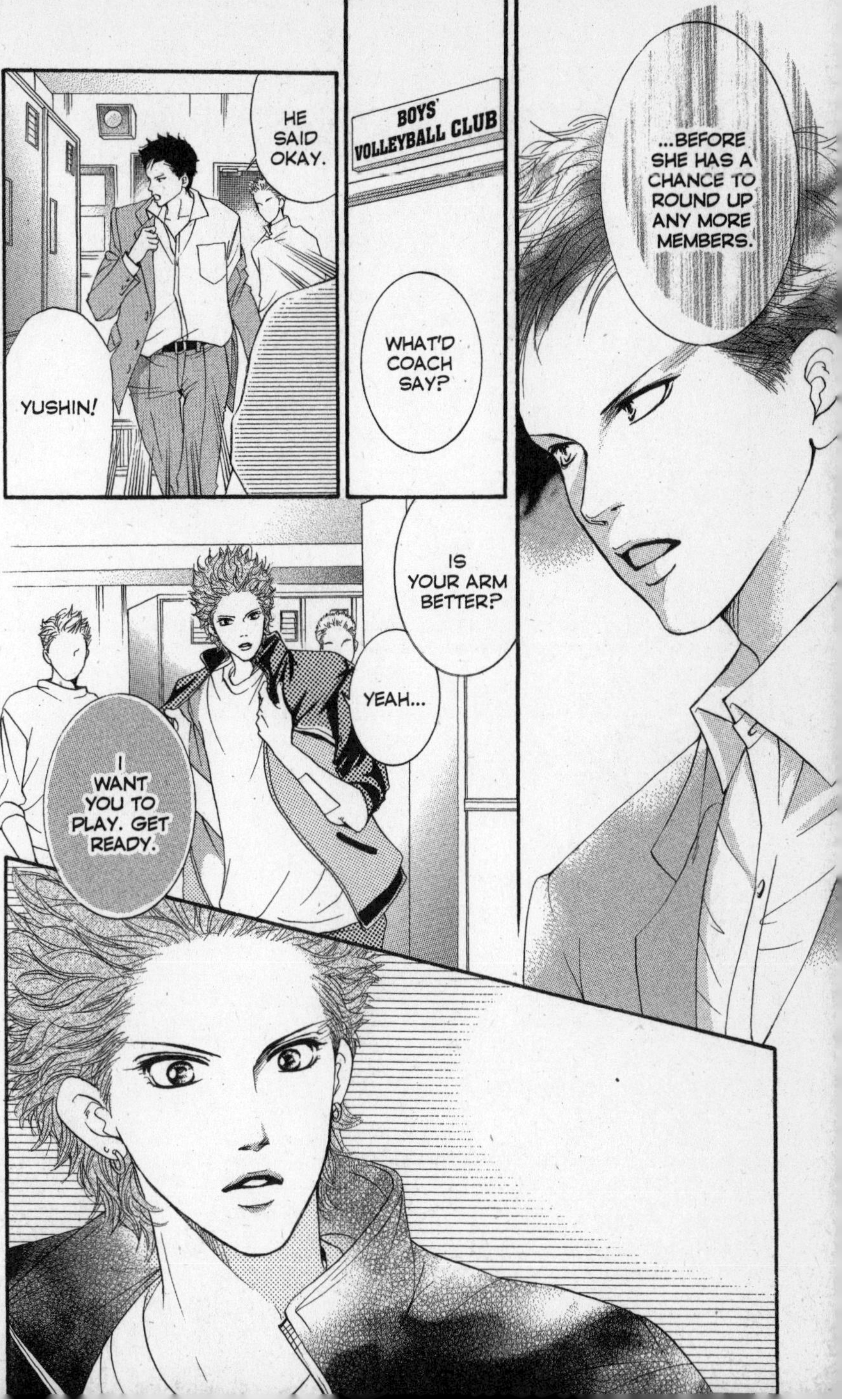
...BEFORE SHE HAS A CHANCE TO ROUND UP ANY MORE MEMBERS.
BOYS' VOLLEYBALL CLUB
WHAT'D COACH SAY?
HE SAID OKAY.
YUSHIN!
IS YOUR ARM BETTER?
YEAH...
I WANT YOU TO PLAY. GET READY.

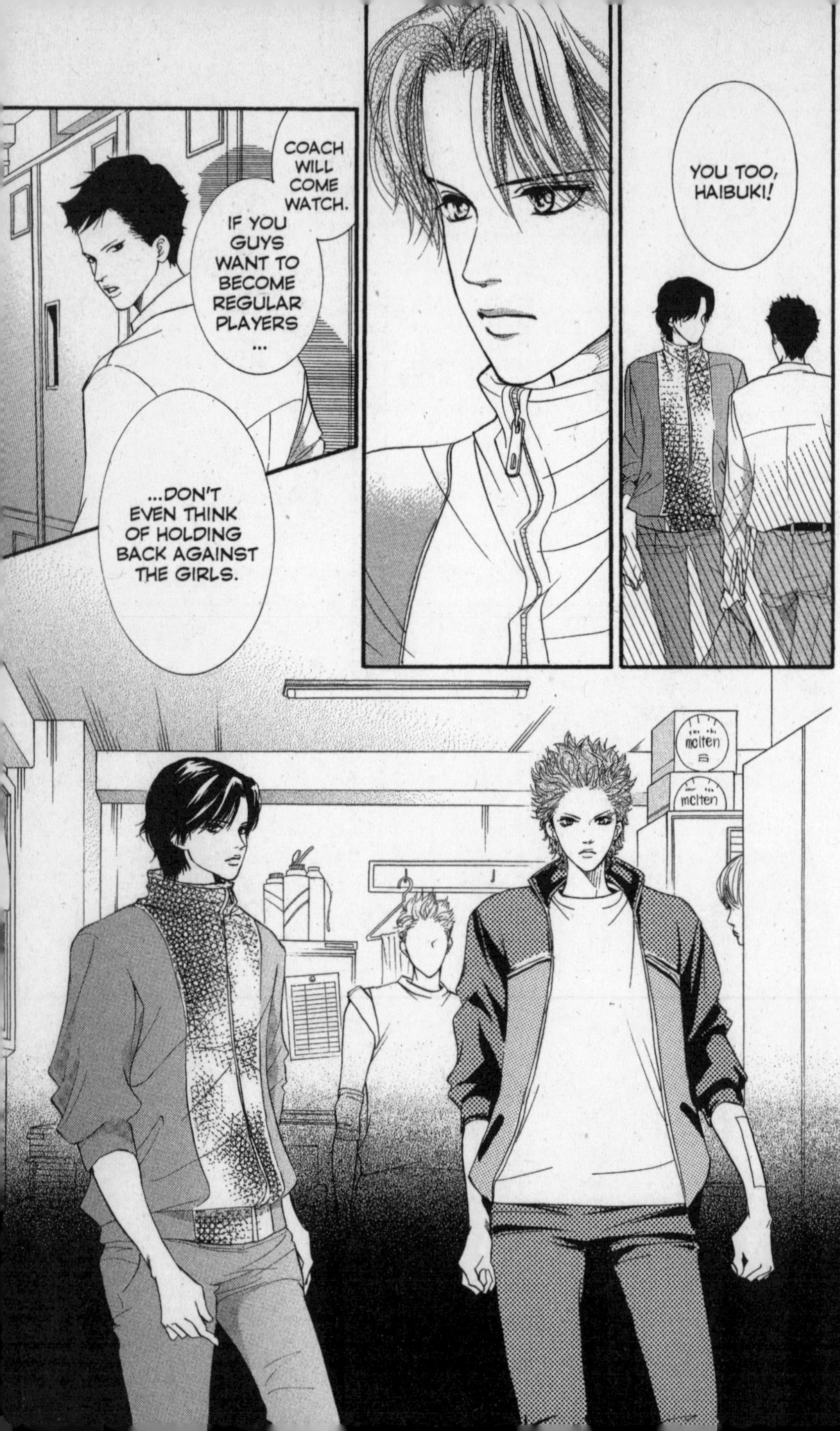
YOU TOO, HAIBUKI!
COACH WILL COME WATCH.
IF YOU GUYS WANT TO BECOME REGULAR PLAYERS ...
...DON'T EVEN THINK OF HOLDING BACK AGAINST THE GIRLS.
molten
molten

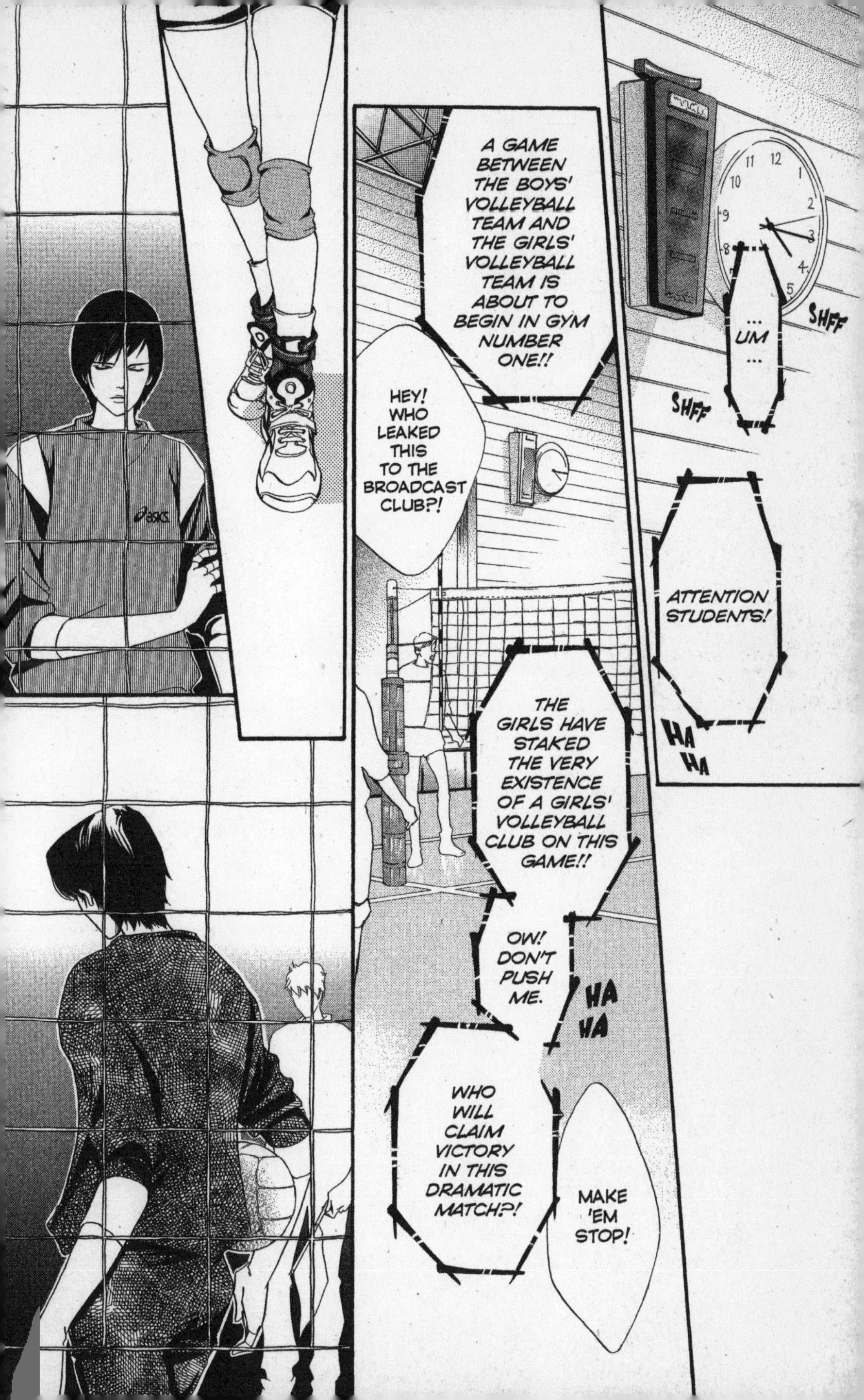
SHFF
... UM ...
SHFF
ATTENTION STUDENTS!
HA HA
A GAME BETWEEN THE BOYS' VOLLEYBALL TEAM AND THE GIRLS' VOLLEYBALL TEAM IS ABOUT TO BEGIN IN GYM NUMBER ONE!!
HEY! WHO LEAKED THIS TO THE BROADCAST CLUB?!
THE GIRLS HAVE STAKED THE VERY EXISTENCE OF A GIRLS' VOLLEYBALL CLUB ON THIS GAME!!
OW! DON'T PUSH ME.
HA HA
WHO WILL CLAIM VICTORY IN THIS DRAMATIC MATCH?!
MAKE 'EM STOP!

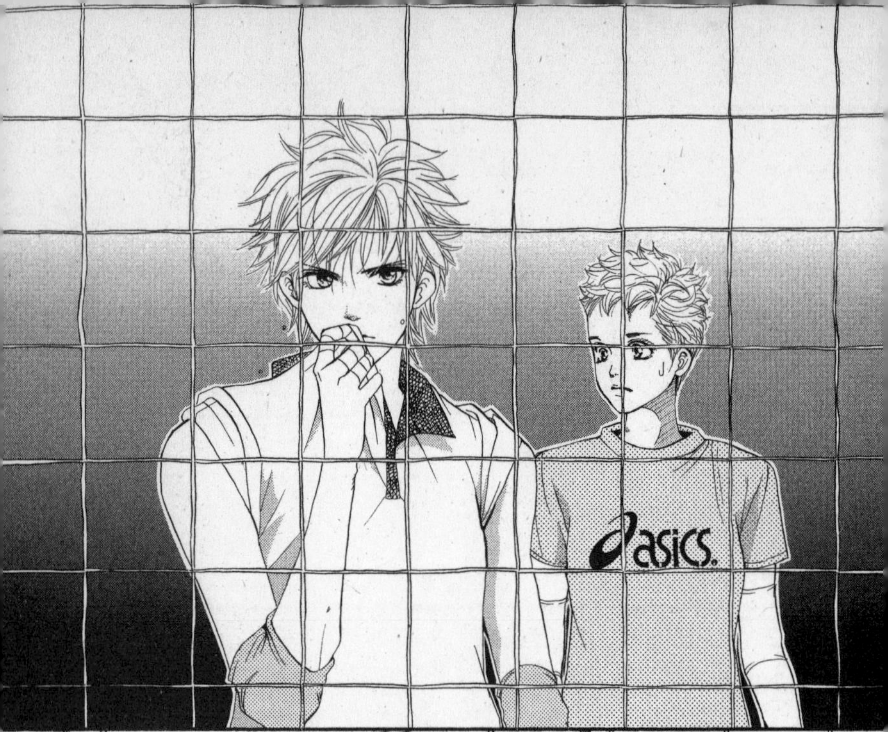
asics

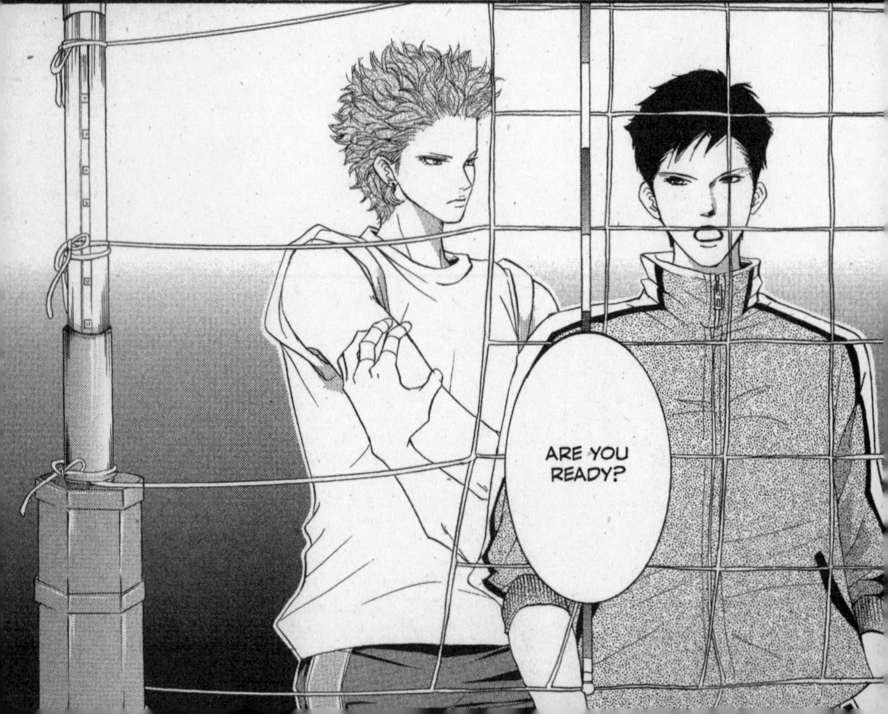
ARE YOU READY?

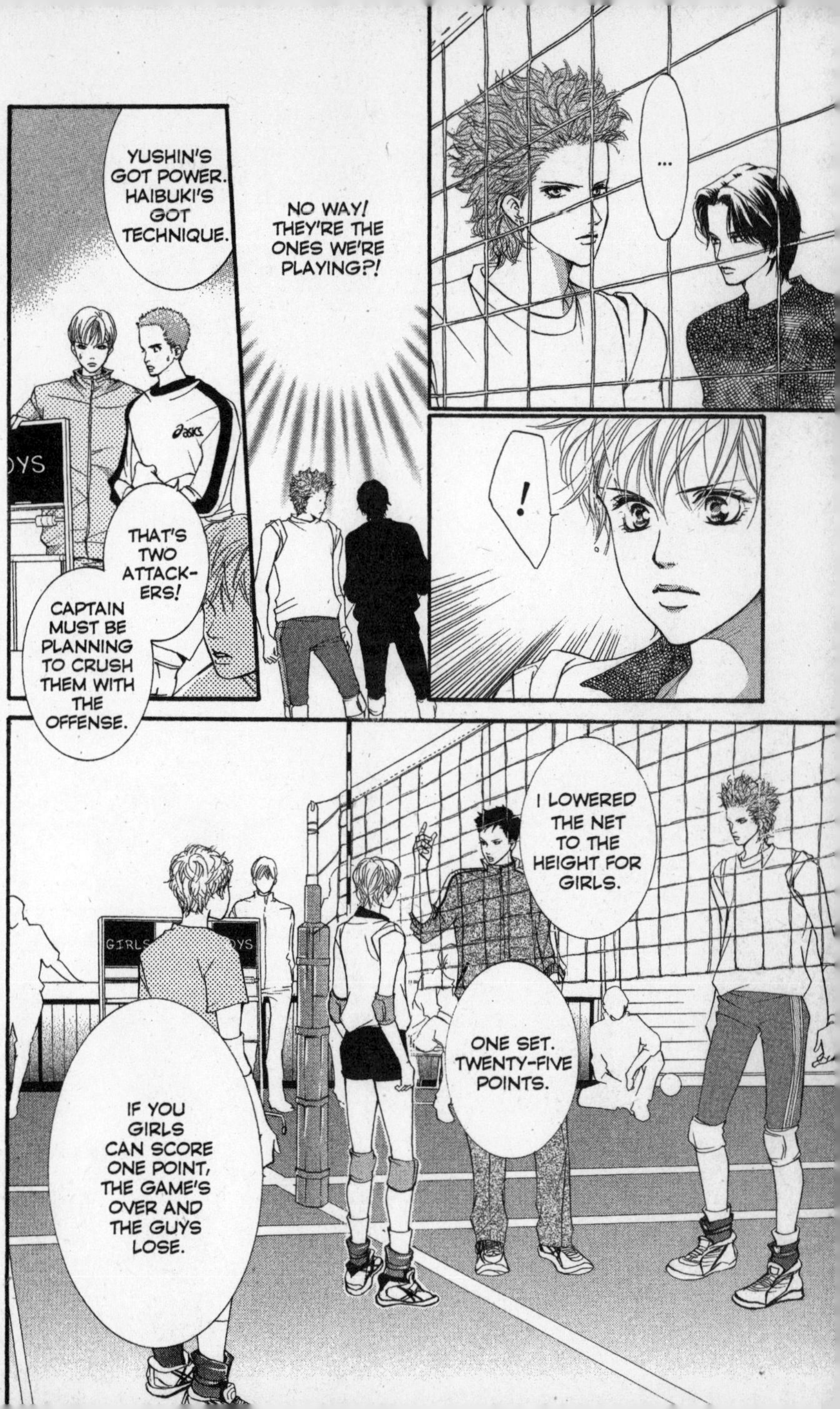
...
!
NO WAY! THEY'RE THE ONES WE'RE PLAYING?!
YUSHIN'S GOT POWER. HAIBUKI'S GOT TECHNIQUE.
THAT'S TWO ATTACKERS!
CAPTAIN MUST BE PLANNING TO CRUSH THEM WITH THE OFFENSE.
I LOWERED THE NET TO THE HEIGHT FOR GIRLS.
ONE SET. TWENTY-FIVE POINTS.
IF YOU GIRLS CAN SCORE ONE POINT, THE GAME'S OVER AND THE GUYS LOSE.

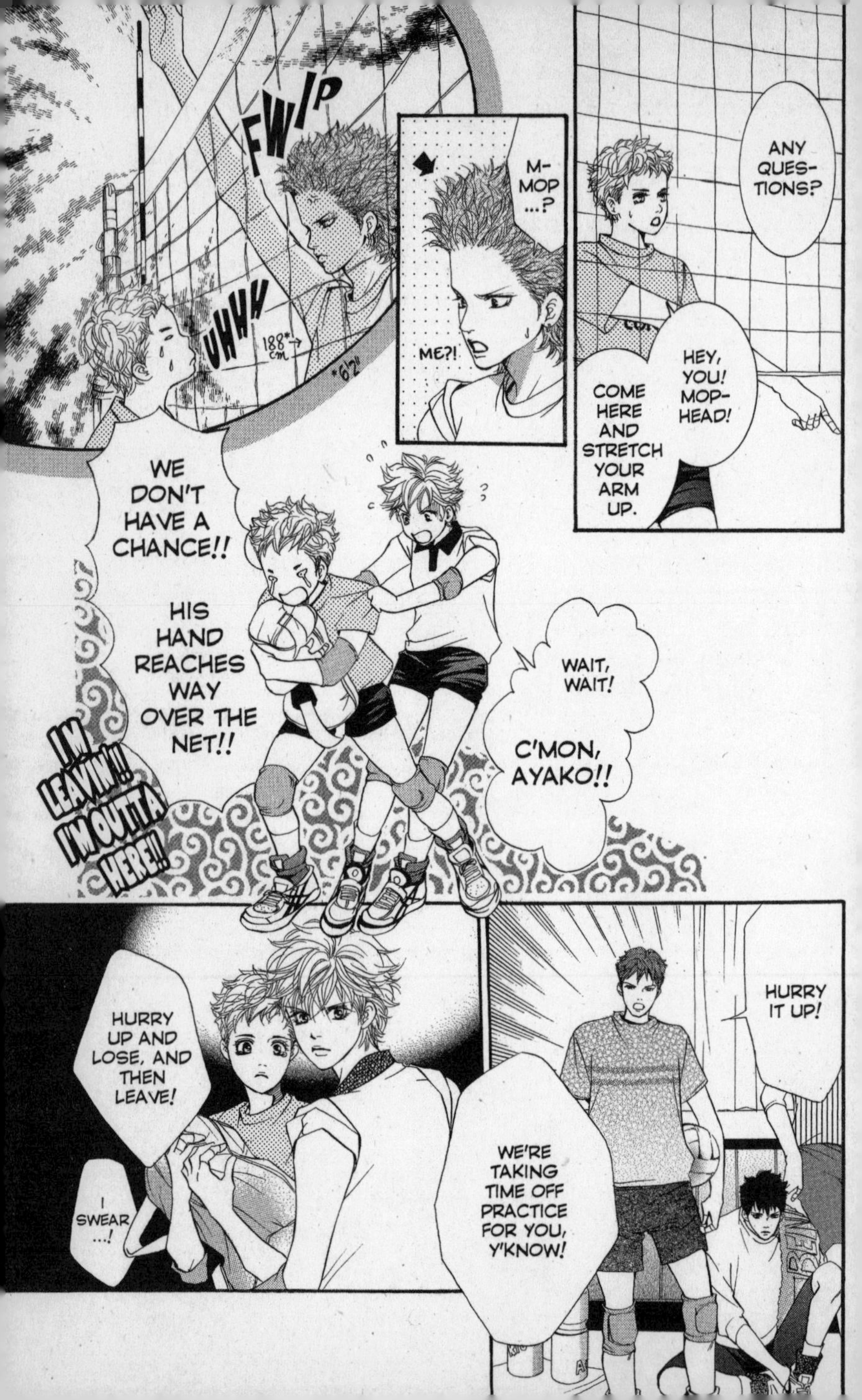
ANY QUES-TIONS?
HEY, YOU! MOP-HEAD!
COME HERE AND STRETCH YOUR ARM UP.
M-MOP ...?
ME?!
FWIP
UHHH
188* cm →
*6'2"
WAIT, WAIT!
C'MON, AYAKO!!
WE DON'T HAVE A CHANCE!!
HIS HAND REACHES WAY OVER THE NET!!
I'M LEAVIN'!! I'M OUTTA HERE!!
HURRY IT UP!
WE'RE TAKING TIME OFF PRACTICE FOR YOU, Y'KNOW!
HURRY UP AND LOSE, AND THEN LEAVE!
I SWEAR ...!

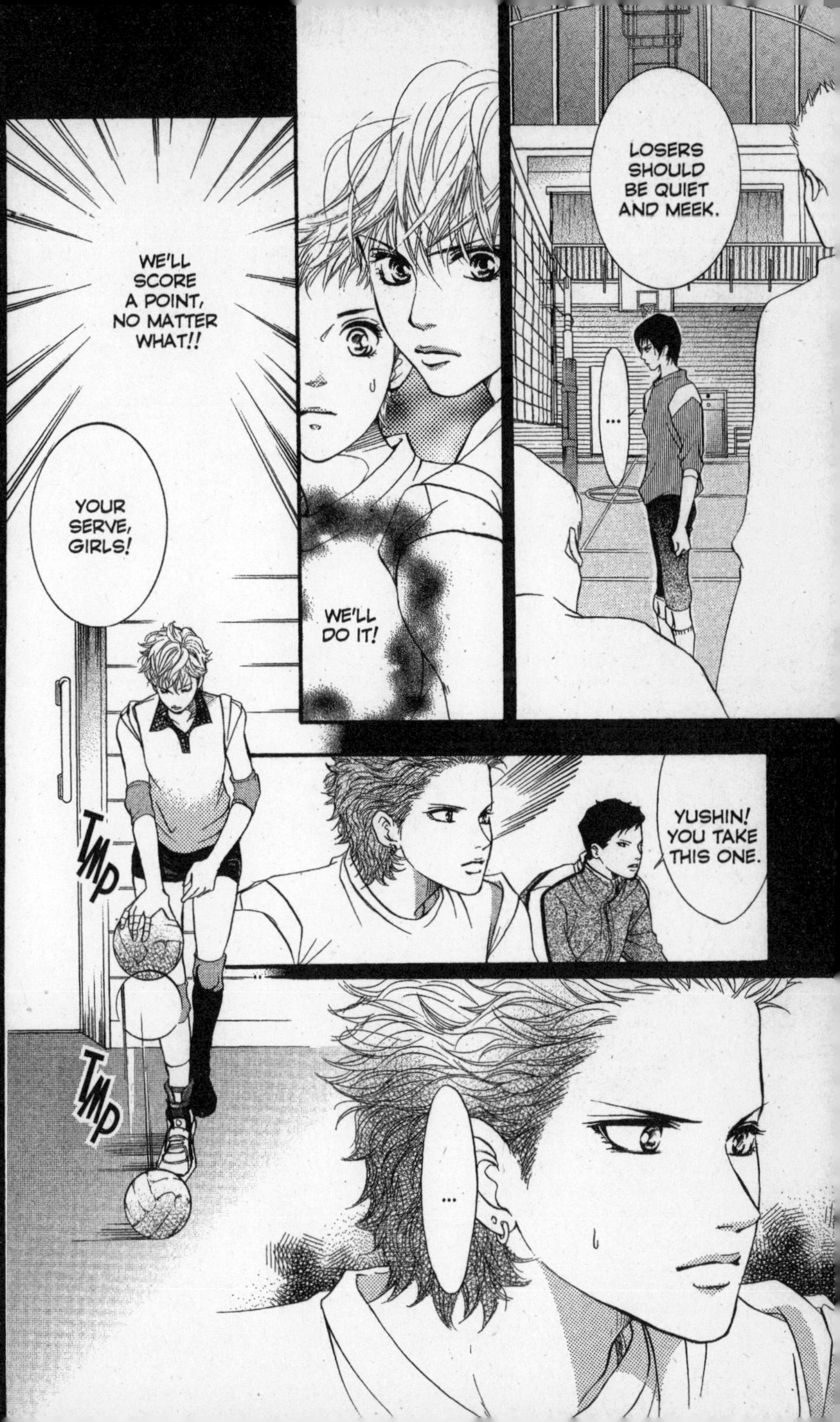
LOSERS SHOULD BE QUIET AND MEEK.
...
WE'LL DO IT!
YUSHIN! YOU TAKE THIS ONE.
...
WE'LL SCORE A POINT, NO MATTER WHAT!!
YOUR SERVE, GIRLS!
TMP
TMP

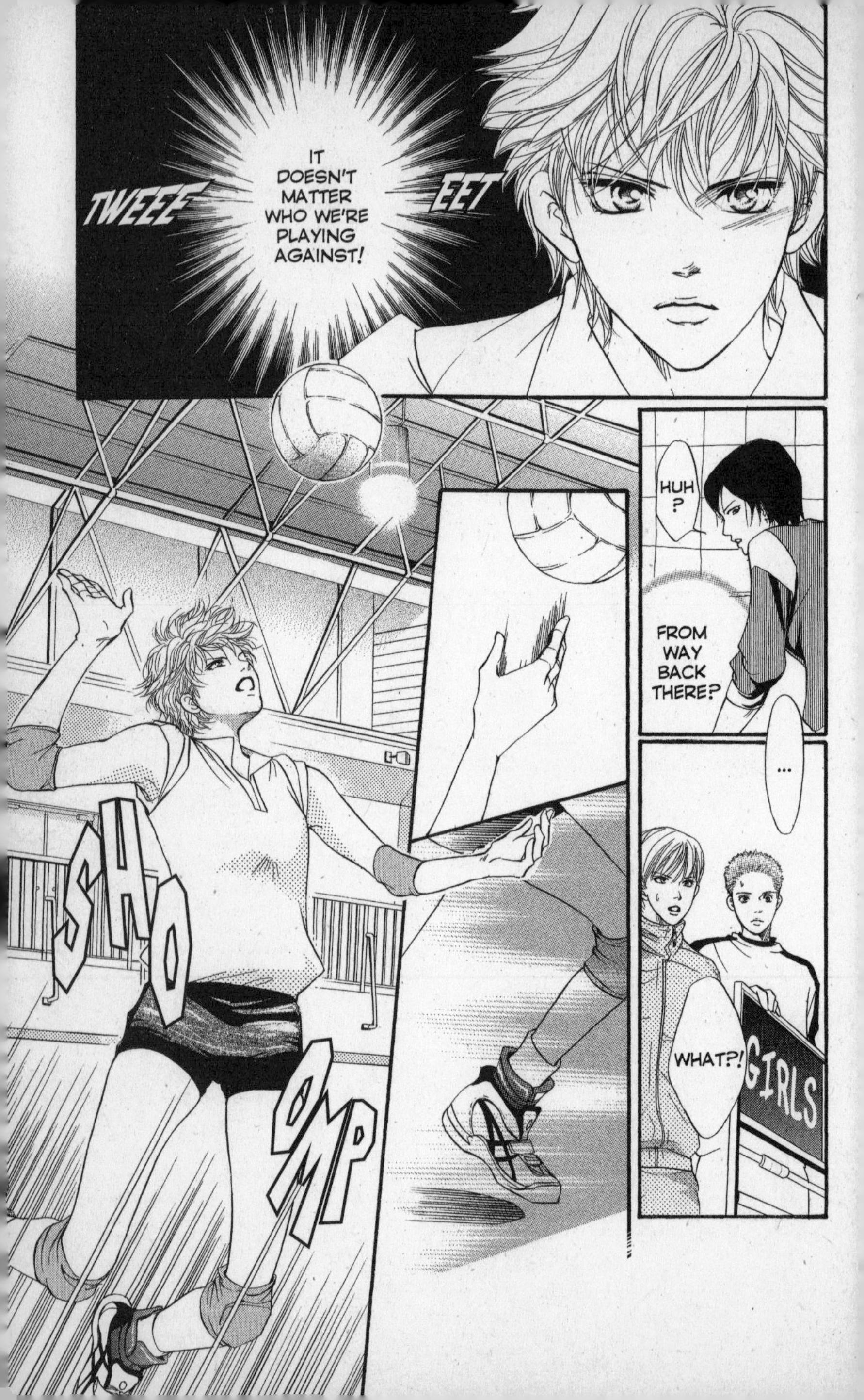
TWEEE EET
IT DOESN'T MATTER WHO WE'RE PLAYING AGAINST!
HUH?
FROM WAY BACK THERE?
...
WHAT?!
GIRLS
SHOOMP

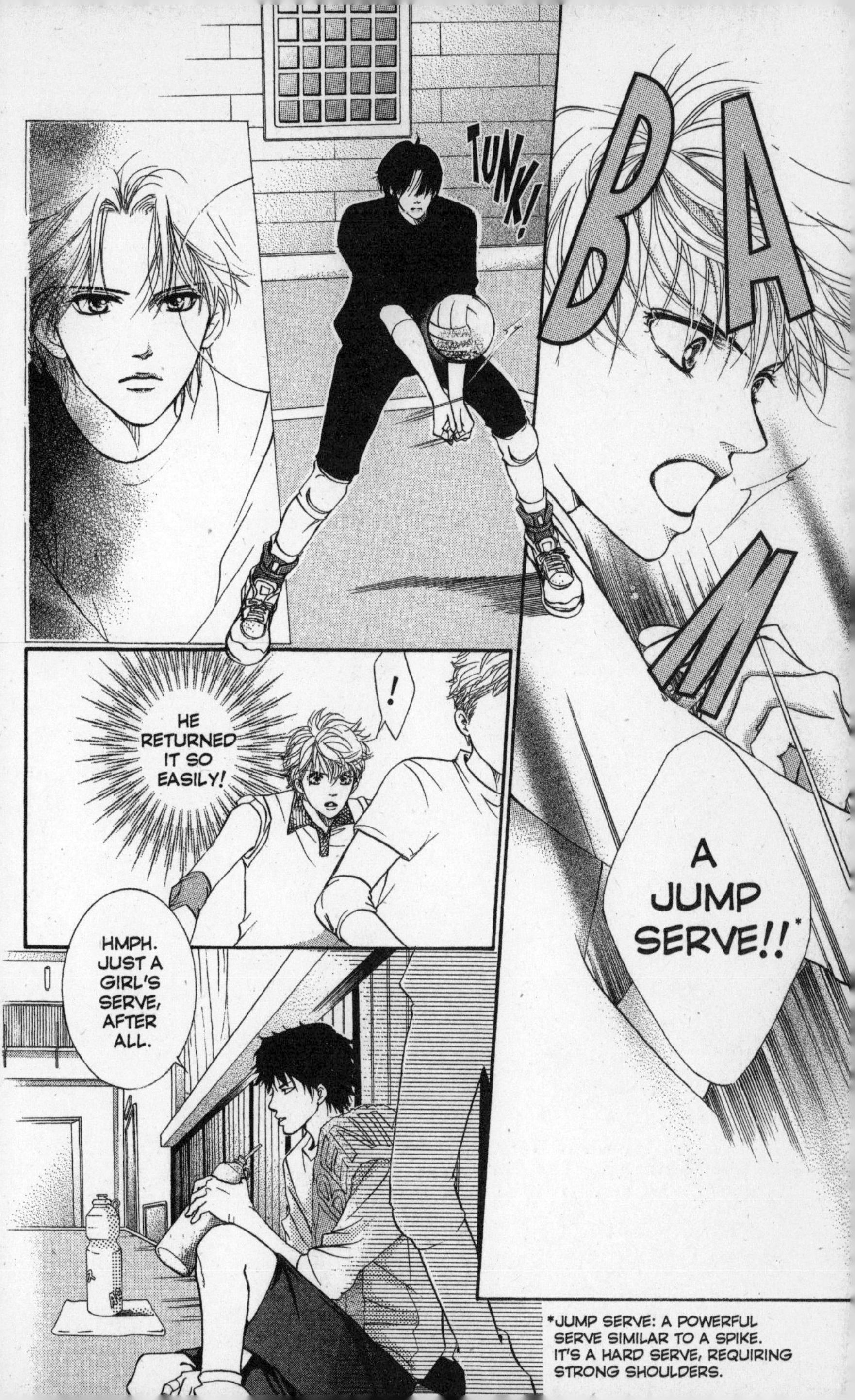
BAM
A JUMP SERVE!!*
TUNK!
!
HE RETURNED IT SO EASILY!
HMPH. JUST A GIRL'S SERVE, AFTER ALL.

*JUMP SERVE: A POWERFUL SERVE SIMILAR TO A SPIKE. IT'S A HARD SERVE, REQUIRING STRONG SHOULDERS.

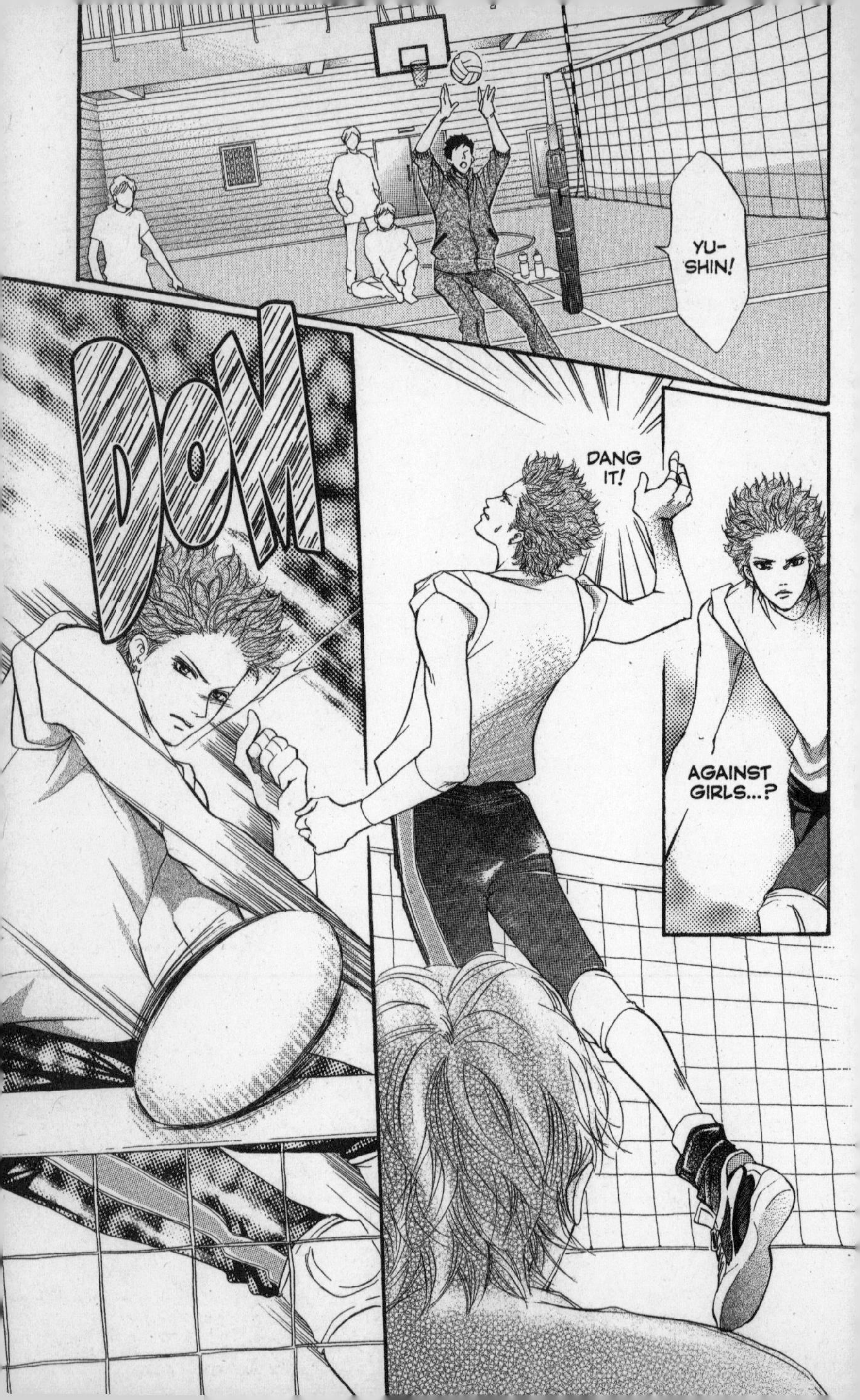
YU-SHIN!
DANG IT!
AGAINST GIRLS...?
DOM

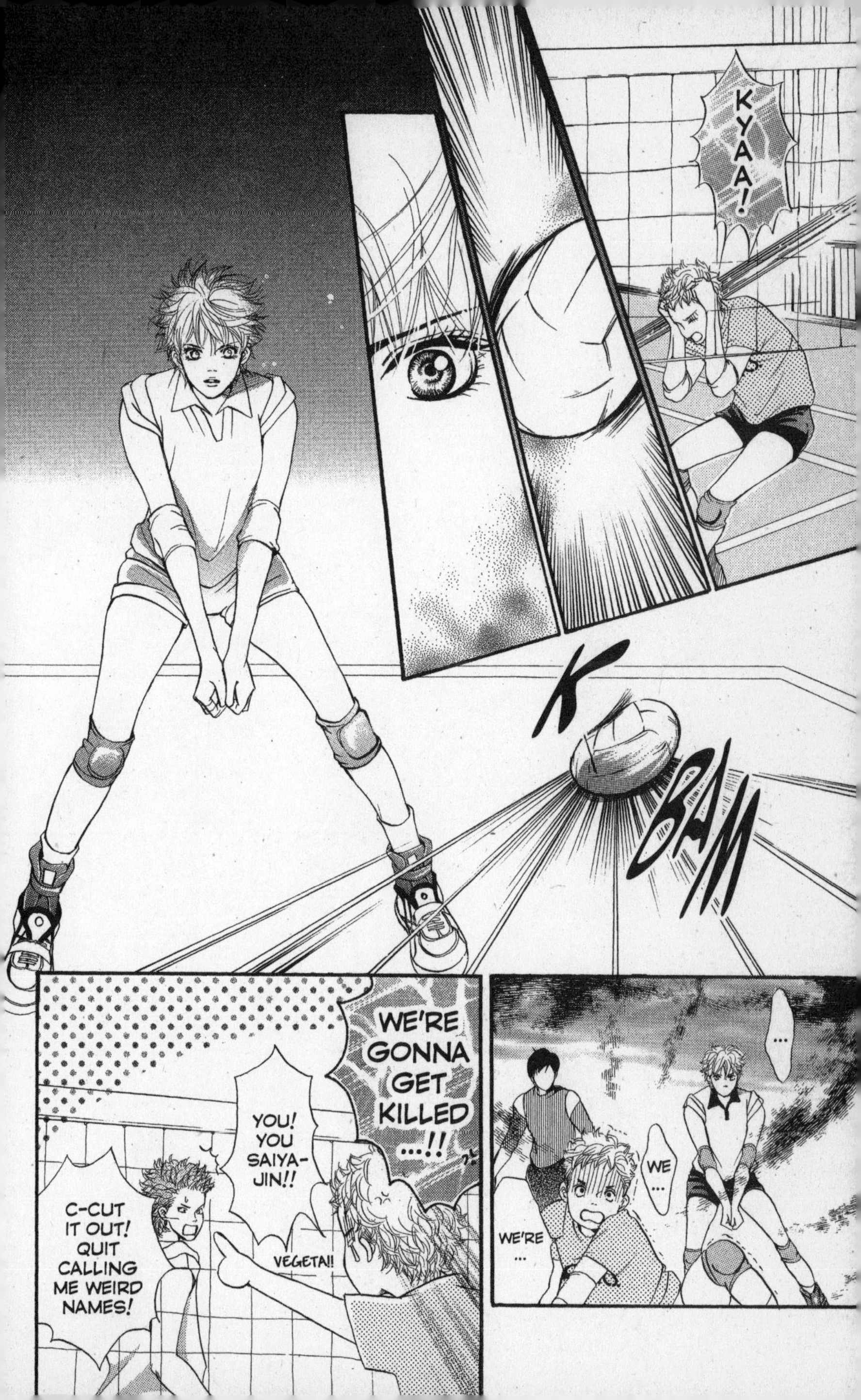
KYAA!
K
BAM
...
WE ...
WE'RE ...
WE'RE GONNA GET KILLED ...!!
YOU! YOU SAIYA-JIN!!
VEGETA!!
C-CUT IT OUT! QUIT CALLING ME WEIRD NAMES!

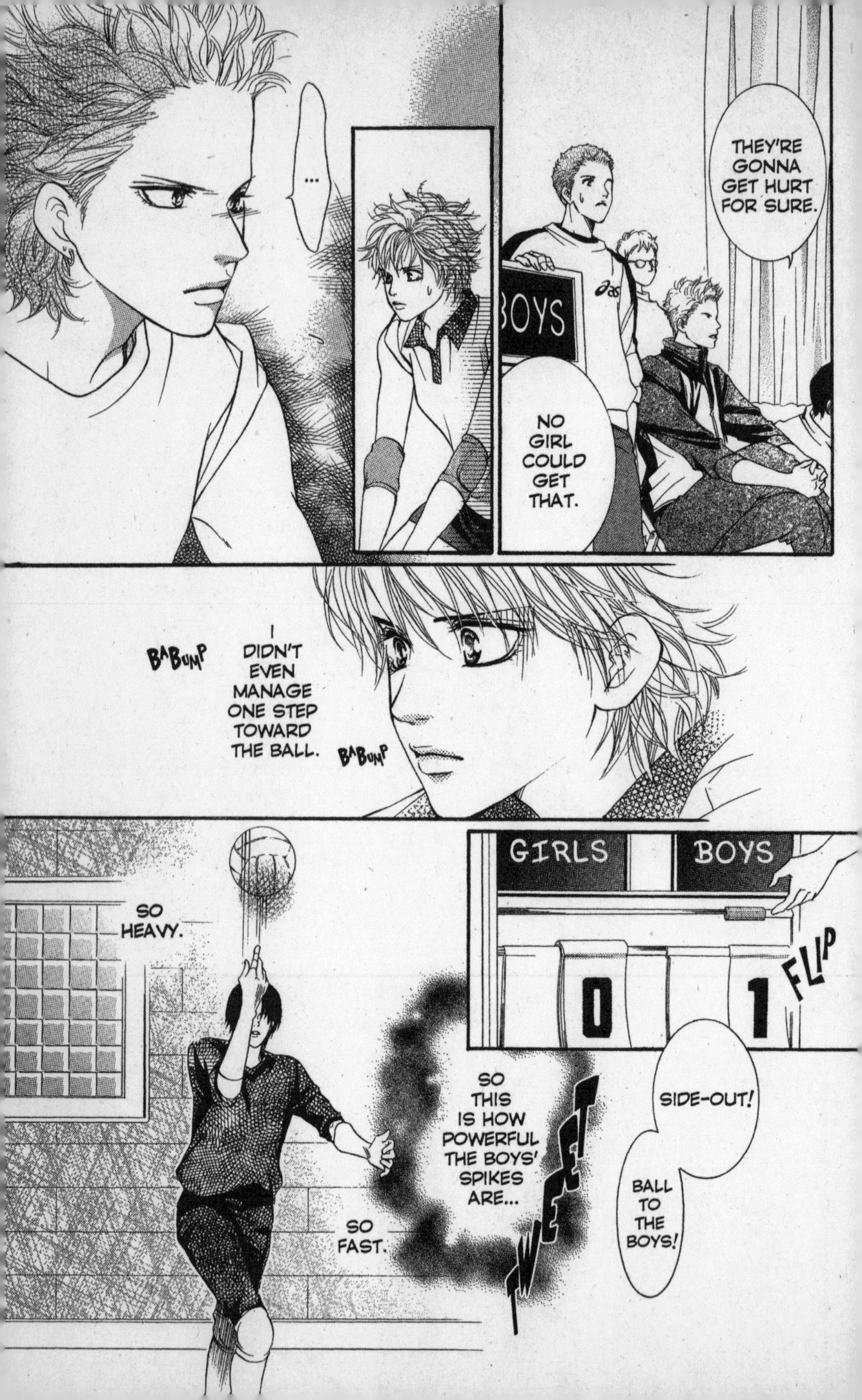
THEY'RE GONNA GET HURT FOR SURE.
NO GIRL COULD GET THAT.
...
BABUMP
I DIDN'T EVEN MANAGE ONE STEP TOWARD THE BALL.
BABUMP
GIRLS
BOYS
0
1
FLIP
SIDE-OUT!
BALL TO THE BOYS!
SO THIS IS HOW POWERFUL THE BOYS' SPIKES ARE...
SO HEAVY.
SO FAST.

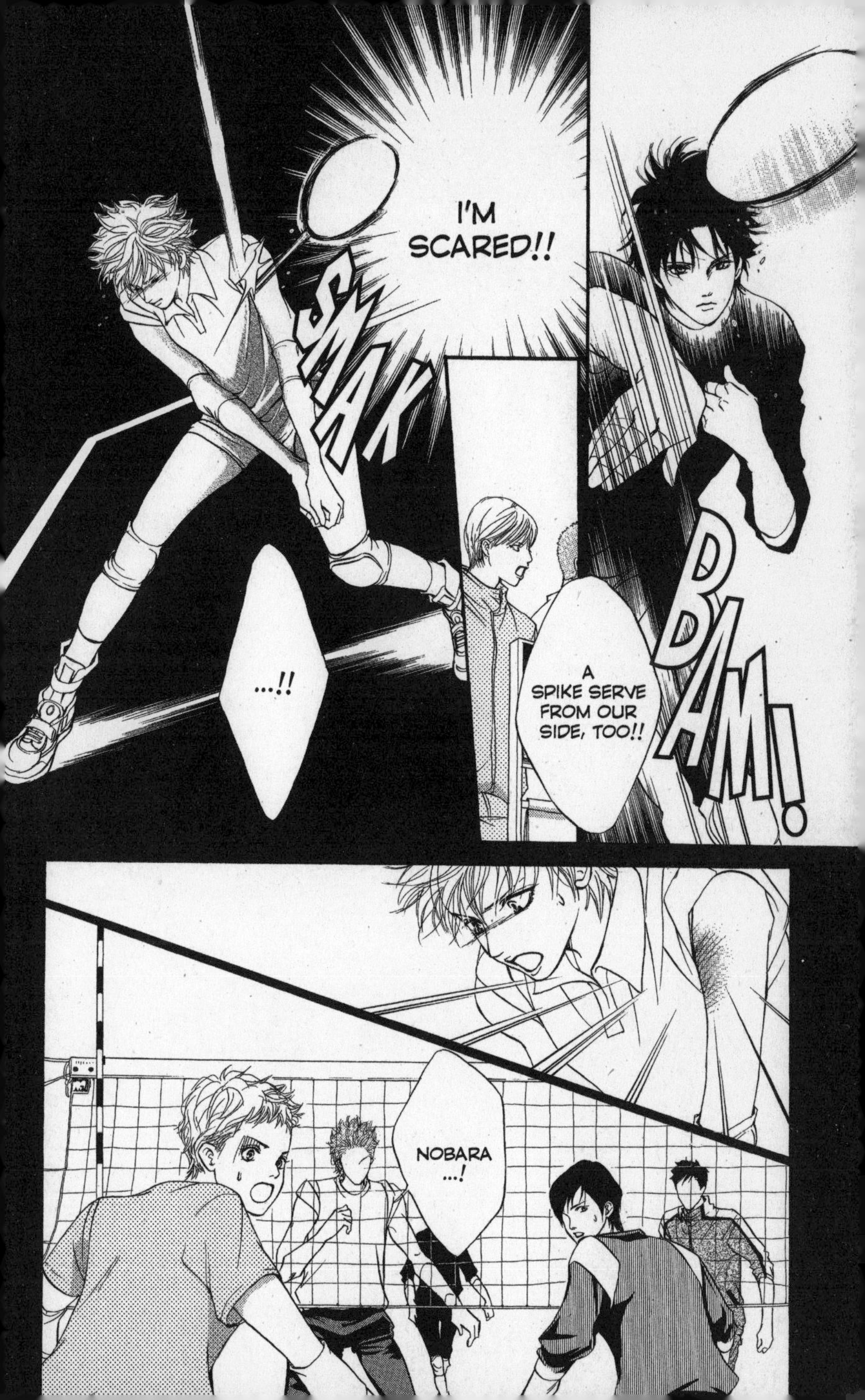
BAM!
A SPIKE SERVE FROM OUR SIDE, TOO!!
I'M SCARED!!
SMAK
...!!
NOBARA ...!

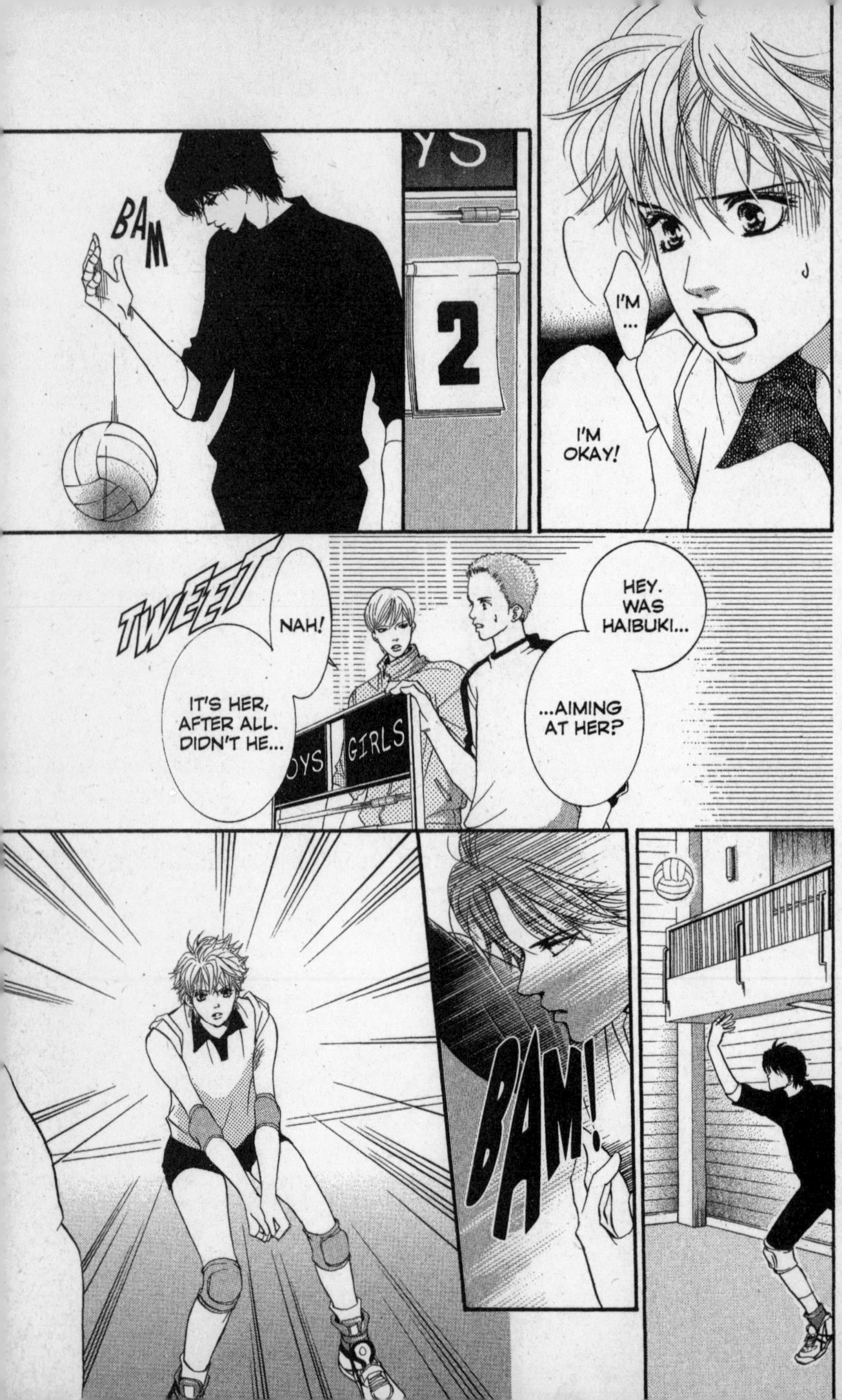
I'M ...
I'M OKAY!
BAM
2
HEY. WAS HAIBUKI...
...AIMING AT HER?
NAH!
TWEET
IT'S HER, AFTER ALL. DIDN'T HE...
GIRLS
BAM!

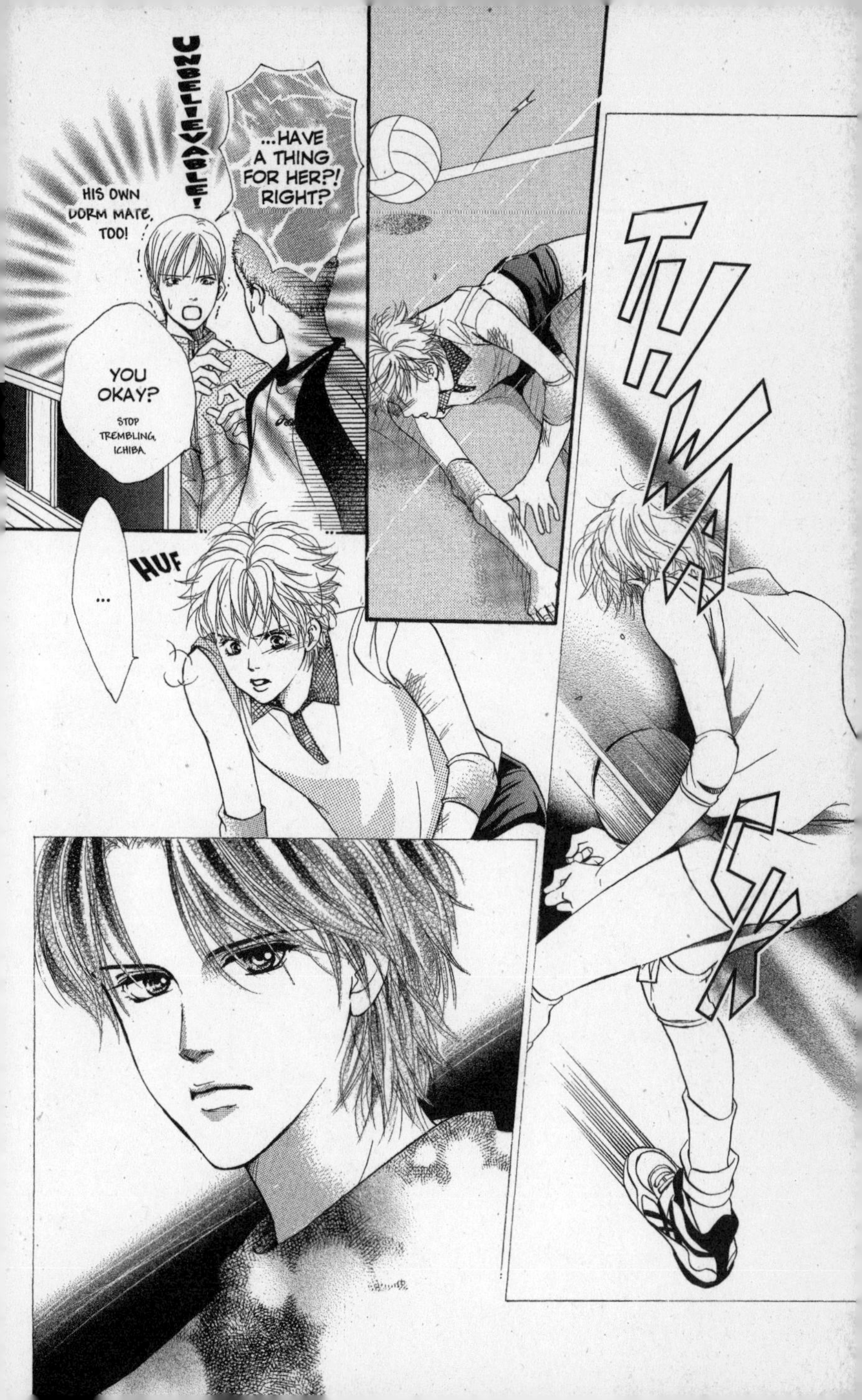
THWACK
...HAVE A THING FOR HER?! RIGHT?
UNBELIEVABLE!
HIS OWN DORM MATE, TOO!
YOU OKAY?
STOP TREMBLING, ICHIBA.
HUF
...

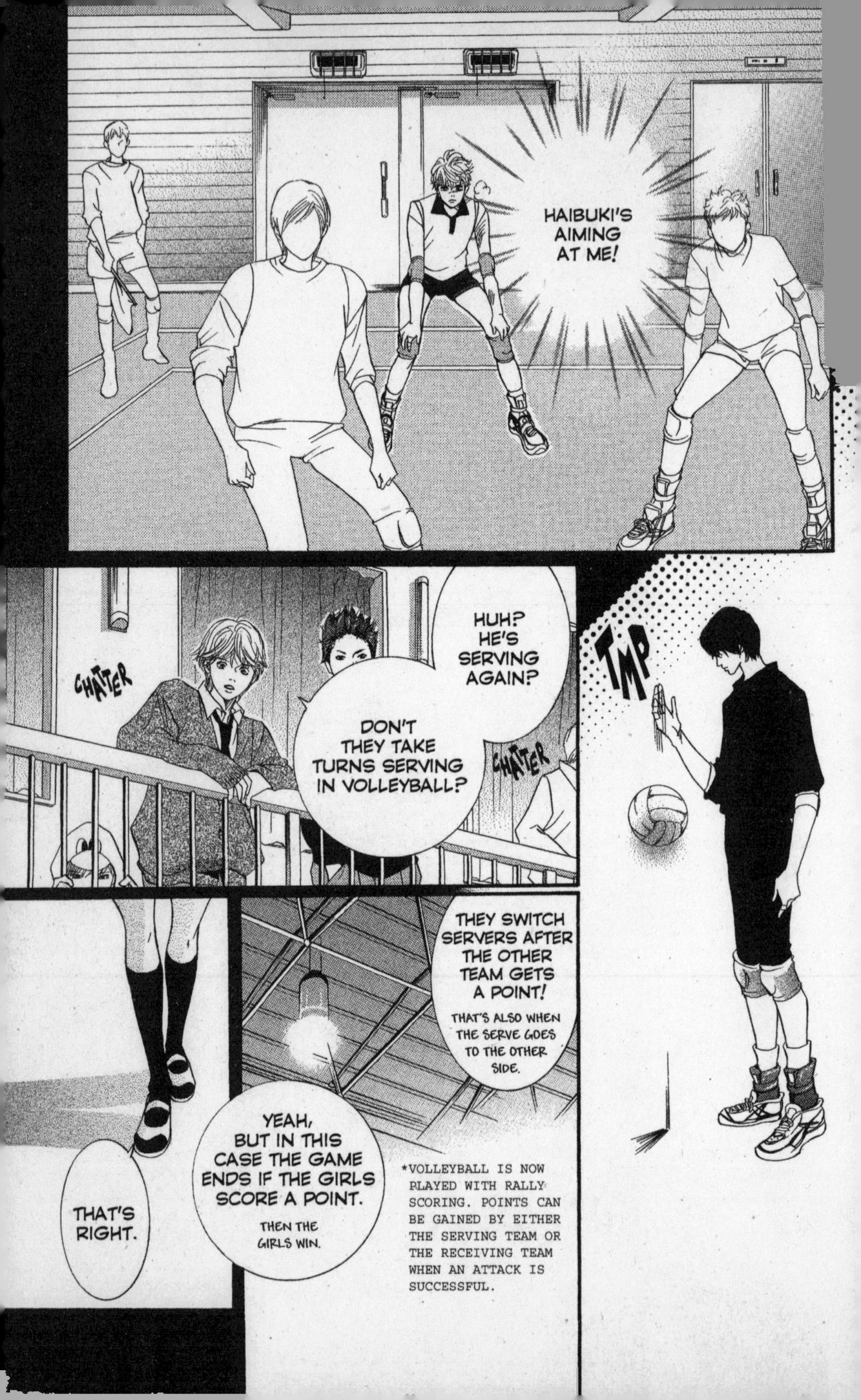
HAIBUKI'S AIMING AT ME!
TMP
HUH? HE'S SERVING AGAIN?
CHATTER
DON'T THEY TAKE TURNS SERVING IN VOLLEYBALL?
CHATTER
THEY SWITCH SERVERS AFTER THE OTHER TEAM GETS A POINT!
THAT'S ALSO WHEN THE SERVE GOES TO THE OTHER SIDE.
YEAH, BUT IN THIS CASE THE GAME ENDS IF THE GIRLS SCORE A POINT.
THEN THE GIRLS WIN.
*VOLLEYBALL IS NOW PLAYED WITH RALLY SCORING. POINTS CAN BE GAINED BY EITHER THE SERVING TEAM OR THE RECEIVING TEAM WHEN AN ATTACK IS SUCCESSFUL.
THAT'S RIGHT.

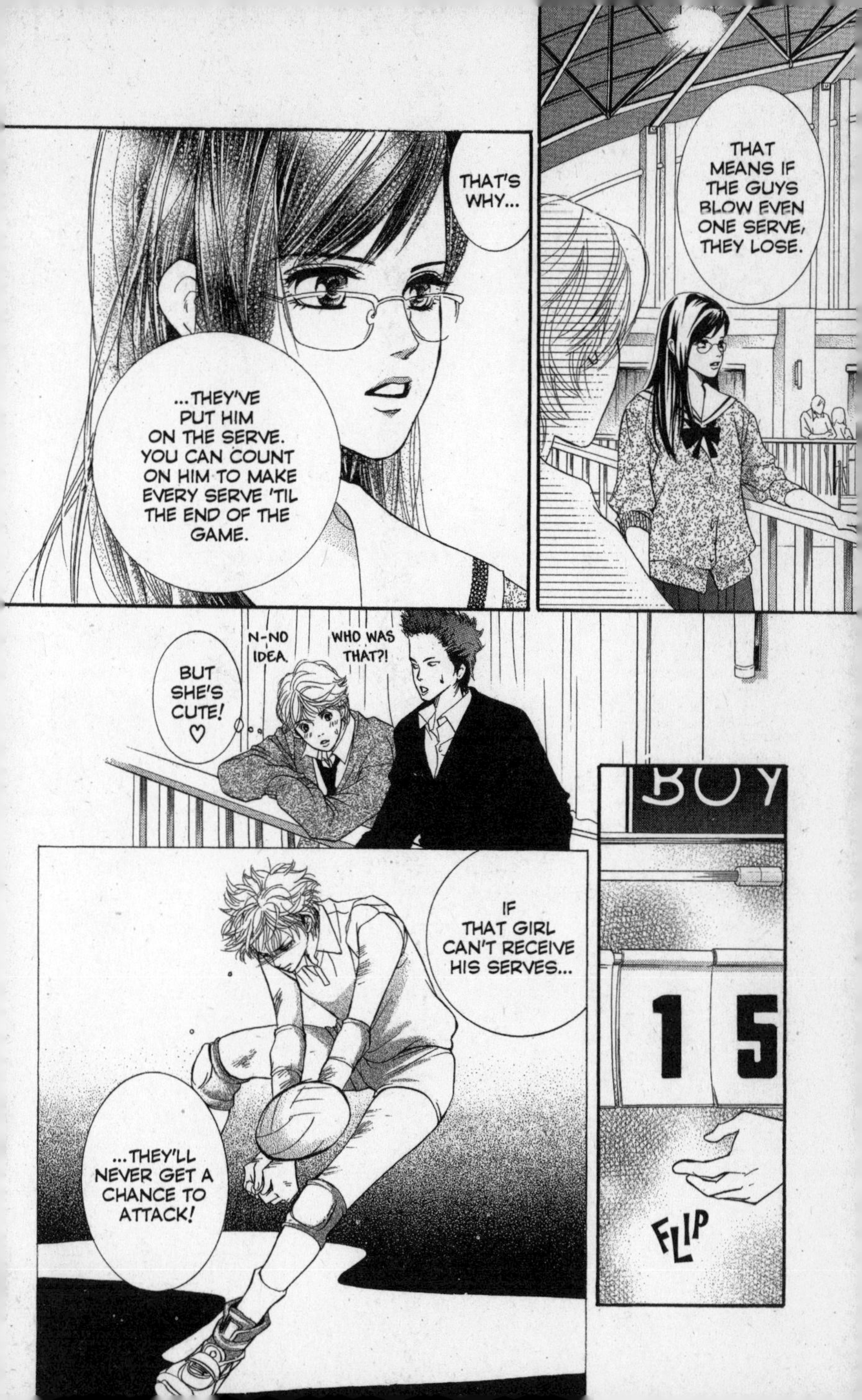
THAT MEANS IF THE GUYS BLOW EVEN ONE SERVE, THEY LOSE.
THAT'S WHY...
...THEY'VE PUT HIM ON THE SERVE. YOU CAN COUNT ON HIM TO MAKE EVERY SERVE 'TIL THE END OF THE GAME.
WHO WAS THAT?!
N-NO IDEA.
BUT SHE'S CUTE! ♡
BOY
15
FLIP
IF THAT GIRL CAN'T RECEIVE HIS SERVES...
...THEY'LL NEVER GET A CHANCE TO ATTACK!

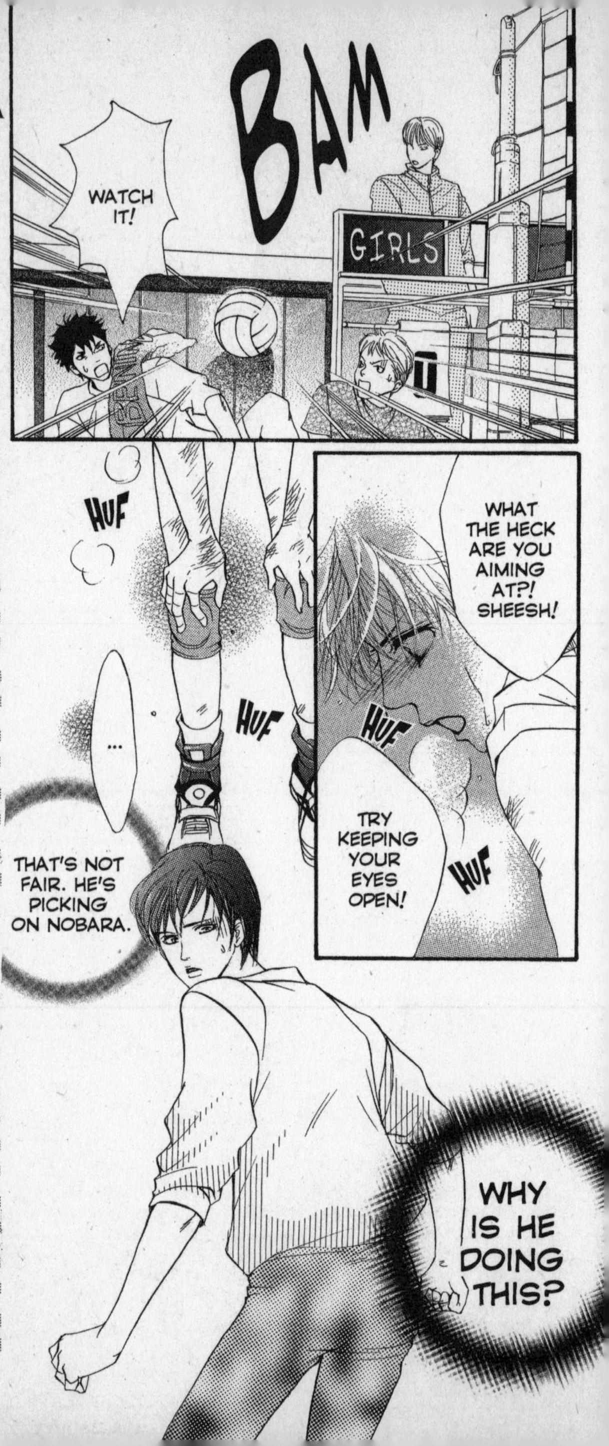
BAM
WATCH IT!
WHAT THE HECK ARE YOU AIMING AT?! SHEESH!
HUF
TRY KEEPING YOUR EYES OPEN!
HUF
HUF
HUF
...
THAT'S NOT FAIR. HE'S PICKING ON NOBARA.
WHY IS HE DOING THIS?

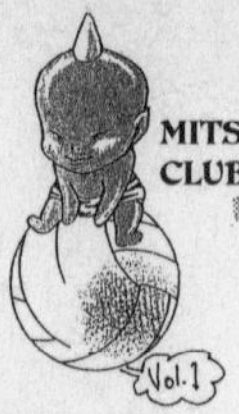
Vol.1

MITSUBA CLUB

--THE END OF SUMMER--

FIREWORKS? HOW NICE. I DID SOME WITH THE WHOLE STAFF, WHILE WORKING ON MY DRAFTS. TWICE, EVEN. IT'S ONE OF THOSE ACTIVITIES THAT MAKES YOU HAPPY TO BE JAPANESE, SENSITIVE TO THE SEASONS. DON'T YOU AGREE?

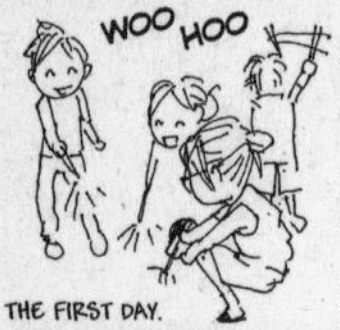
WOO HOO

THE FIRST DAY.
IN A NEARBY PARKING LOT WE LIT SPARKLERS DECORATED WITH AN IMAGE OF A CREEPY GREEN HAMSTER.
ON THE SECOND DAY MY PET CAT CHIRO DID THE FIREWORKS WITH US. BUT CHIRO SEEMED SCARED OF THE FIREWORKS AND BURIED HIS HEAD BETWEEN MY ARM AND MY BODY.

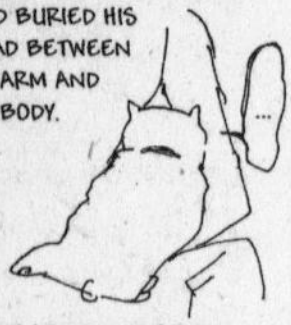
...

IT TUGGED AT MY HEART.
THE KIND THAT SHOOTS UP IS NICE TOO, DON'T YOU THINK? HUNDREDS OF EXPLOSIONS OF FIREWORKS, LIGHTING UP THE NIGHT SKY--FIREWORKS PAINSTAKINGLY CREATED BY CRAFTSMEN.

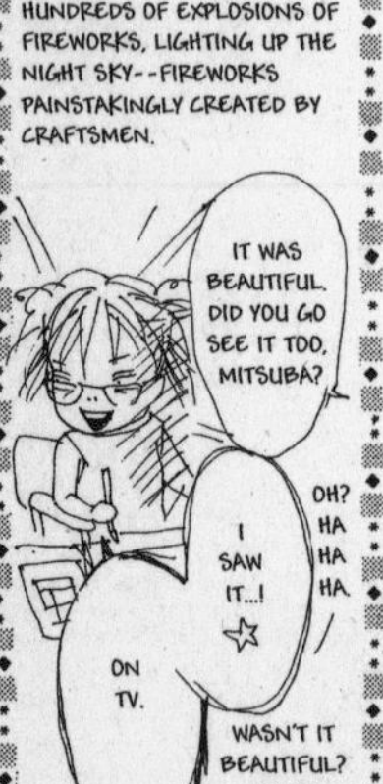
IT WAS BEAUTIFUL. DID YOU GO SEE IT TOO, MITSUBA?
OH? HA HA HA.
I SAW IT...! ☆
ON TV.
WASN'T IT BEAUTIFUL? HA HA.
THE END.

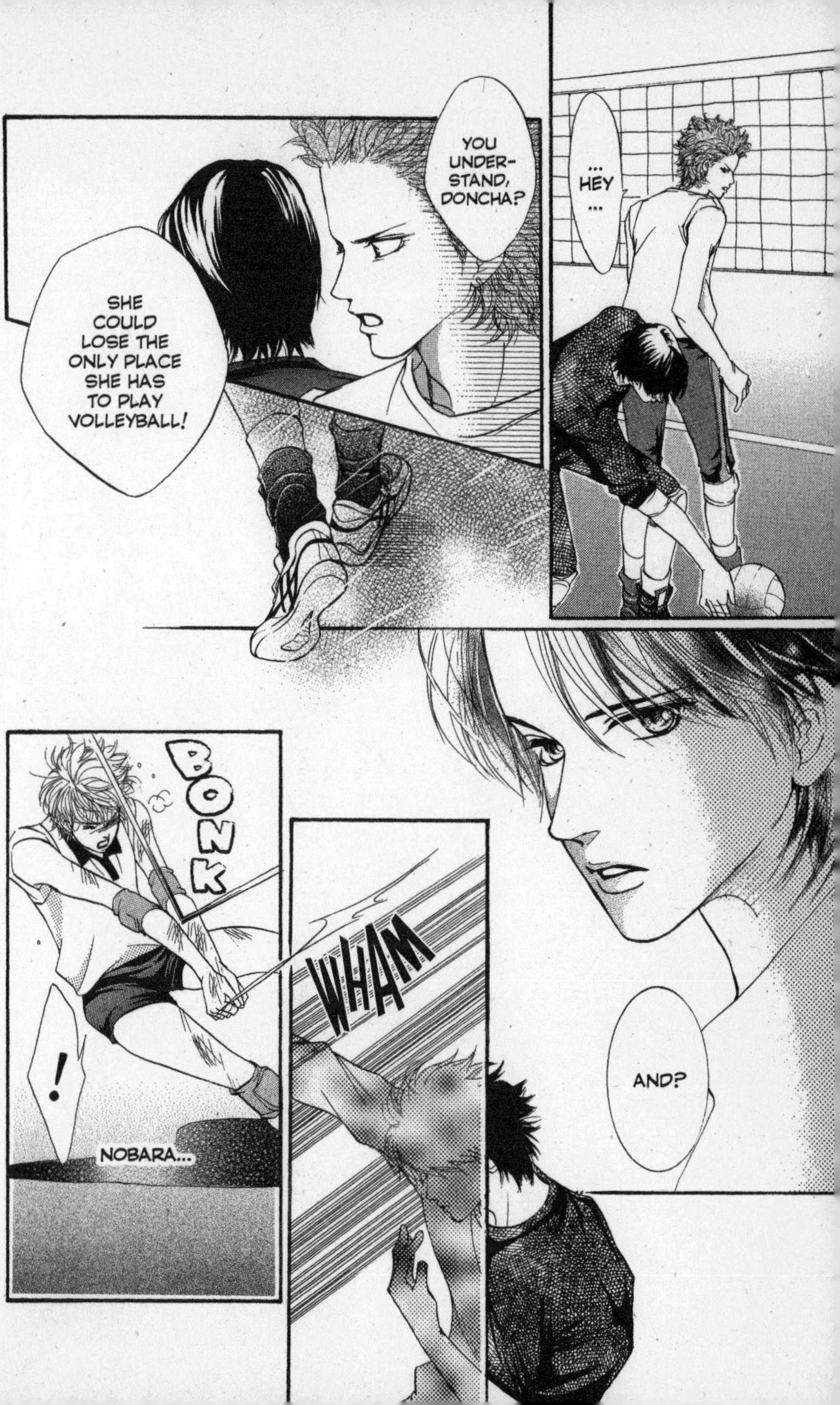
...HEY...
YOU UNDER-STAND, DONCHA?
SHE COULD LOSE THE ONLY PLACE SHE HAS TO PLAY VOLLEYBALL!
AND?
WHAM
BONK
!
NOBARA...

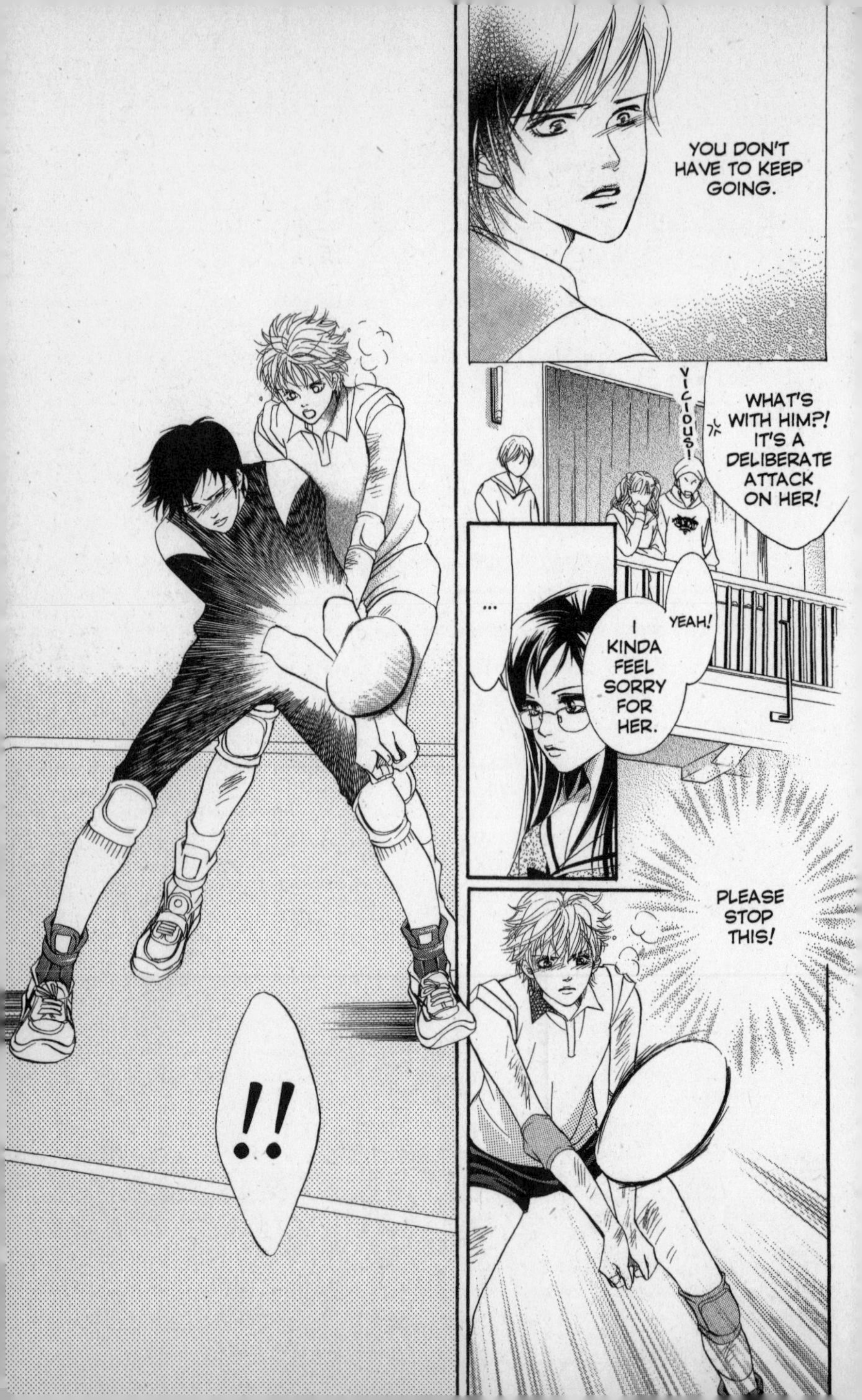
YOU DON'T HAVE TO KEEP GOING.
VICIOUS!
WHAT'S WITH HIM?! IT'S A DELIBERATE ATTACK ON HER!
YEAH!
I KINDA FEEL SORRY FOR HER.
...
PLEASE STOP THIS!
!!

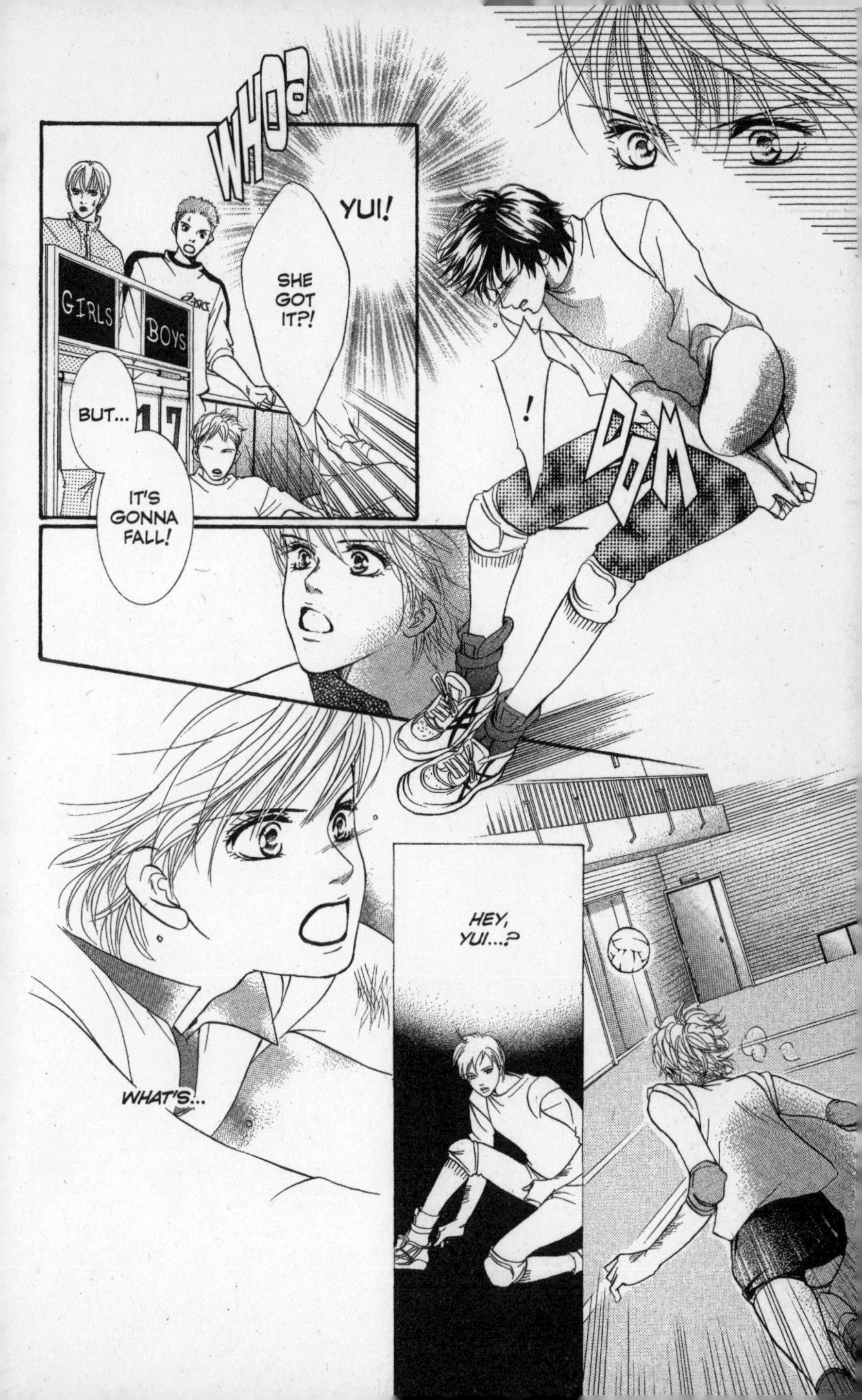
!
DOM DOM
WHOA
YUI!
SHE GOT IT?!
GIRLS
BOYS
BUT...
IT'S GONNA FALL!
HEY, YUI...?
WHAT'S...

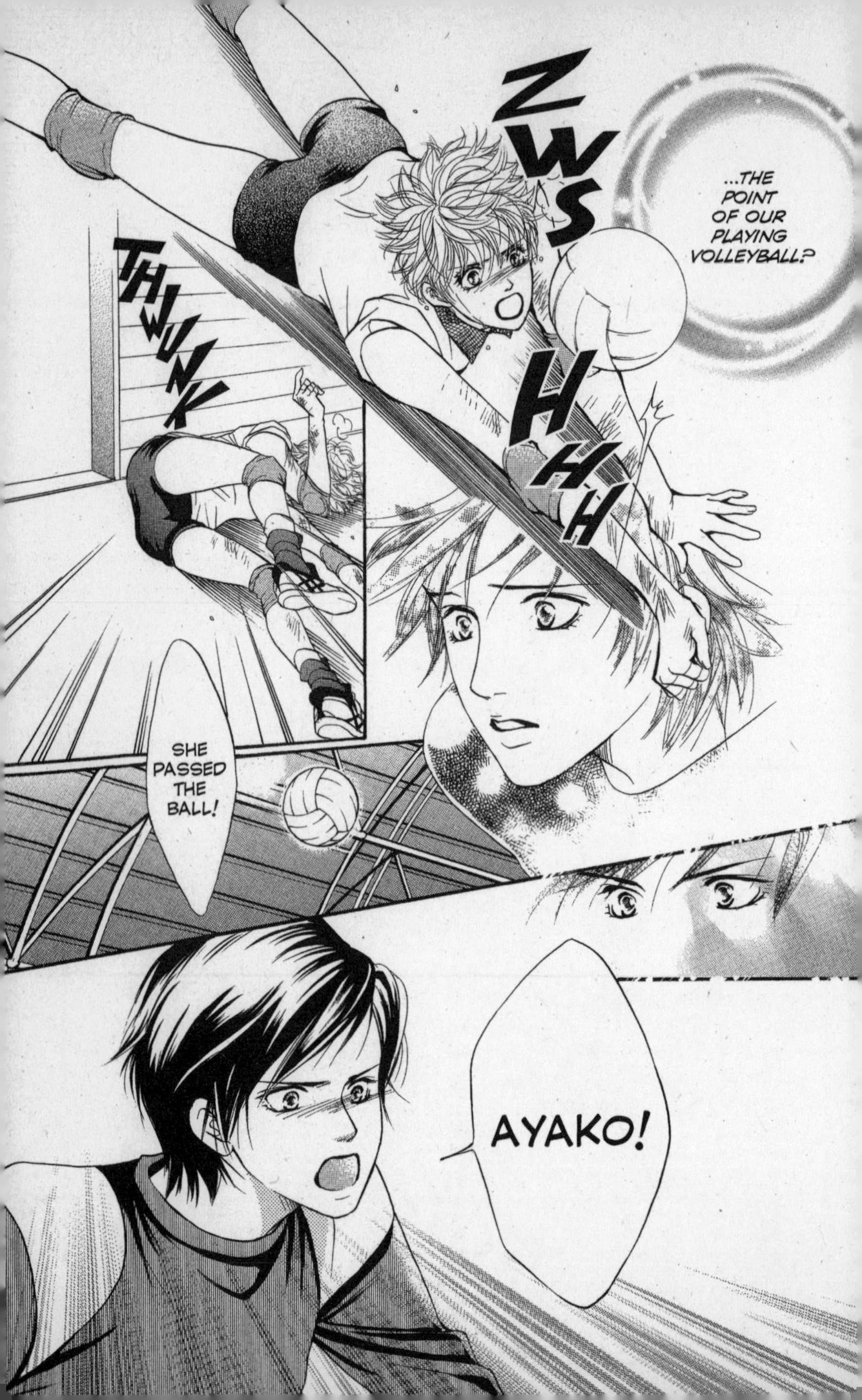
...THE POINT OF OUR PLAYING VOLLEYBALL?
ZWSHHHH
THWUNK
SHE PASSED THE BALL!
AYAKO!

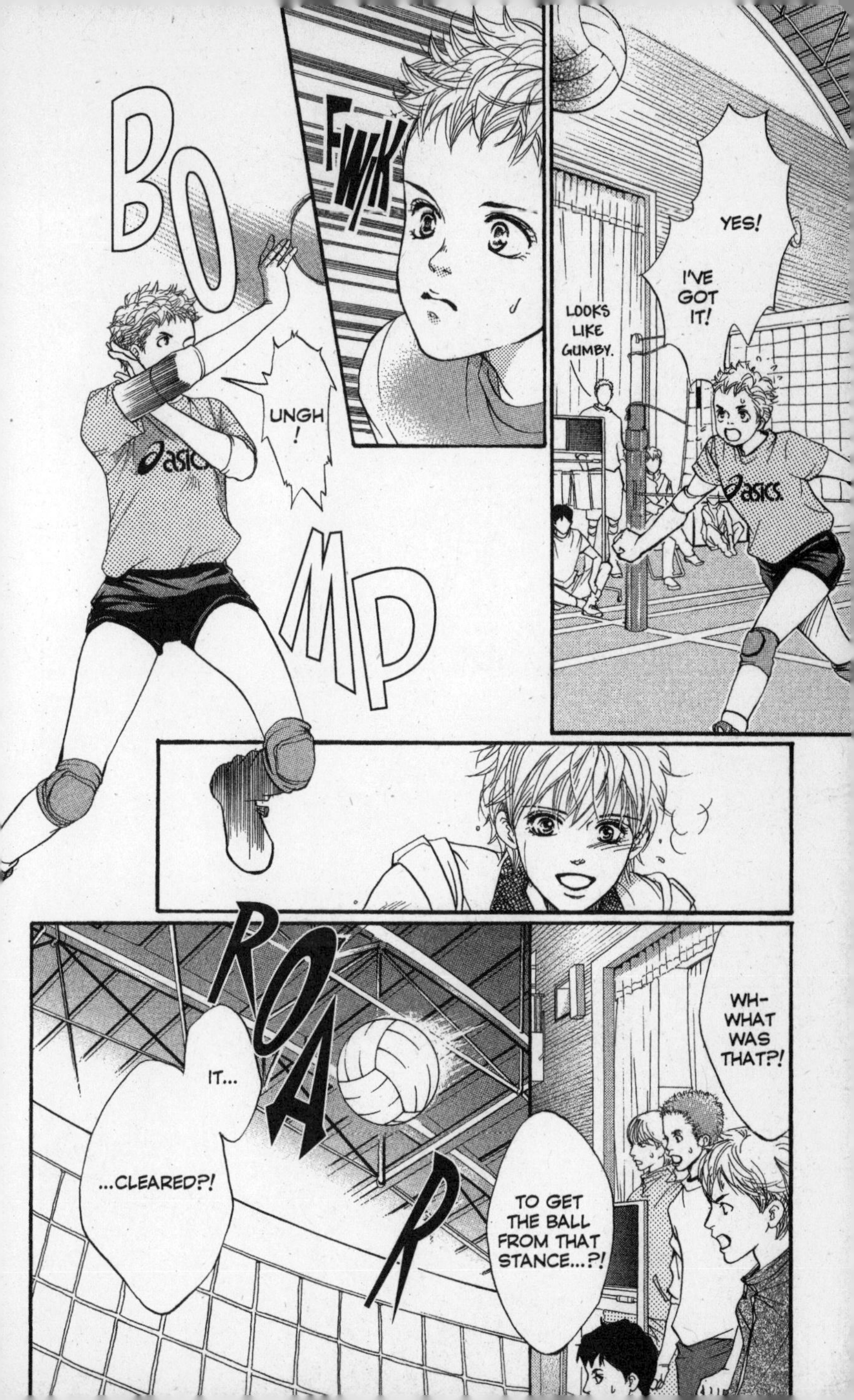
YES!
I'VE GOT IT!
LOOKS LIKE GUMBY.
FWK
BOMP
UNGH!
WH-WHAT WAS THAT?!
TO GET THE BALL FROM THAT STANCE...?!
ROAR
IT...
...CLEARED?!

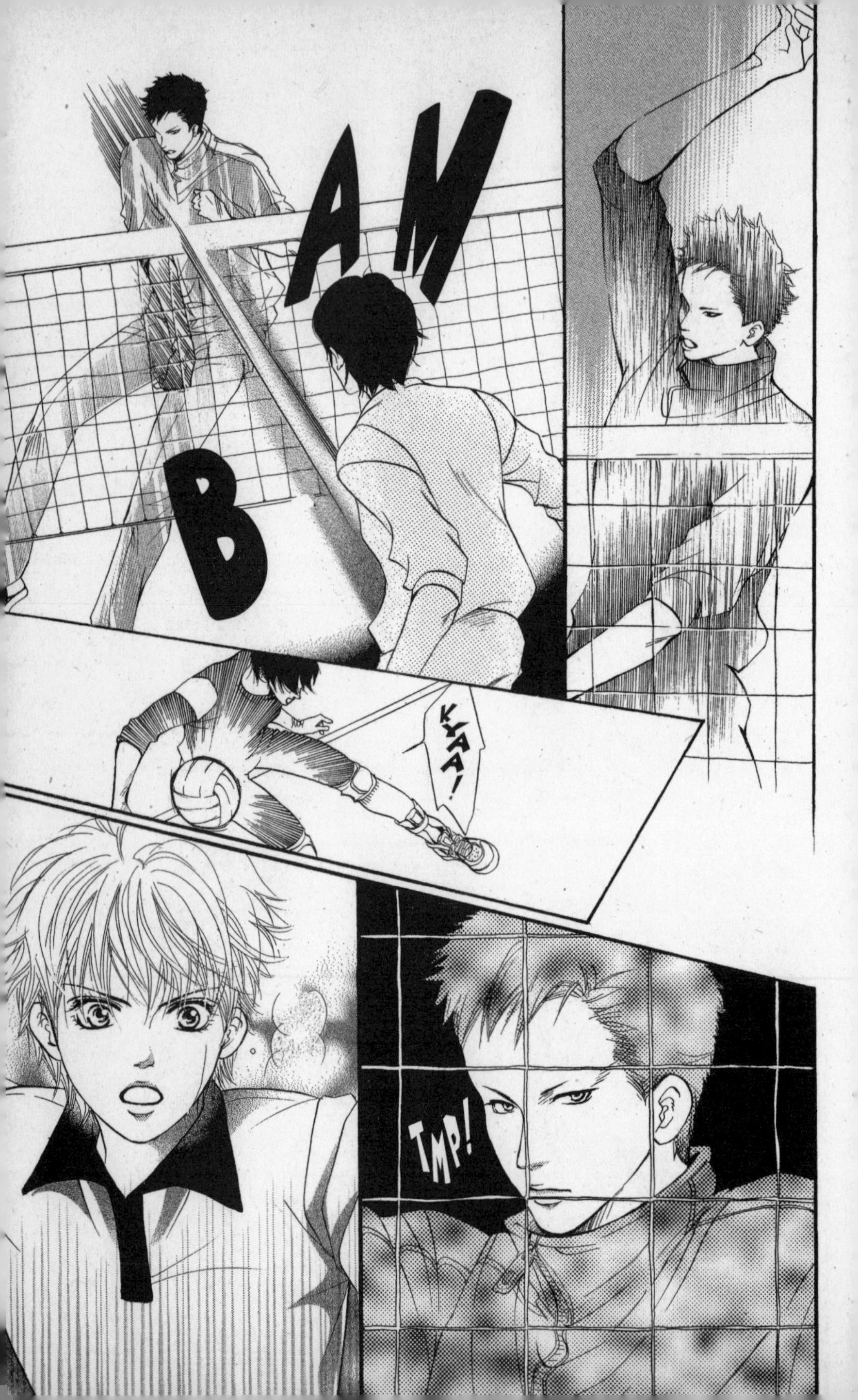
BAM
KYAA!
TMP!

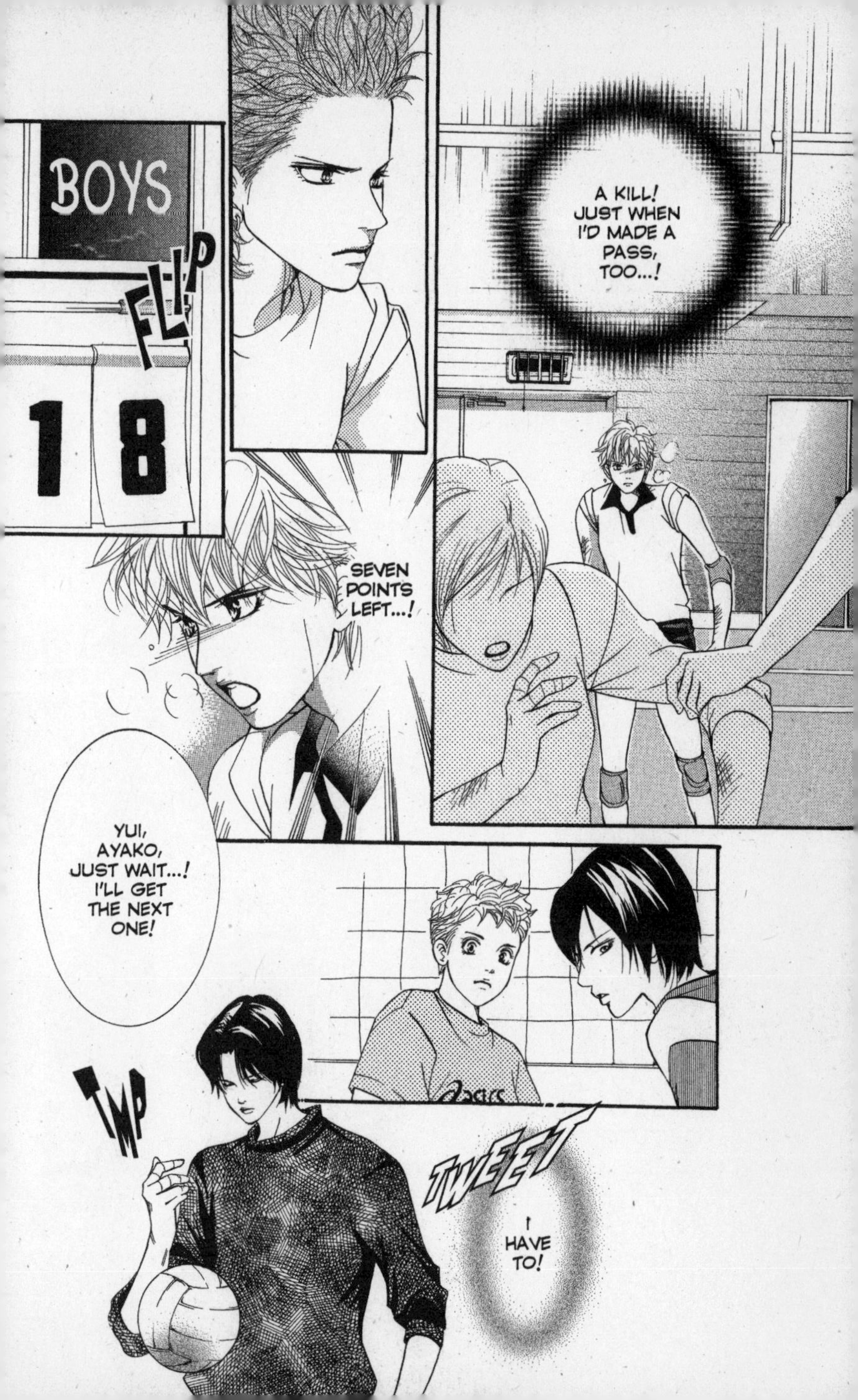
A KILL! JUST WHEN I'D MADE A PASS, TOO...!
BOYS
FLIP
18
SEVEN POINTS LEFT...!
YUI, AYAKO, JUST WAIT...! I'LL GET THE NEXT ONE!
TWEET
I HAVE TO!
TMP

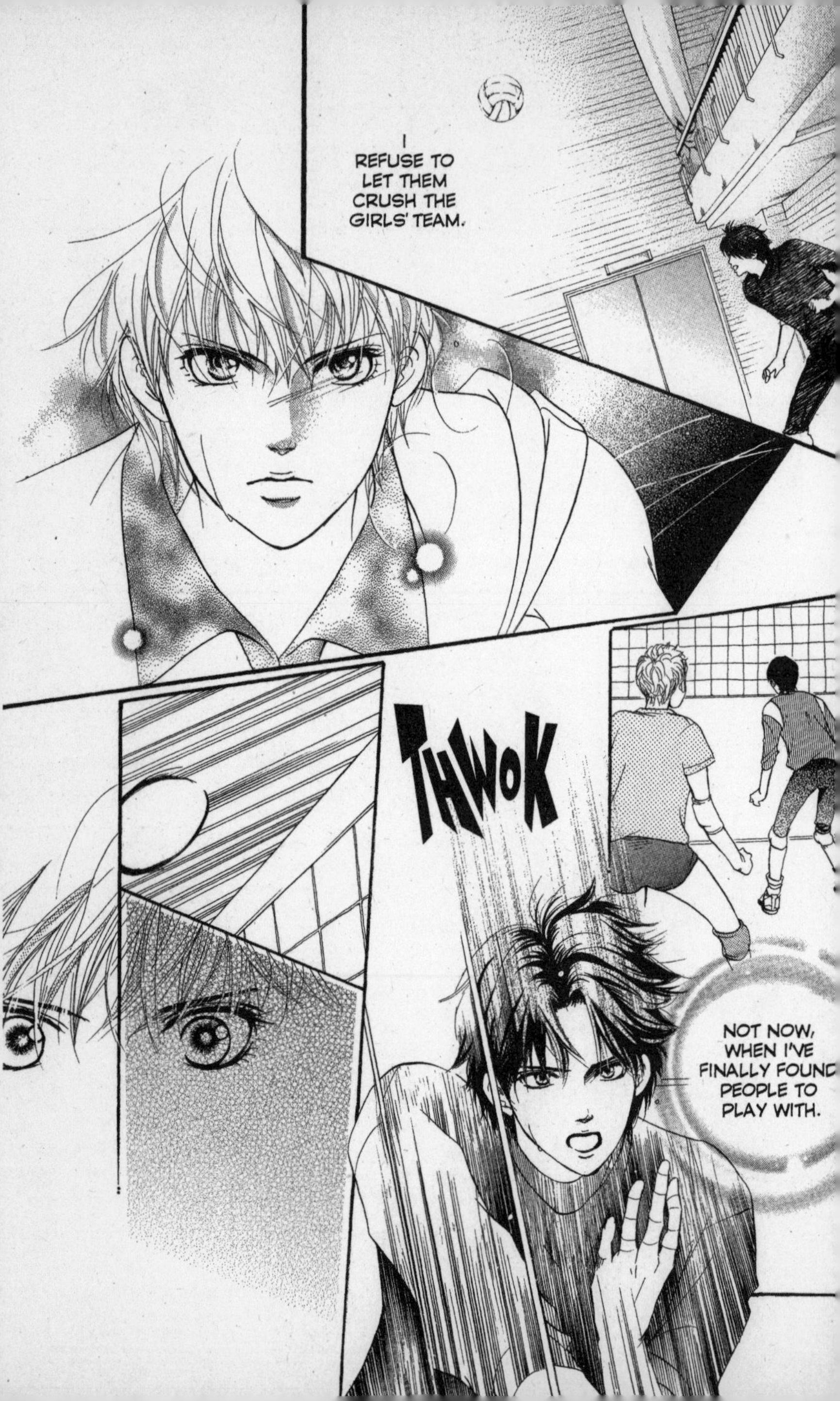
I REFUSE TO LET THEM CRUSH THE GIRLS' TEAM.
THWOK
NOT NOW, WHEN I'VE FINALLY FOUND PEOPLE TO PLAY WITH.

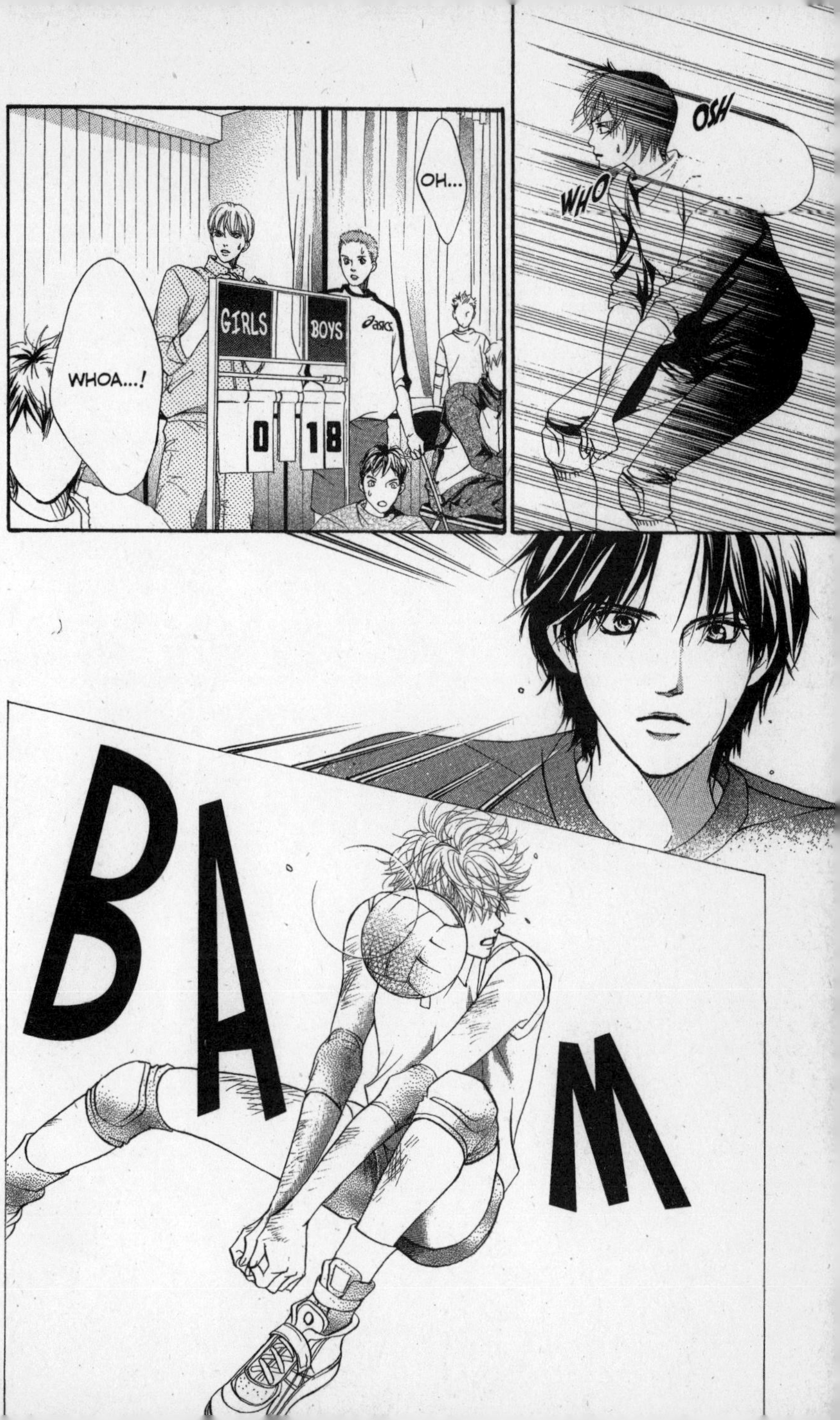
WHO
OSH
OH...
WHOA...!
GIRLS
BOYS
0
18
BAM

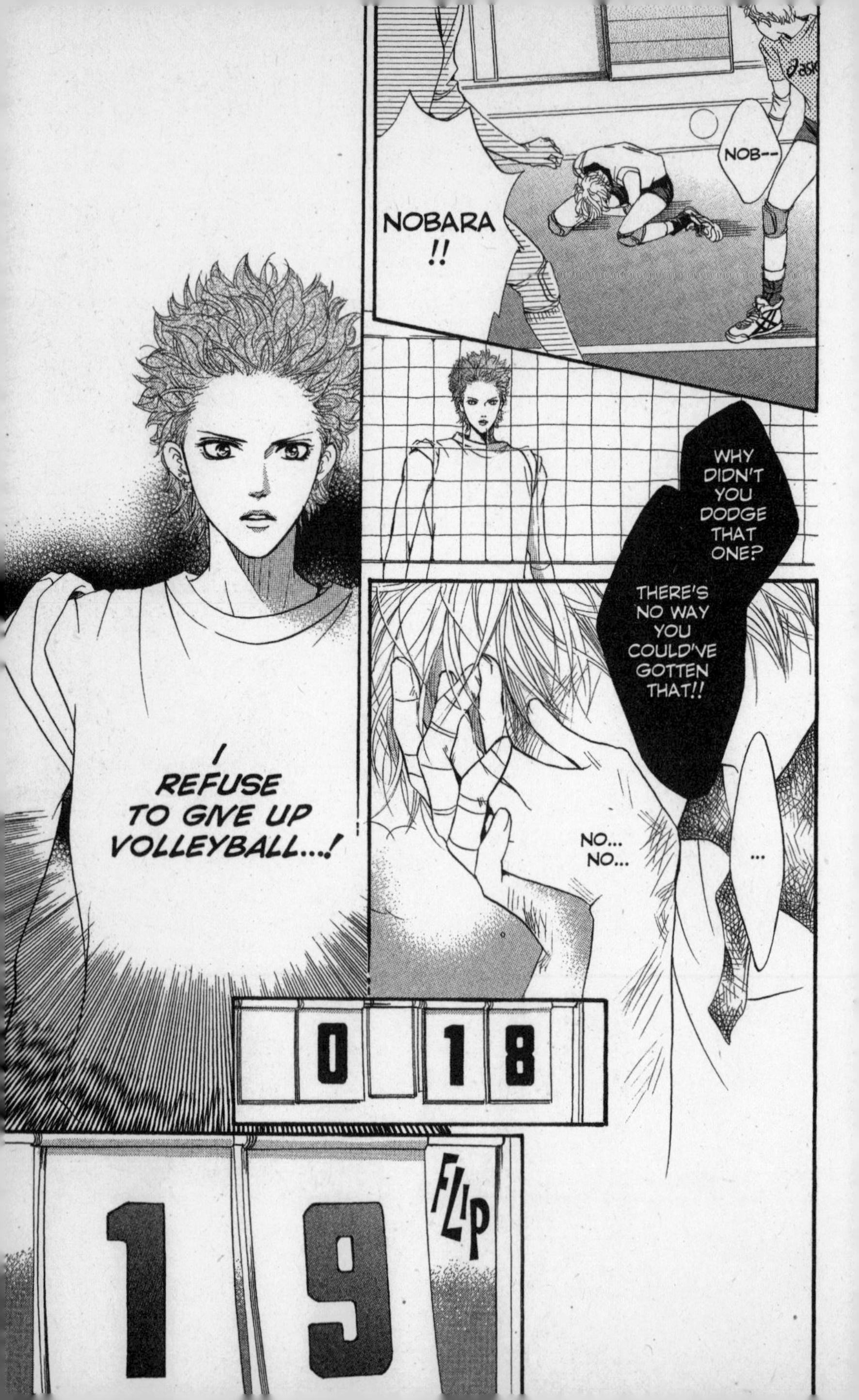
NOB--
NOBARA !!
WHY DIDN'T YOU DODGE THAT ONE?
THERE'S NO WAY YOU COULD'VE GOTTEN THAT!!
...
NO... NO...
I REFUSE TO GIVE UP VOLLEYBALL...!
0 18
FLIP
1 9

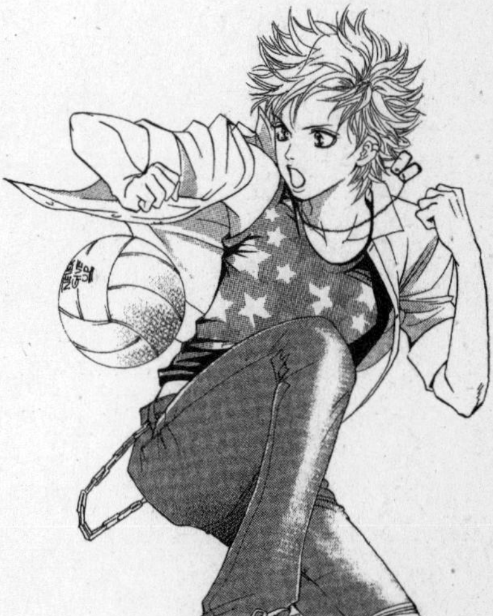

Crimson Hero

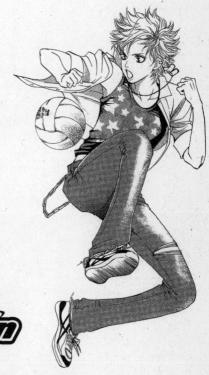

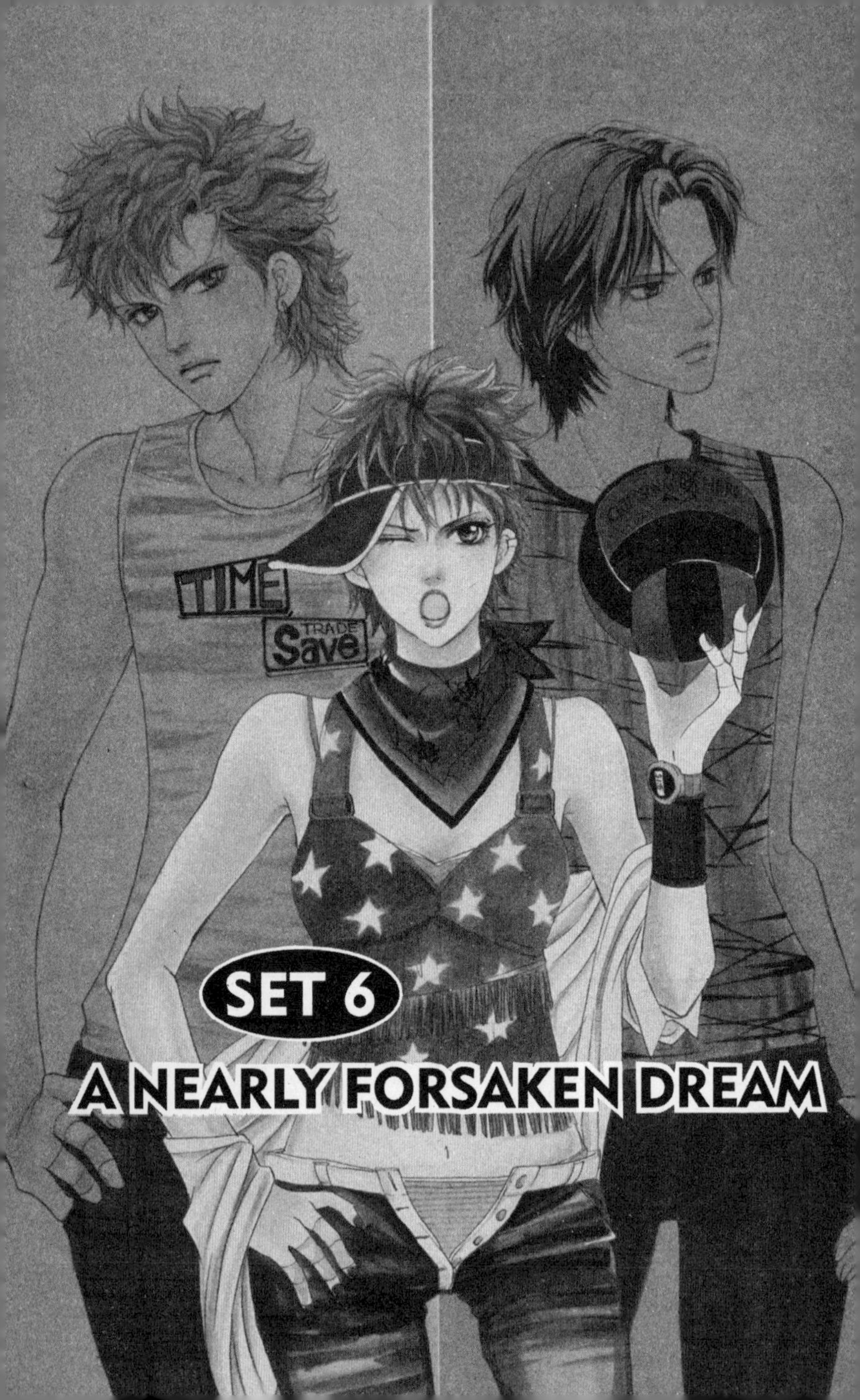
TIME
TRADE
Save
SET 6
A NEARLY FORSAKEN DREAM

Crimson Hero

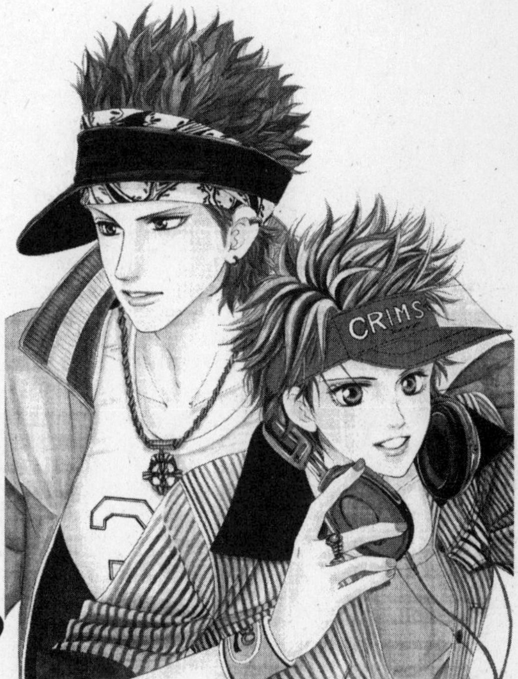
CRIMS

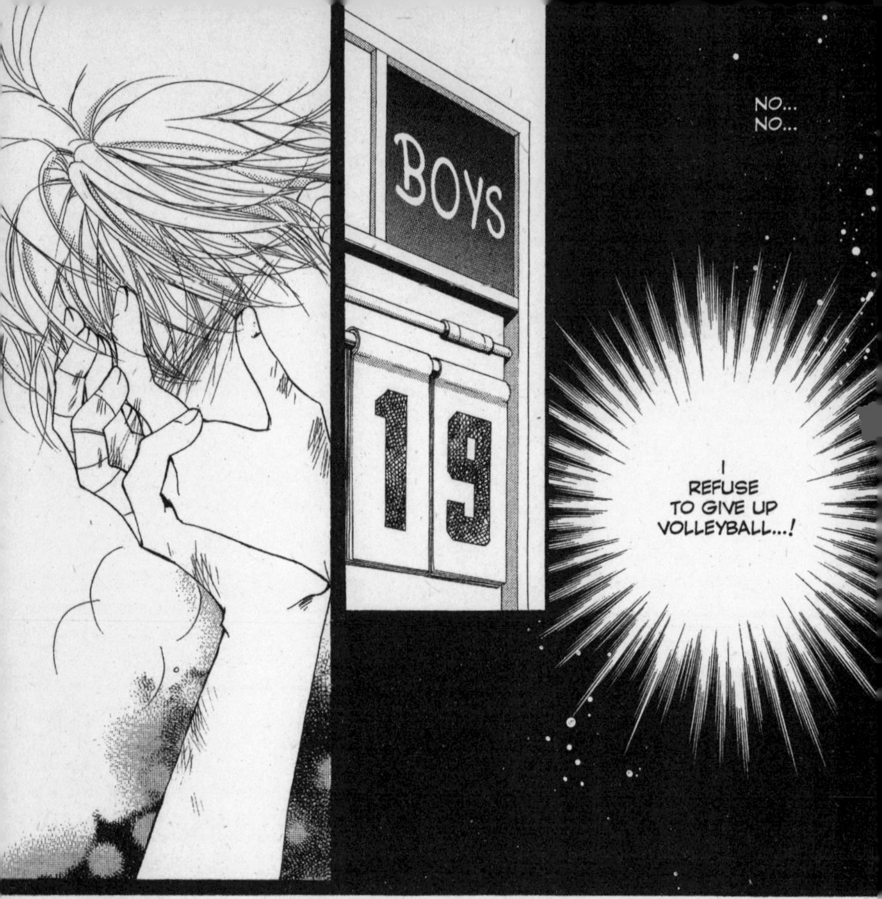
NO...
NO...
I REFUSE TO GIVE UP VOLLEYBALL...!
BOYS
19

THE MAKING OF CRIMSON HERO

Vol. 2

CONTINUED FROM VOL. 1...

IT STARTED WITH THE PROCESSIONAL ENTRANCE OF THE PLAYERS AND THE OPENING CEREMONY. TAKANASHI WAS QUITE SURPRISED AT THE PROCESSIONAL, WONDERING IF THEY REHEARSED THAT TOO. IT WAS AMAZING-- THEY MARCHED IN PERFECT ALIGNMENT.

BUT THERE WERE A COUPLE OF FLUSTERED GIRLS MIXED IN, STICKING OUT THEIR ARM ON THE SAME SIDE AS THEIR LEG. IT WAS CUTE.

AFTER THE OPENING CEREMONY, THE J-POP BAND ARASHI CAME OUT. A CLAMOR AROSE IN THE ARENA. THE LIGHTS WENT OUT AND THE STADIUM ERUPTED WITH SCREAMS OF "KYAAAA!!!"

WHAT IS IT?! WHAT HAP-PENED?!

I'M BUDDIES WITH ARASHI.

KYAAA!!

BY THE WAY, NINOMIYA IS THE ONLY BAND MEMBER WHOSE NAME I KNOW. (SORRY.)

↖ BABO, THE MASCOT.

THEN THE GAMES BEGAN. TAKANASHI FOUND A HERO WITHIN SECONDS. THE INSTANT SHE LAID HER EYES ON HIM SHE THOUGHT, "AH, IT'S HIM. NO DOUBT ABOUT IT."

THAT'S RIGHT. SEE, HE KIND OF LOOKED LIKE YUSHIN. AT ANY RATE, I THOUGHT SO. HE WAS THE TEAM ACE AND SHOUTED THE MOST. WHEN HE GOT ACED BY A SERVE HE'D GET SO FRUSTRATED. EVEN WE SPECTATORS FELT HIS ANGUISH. HE WAS SO FRANK AND OPEN. UNFORTUNATELY, HIS SCHOOL WAS ELIMINATED IN THREE ROUNDS. TAKANASHI HOPED THEY'D WIN AT THE REGIONALS AGAIN NEXT YEAR SO SHE COULD ENCOUNTER HIS POWER AND HONEST DIRECTNESS ONCE AGAIN. AH, YOUR PLAYING BRINGS TEARS TO MY EYES.

OVER 190 CM. SO TALL...

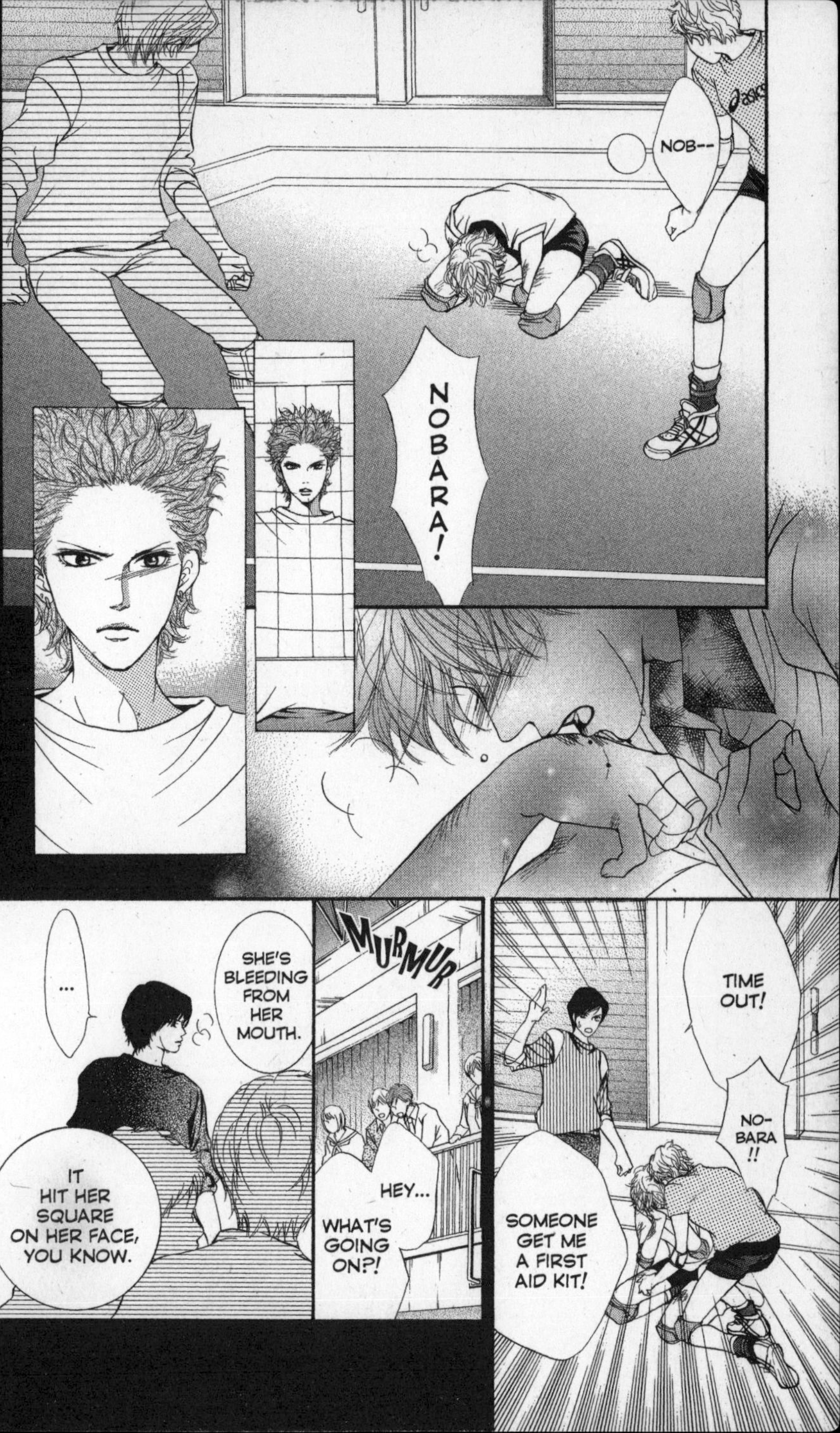
NOB--
NOBARA!
TIME OUT!
NO-BARA!!
SOMEONE GET ME A FIRST AID KIT!
MURMUR
HEY...
WHAT'S GOING ON?!
SHE'S BLEEDING FROM HER MOUTH.
...
IT HIT HER SQUARE ON HER FACE, YOU KNOW.

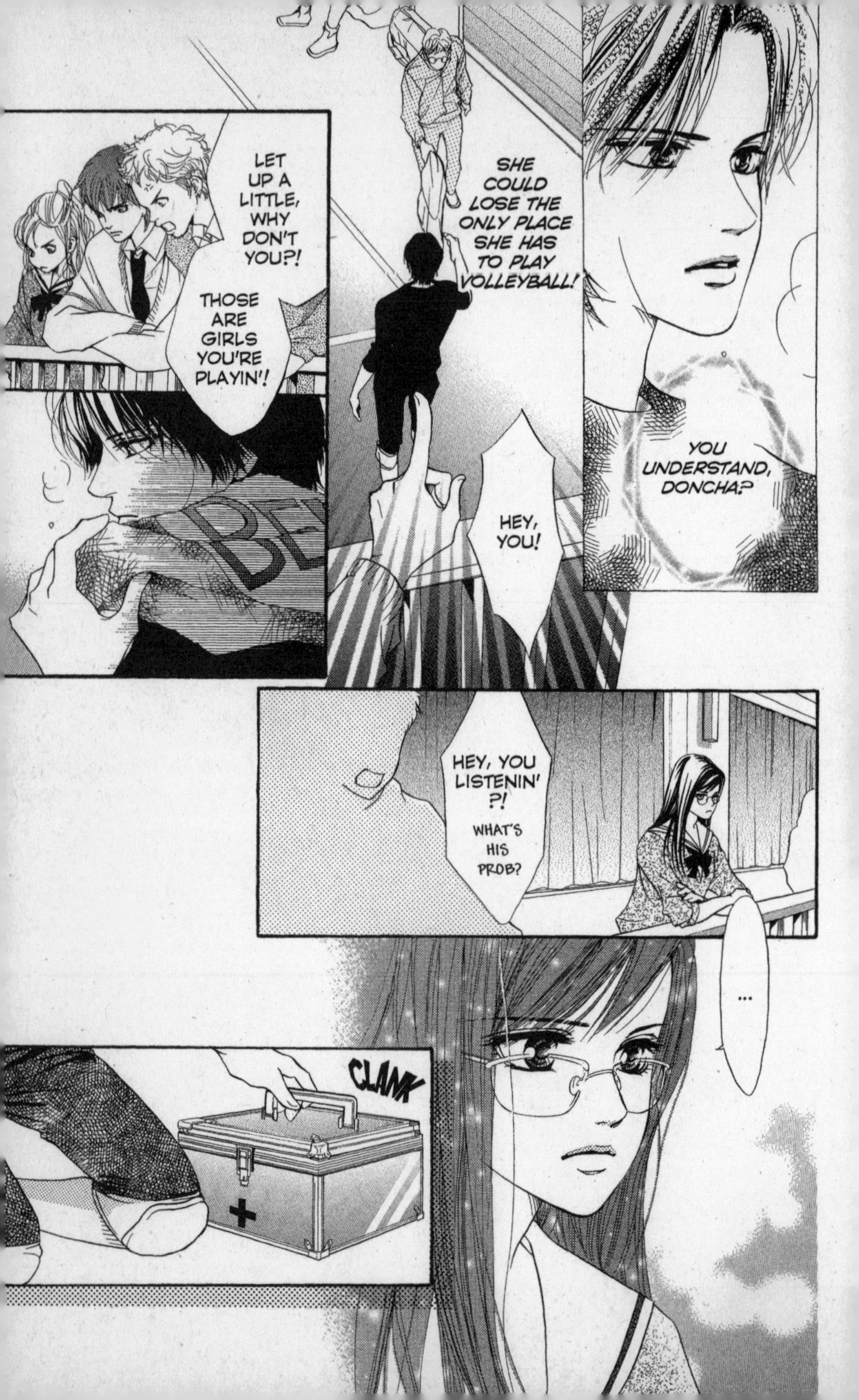
SHE COULD LOSE THE ONLY PLACE SHE HAS TO PLAY VOLLEYBALL!
YOU UNDERSTAND, DONCHA?
HEY, YOU!
LET UP A LITTLE, WHY DON'T YOU?!
THOSE ARE GIRLS YOU'RE PLAYIN'!
HEY, YOU LISTENIN' ?!
WHAT'S HIS PROB?
...
CLANK

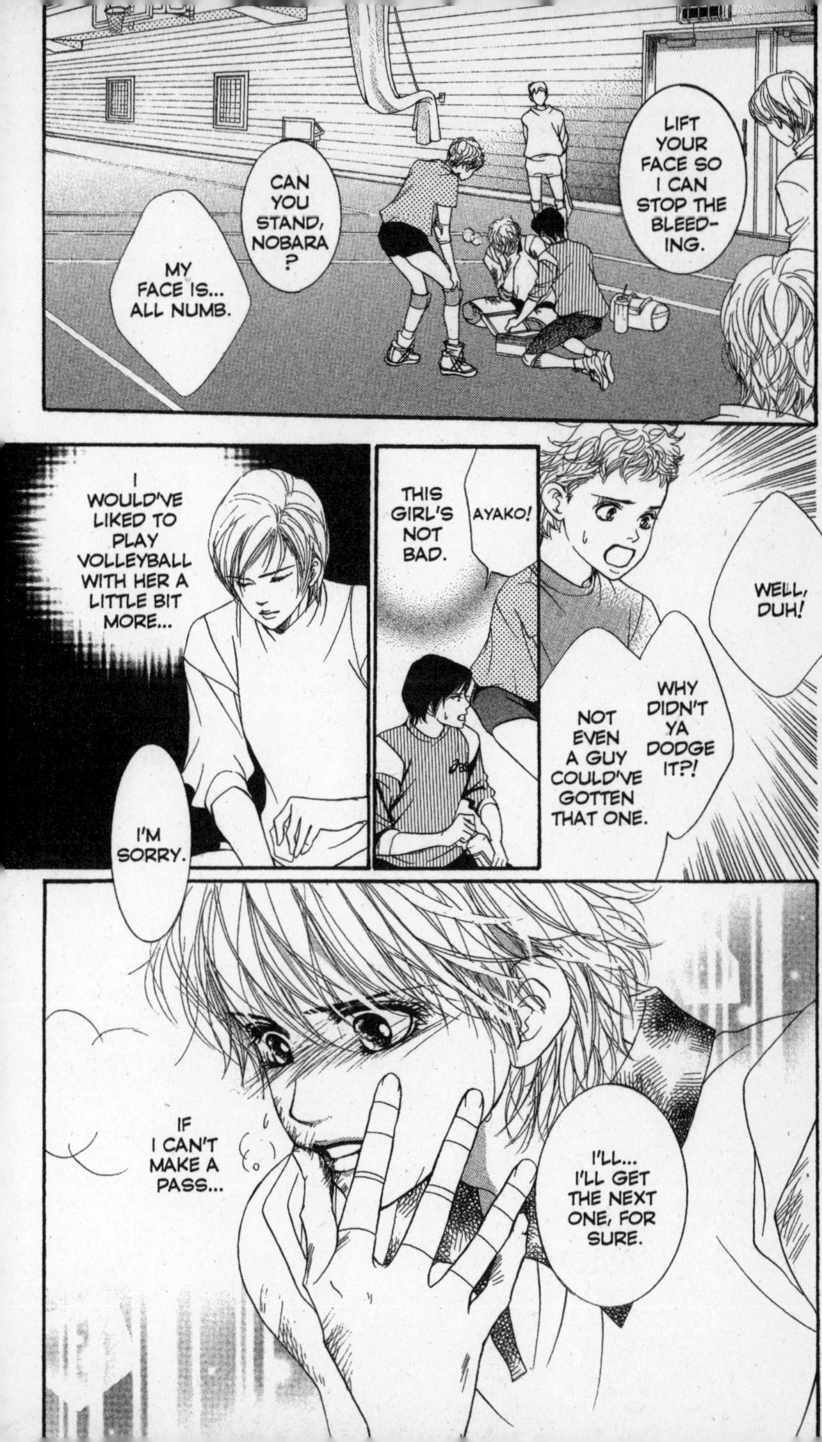
LIFT YOUR FACE SO I CAN STOP THE BLEED-ING.
CAN YOU STAND, NOBARA?
MY FACE IS... ALL NUMB.
WELL, DUH!
WHY DIDN'T YA DODGE IT?!
NOT EVEN A GUY COULD'VE GOTTEN THAT ONE.
AYAKO!
THIS GIRL'S NOT BAD.
I WOULD'VE LIKED TO PLAY VOLLEYBALL WITH HER A LITTLE BIT MORE...
I'M SORRY.
I'LL... I'LL GET THE NEXT ONE, FOR SURE.
IF I CAN'T MAKE A PASS...

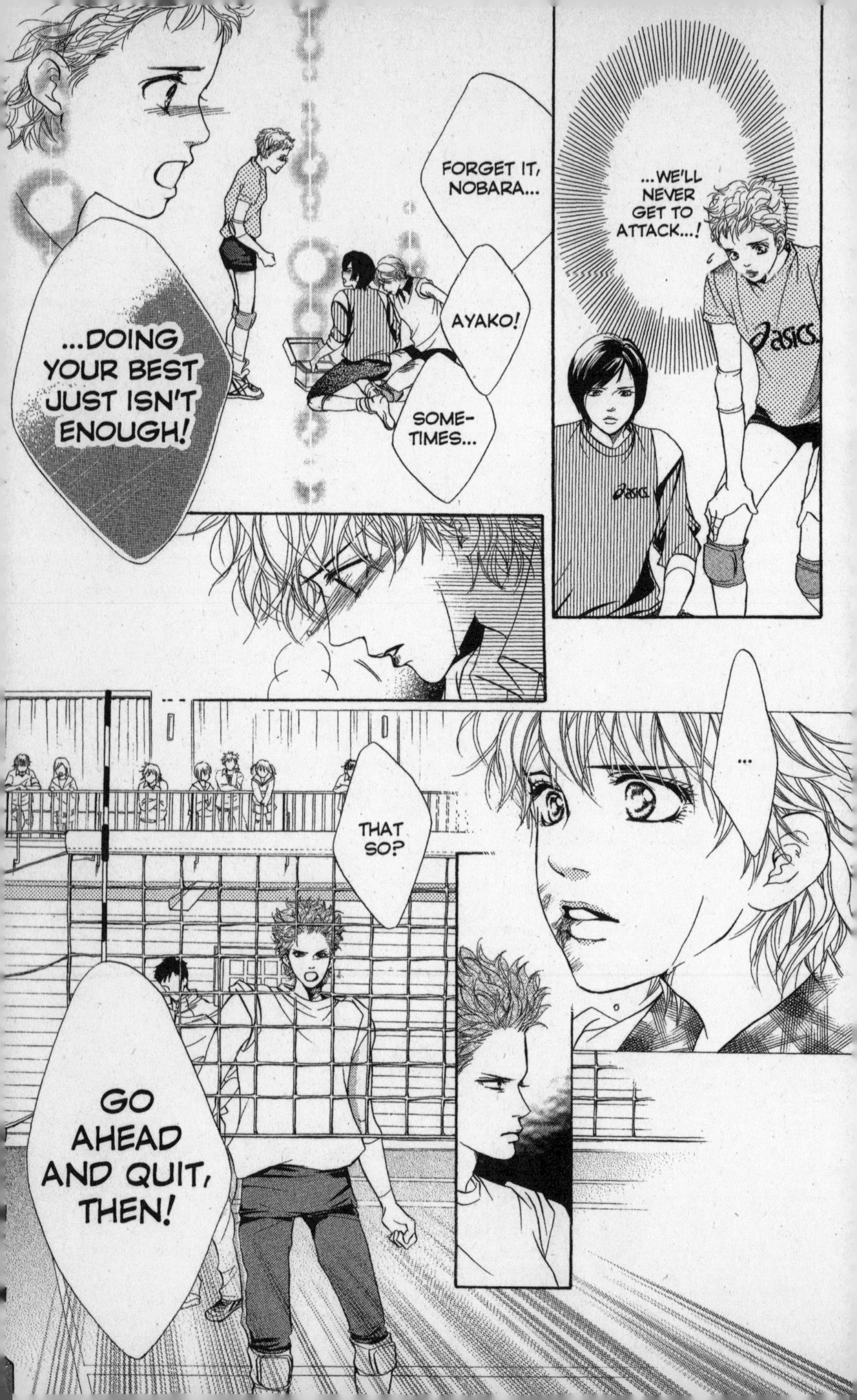
...WE'LL NEVER GET TO ATTACK...!
FORGET IT, NOBARA...
AYAKO!
SOME-TIMES...
...DOING YOUR BEST JUST ISN'T ENOUGH!
...
THAT SO?
GO AHEAD AND QUIT, THEN!

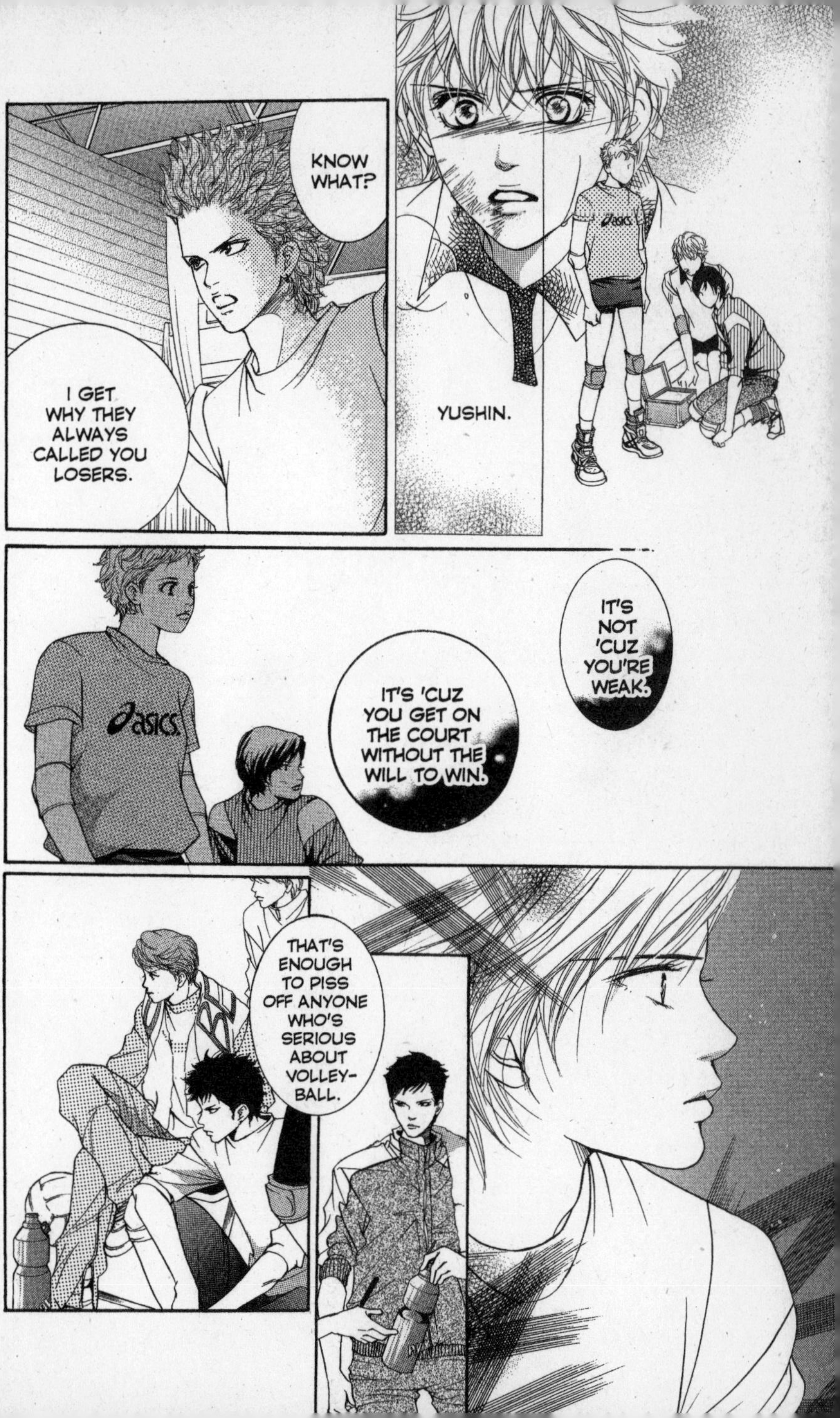
YUSHIN.
KNOW WHAT?
I GET WHY THEY ALWAYS CALLED YOU LOSERS.
IT'S NOT 'CUZ YOU'RE WEAK.
IT'S 'CUZ YOU GET ON THE COURT WITHOUT THE WILL TO WIN.
THAT'S ENOUGH TO PISS OFF ANYONE WHO'S SERIOUS ABOUT VOLLEY-BALL.

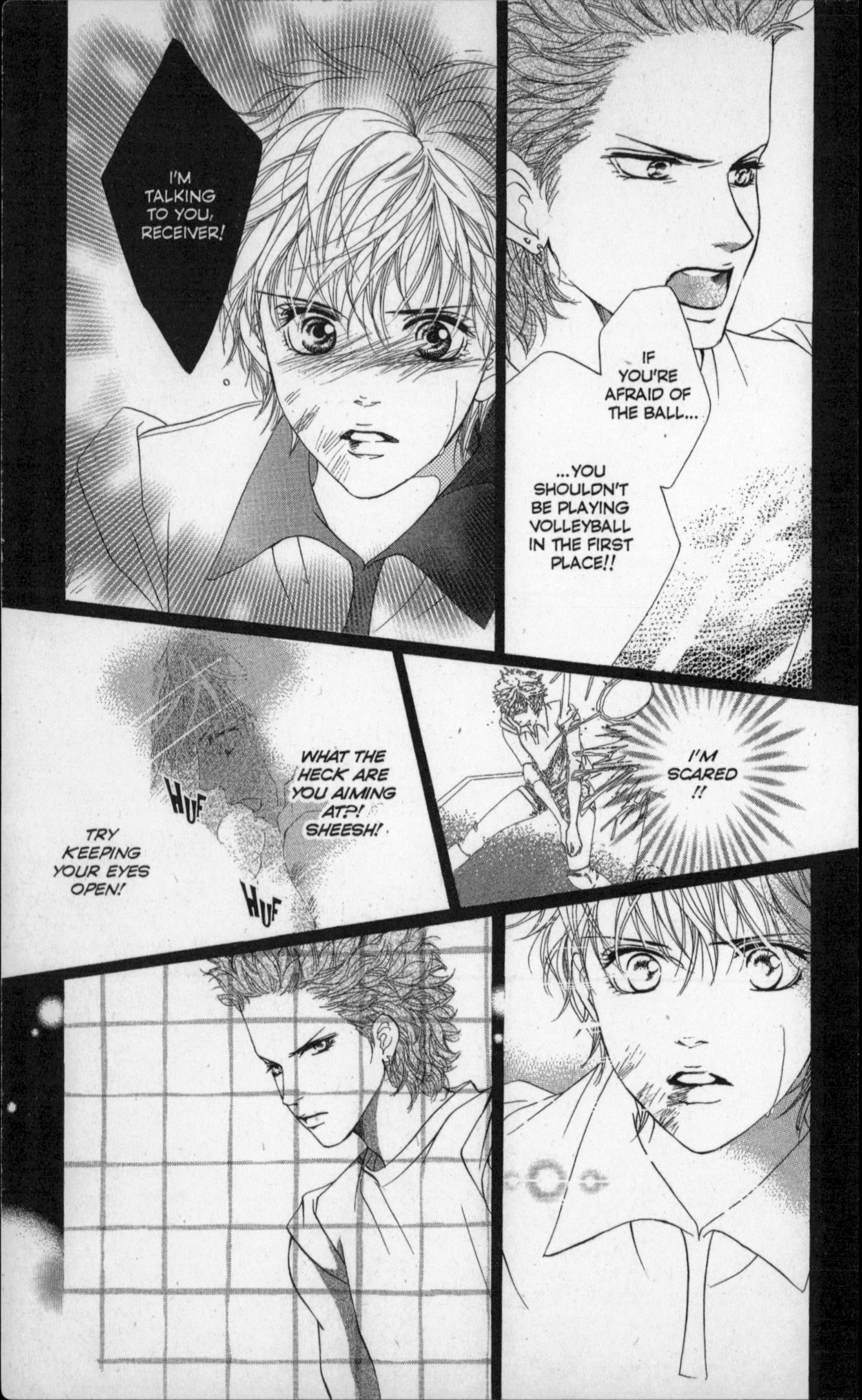
IF YOU'RE AFRAID OF THE BALL...
...YOU SHOULDN'T BE PLAYING VOLLEYBALL IN THE FIRST PLACE!!
I'M TALKING TO YOU, RECEIVER!
I'M SCARED!!
WHAT THE HECK ARE YOU AIMING AT?! SHEESH!
HUF
TRY KEEPING YOUR EYES OPEN!
HUF

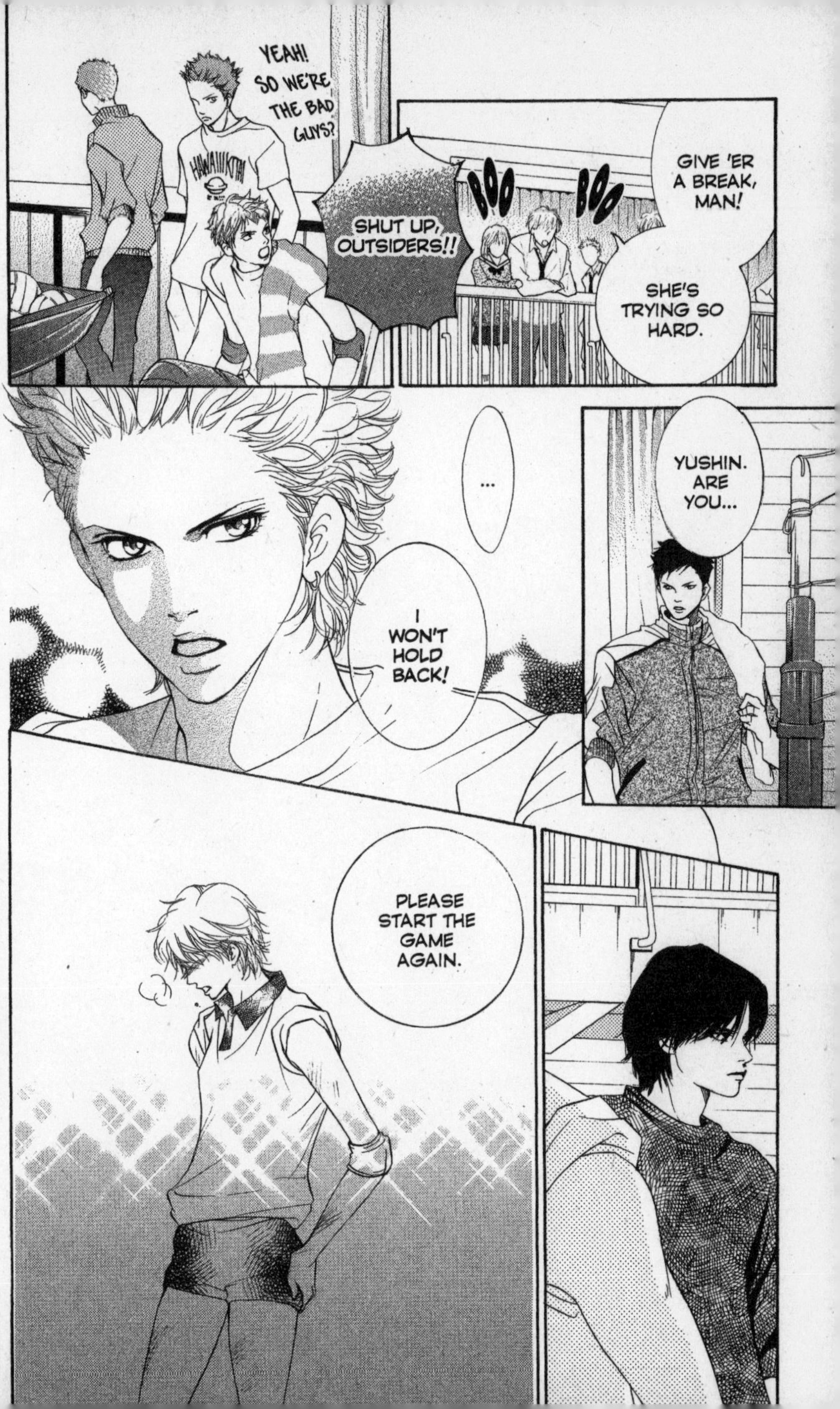
BOO
BOO
GIVE 'ER A BREAK, MAN!
SHE'S TRYING SO HARD.
SHUT UP, OUTSIDERS!!
YEAH! SO WE'RE THE BAD GUYS?
YUSHIN. ARE YOU...
...
I WON'T HOLD BACK!
PLEASE START THE GAME AGAIN.

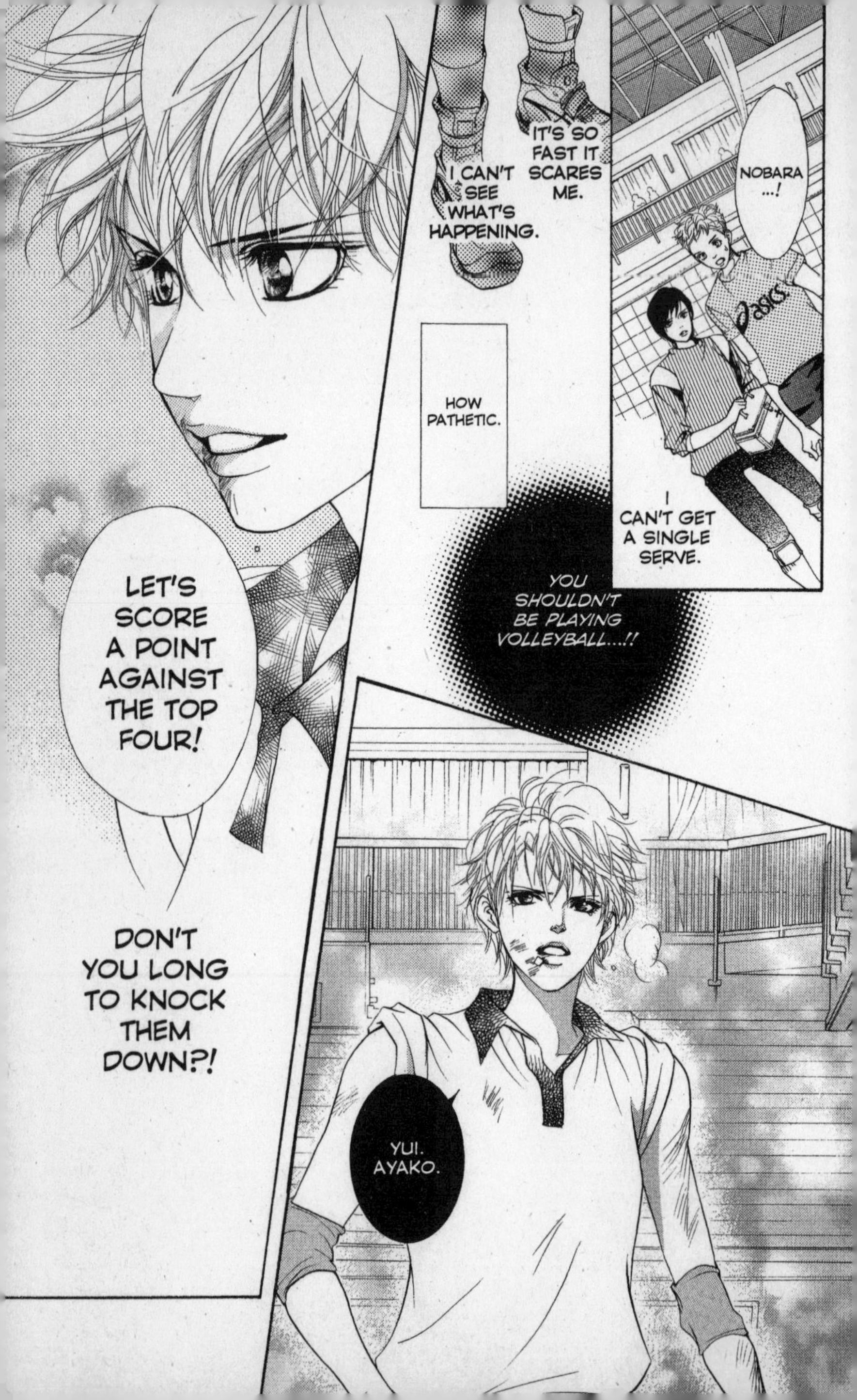
NOBARA ...!
I CAN'T GET A SINGLE SERVE.
IT'S SO FAST IT SCARES ME.
I CAN'T SEE WHAT'S HAPPENING.
HOW PATHETIC.
YOU SHOULDN'T BE PLAYING VOLLEYBALL...!!
YUI. AYAKO.
LET'S SCORE A POINT AGAINST THE TOP FOUR!
DON'T YOU LONG TO KNOCK THEM DOWN?!

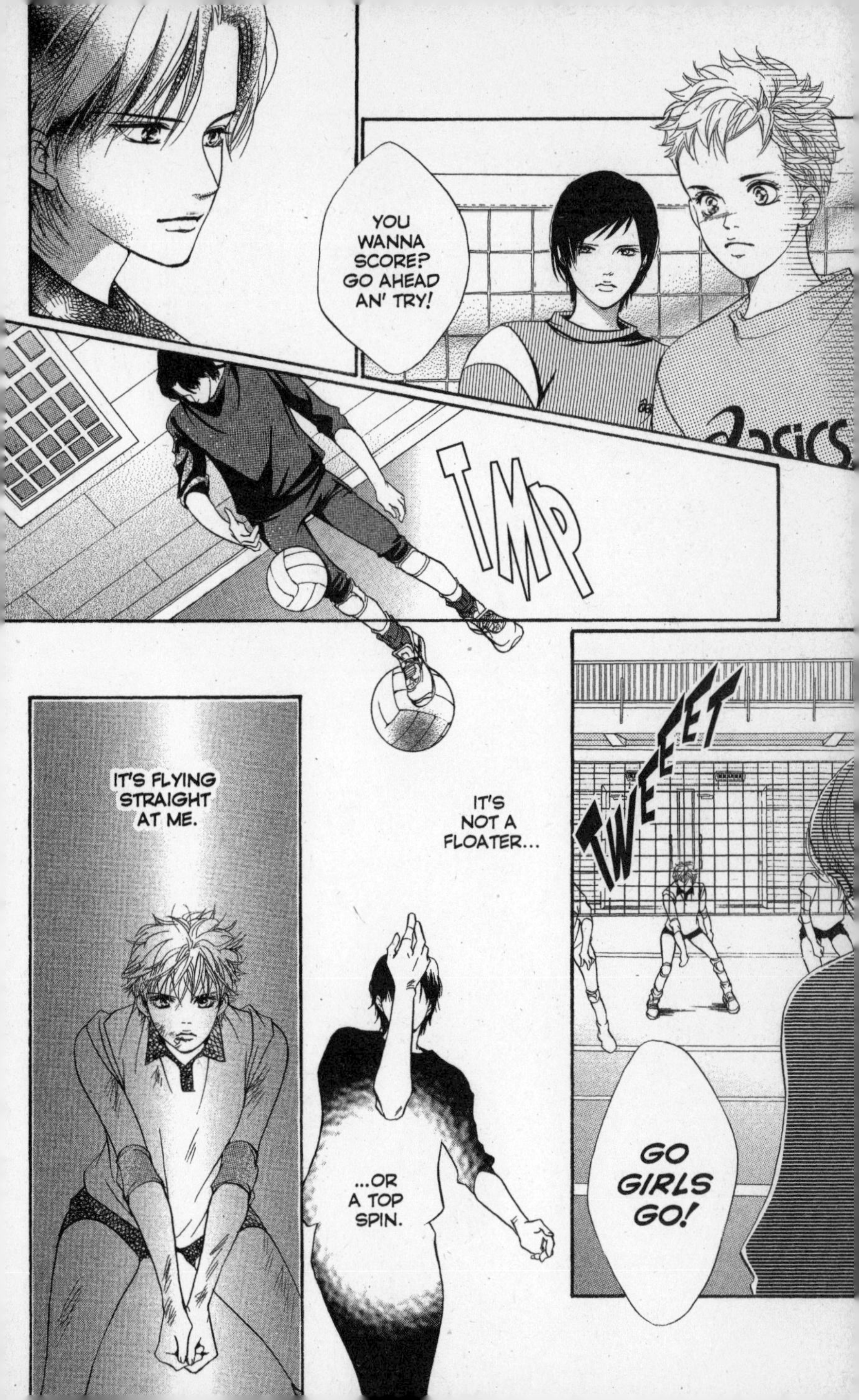
YOU WANNA SCORE? GO AHEAD AN' TRY!
TMP
TWEEET
GO GIRLS GO!
IT'S NOT A FLOATER...
...OR A TOP SPIN.
IT'S FLYING STRAIGHT AT ME.

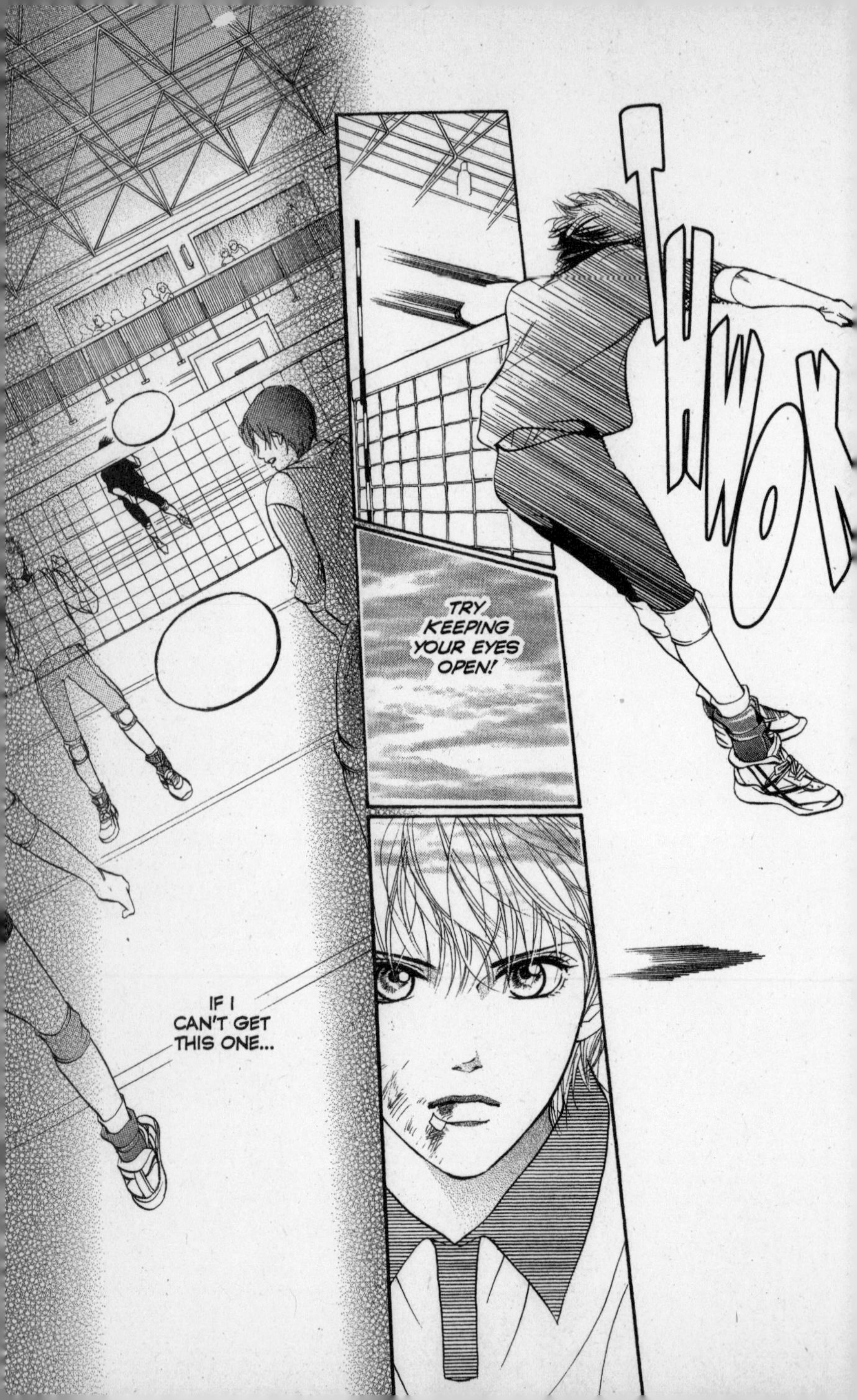
THWOCK
TRY KEEPING YOUR EYES OPEN!
IF I CAN'T GET THIS ONE...

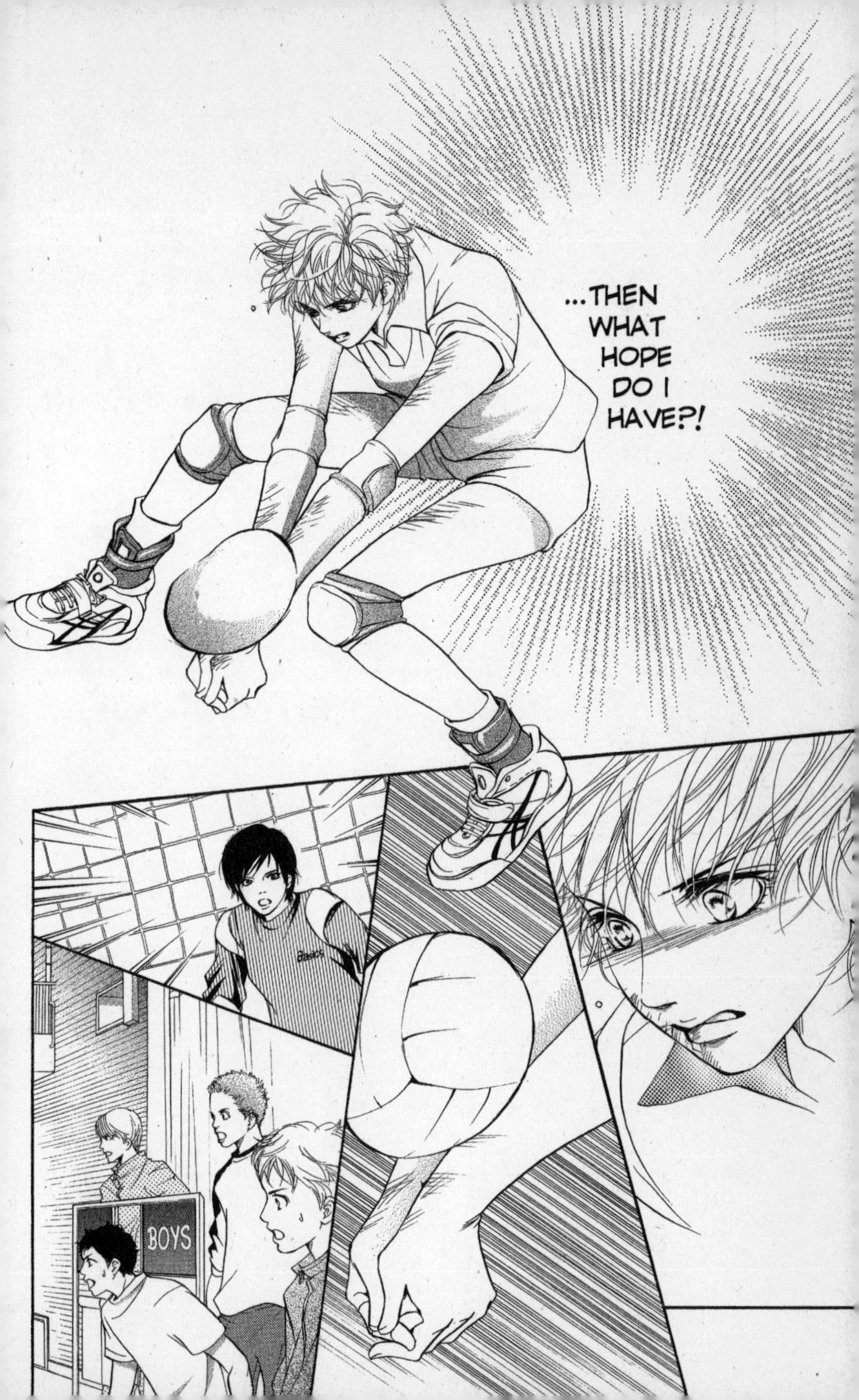
...THEN WHAT HOPE DO I HAVE?!
BOYS

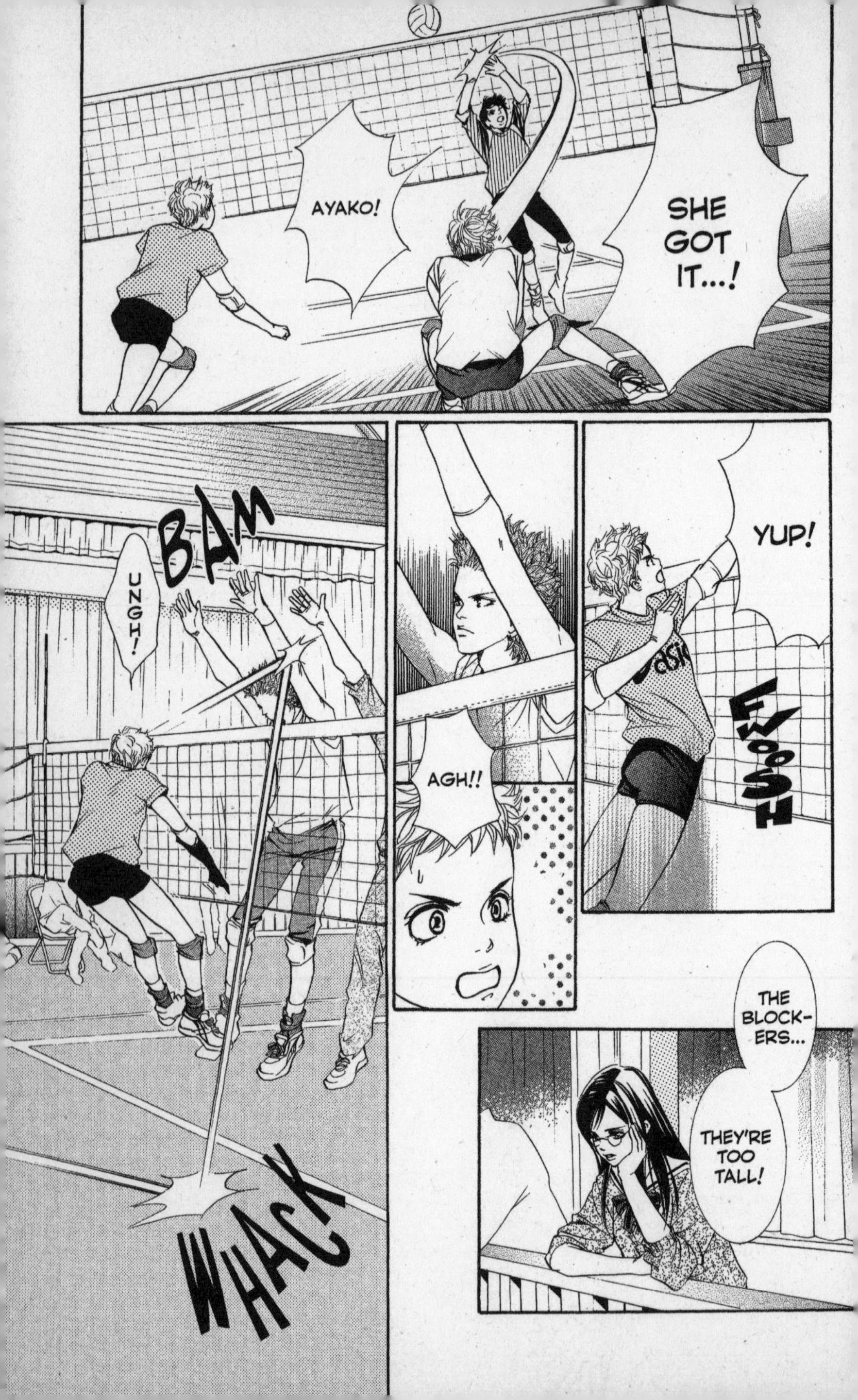
SHE GOT IT...!
AYAKO!
YUP!
FWOOSH
AGH!!
THE BLOCKERS...
THEY'RE TOO TALL!
BAM
UNGH!
WHACK

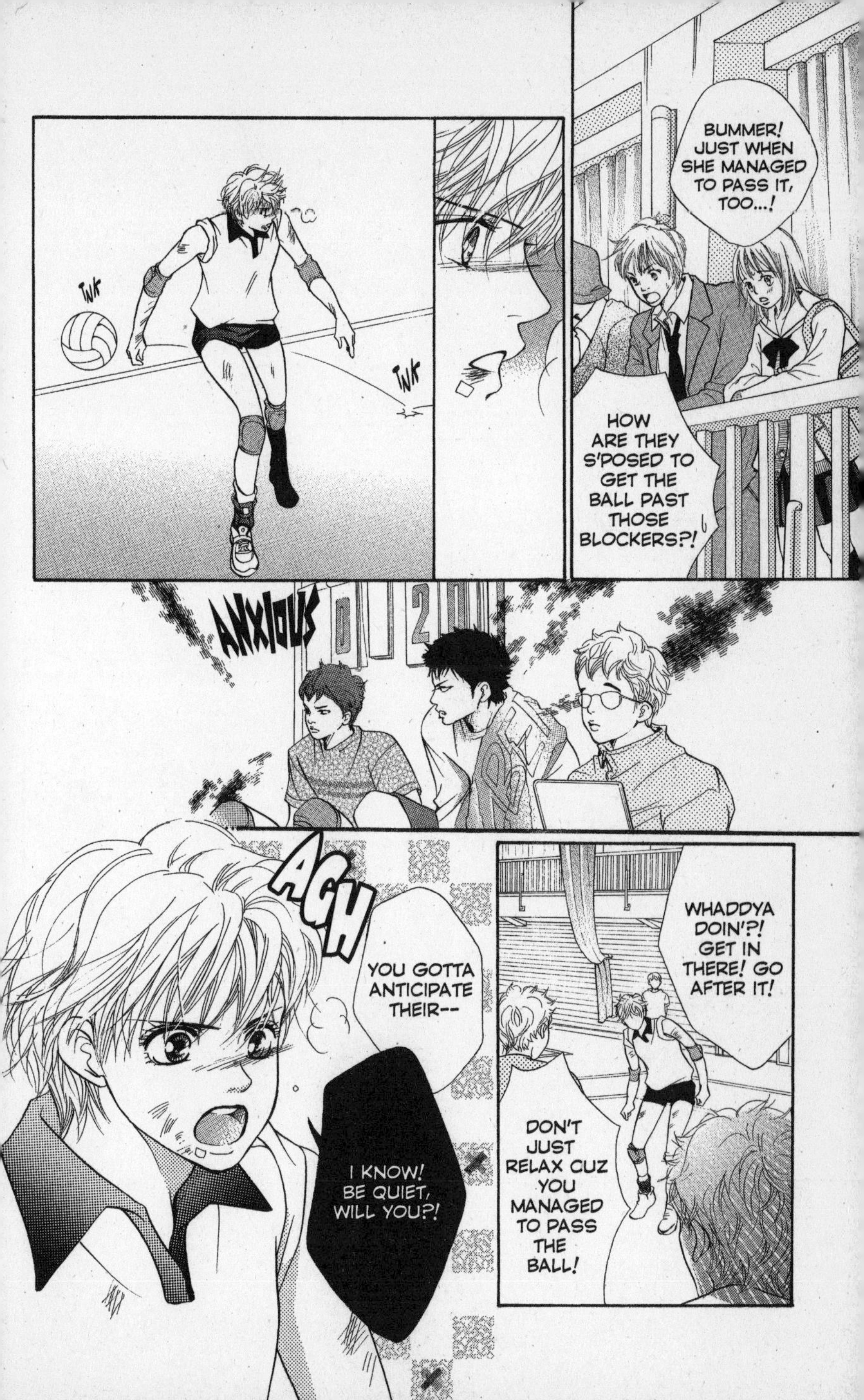
BUMMER! JUST WHEN SHE MANAGED TO PASS IT, TOO...!
HOW ARE THEY S'POSED TO GET THE BALL PAST THOSE BLOCKERS?!
TNK
TNK
ANXIOUS
WHADDYA DOIN'?! GET IN THERE! GO AFTER IT!
DON'T JUST RELAX CUZ YOU MANAGED TO PASS THE BALL!
AGH
YOU GOTTA ANTICIPATE THEIR--
I KNOW! BE QUIET, WILL YOU?!

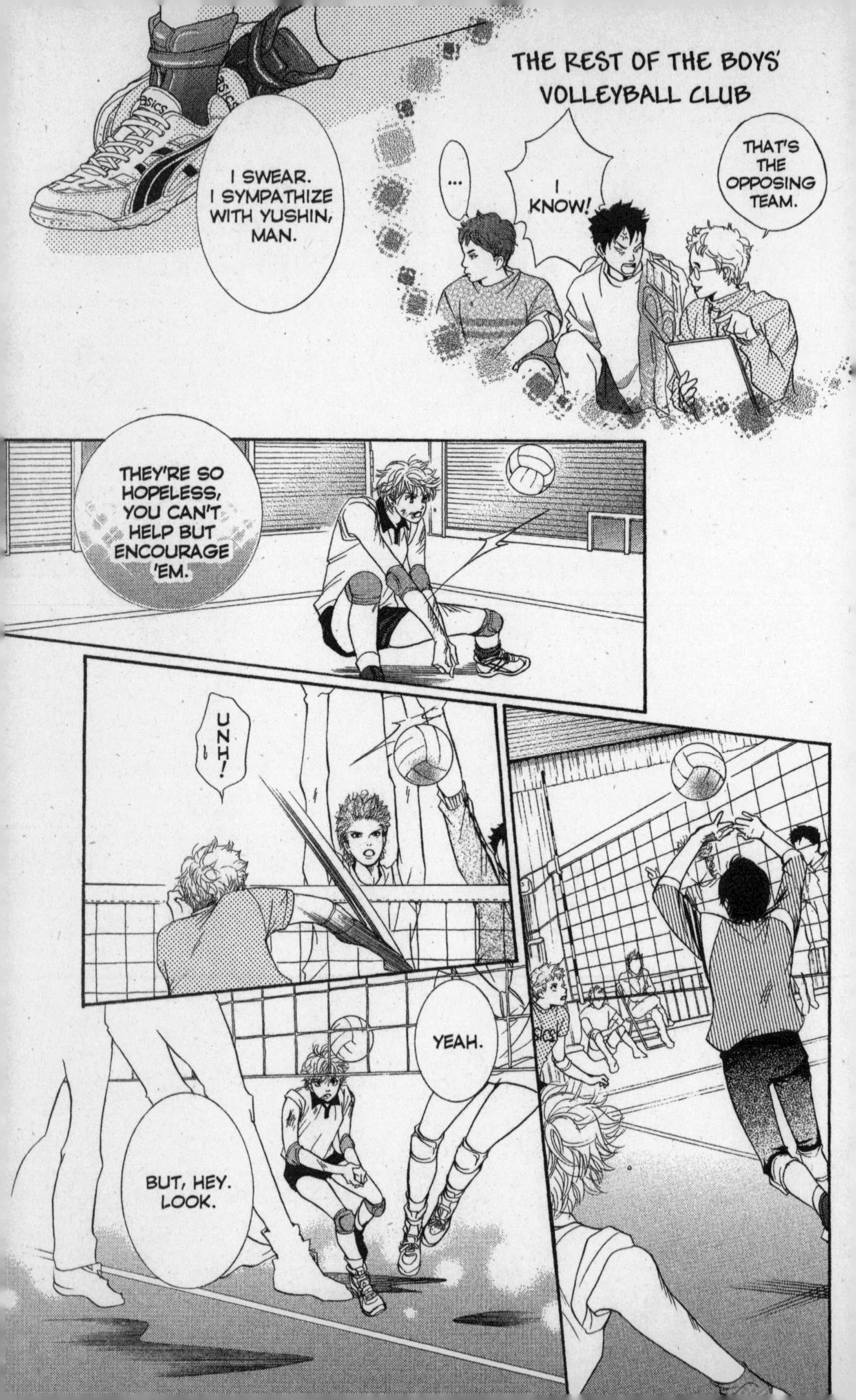
THE REST OF THE BOYS' VOLLEYBALL CLUB
THAT'S THE OPPOSING TEAM.
I KNOW!
...
I SWEAR. I SYMPATHIZE WITH YUSHIN, MAN.
THEY'RE SO HOPELESS, YOU CAN'T HELP BUT ENCOURAGE 'EM.
UNH!
YEAH.
BUT, HEY. LOOK.

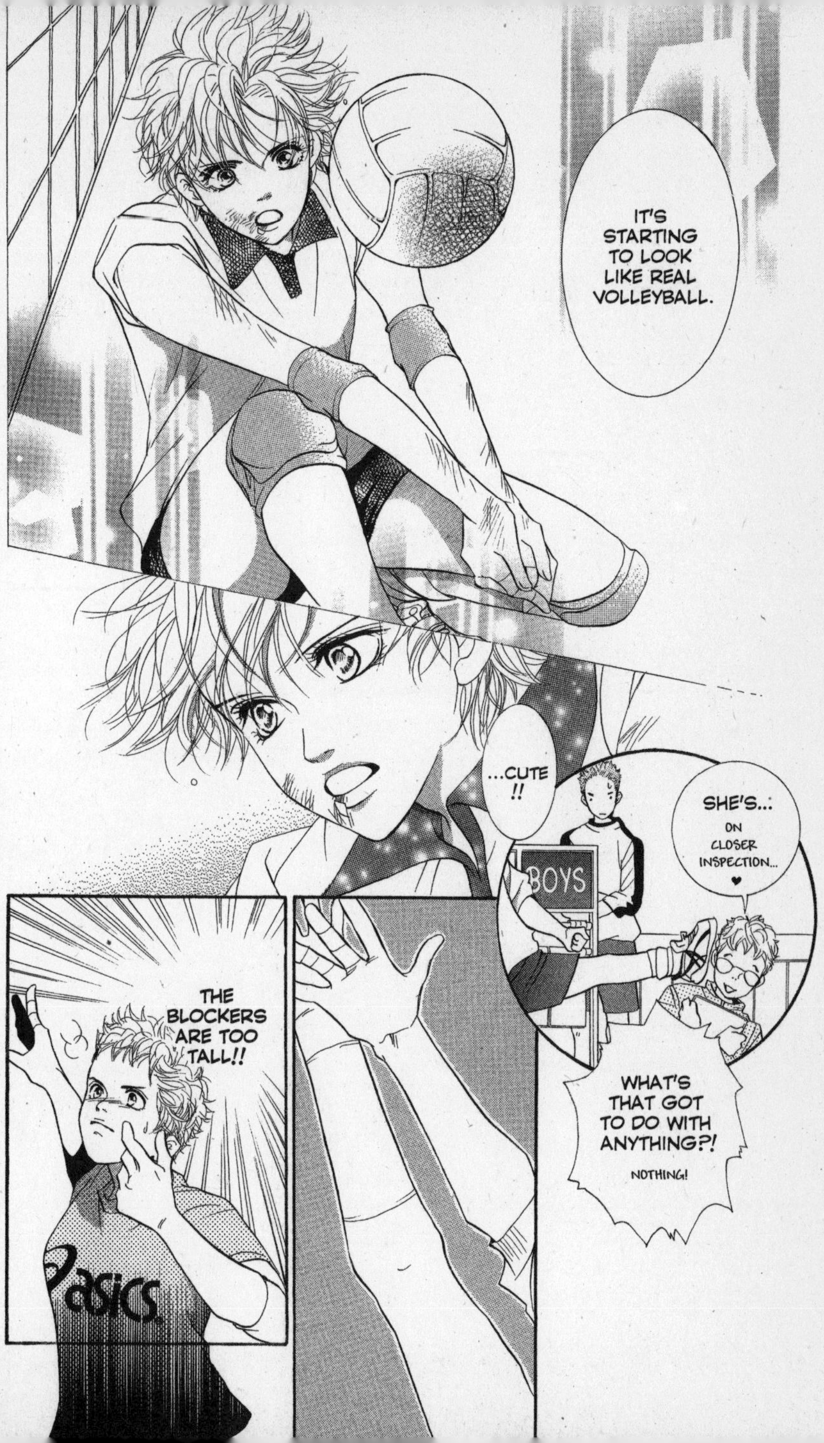
IT'S STARTING TO LOOK LIKE REAL VOLLEYBALL.
SHE'S... ON CLOSER INSPECTION... ♥
...CUTE!!
BOYS
WHAT'S THAT GOT TO DO WITH ANYTHING?!
NOTHING!
THE BLOCKERS ARE TOO TALL!!
asics

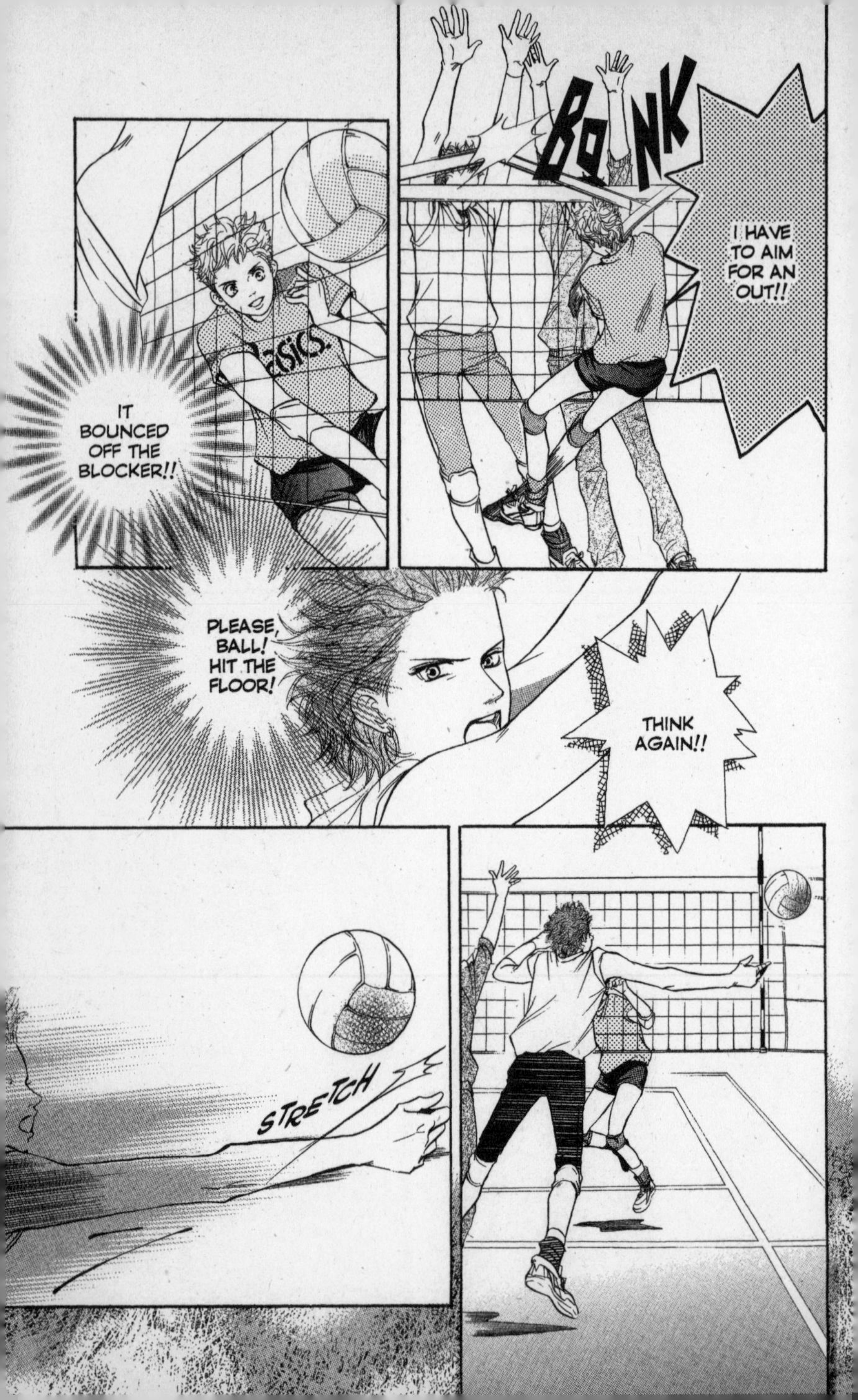
BONK
I HAVE TO AIM FOR AN OUT!!
IT BOUNCED OFF THE BLOCKER!!
PLEASE, BALL! HIT THE FLOOR!
THINK AGAIN!!
STRETCH

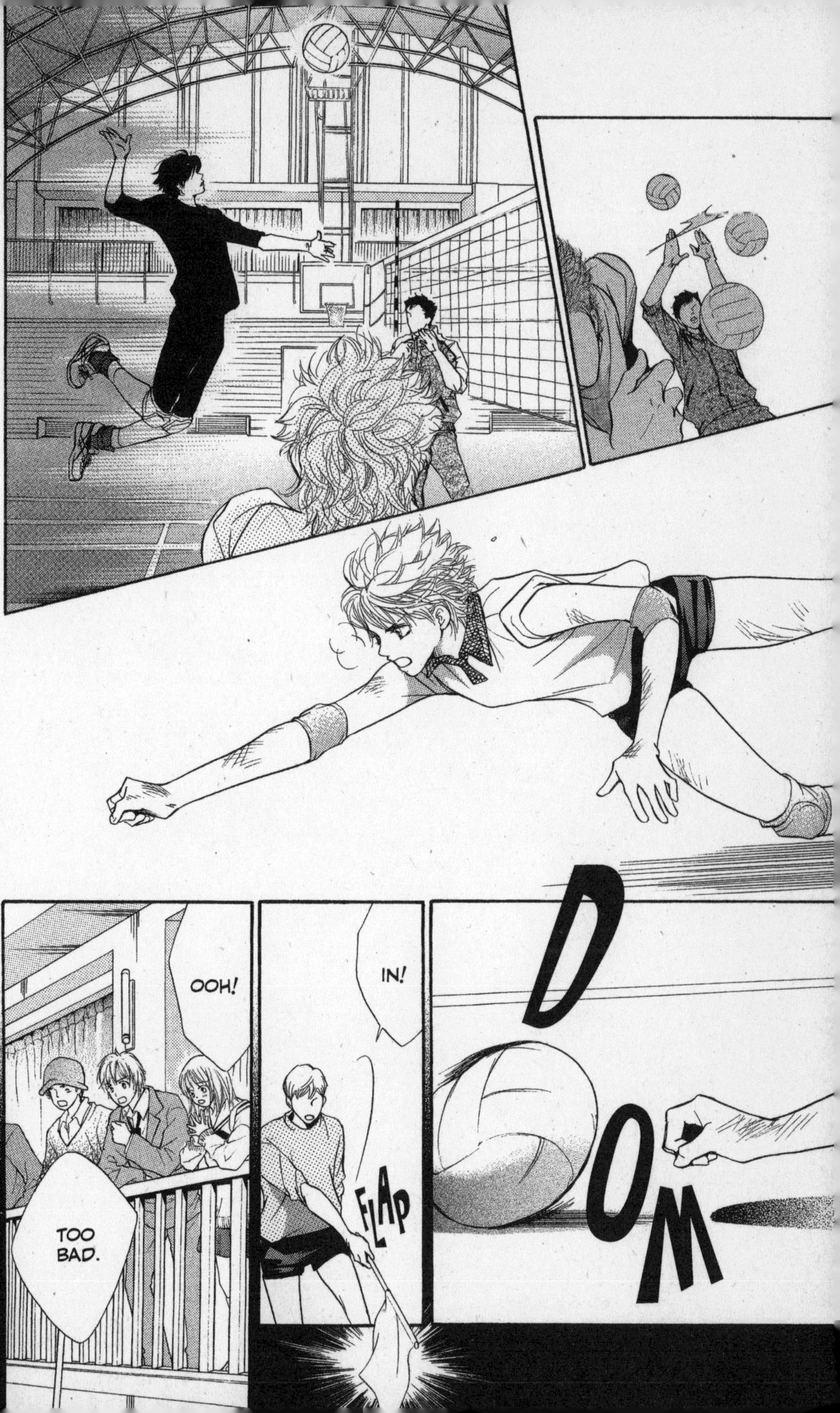
DOM
IN!
FLAP
OOH!
TOO BAD.

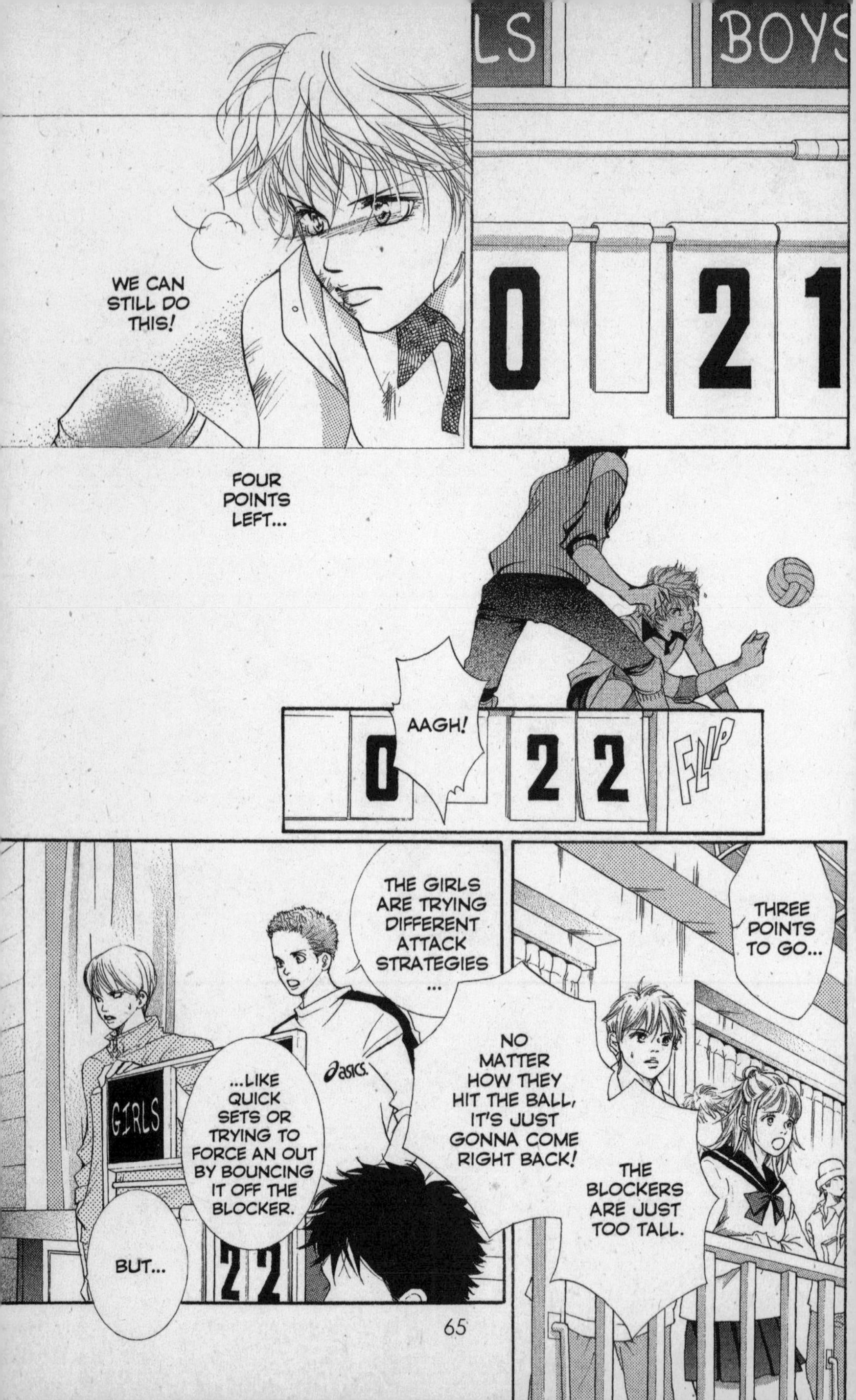
LS
BOYS
0 21
WE CAN STILL DO THIS!
FOUR POINTS LEFT...
AAGH!
0 22
FLIP
THREE POINTS TO GO...
THE GIRLS ARE TRYING DIFFERENT ATTACK STRATEGIES...
...LIKE QUICK SETS OR TRYING TO FORCE AN OUT BY BOUNCING IT OFF THE BLOCKER.
GIRLS
BUT...
NO MATTER HOW THEY HIT THE BALL, IT'S JUST GONNA COME RIGHT BACK!
THE BLOCKERS ARE JUST TOO TALL.

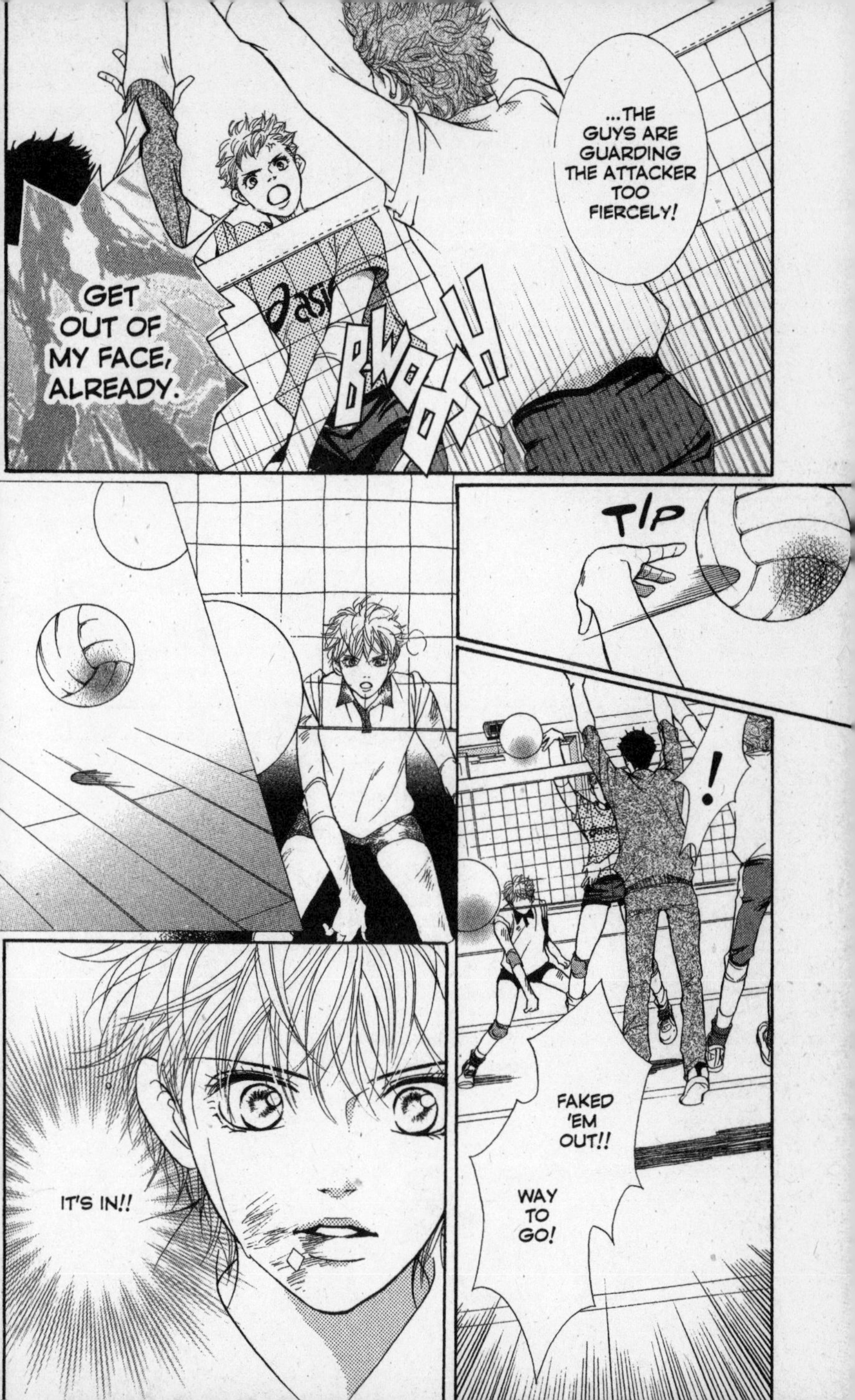
...THE GUYS ARE GUARDING THE ATTACKER TOO FIERCELY!
BWOOSH
GET OUT OF MY FACE, ALREADY.
T/P
!
FAKED 'EM OUT!!
WAY TO GO!
IT'S IN!!

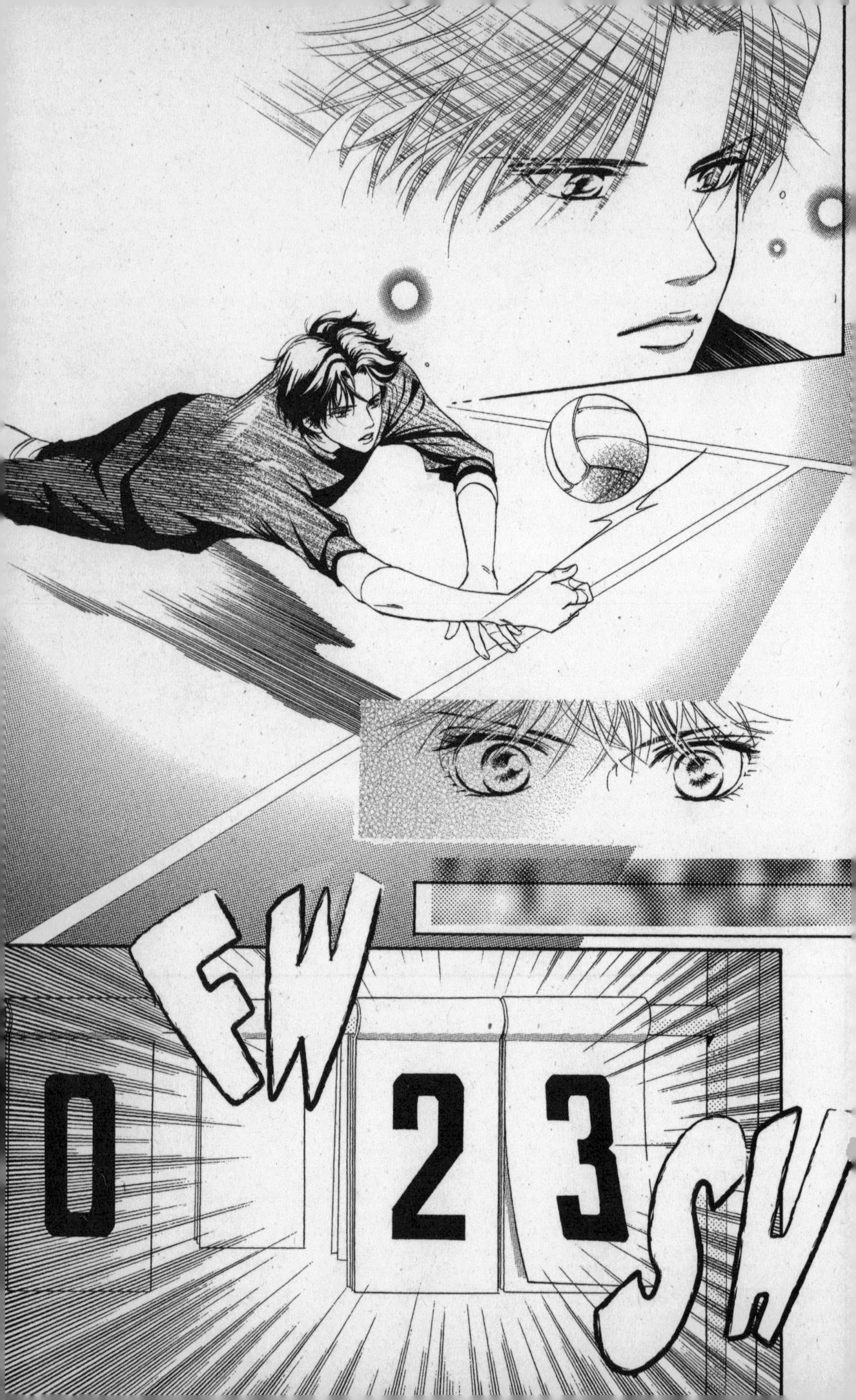
FW
SH
0
23

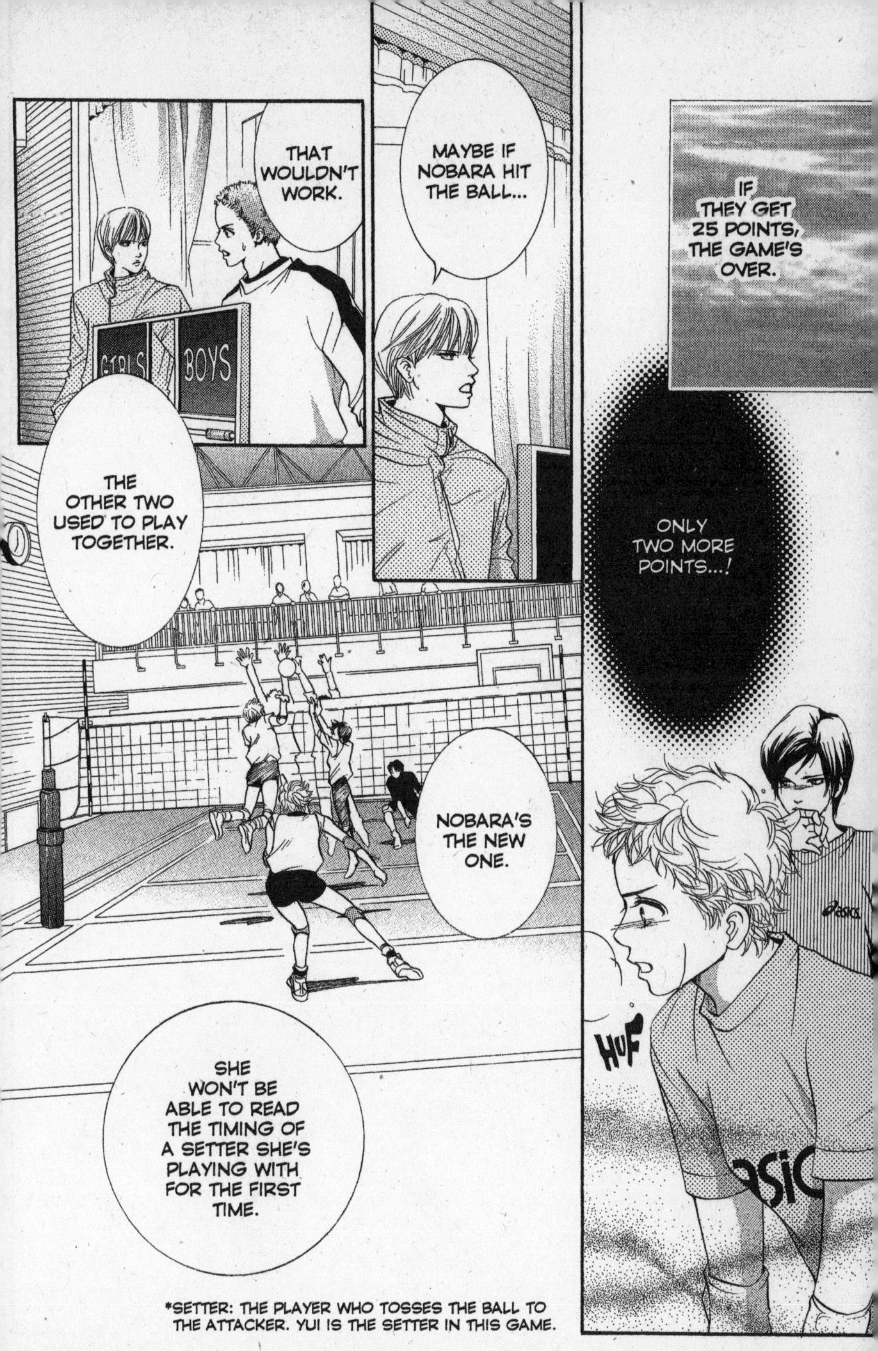
IF THEY GET 25 POINTS, THE GAME'S OVER.
ONLY TWO MORE POINTS...!
HUF
MAYBE IF NOBARA HIT THE BALL...
THAT WOULDN'T WORK.
GIRLS
BOYS
THE OTHER TWO USED TO PLAY TOGETHER.
NOBARA'S THE NEW ONE.
SHE WON'T BE ABLE TO READ THE TIMING OF A SETTER SHE'S PLAYING WITH FOR THE FIRST TIME.

*SETTER: THE PLAYER WHO TOSSES THE BALL TO THE ATTACKER. YUI IS THE SETTER IN THIS GAME.

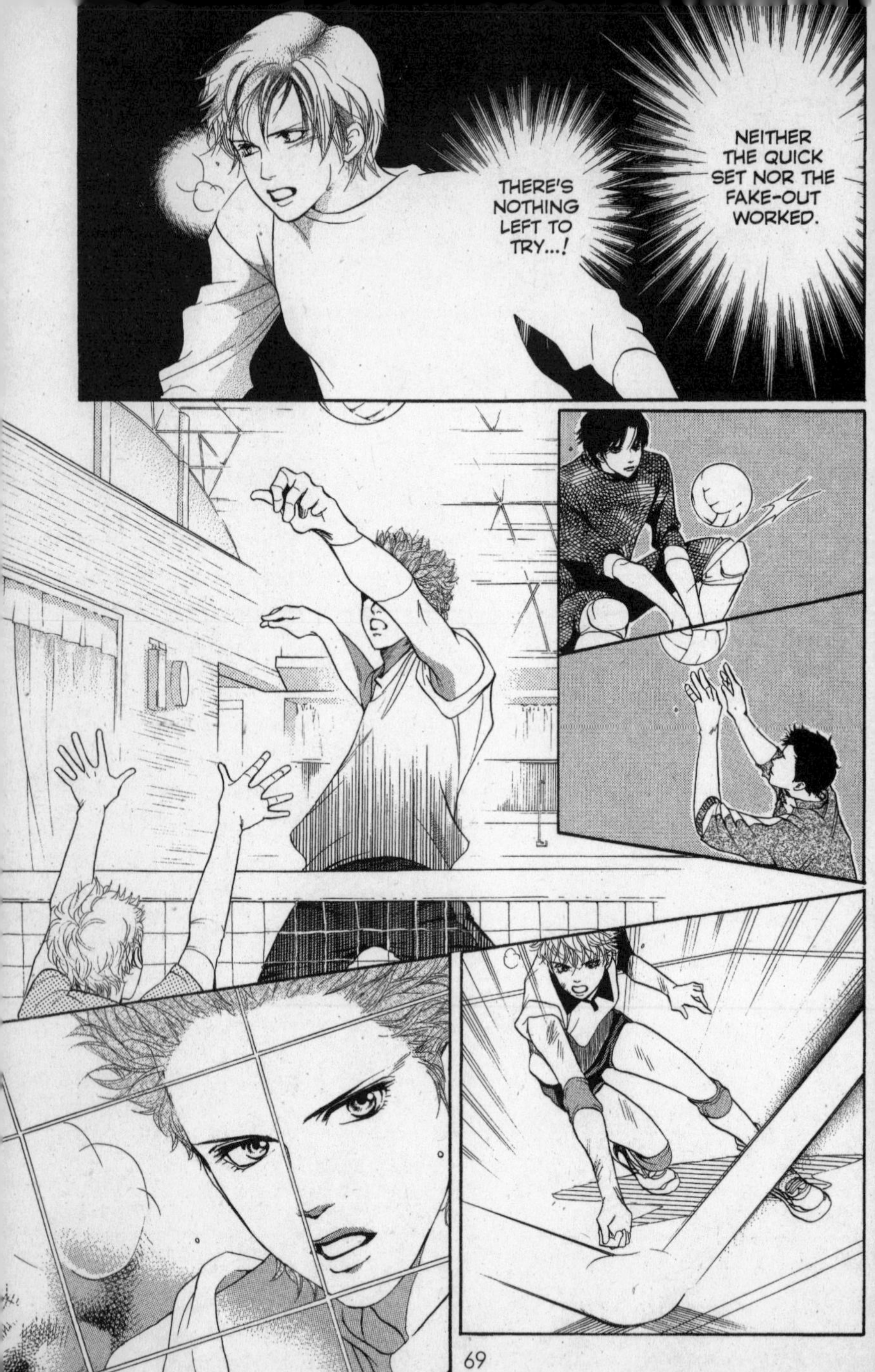
NEITHER THE QUICK SET NOR THE FAKE-OUT WORKED.
THERE'S NOTHING LEFT TO TRY...!

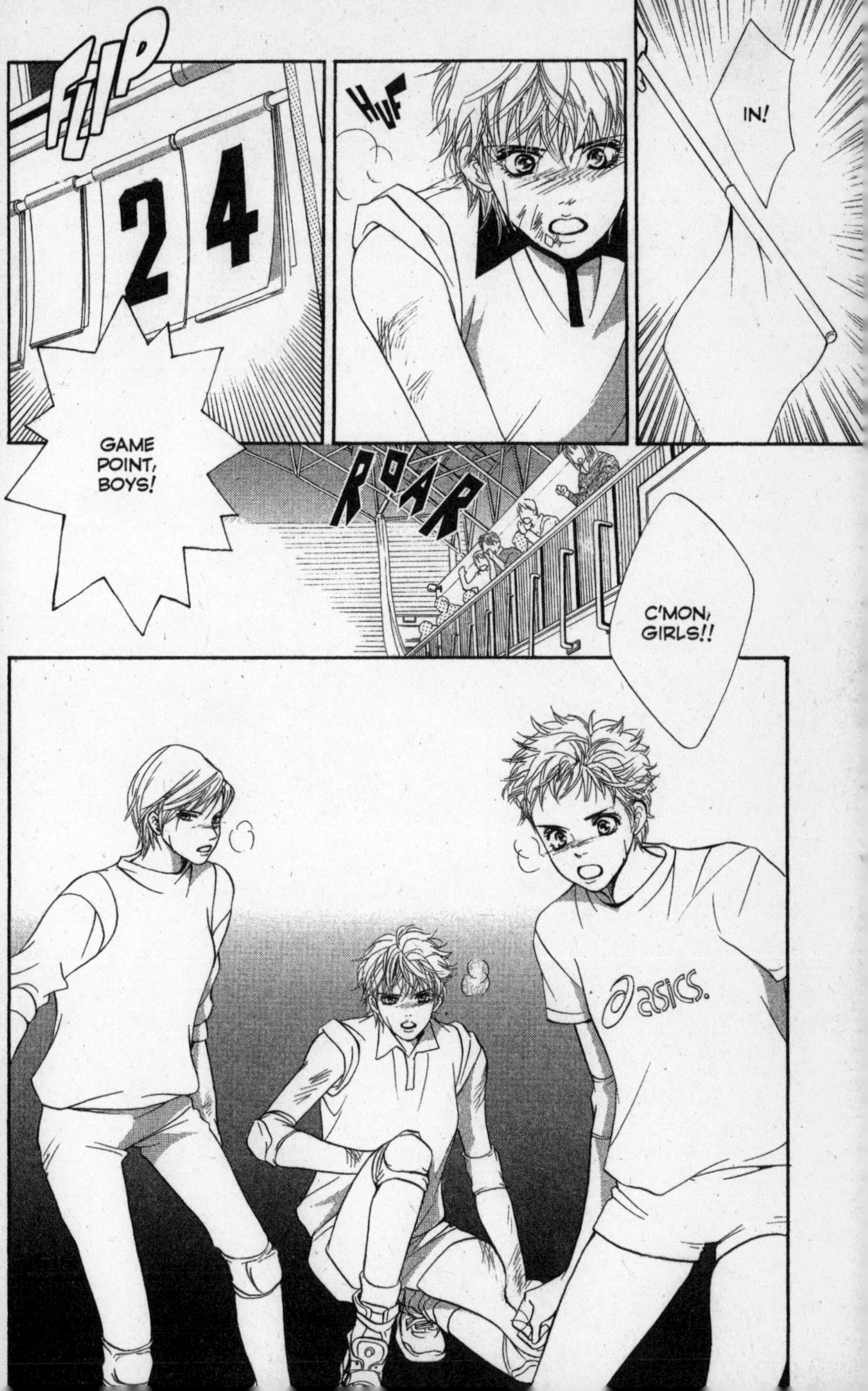
IN!
HUF
FLIP
24
C'MON, GIRLS!!
ROAR
GAME POINT, BOYS!
asics.

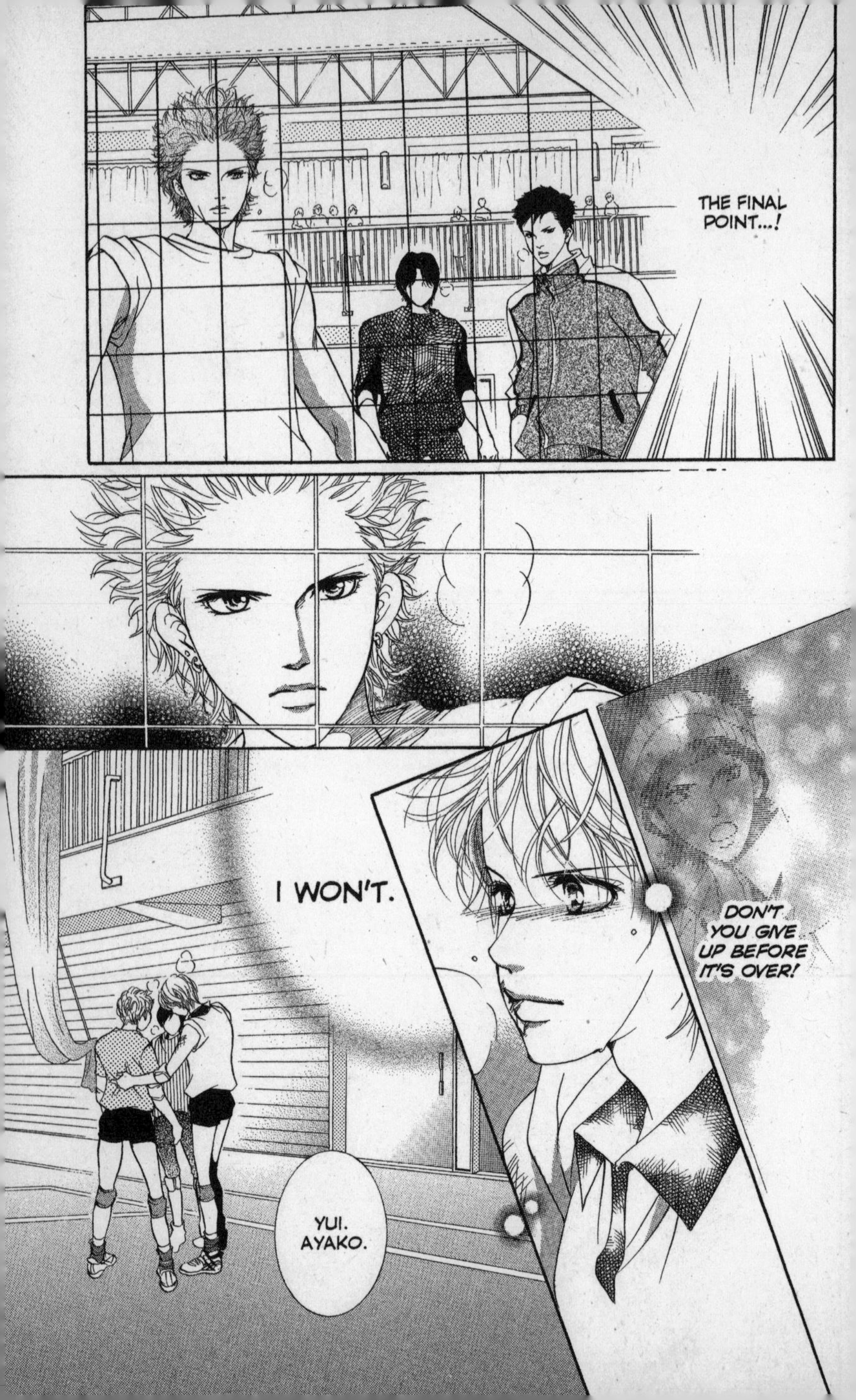
THE FINAL POINT...!
DON'T YOU GIVE UP BEFORE IT'S OVER!
I WON'T.
YUI. AYAKO.

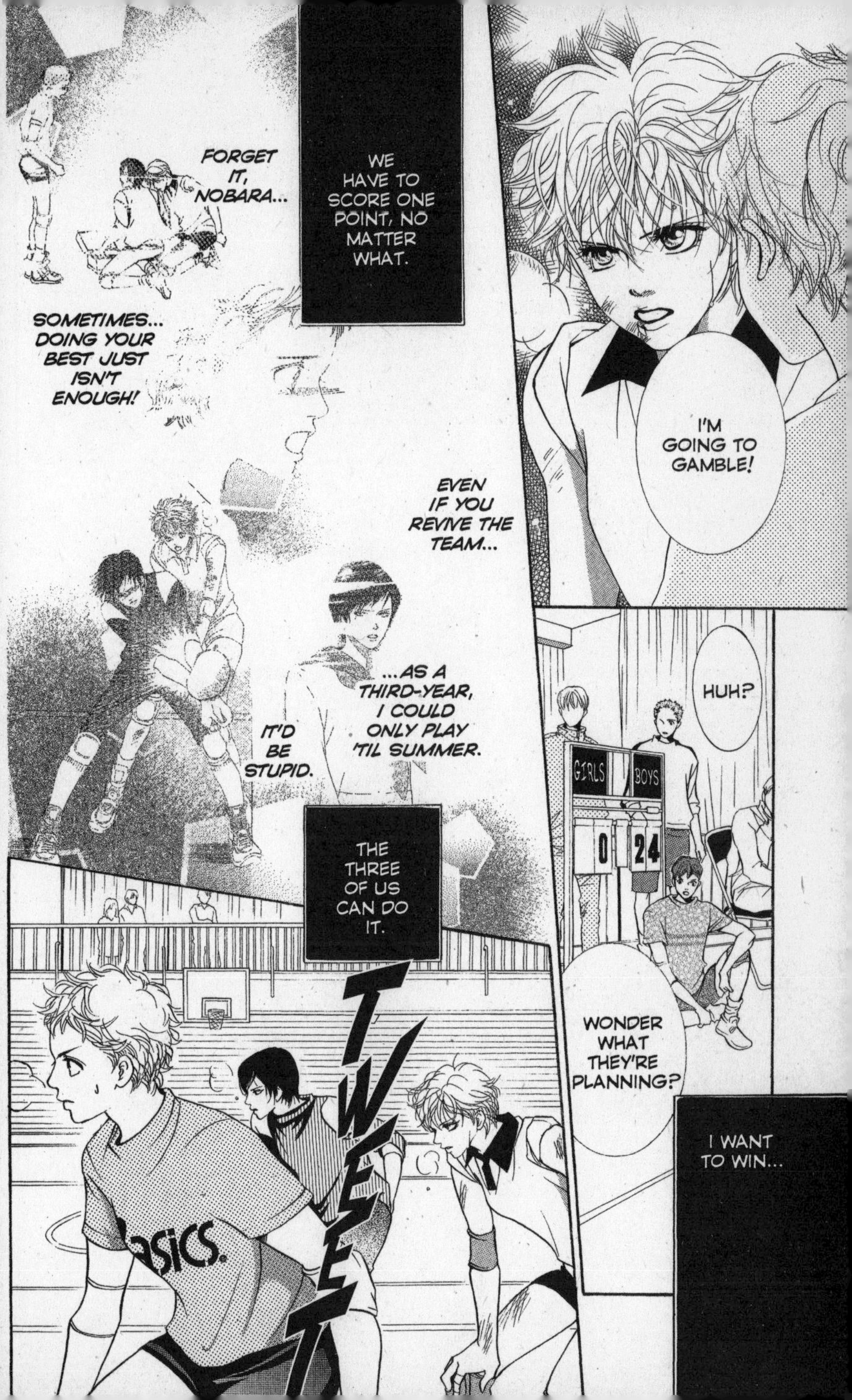
I'M GOING TO GAMBLE!
WE HAVE TO SCORE ONE POINT, NO MATTER WHAT.
FORGET IT, NOBARA...
SOMETIMES... DOING YOUR BEST JUST ISN'T ENOUGH!
EVEN IF YOU REVIVE THE TEAM...
...AS A THIRD-YEAR, I COULD ONLY PLAY 'TIL SUMMER.
IT'D BE STUPID.
HUH?
GIRLS
BOYS
0
24
WONDER WHAT THEY'RE PLANNING?
I WANT TO WIN...
THE THREE OF US CAN DO IT.
TWEET
asics

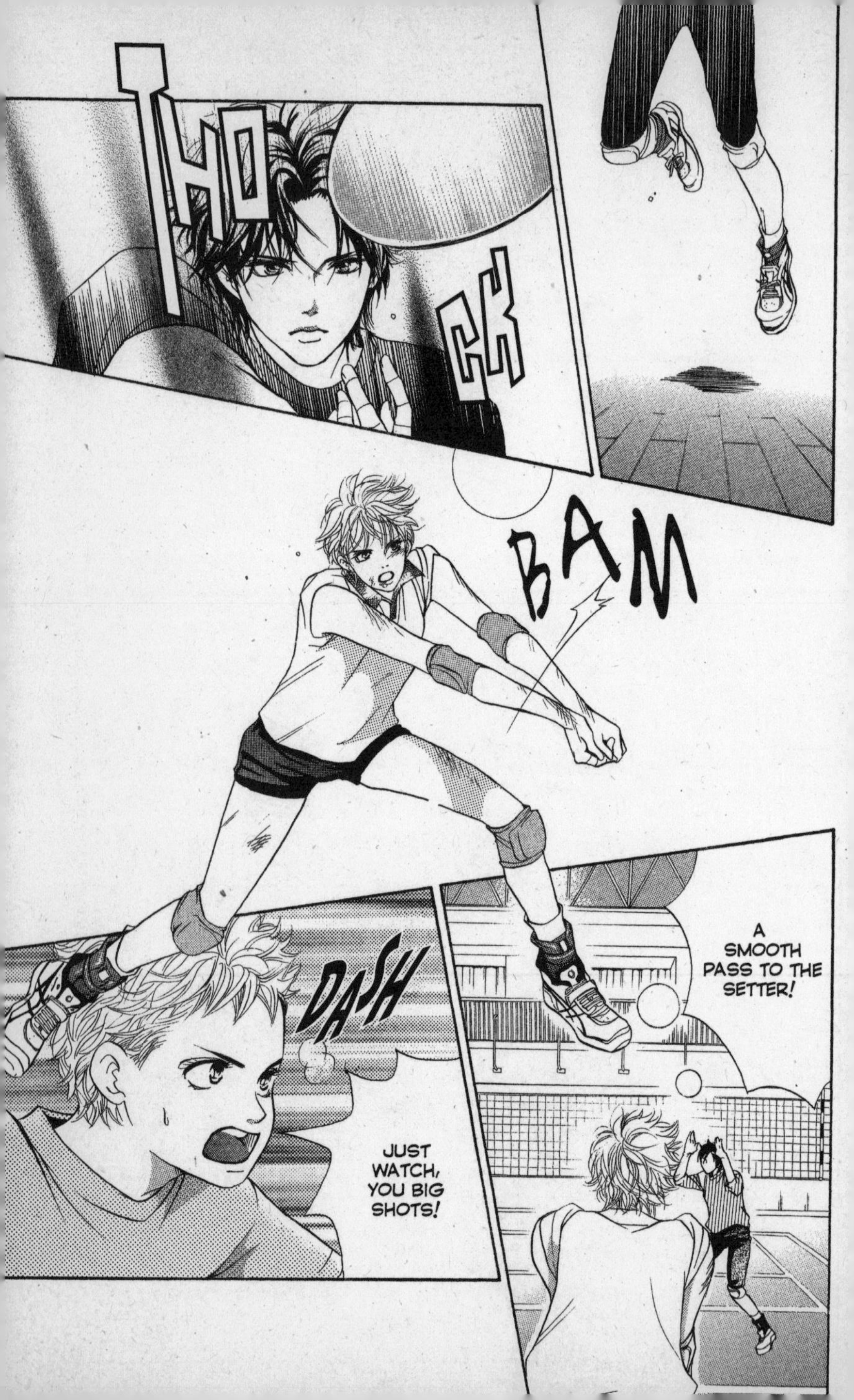
THOCK
BAM
A SMOOTH PASS TO THE SETTER!
DASH
JUST WATCH, YOU BIG SHOTS!

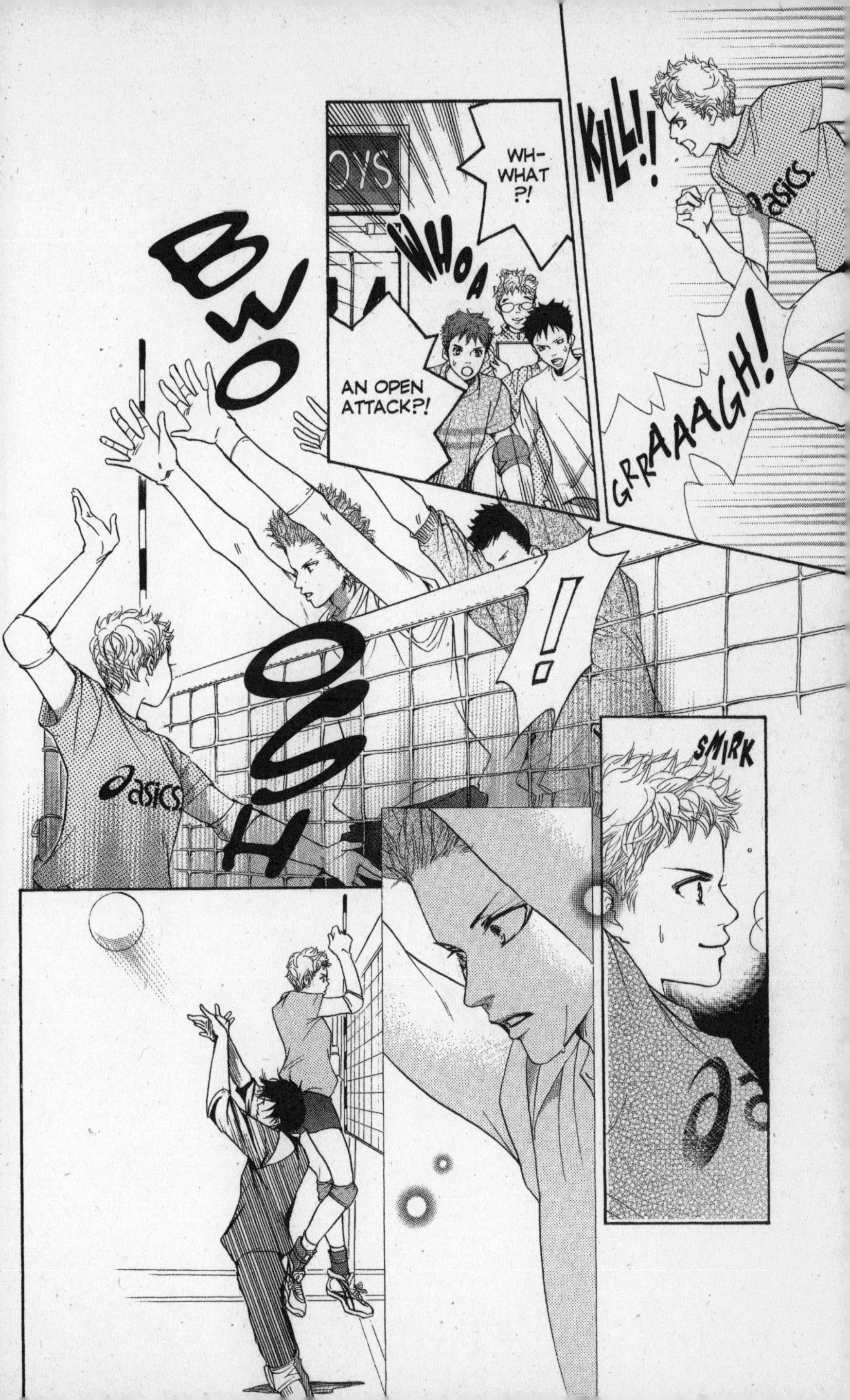
KILL!!
GRRAAAGH!
WHOA
WH-WHAT?!
AN OPEN ATTACK?!
BWO
!
SMIRK

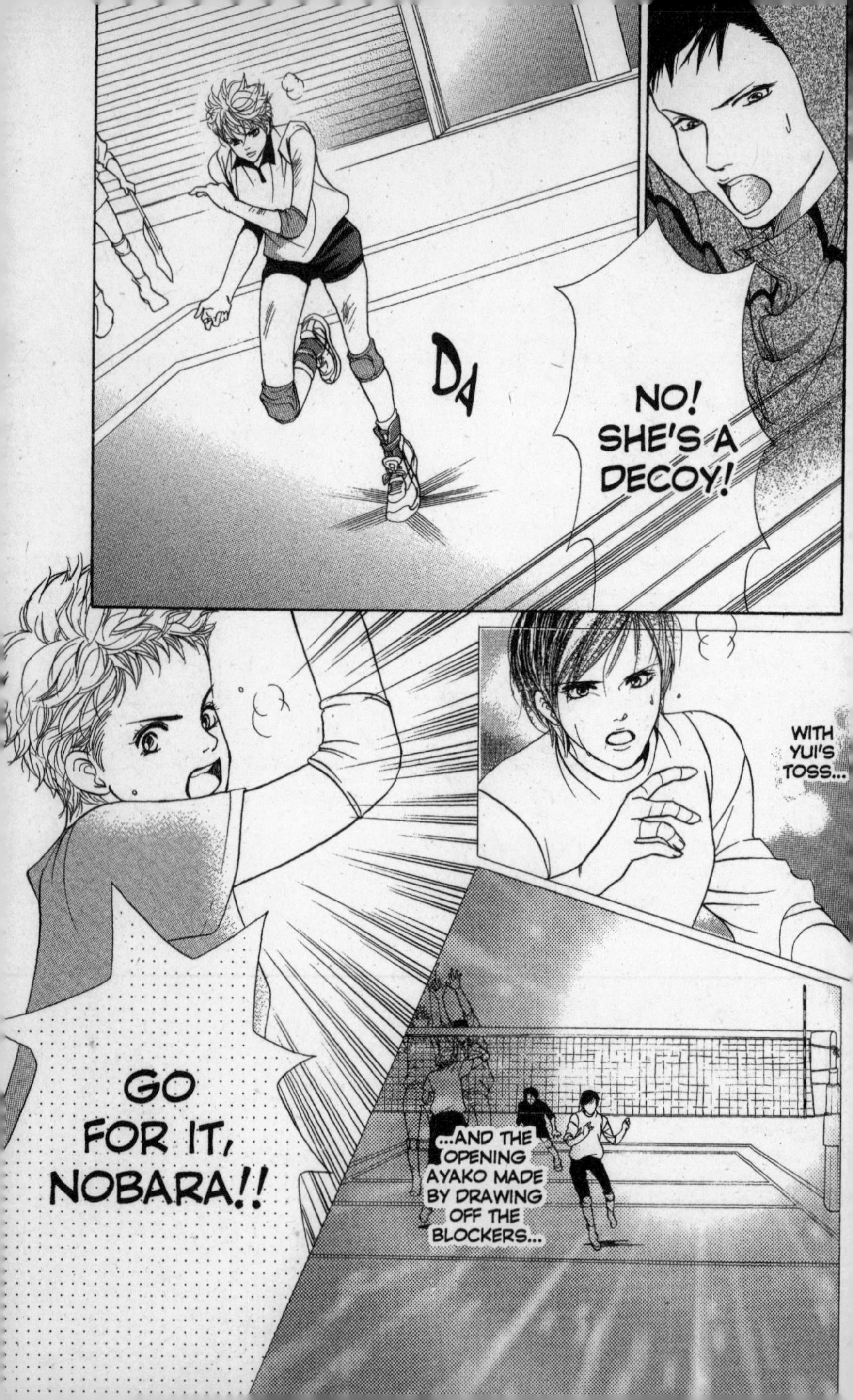

NO! SHE'S A DECOY!
DA
WITH YUI'S TOSS...
...AND THE OPENING AYAKO MADE BY DRAWING OFF THE BLOCKERS...
GO FOR IT, NOBARA!!

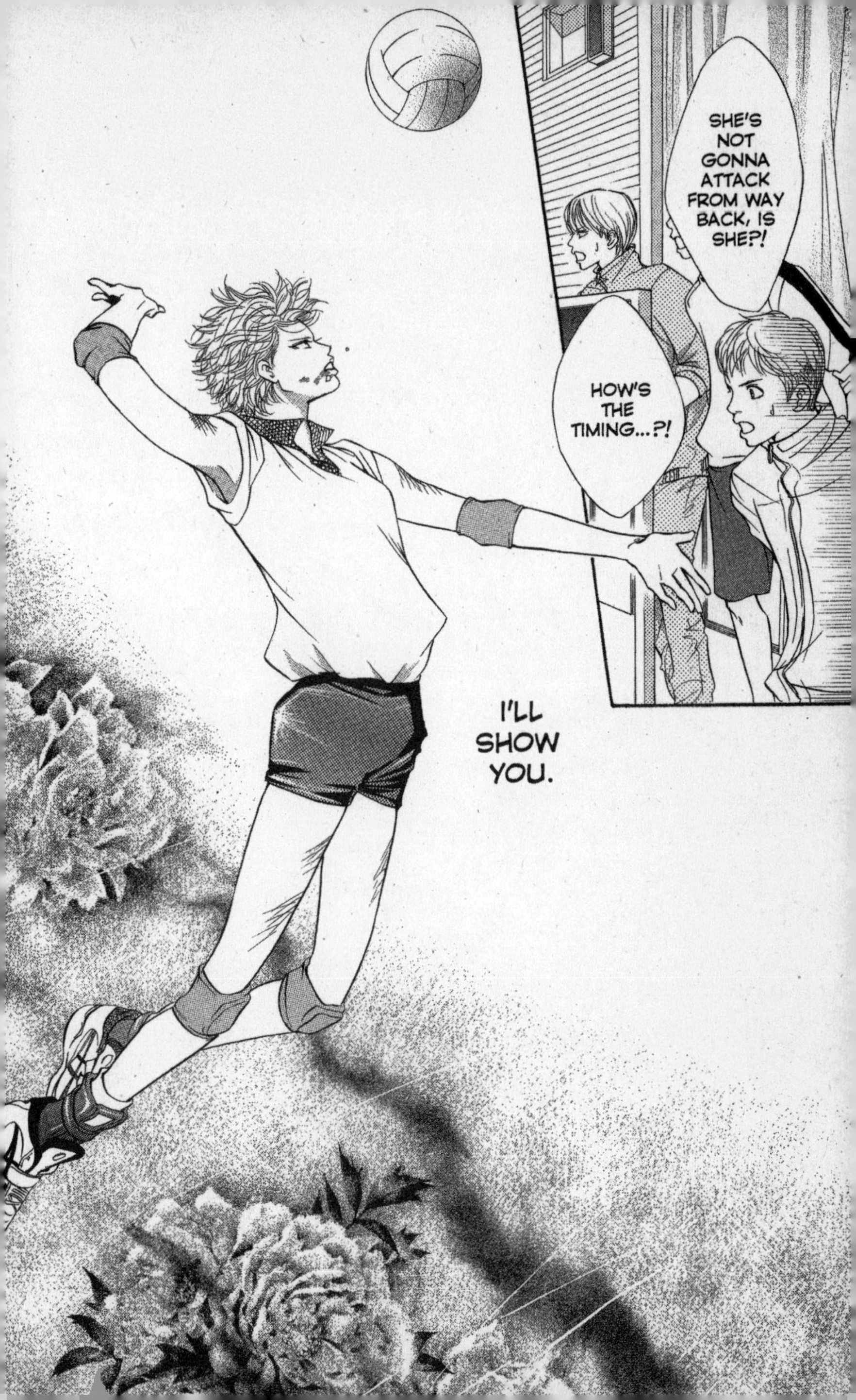
SHE'S NOT GONNA ATTACK FROM WAY BACK, IS SHE?!
HOW'S THE TIMING...?!
I'LL SHOW YOU.

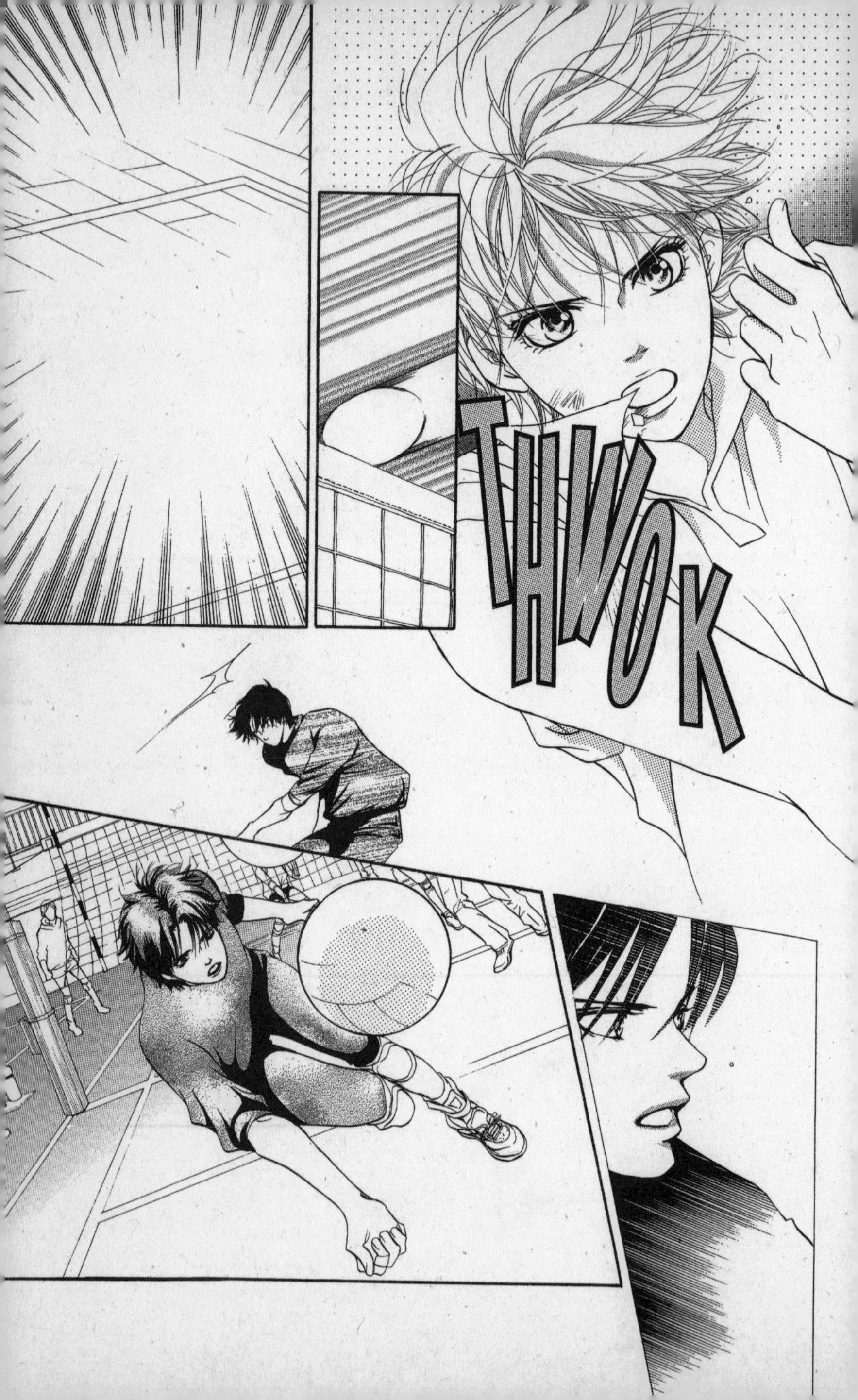
THWOK

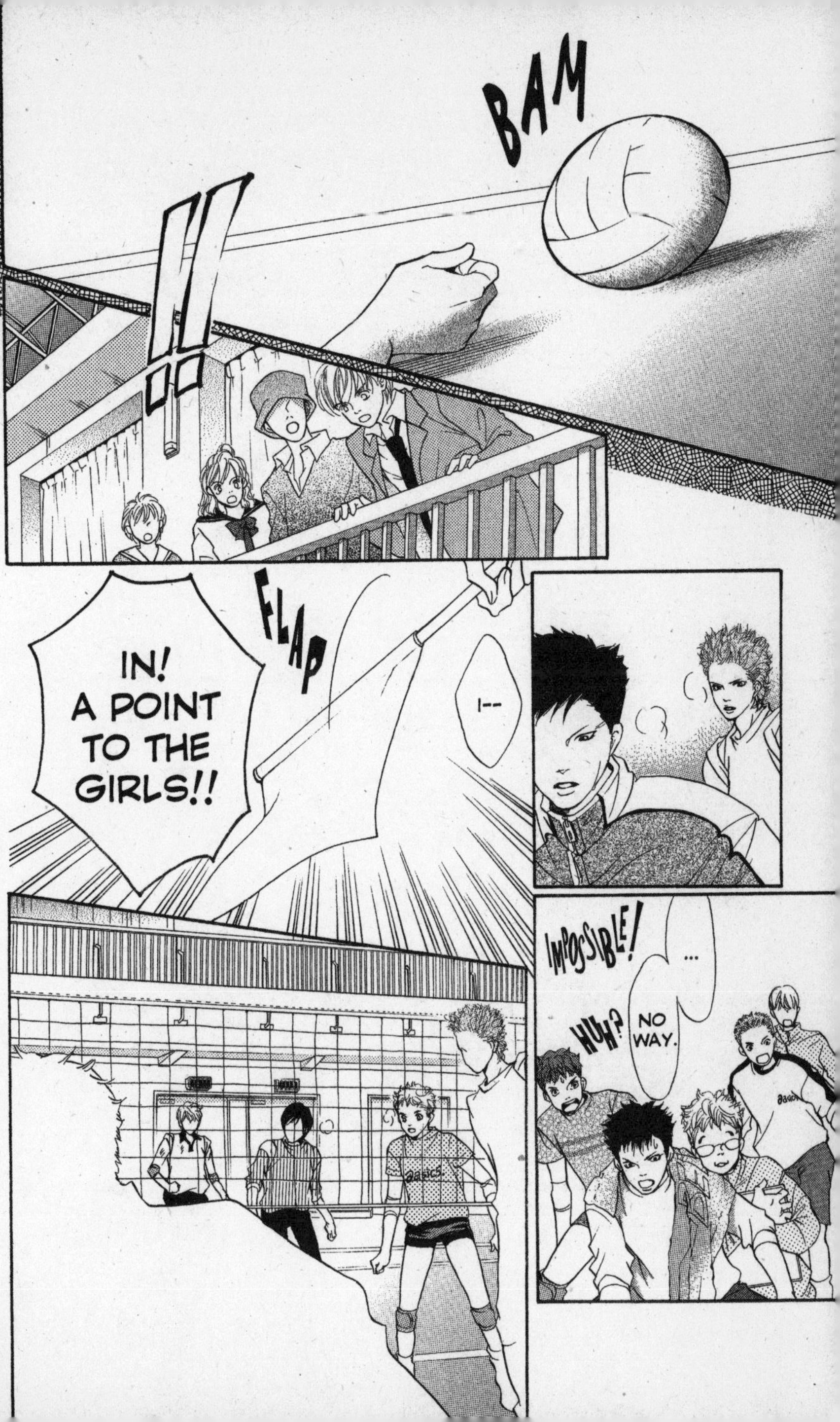
BAM
!!
FLAP
I--
IN! A POINT TO THE GIRLS!!
...
NO WAY.
HUH?
IMPOSSIBLE!

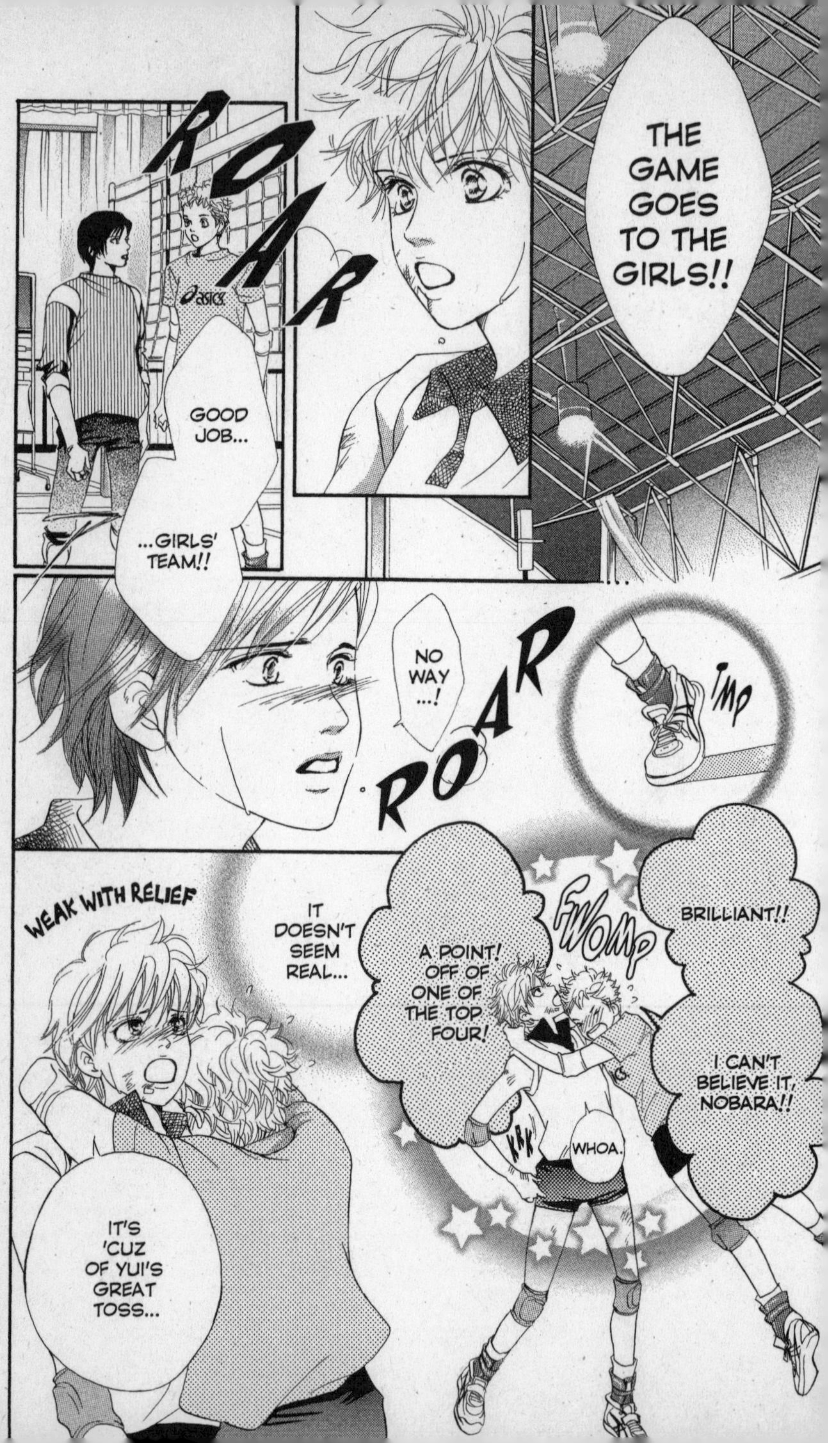
THE GAME GOES TO THE GIRLS!!
ROAR
GOOD JOB...
...GIRLS' TEAM!!
...
TMP
ROAR
NO WAY ...!
BRILLIANT!!
I CAN'T BELIEVE IT, NOBARA!!
FWOMP
A POINT! OFF OF ONE OF THE TOP FOUR!
WHOA.
KRK
IT DOESN'T SEEM REAL...
WEAK WITH RELIEF
IT'S 'CUZ OF YUI'S GREAT TOSS...

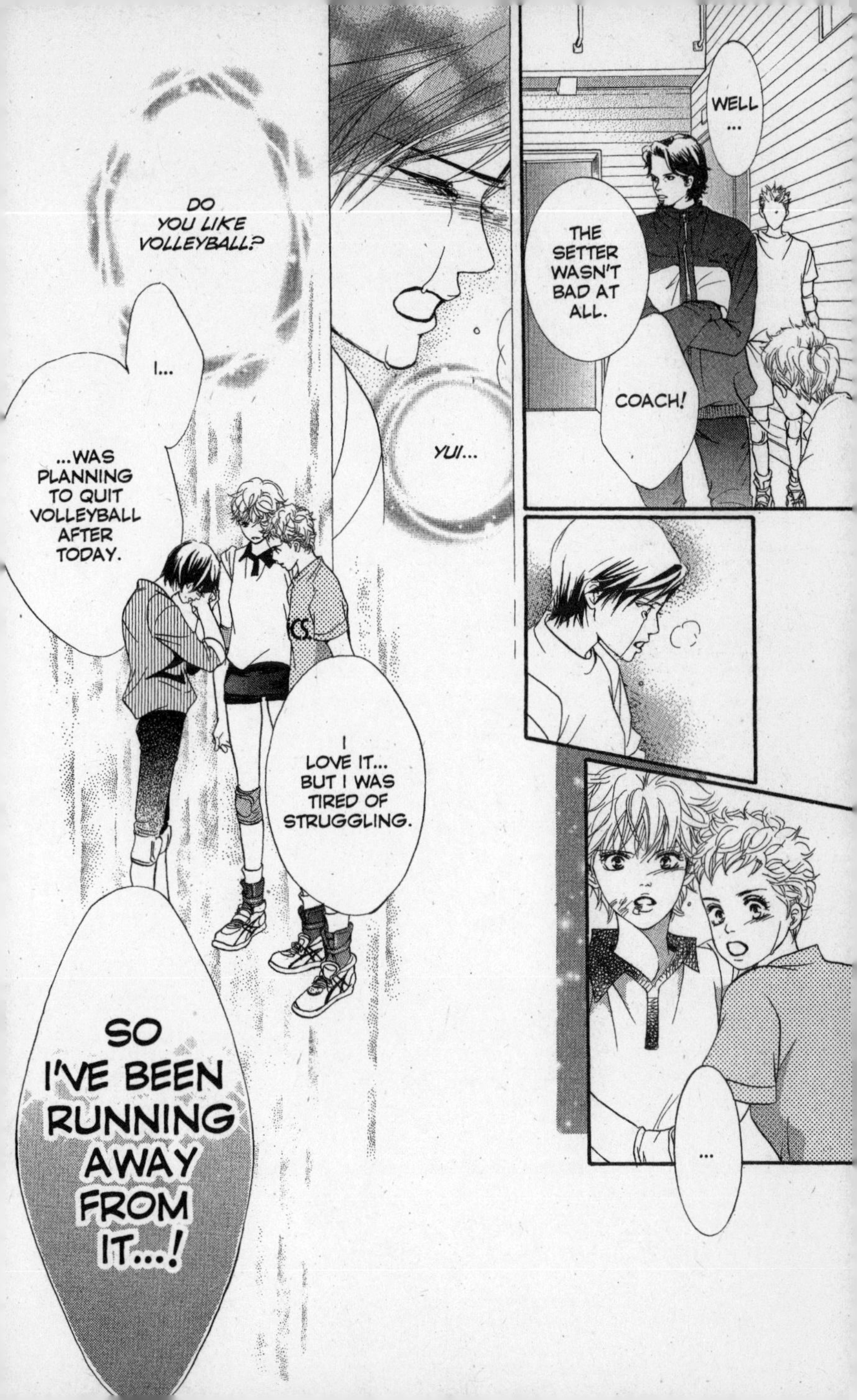
WELL ...
THE SETTER WASN'T BAD AT ALL.
COACH!
...
YUI...
DO YOU LIKE VOLLEYBALL?
I...
...WAS PLANNING TO QUIT VOLLEYBALL AFTER TODAY.
I LOVE IT... BUT I WAS TIRED OF STRUGGLING.
SO I'VE BEEN RUNNING AWAY FROM IT...!

MITSUBA CLUB

Vol. 2

RABBIT CAT

CHIRO HAS A COTTONTAIL. AND THE BLACK MARKINGS THAT HE HAD ON HIS HEAD AS A KITTEN FADED ALMOST TO WHITE AS HE GREW, SO FROM BEHIND HE LOOKS LIKE A RABBIT.

MEOW

HEY RABBIT-CAT!

RABBIT PRINCE!

HERE, CHIRO.

YOOHOO, WHITE CREATURE!

HE HAS LOTS OF NICKNAMES. THERE WAS THIS GUY THAT ONCE SAID, "RABBITS AND STRAWBERRIES ARE, LIKE, THE SAME TO ME." (MAYBE HE MEANT THEY'RE CUTE IN THE SAME WAY.) SO FOR A WHILE I EVEN CALLED THE CAT "STRAWBERRY."

CHIRO, AGE 2 1/2.

CHIRO HATES HOSPITALS. HE BRISTLES AND HIS HAIRS STAND ON END WHEN HE FACES DOCTORS.

CHIRO MEOWING AT A BIRD OUTSIDE THE WINDOW. YOU'RE A SHELTERED LITTLE PRINCE SO YOU DON'T HAVE A CHANCE AGAINST THAT CROW.

MEOOOW

MENACING LOOK

CHIRO SLEEPS IN THE MIDDLE OF MY DESK ALMOST 24 HOURS A DAY WHEN I'M APPLYING SCREEN TONES BEFORE A DEADLINE.

CHIRO STANDS GUARD AT THE ENTRANCE WHEN GUESTS VISIT.

CHIRO IS ALWAYS EYEING MY DRINK. HE STICKS HIS FACE RIGHT INTO THE CUP.

CHIRO, ARE YOU HAPPY?

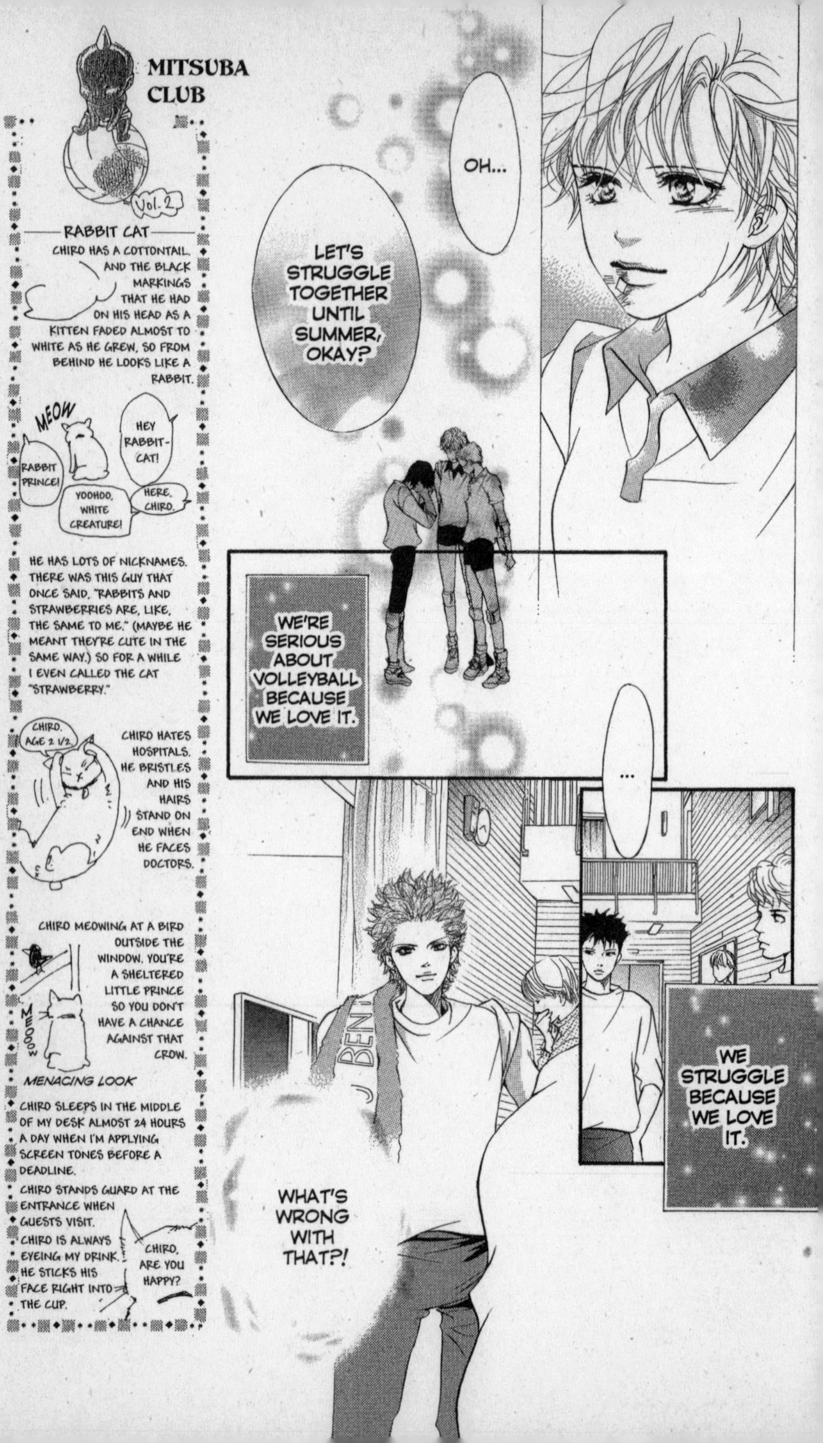
OH...
LET'S STRUGGLE TOGETHER UNTIL SUMMER, OKAY?
WE'RE SERIOUS ABOUT VOLLEYBALL BECAUSE WE LOVE IT.
...
WE STRUGGLE BECAUSE WE LOVE IT.
WHAT'S WRONG WITH THAT?!

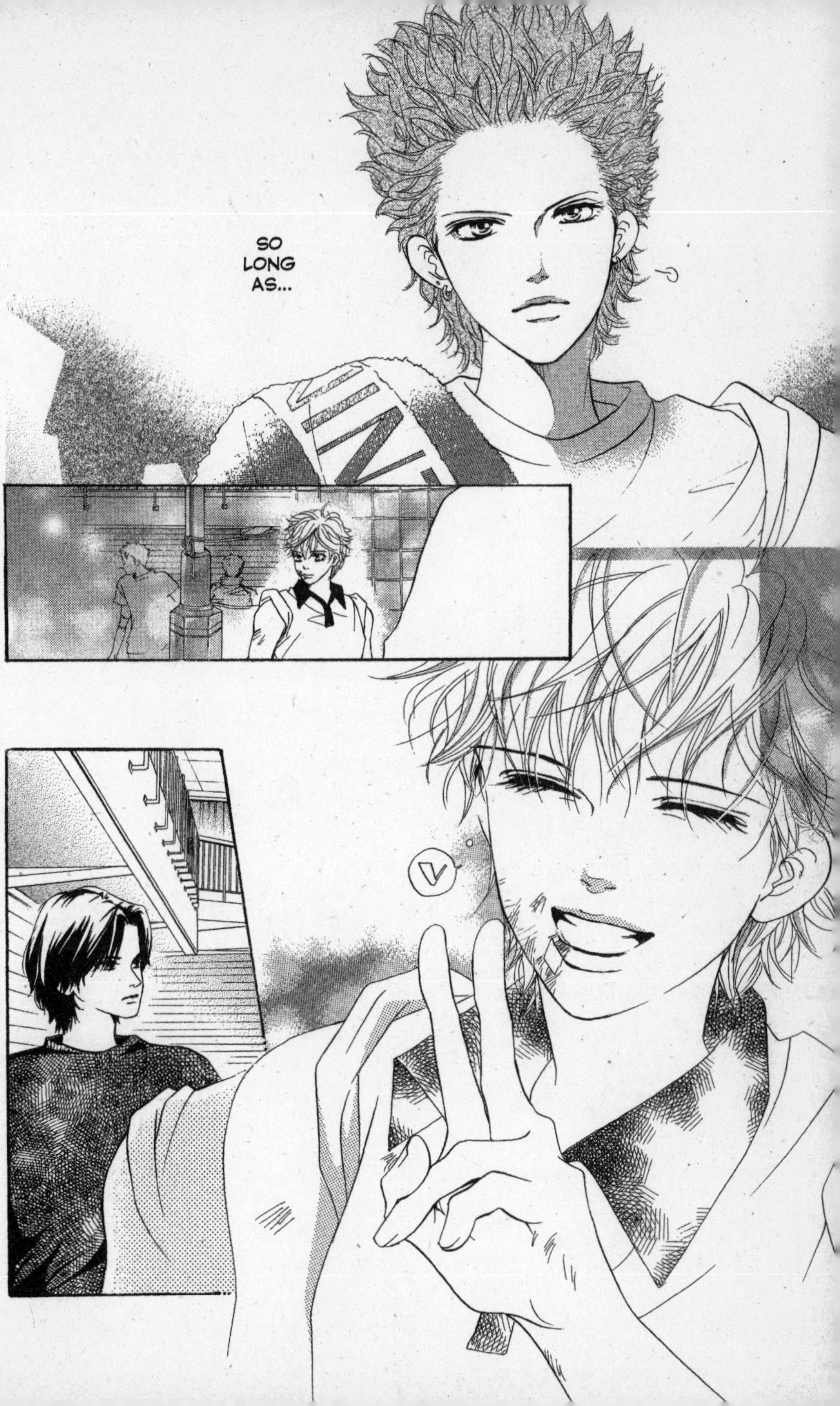
SO LONG AS...

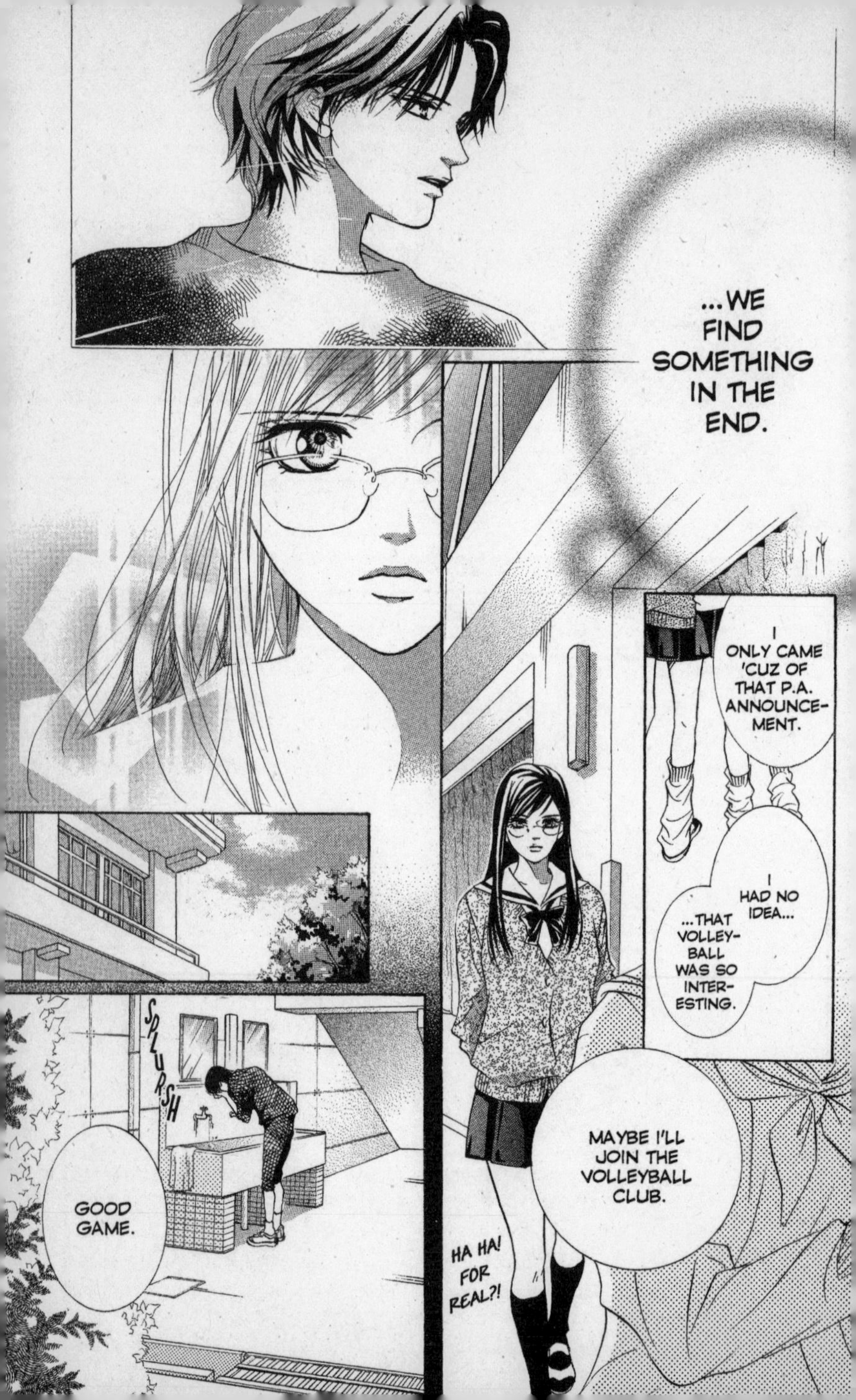

...WE FIND SOMETHING IN THE END.
I ONLY CAME 'CUZ OF THAT P.A. ANNOUNCEMENT.
I HAD NO IDEA...
...THAT VOLLEY-BALL WAS SO INTER-ESTING.
MAYBE I'LL JOIN THE VOLLEYBALL CLUB.
HA HA! FOR REAL?!
SPLURSH
GOOD GAME.

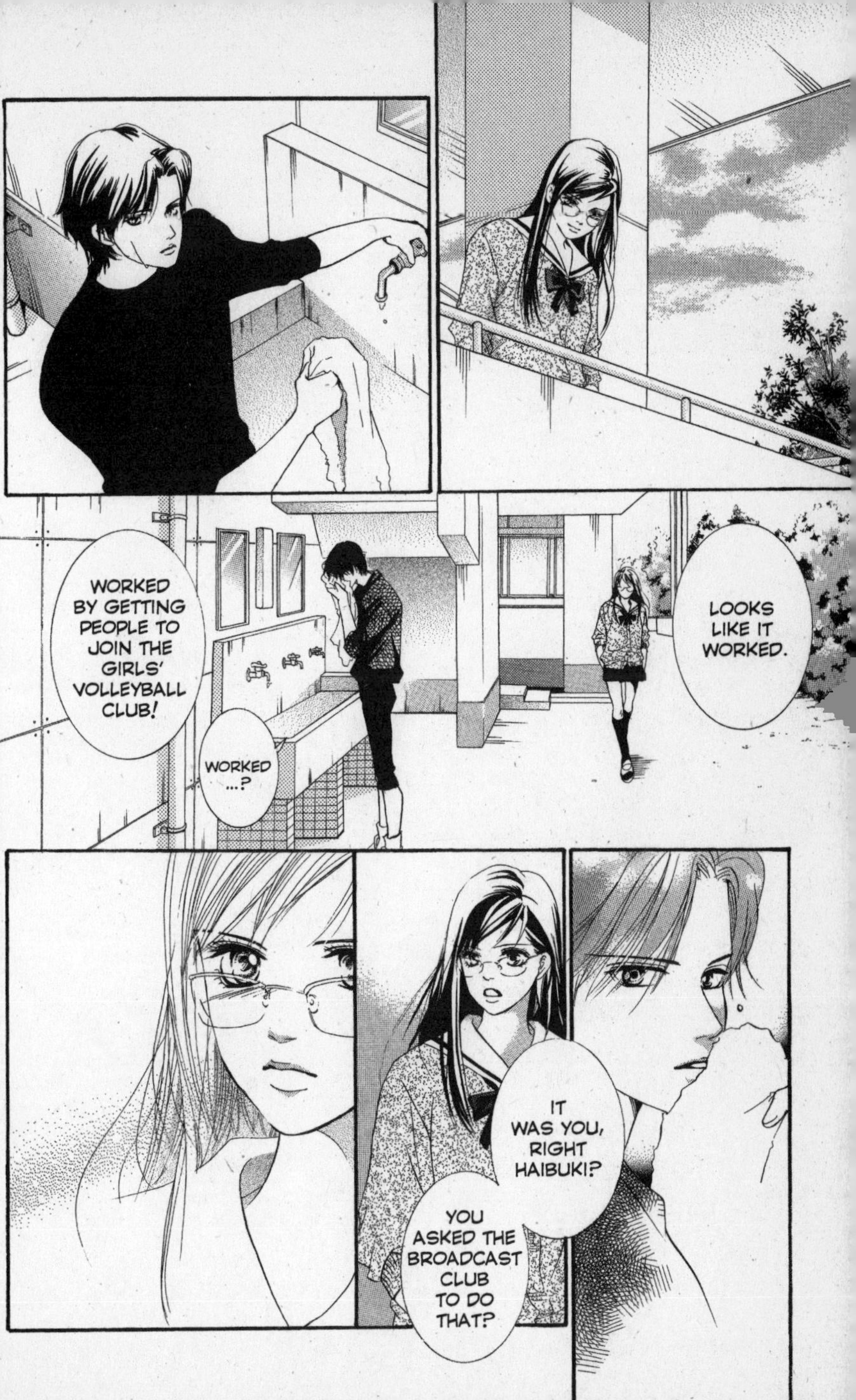
LOOKS LIKE IT WORKED.
WORKED ...?
WORKED BY GETTING PEOPLE TO JOIN THE GIRLS' VOLLEYBALL CLUB!
IT WAS YOU, RIGHT HAIBUKI?
YOU ASKED THE BROADCAST CLUB TO DO THAT?

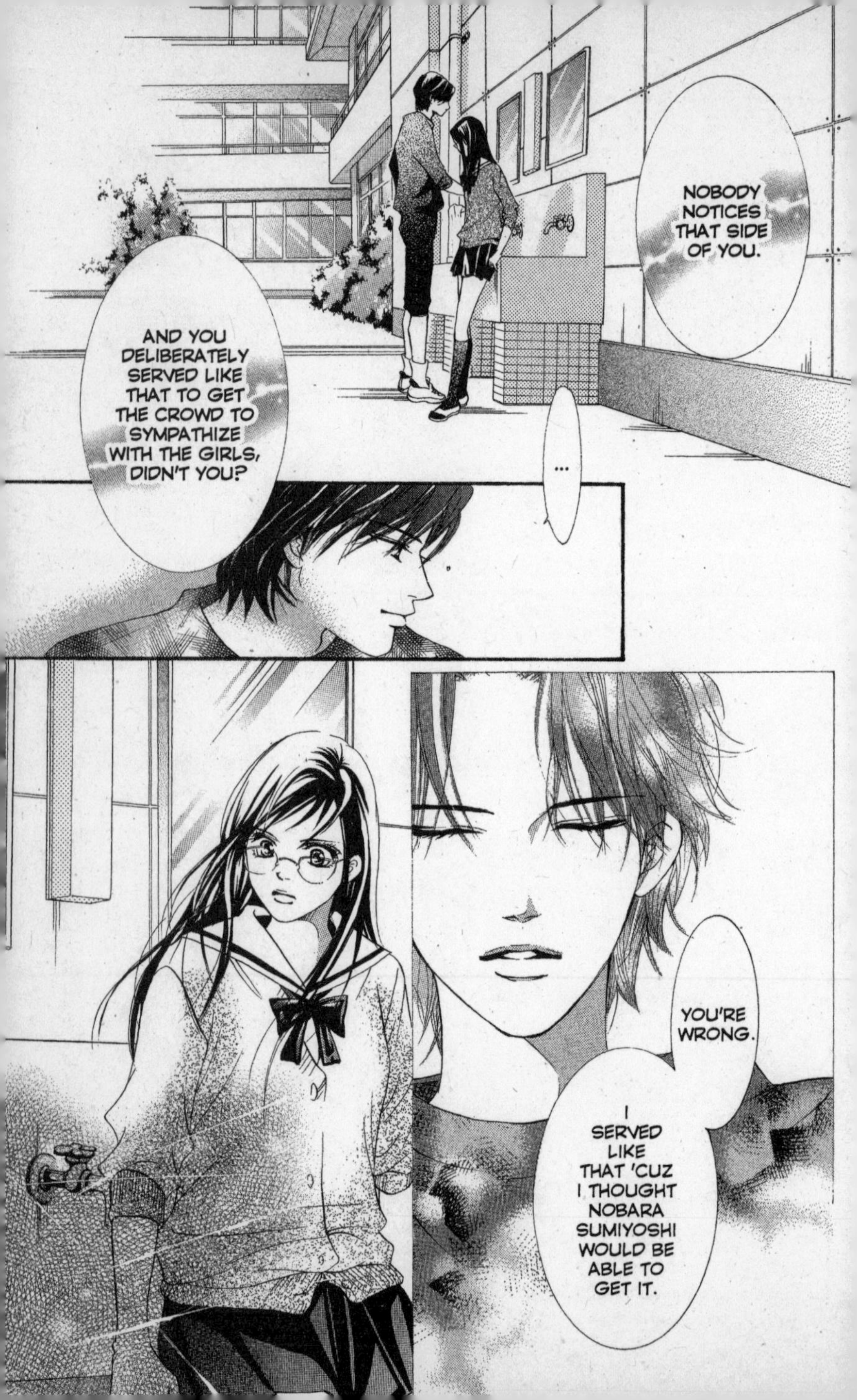
NOBODY NOTICES THAT SIDE OF YOU.
AND YOU DELIBERATELY SERVED LIKE THAT TO GET THE CROWD TO SYMPATHIZE WITH THE GIRLS, DIDN'T YOU?
...
YOU'RE WRONG.
I SERVED LIKE THAT 'CUZ I THOUGHT NOBARA SUMIYOSHI WOULD BE ABLE TO GET IT.

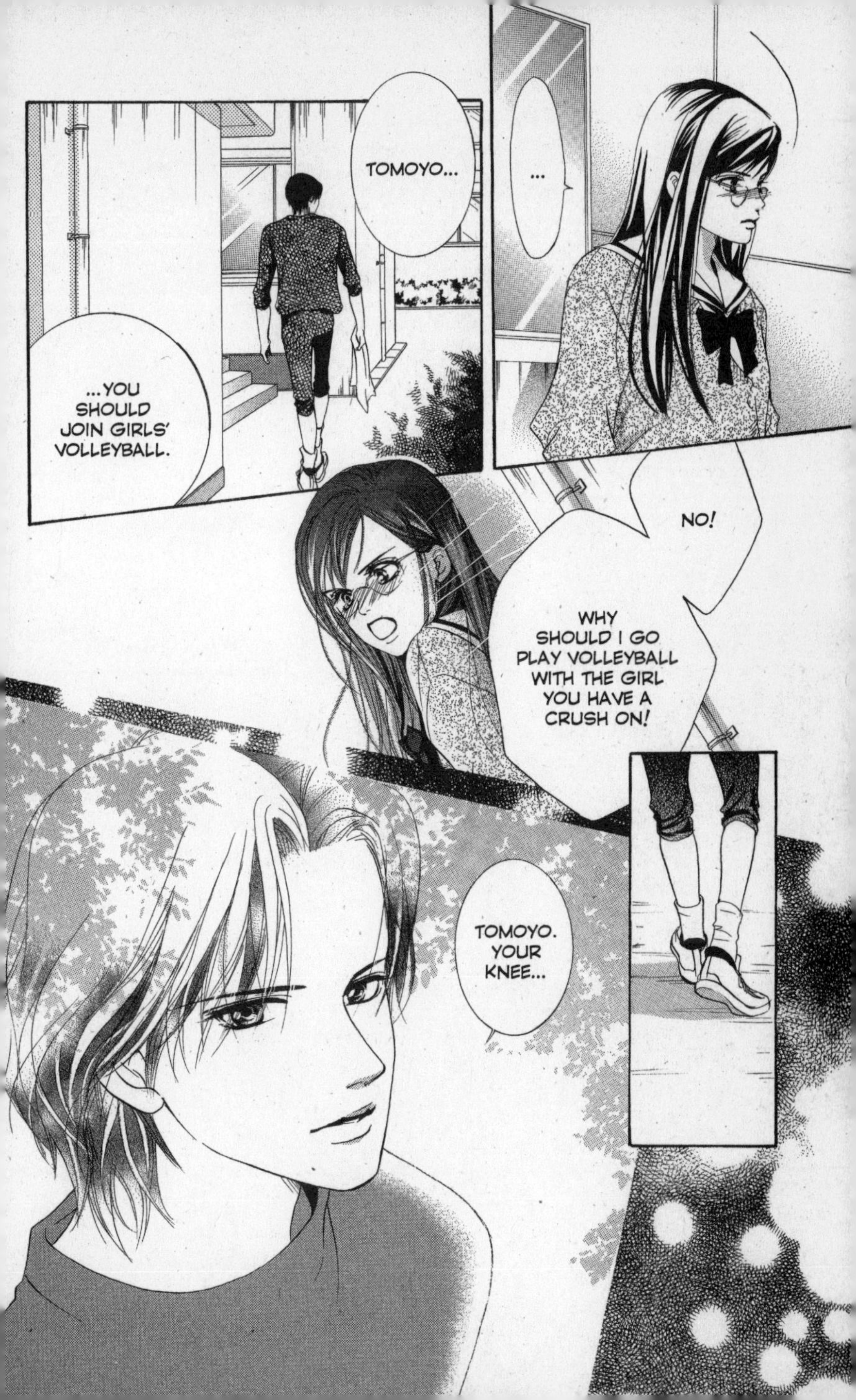
...
TOMOYO...
...YOU SHOULD JOIN GIRLS' VOLLEYBALL.
NO!
WHY SHOULD I GO PLAY VOLLEYBALL WITH THE GIRL YOU HAVE A CRUSH ON!
TOMOYO. YOUR KNEE...

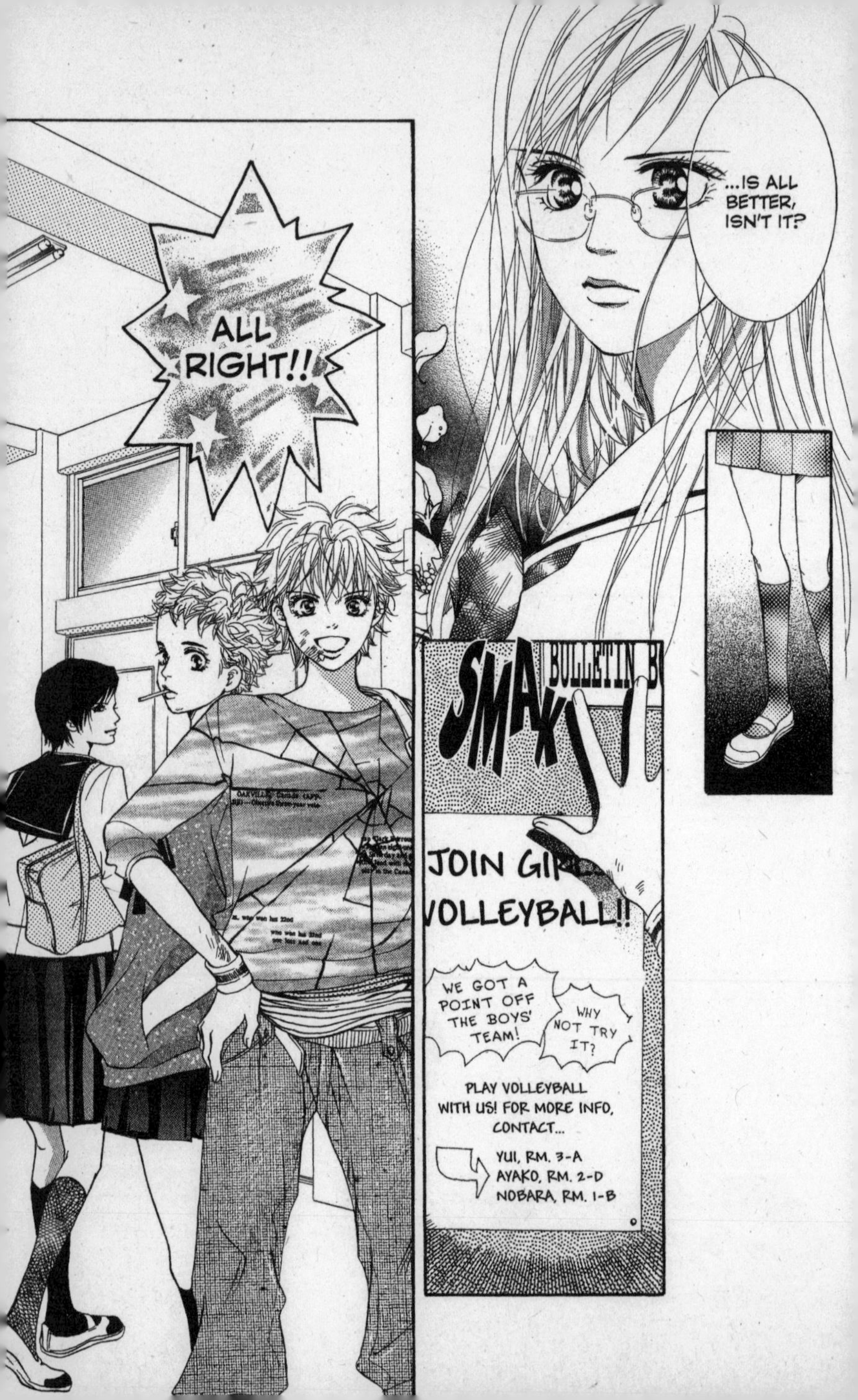
...IS ALL BETTER, ISN'T IT?
SMAK
BULLETIN B
JOIN GIR
VOLLEYBALL!!
WE GOT A POINT OFF THE BOYS' TEAM!
WHY NOT TRY IT?
PLAY VOLLEYBALL WITH US! FOR MORE INFO, CONTACT...
YUI, RM. 3-A
AYAKO, RM. 2-D
NOBARA, RM. 1-B
ALL RIGHT!!

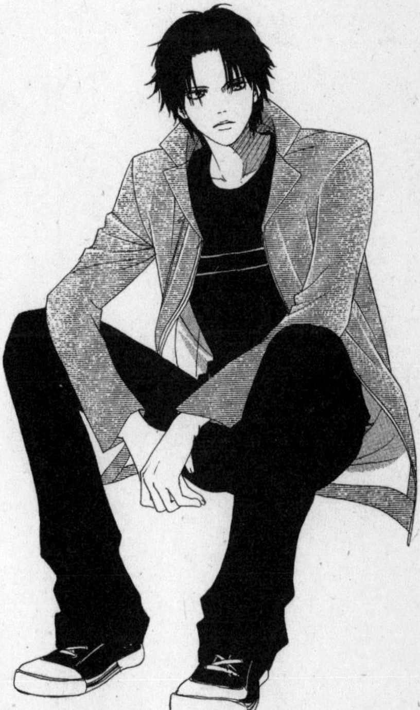

Crimson Hero

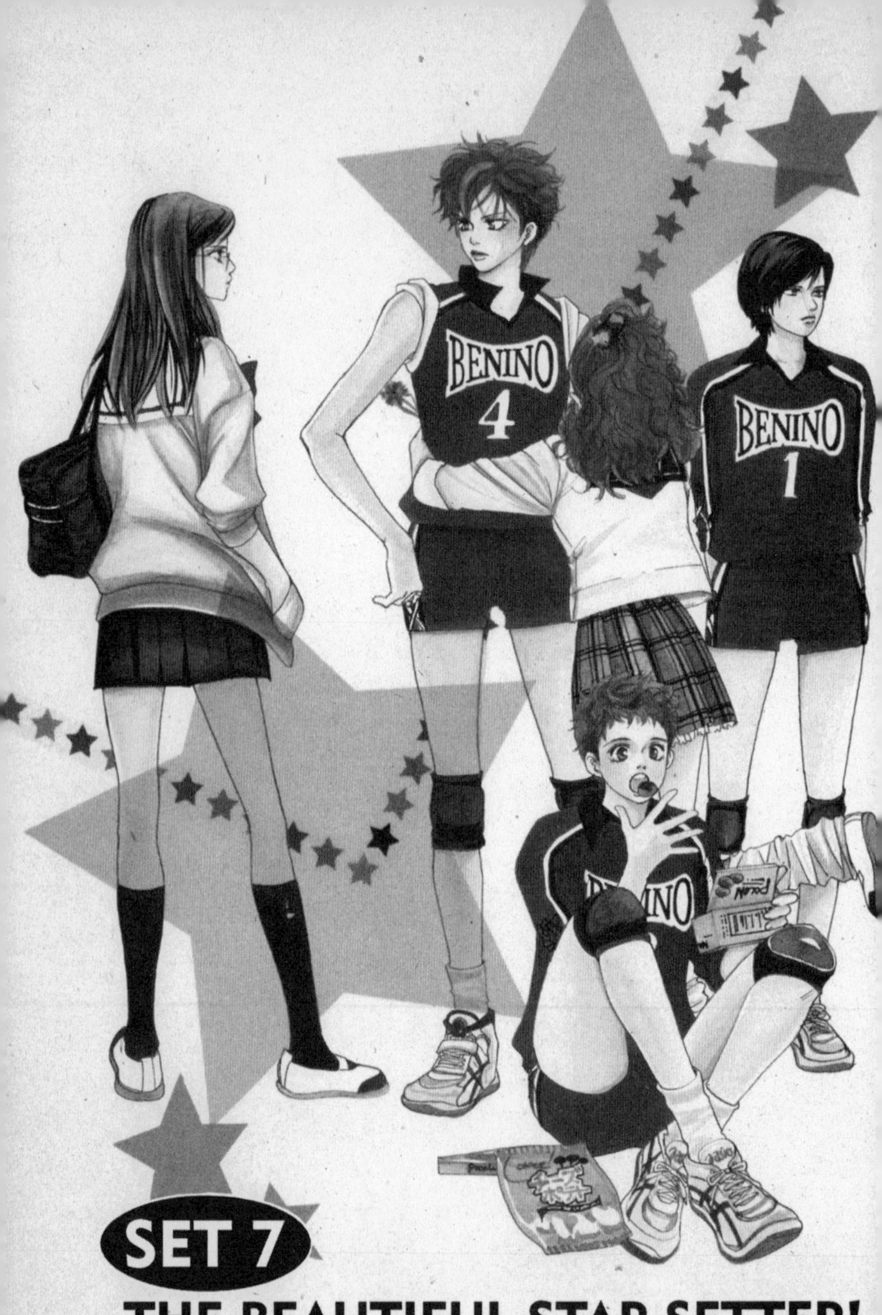
BENINO
4
BENINO
1

SET 7
THE BEAUTIFUL STAR SETTER!

Crimson Hero

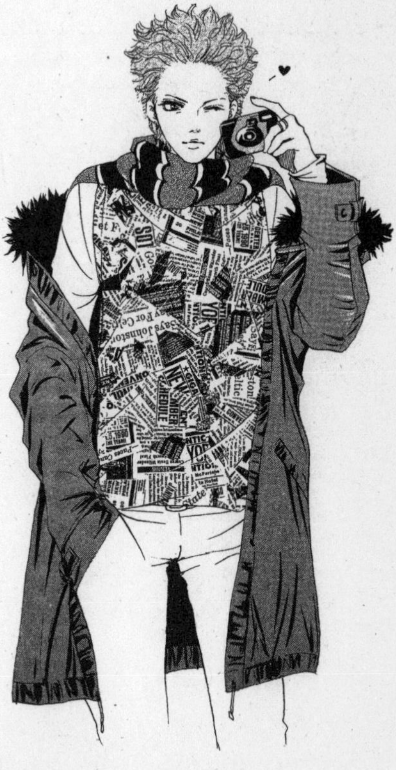

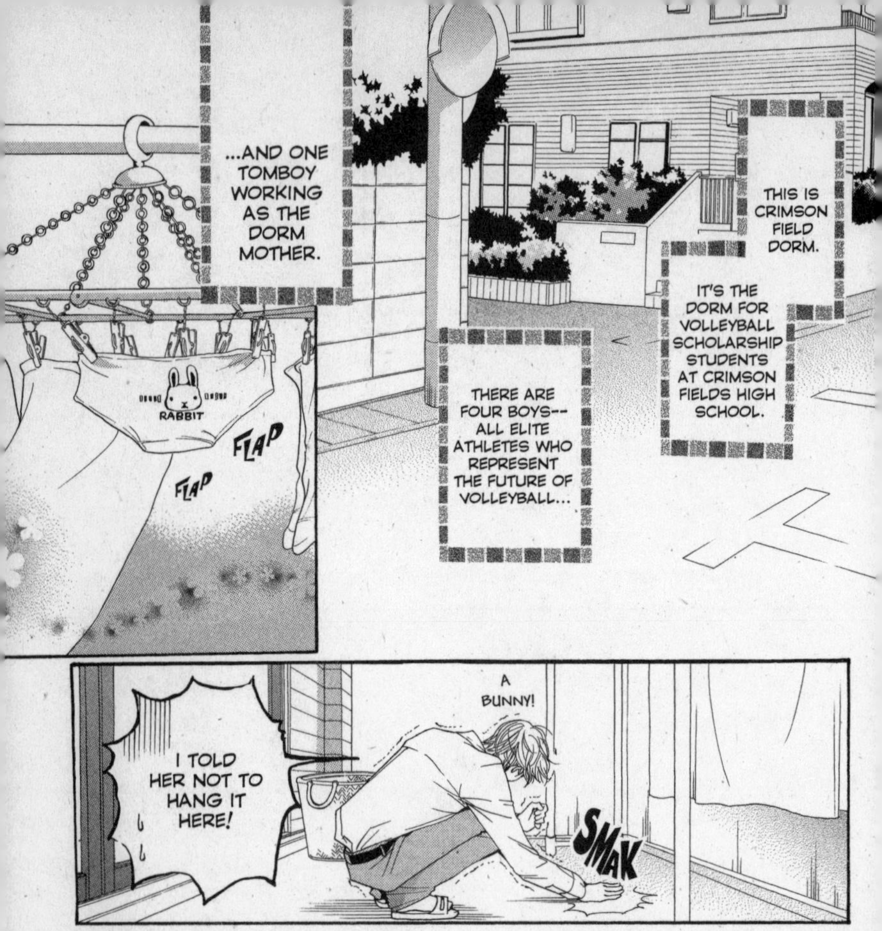
THIS IS CRIMSON FIELD DORM.
IT'S THE DORM FOR VOLLEYBALL SCHOLARSHIP STUDENTS AT CRIMSON FIELDS HIGH SCHOOL.
THERE ARE FOUR BOYS-- ALL ELITE ATHLETES WHO REPRESENT THE FUTURE OF VOLLEYBALL...
...AND ONE TOMBOY WORKING AS THE DORM MOTHER.
RABBIT
FLAP
FLAP
A BUNNY!
SMAK
I TOLD HER NOT TO HANG IT HERE!

THE MAKING OF CRIMSON HERO

Vol. 3

I REALLY DO FIND VOLLEYBALL INTERESTING. SOME PEOPLE MAKE COMMENTS LIKE "THAT PLAY WAS AMAZING," OR "WHAT A CLEVER PLAY." THAT'S ONE WAY TO ENJOY VOLLEYBALL, BUT MY GAZE INVARIABLY GOES TO THE KIDS WHO PLAY SUPPORTING ROLES. ONLY A SELECT FEW EVER GET TO PLAY AT THE SPRING HIGH SCHOOL VOLLEYBALL TOURNAMENT. OF COURSE, THOSE KIDS ARE SPLENDID TOO. BUT I'M DRAWN TO THINGS LIKE THE EARNEST EXPRESSION ON THE BENCH PLAYER HANDING TOWELS TO THE STARTERS DURING TIME OUTS...

...OR THE CLUB MEMBERS WHO DIDN'T MAKE IT ON THE BENCH, SITTING WITH THE SUPPORTERS IN THE STANDS...

...OR HOW THE PLAYERS ON THE COURT FEEL ABOUT THE HEAVY EXPECTATIONS OF THE OTHERS.

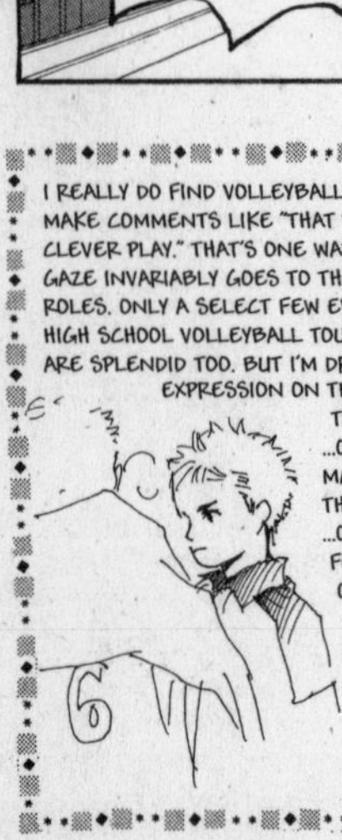

I THINK THERE ARE ALL SORTS OF KIDS. I EVEN WONDER HOW IT FEELS TO BE THE KID WHO QUIT THE VOLLEYBALL CLUB PARTWAY THROUGH AND WATCHES THE SPRING HIGH SCHOOL VOLLEYBALL TOURNAMENT AT HOME.

I THINK I'M DRAWN TO THE SIMPLE, UNCOMPLICATED FEELINGS OF THESE KIDS THAT SUPPORT VOLLEYBALL. I HOPE I CAN CONVEY THOSE FEELINGS THROUGH MY DEPICTIONS. DON'T YOU THINK EVEN THE MOST CYNICAL KID HARBORS FEELINGS THAT WOULD BE EMBARRASSING TO ADMIT OUT LOUD? I'M SURE OF IT. THAT'S WHAT I BELIEVE. EVEN IN THIS ERA WHERE MORE AND MORE CRIMES ARE COMMITTED BY MINORS.

I DON'T THINK ADULTS HAVE THESE FEELINGS. ADULTS ARE TOO CONCERNED ABOUT THEIR OWN INTERESTS. THAT INCLUDES ME.

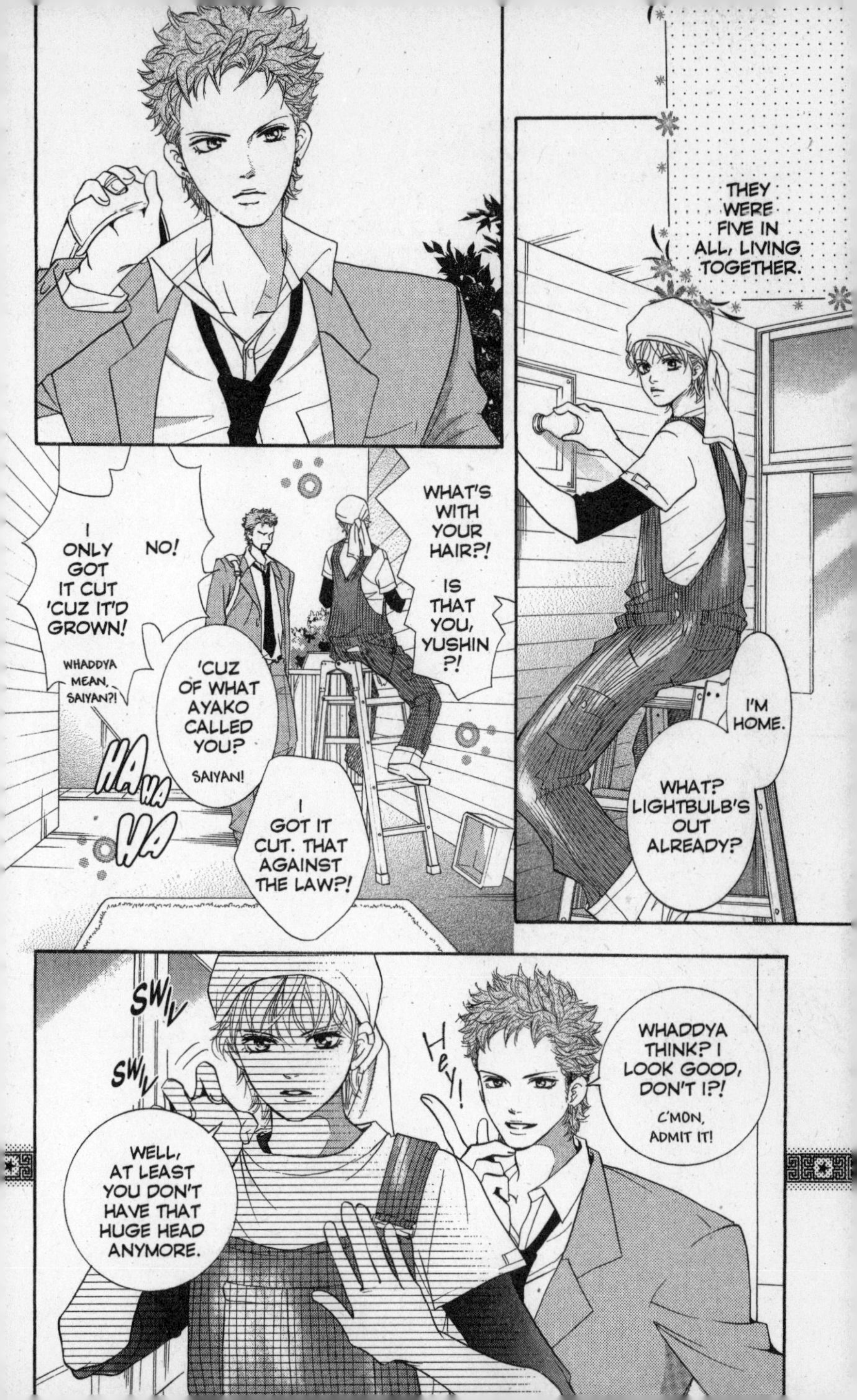
THEY WERE FIVE IN ALL, LIVING TOGETHER.
I'M HOME.
WHAT? LIGHTBULB'S OUT ALREADY?
WHAT'S WITH YOUR HAIR?!
IS THAT YOU, YUSHIN?!
I GOT IT CUT. THAT AGAINST THE LAW?!
'CUZ OF WHAT AYAKO CALLED YOU?
SAIYAN!
NO!
I ONLY GOT IT CUT 'CUZ IT'D GROWN!
WHADDYA MEAN, SAIYAN?!
HA HA HA
WHADDYA THINK? I LOOK GOOD, DON'T I?!
C'MON, ADMIT IT!
Hey!
SWIV
SWIV
WELL, AT LEAST YOU DON'T HAVE THAT HUGE HEAD ANYMORE.

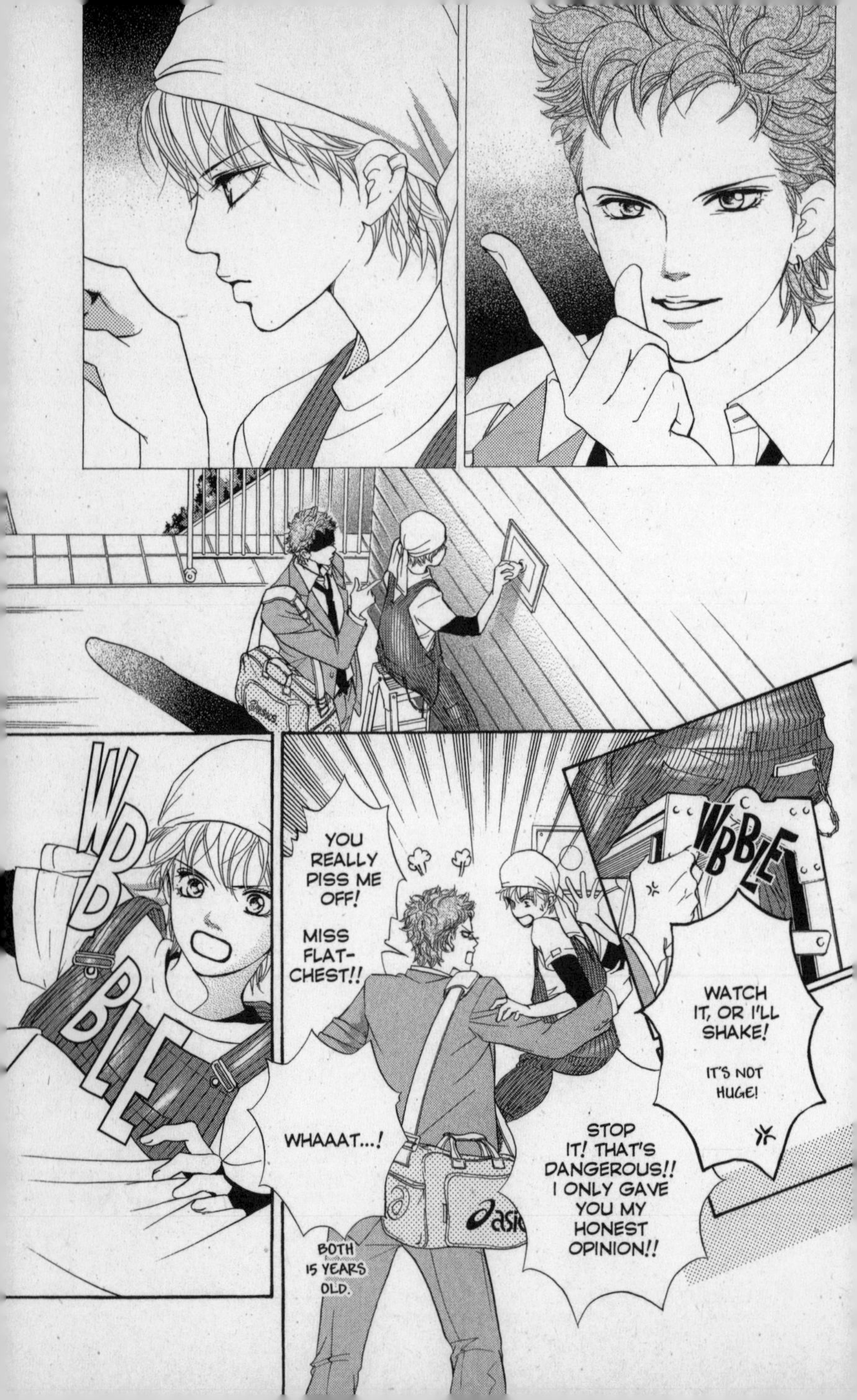
WBBLE
WATCH IT, OR I'LL SHAKE!
IT'S NOT HUGE!
YOU REALLY PISS ME OFF!
MISS FLAT-CHEST!!
STOP IT! THAT'S DANGEROUS!! I ONLY GAVE YOU MY HONEST OPINION!!
WHAAAT...!
BOTH 15 YEARS OLD.
asics

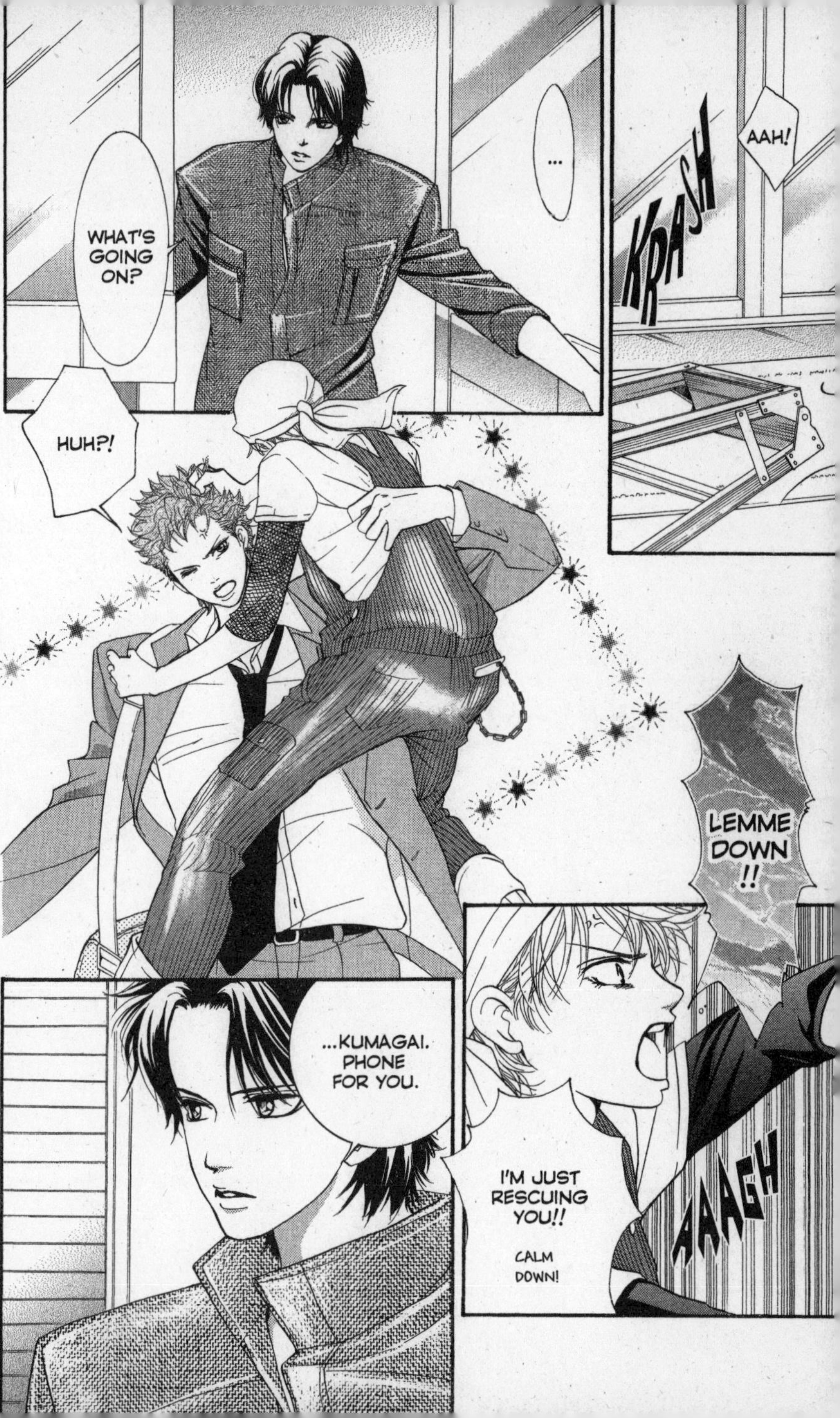
KRASH
AAH!
...
WHAT'S GOING ON?
HUH?!
LEMME DOWN!!
AAAGH
I'M JUST RESCUING YOU!!
CALM DOWN!
...KUMAGAI. PHONE FOR YOU.

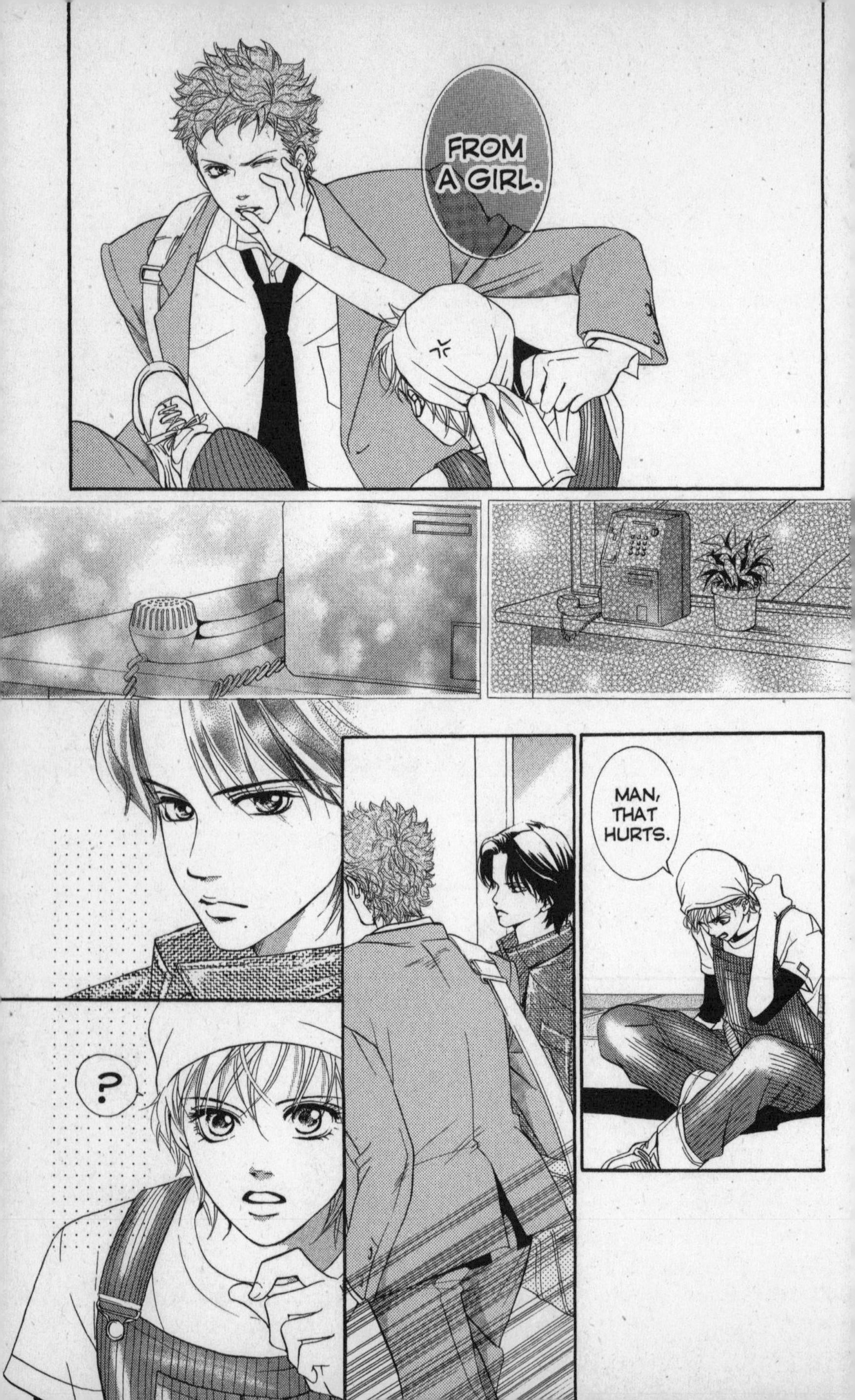
FROM A GIRL.
MAN, THAT HURTS.
?

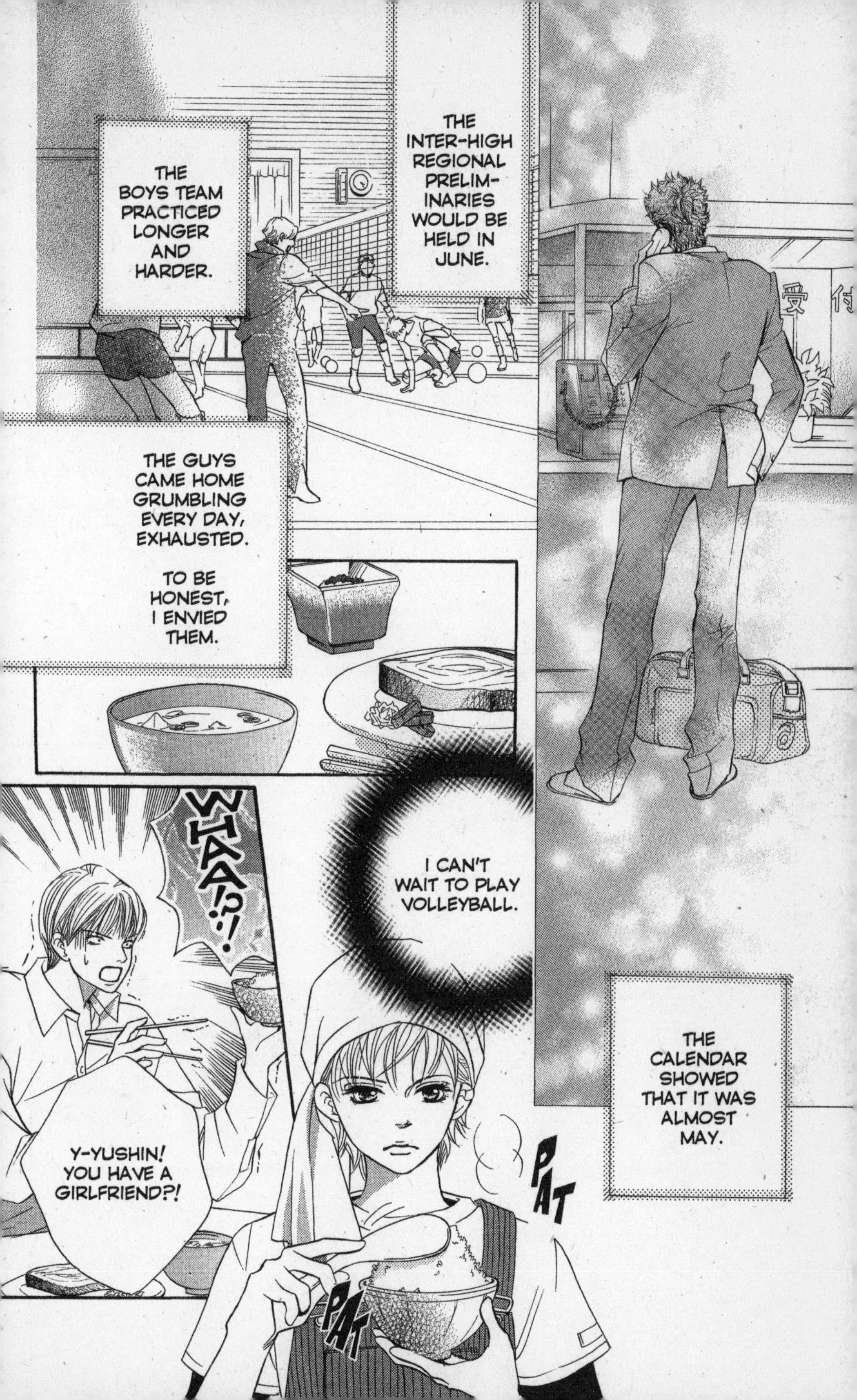
THE CALENDAR SHOWED THAT IT WAS ALMOST MAY.
THE INTER-HIGH REGIONAL PRELIM-INARIES WOULD BE HELD IN JUNE.
THE BOYS TEAM PRACTICED LONGER AND HARDER.
THE GUYS CAME HOME GRUMBLING EVERY DAY, EXHAUSTED.
TO BE HONEST, I ENVIED THEM.
I CAN'T WAIT TO PLAY VOLLEYBALL.
PAT
WHAA!?!
Y-YUSHIN! YOU HAVE A GIRLFRIEND?!
PAT

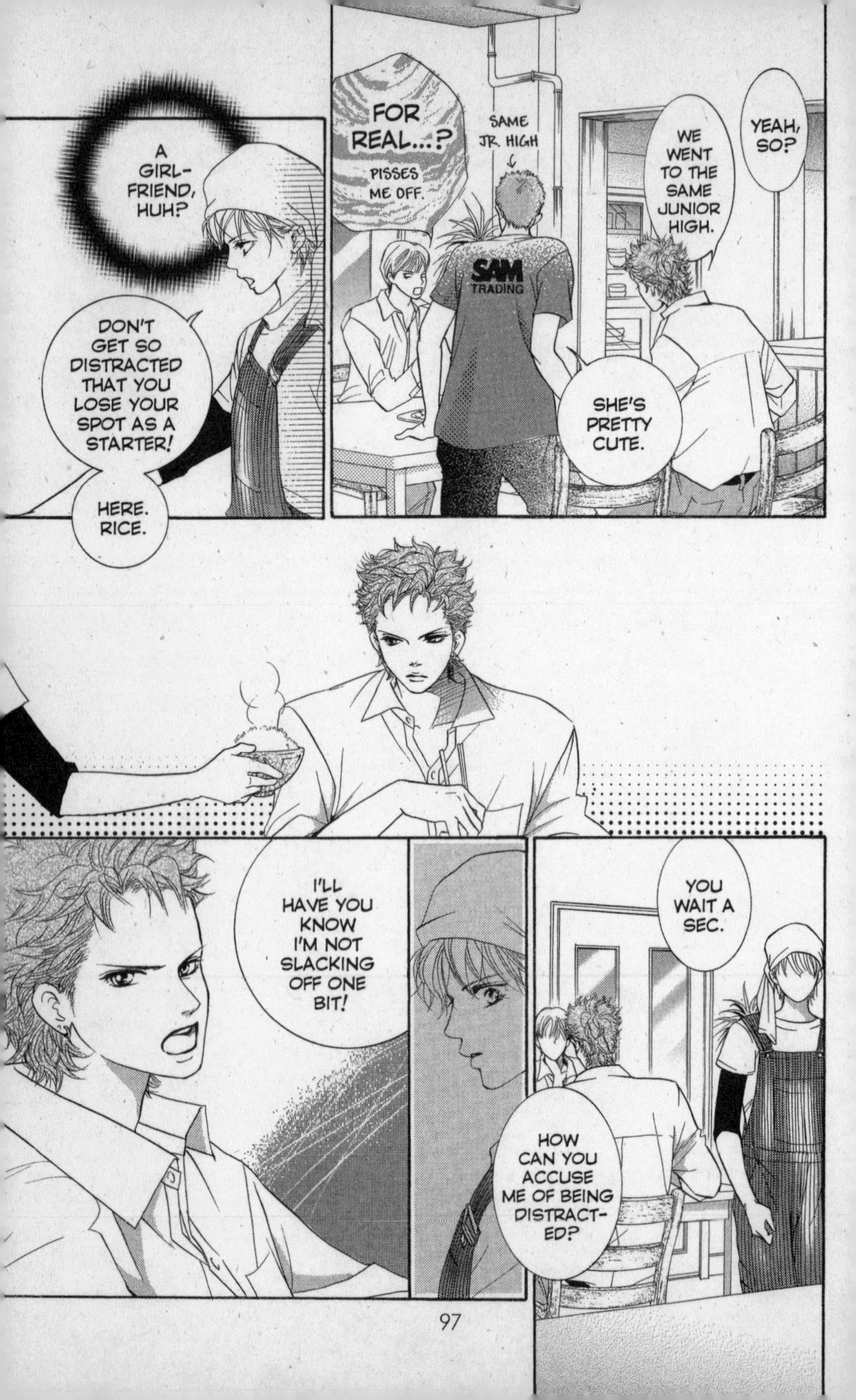
YEAH, SO?
WE WENT TO THE SAME JUNIOR HIGH.
SAME JR. HIGH
SAM TRADING
FOR REAL...?
PISSES ME OFF.
SHE'S PRETTY CUTE.
A GIRL-FRIEND, HUH?
DON'T GET SO DISTRACTED THAT YOU LOSE YOUR SPOT AS A STARTER!
HERE. RICE.
YOU WAIT A SEC.
HOW CAN YOU ACCUSE ME OF BEING DISTRACT-ED?
I'LL HAVE YOU KNOW I'M NOT SLACKING OFF ONE BIT!

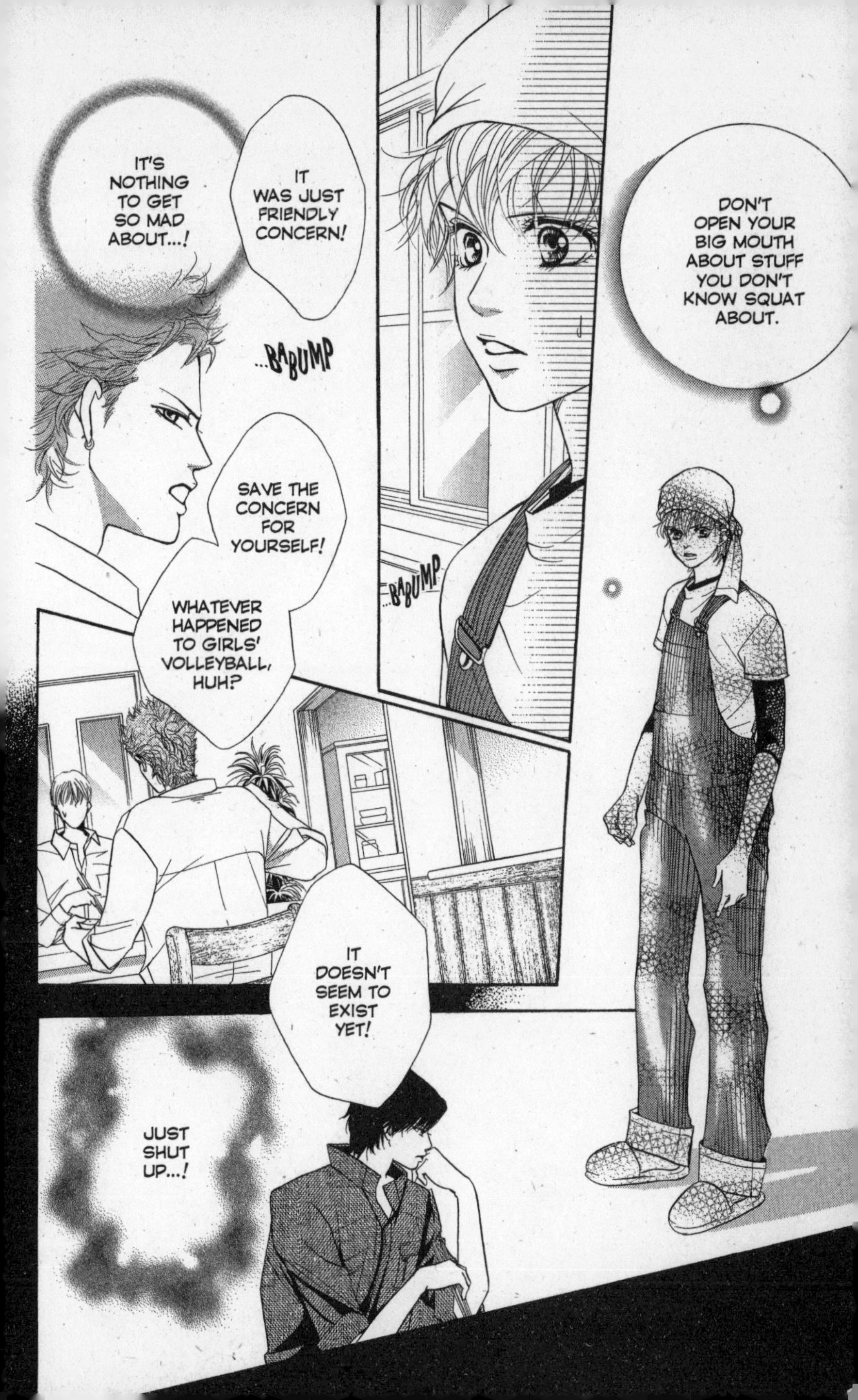

DON'T OPEN YOUR BIG MOUTH ABOUT STUFF YOU DON'T KNOW SQUAT ABOUT.
IT WAS JUST FRIENDLY CONCERN!
IT'S NOTHING TO GET SO MAD ABOUT...!
...BABUMP
...BABUMP
SAVE THE CONCERN FOR YOURSELF!
WHATEVER HAPPENED TO GIRLS' VOLLEYBALL, HUH?
IT DOESN'T SEEM TO EXIST YET!
JUST SHUT UP...!

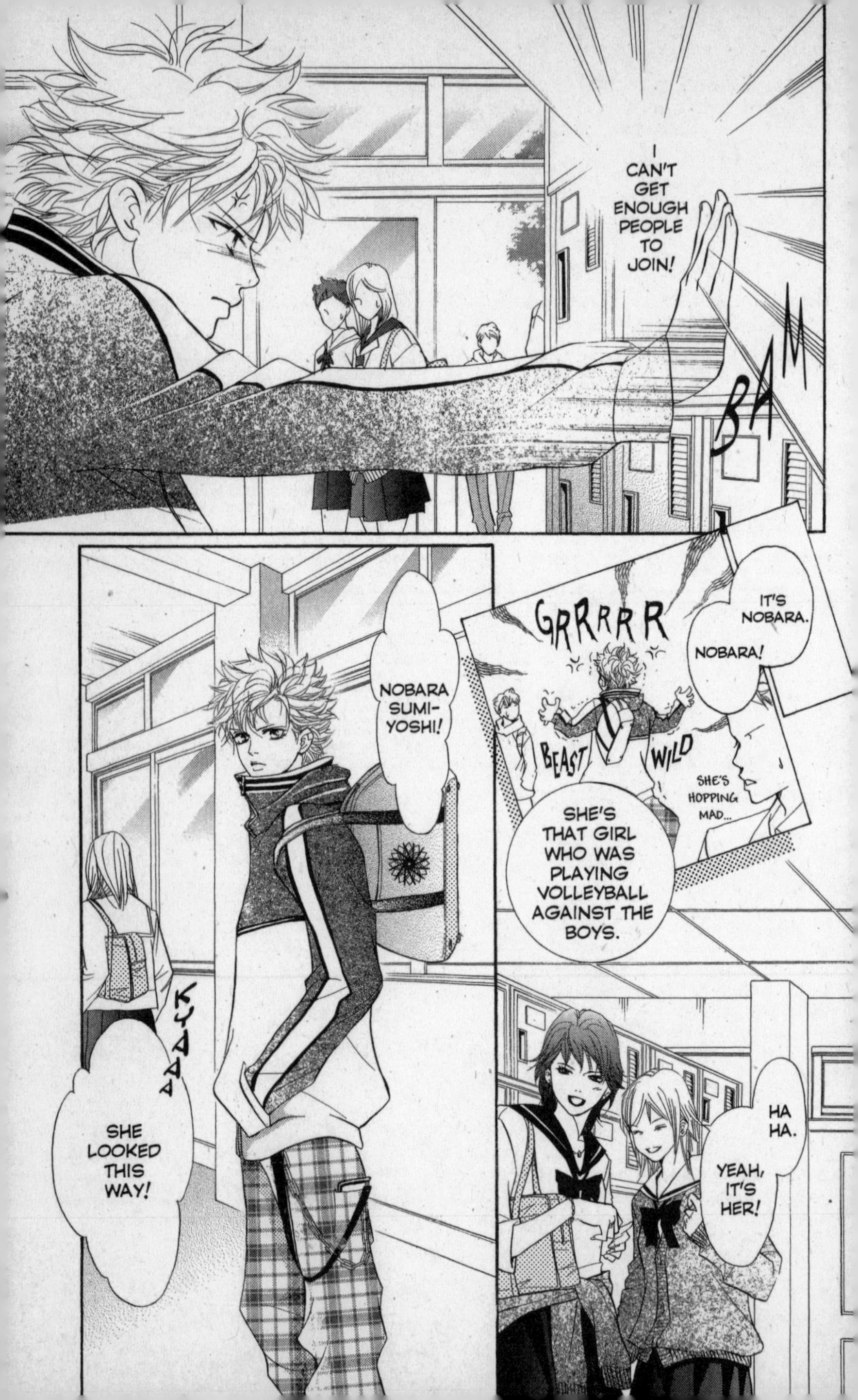
I CAN'T GET ENOUGH PEOPLE TO JOIN!
BAM
IT'S NOBARA.
NOBARA!
GRRRRR
BEAST
WILD
SHE'S HOPPING MAD...
SHE'S THAT GIRL WHO WAS PLAYING VOLLEYBALL AGAINST THE BOYS.
HA HA.
YEAH, IT'S HER!
NOBARA SUMI-YOSHI!
KYAAAA
SHE LOOKED THIS WAY!

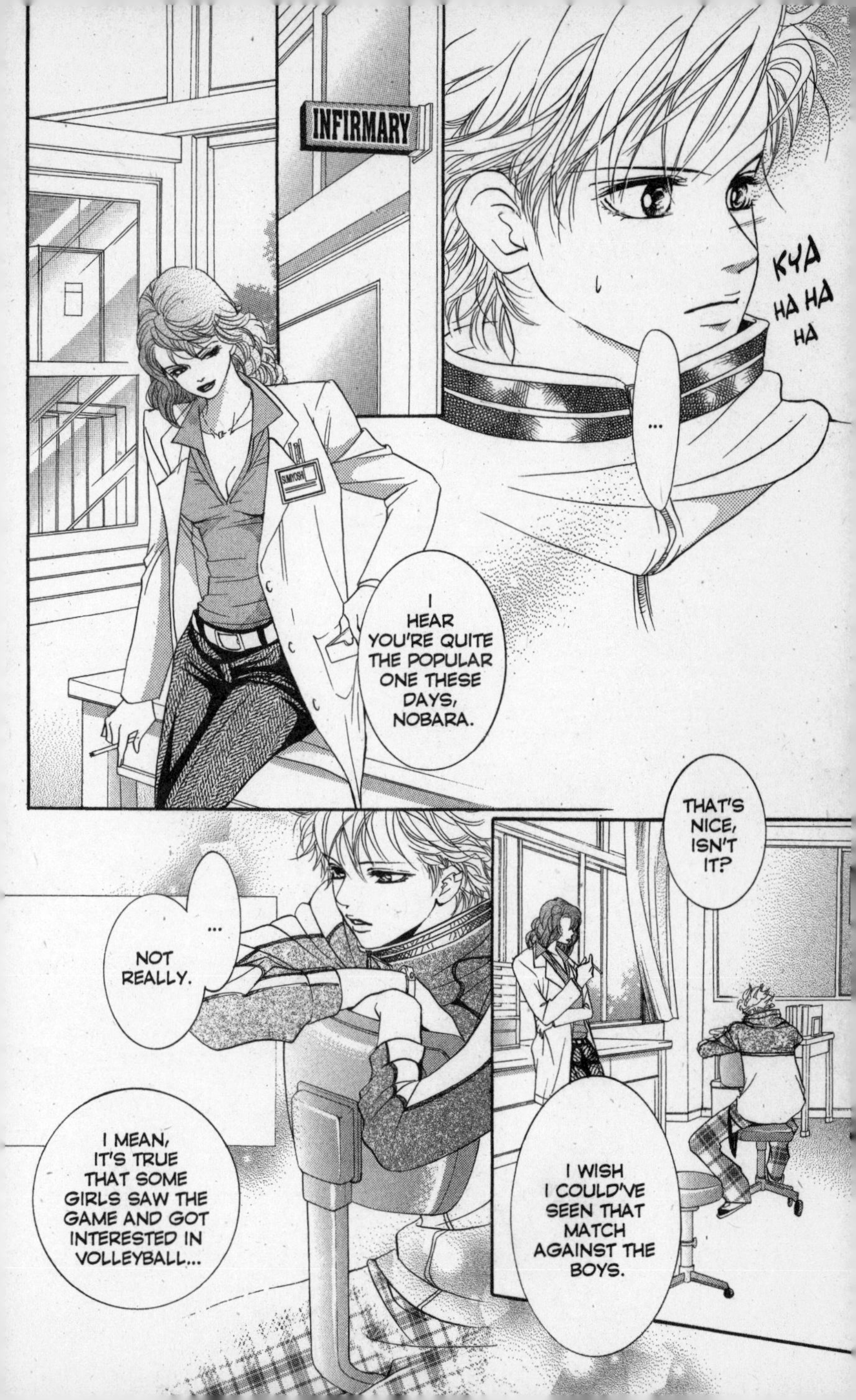
KYA HA HA HA
...
INFIRMARY
I HEAR YOU'RE QUITE THE POPULAR ONE THESE DAYS, NOBARA.
THAT'S NICE, ISN'T IT?
I WISH I COULD'VE SEEN THAT MATCH AGAINST THE BOYS.
... NOT REALLY.
I MEAN, IT'S TRUE THAT SOME GIRLS SAW THE GAME AND GOT INTERESTED IN VOLLEYBALL...

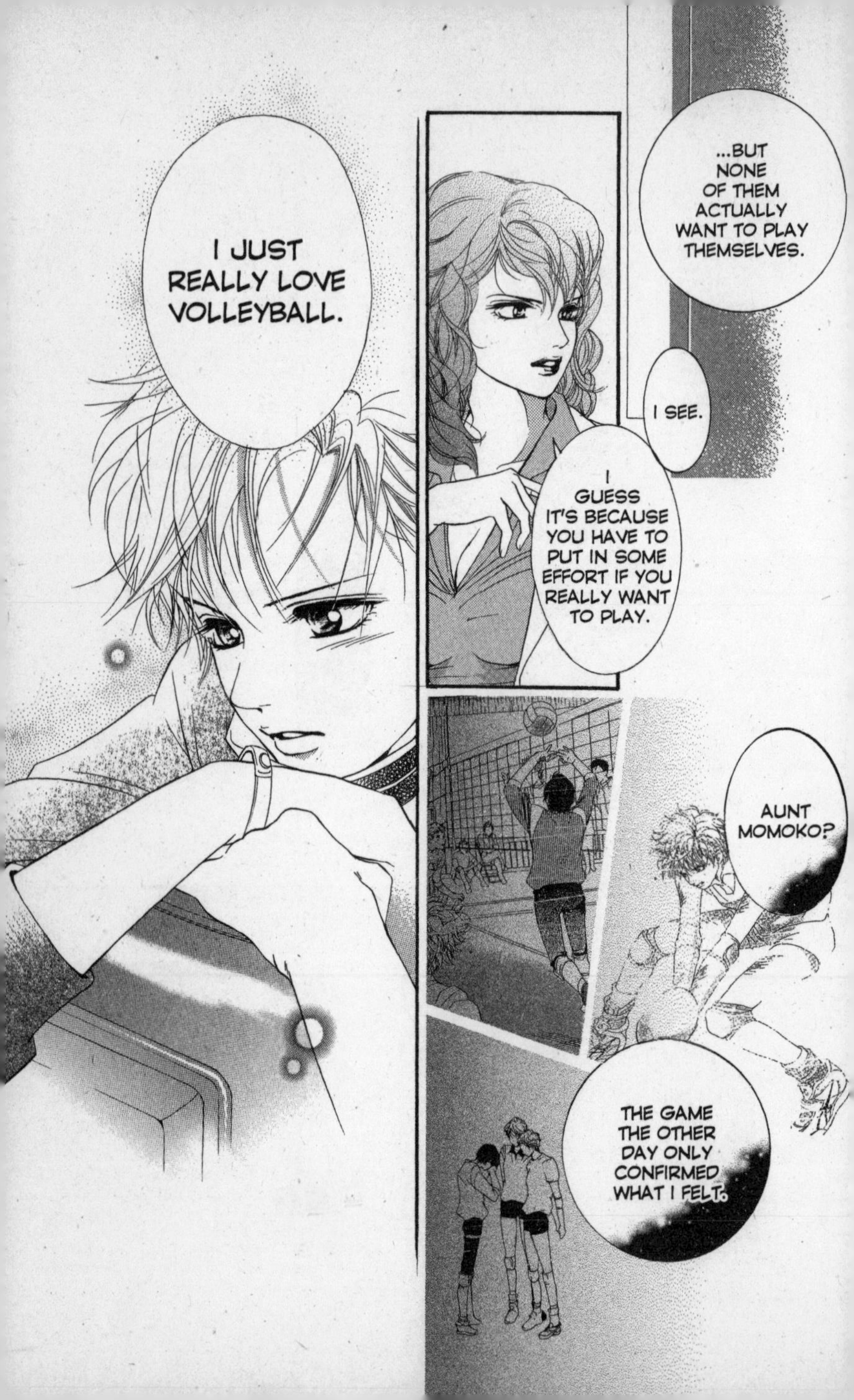
...BUT NONE OF THEM ACTUALLY WANT TO PLAY THEMSELVES.
I SEE.
I GUESS IT'S BECAUSE YOU HAVE TO PUT IN SOME EFFORT IF YOU REALLY WANT TO PLAY.
AUNT MOMOKO?
THE GAME THE OTHER DAY ONLY CONFIRMED WHAT I FELT.
I JUST REALLY LOVE VOLLEYBALL.

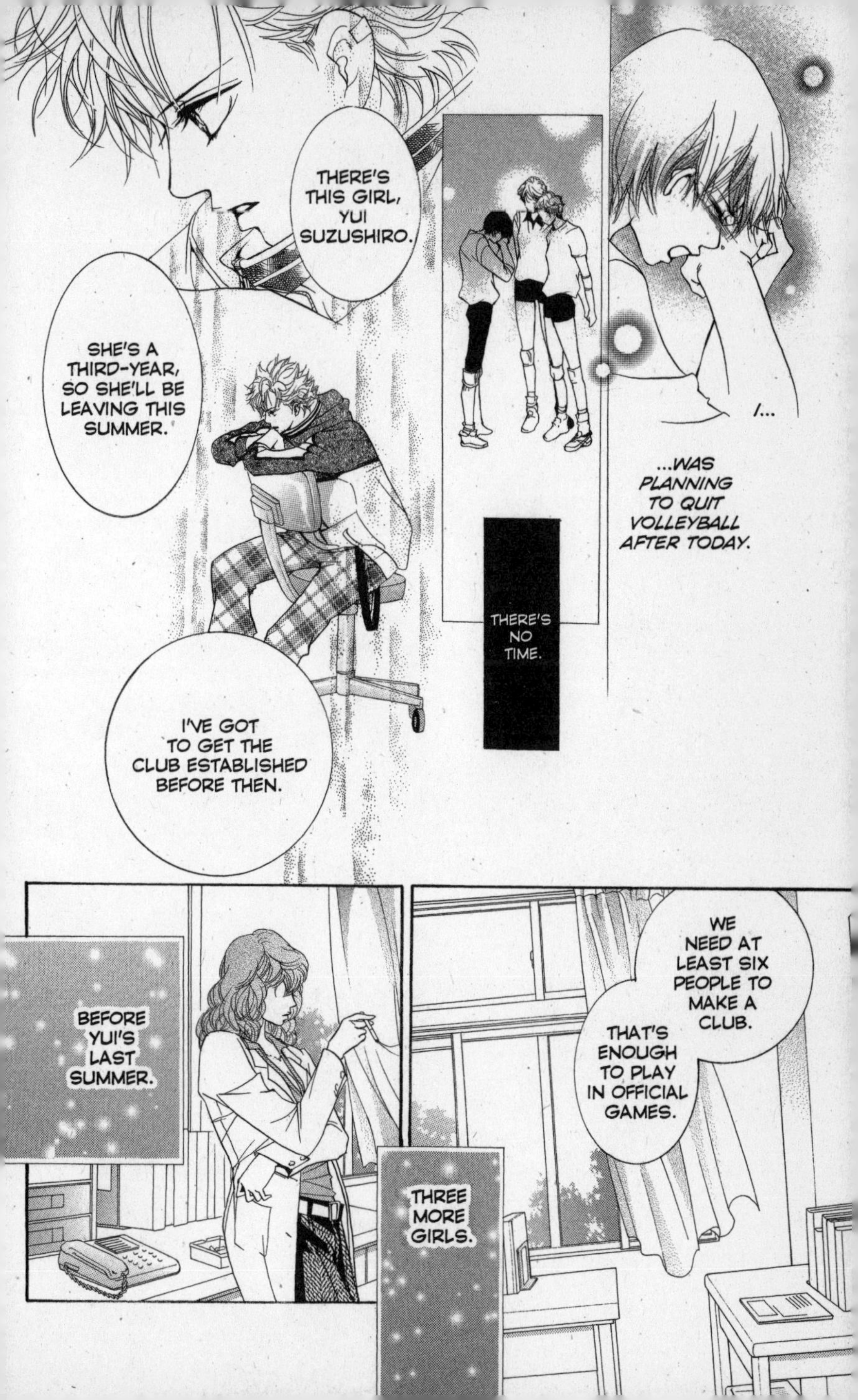
I...
...WAS PLANNING TO QUIT VOLLEYBALL AFTER TODAY.
THERE'S NO TIME.
THERE'S THIS GIRL, YUI SUZUSHIRO.
SHE'S A THIRD-YEAR, SO SHE'LL BE LEAVING THIS SUMMER.
I'VE GOT TO GET THE CLUB ESTABLISHED BEFORE THEN.
WE NEED AT LEAST SIX PEOPLE TO MAKE A CLUB.
THAT'S ENOUGH TO PLAY IN OFFICIAL GAMES.
THREE MORE GIRLS.
BEFORE YUI'S LAST SUMMER.

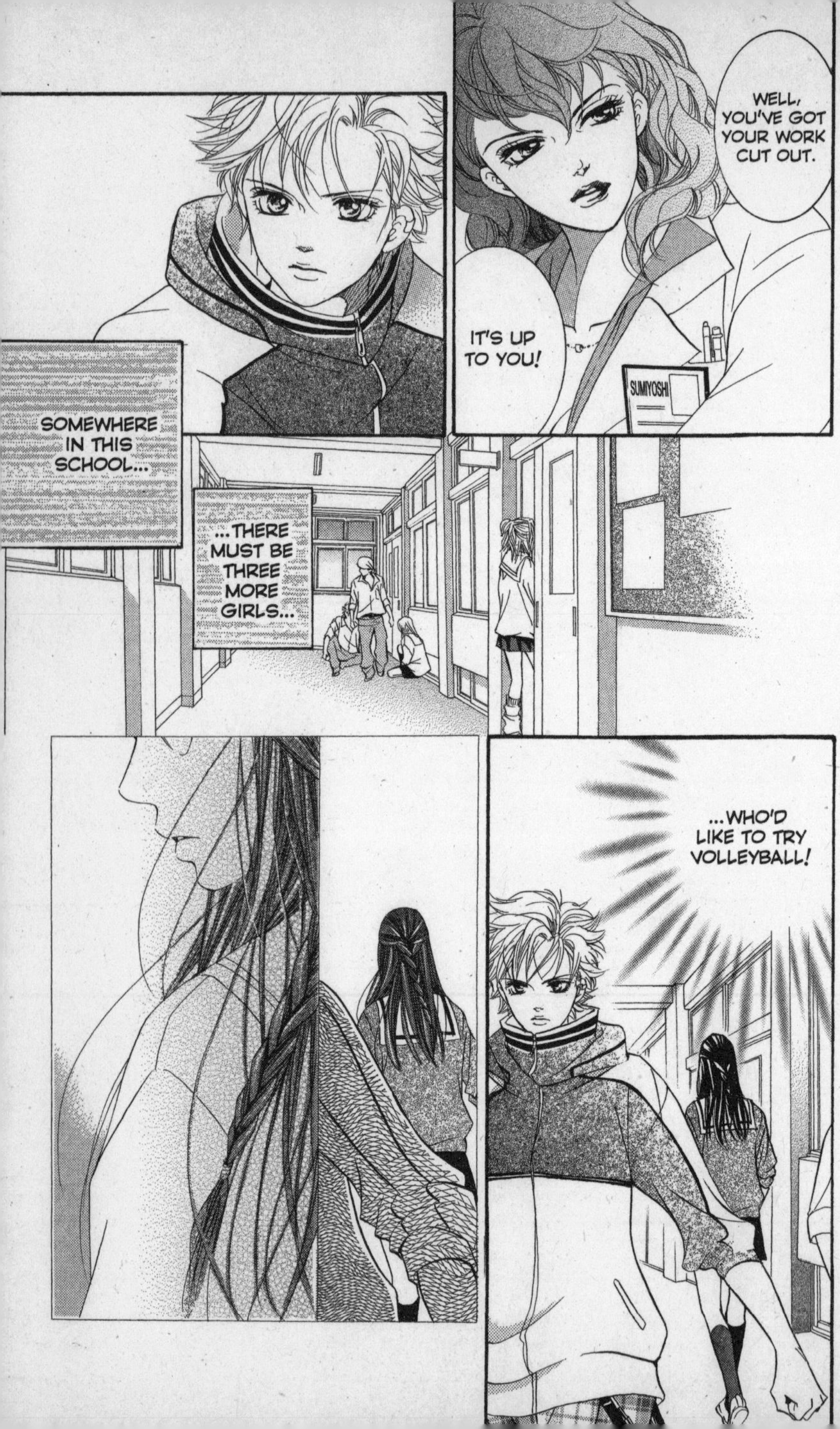
WELL, YOU'VE GOT YOUR WORK CUT OUT.
IT'S UP TO YOU!
SUMIYOSHI
SOMEWHERE IN THIS SCHOOL...
...THERE MUST BE THREE MORE GIRLS...
...WHO'D LIKE TO TRY VOLLEYBALL!

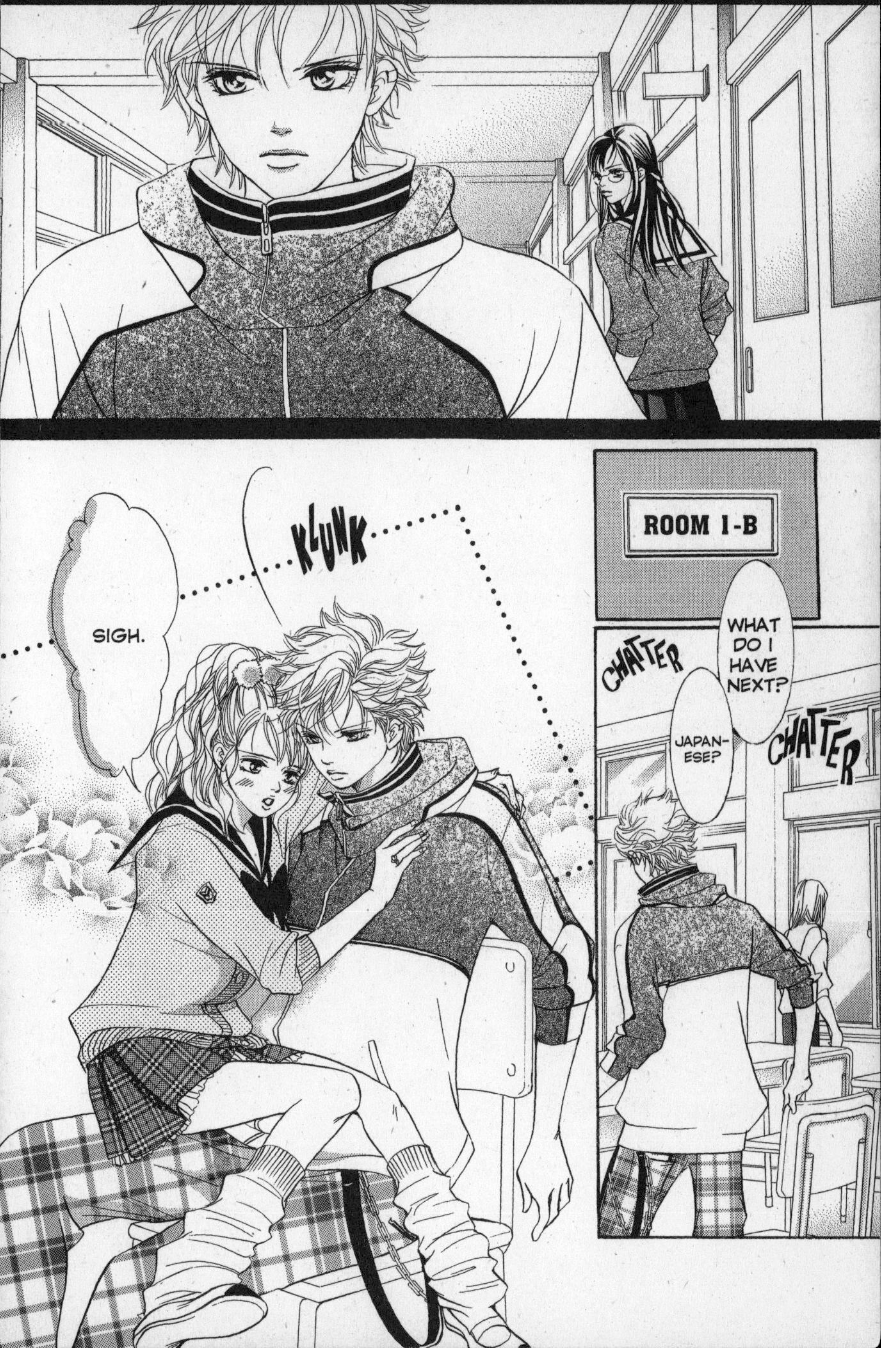
ROOM 1-B
WHAT DO I HAVE NEXT?
CHATTER
JAPAN-ESE?
CHATTER
KLUNK
SIGH.

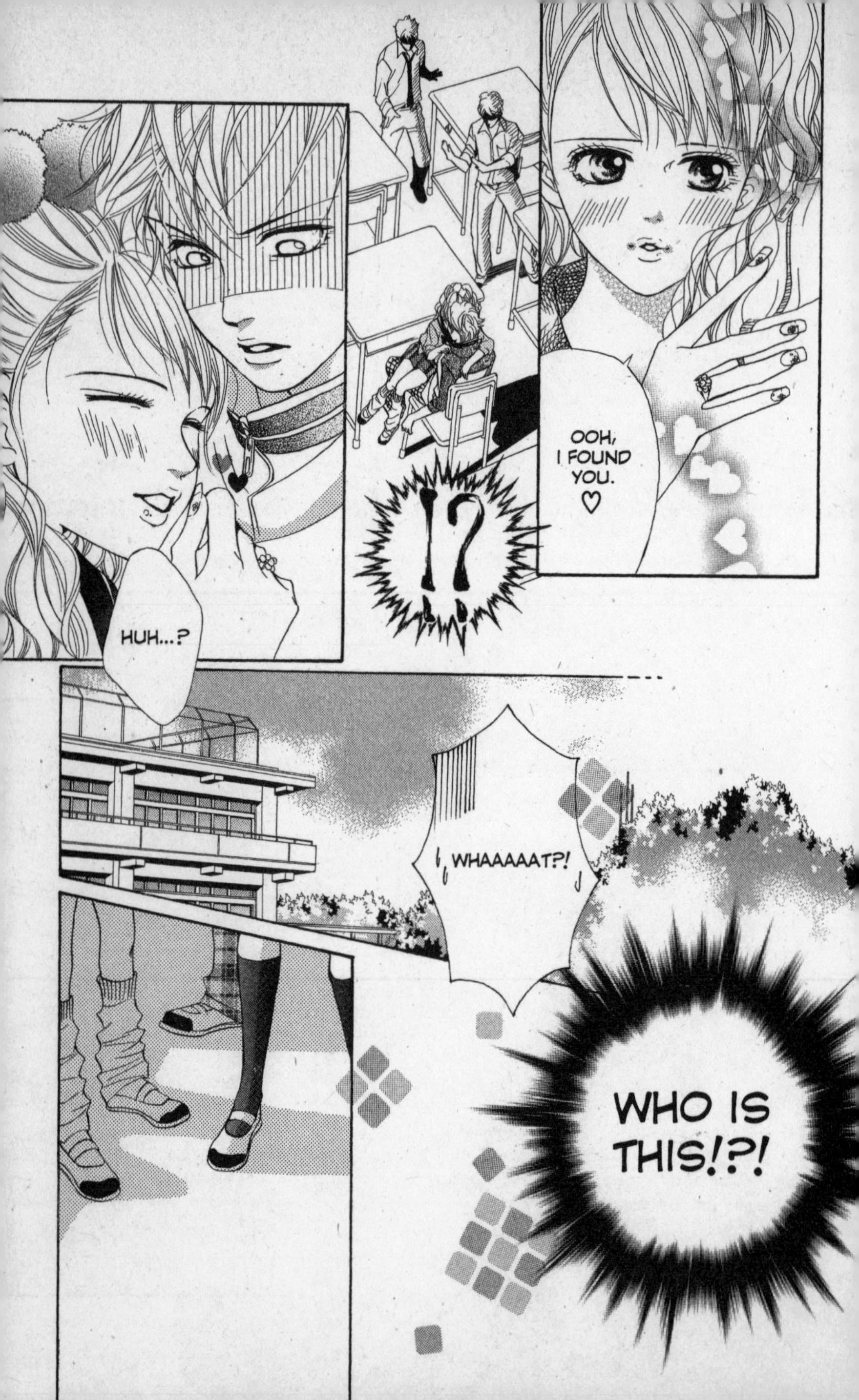
OOH, I FOUND YOU. ♡
!?
HUH...?
WHAAAAAT?!
WHO IS THIS!?!

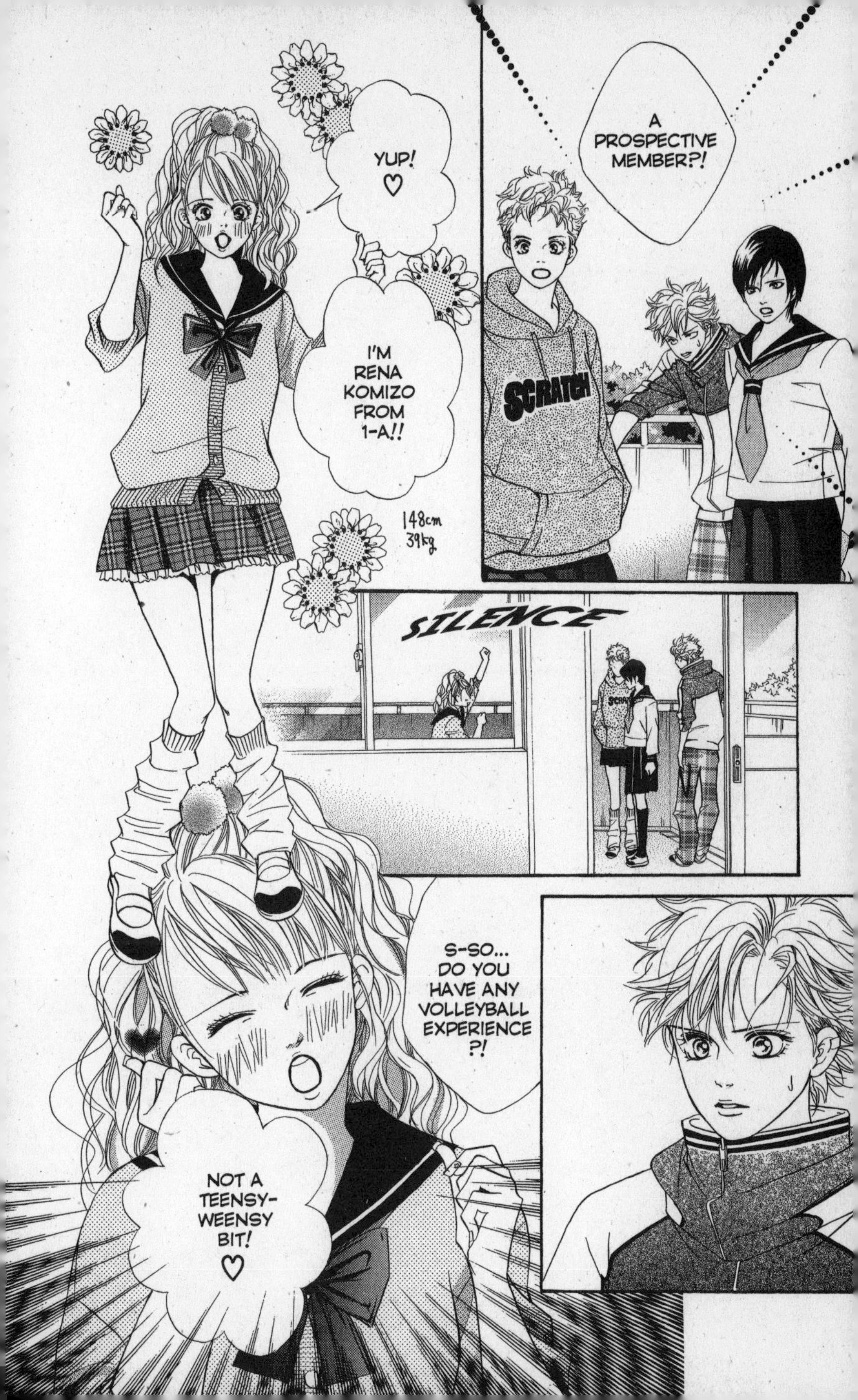
A PROSPECTIVE MEMBER?!
YUP! ♡
I'M RENA KOMIZO FROM 1-A!!
148cm 39kg
SILENCE
S-SO... DO YOU HAVE ANY VOLLEYBALL EXPERIENCE?!
NOT A TEENSY-WEENSY BIT! ♡

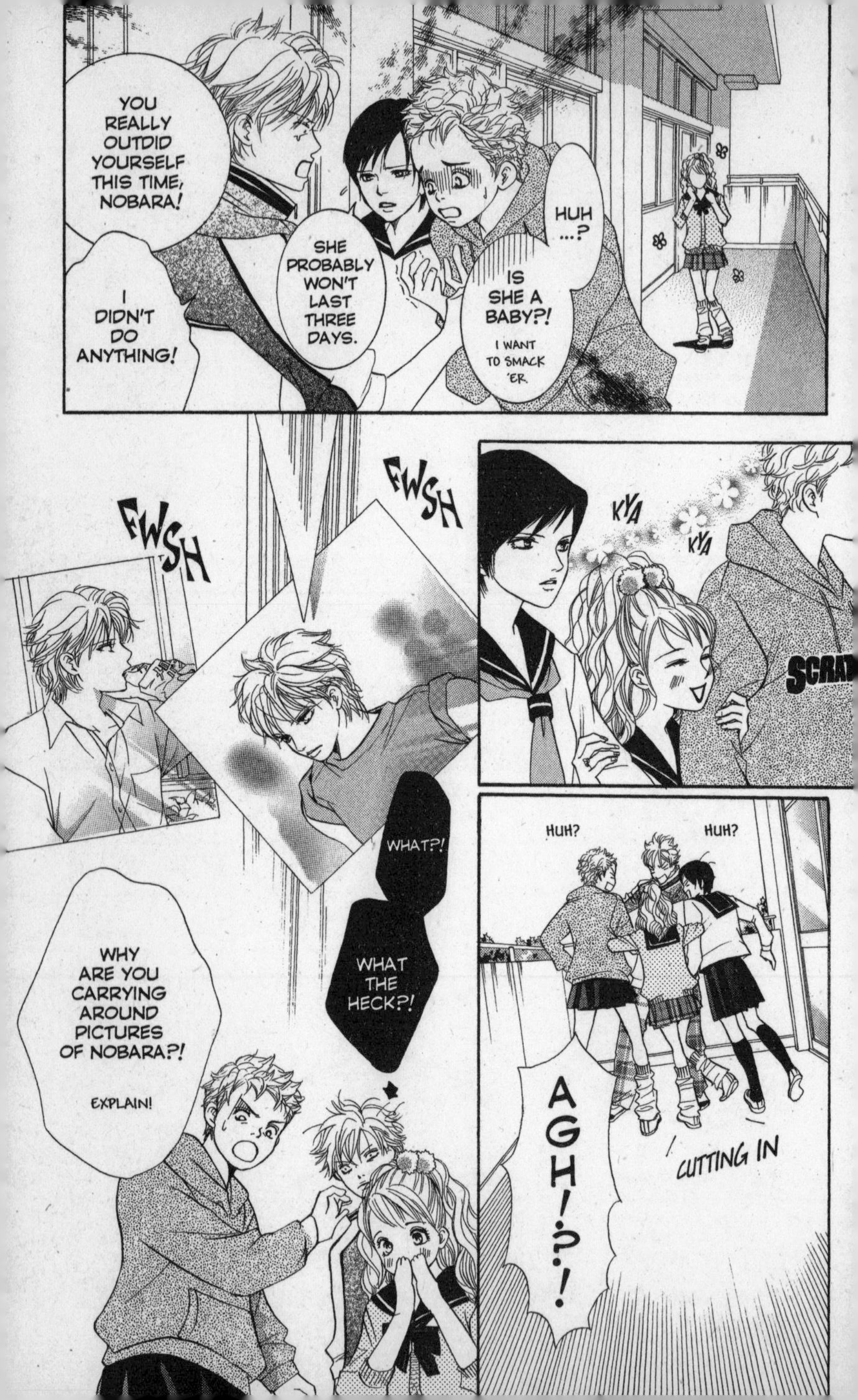
HUH ...?
IS SHE A BABY?!
I WANT TO SMACK 'ER.
SHE PROBABLY WON'T LAST THREE DAYS.
YOU REALLY OUTDID YOURSELF THIS TIME, NOBARA!
I DIDN'T DO ANYTHING!
KYA
KYA
SCRAT
HUH?
HUH?
CUTTING IN
AGH!?!
FWSH
FWSH
WHAT?!
WHAT THE HECK?!
WHY ARE YOU CARRYING AROUND PICTURES OF NOBARA?!
EXPLAIN!

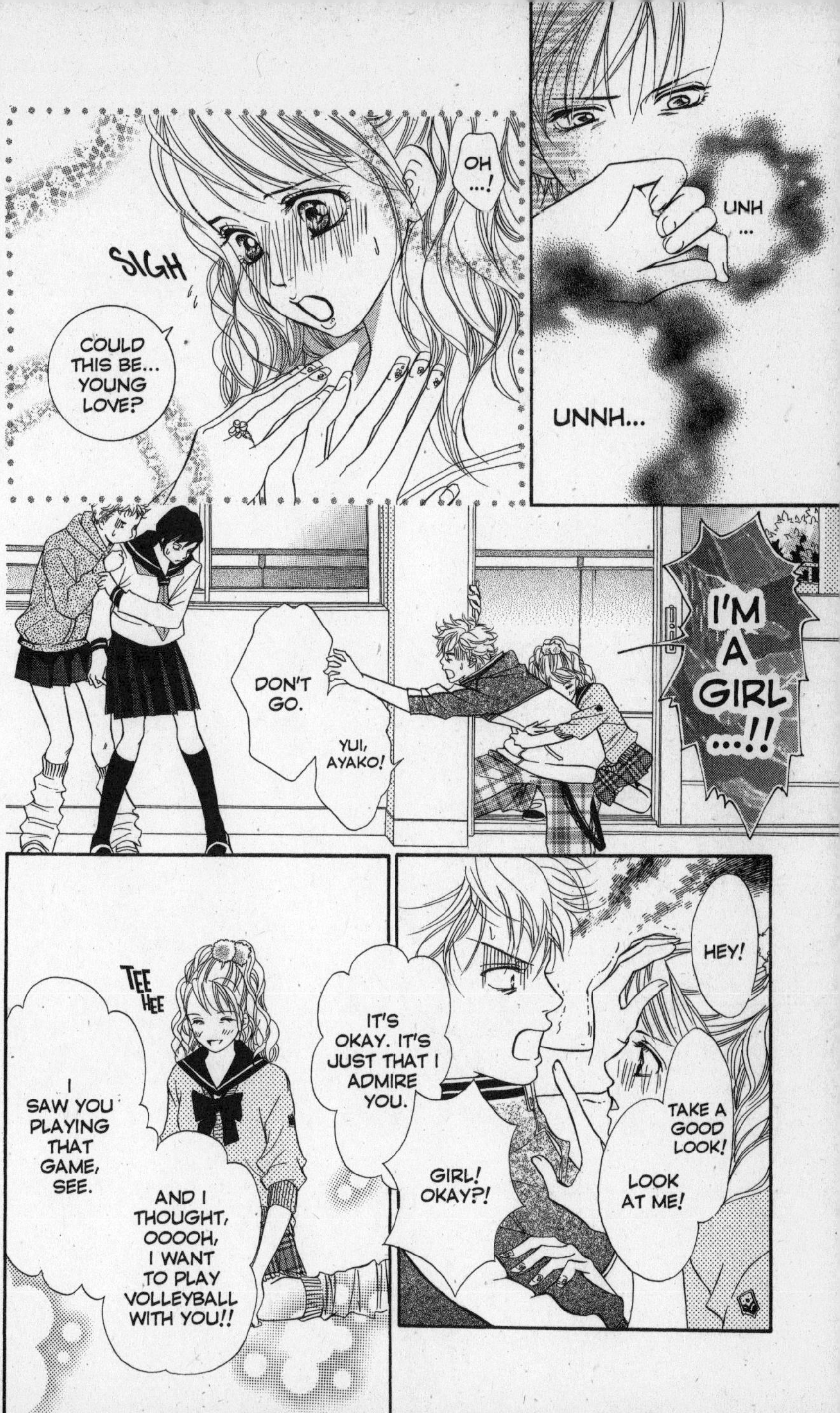
UNH ...
UNNH...
OH ...!
SIGH
COULD THIS BE... YOUNG LOVE?
I'M A GIRL ...!!
YUI, AYAKO!
DON'T GO.
HEY!
TAKE A GOOD LOOK!
LOOK AT ME!
GIRL! OKAY?!
IT'S OKAY. IT'S JUST THAT I ADMIRE YOU.
TEE HEE
I SAW YOU PLAYING THAT GAME, SEE.
AND I THOUGHT, OOOOH, I WANT TO PLAY VOLLEYBALL WITH YOU!!

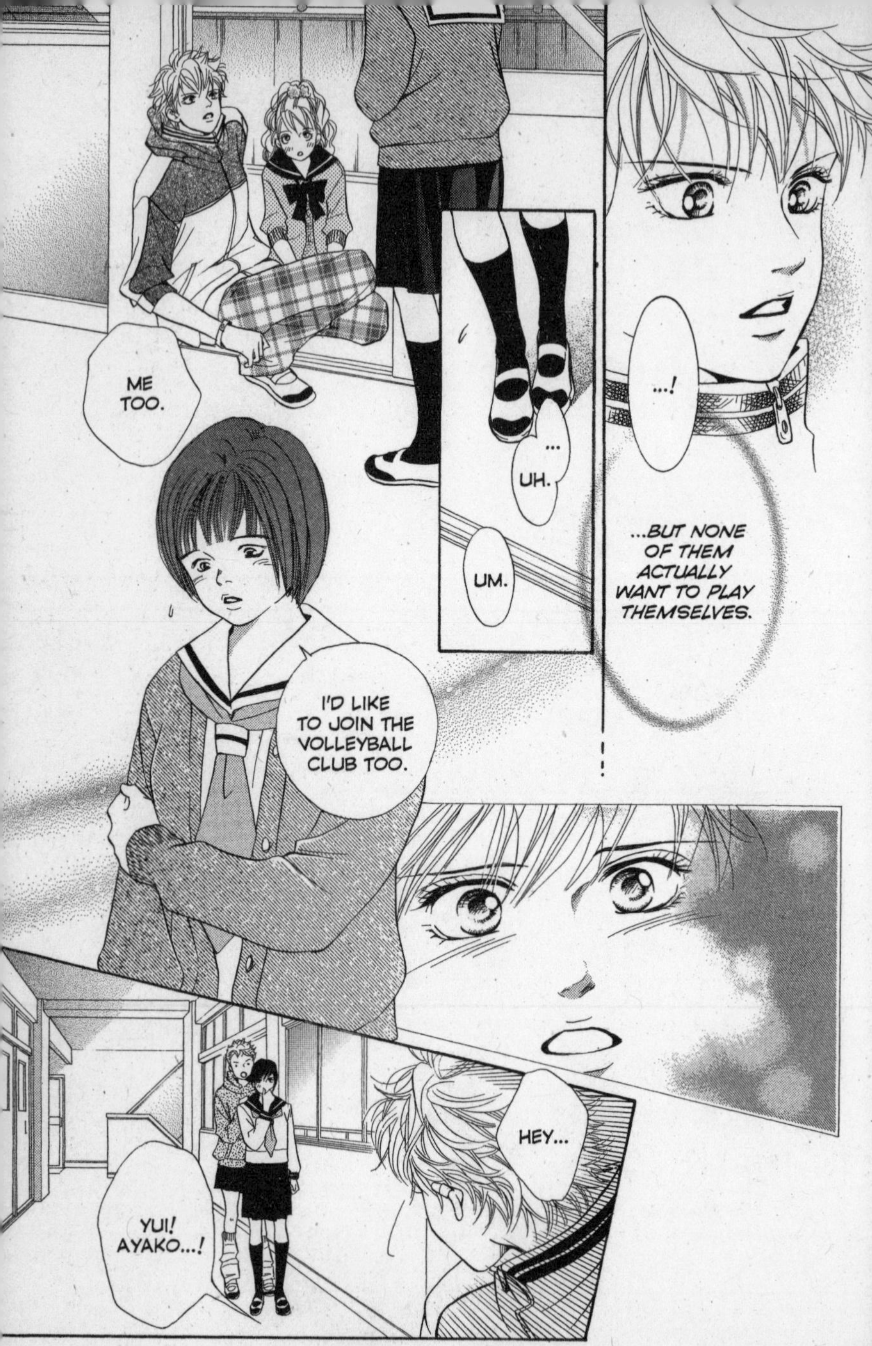
...!
...BUT NONE OF THEM ACTUALLY WANT TO PLAY THEMSELVES.
... UH.
UM.
ME TOO.
I'D LIKE TO JOIN THE VOLLEYBALL CLUB TOO.
HEY...
YUI! AYAKO...!

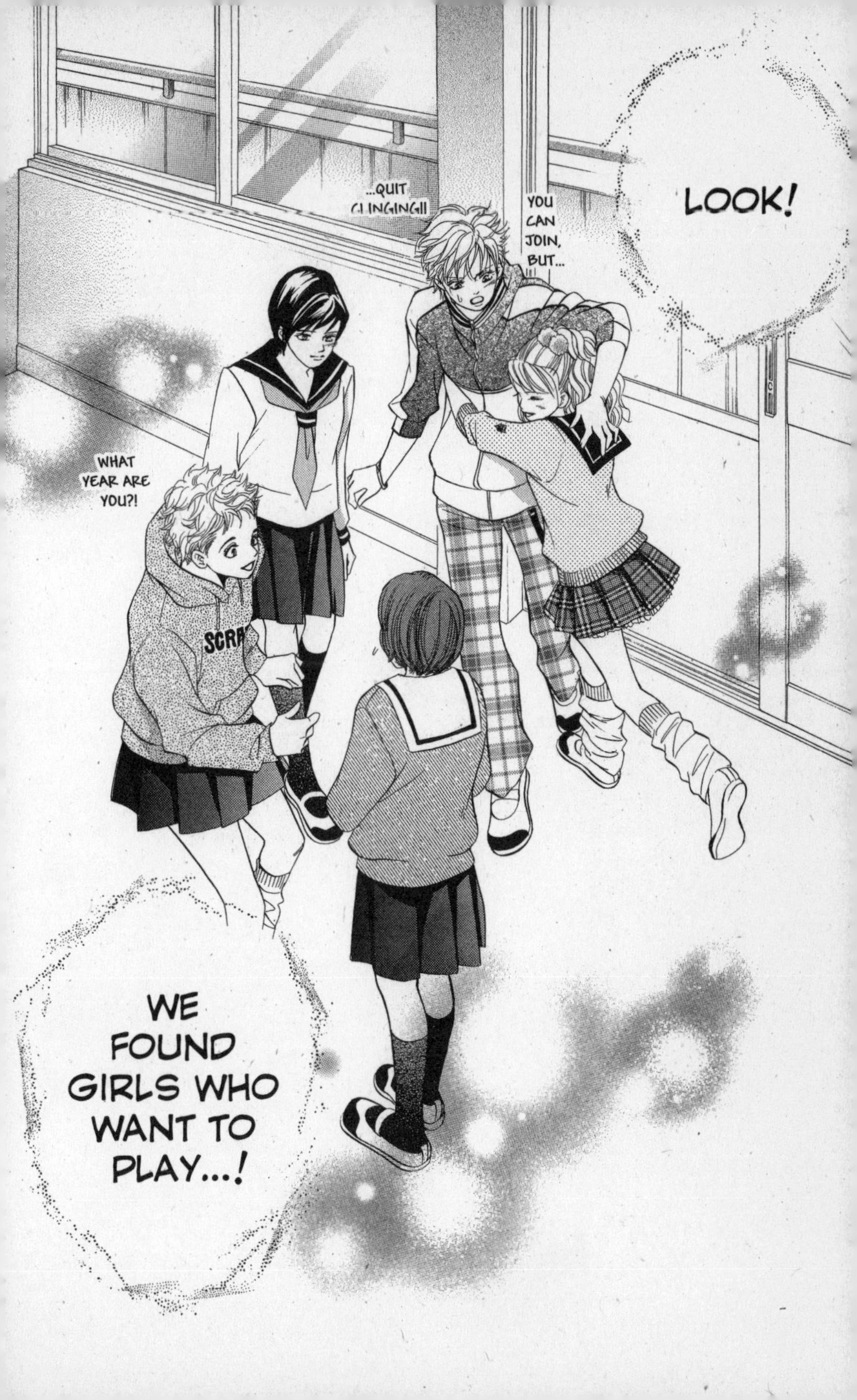
LOOK!
YOU CAN JOIN, BUT...
...QUIT CLINGING!!
WHAT YEAR ARE YOU?!
WE FOUND GIRLS WHO WANT TO PLAY...!

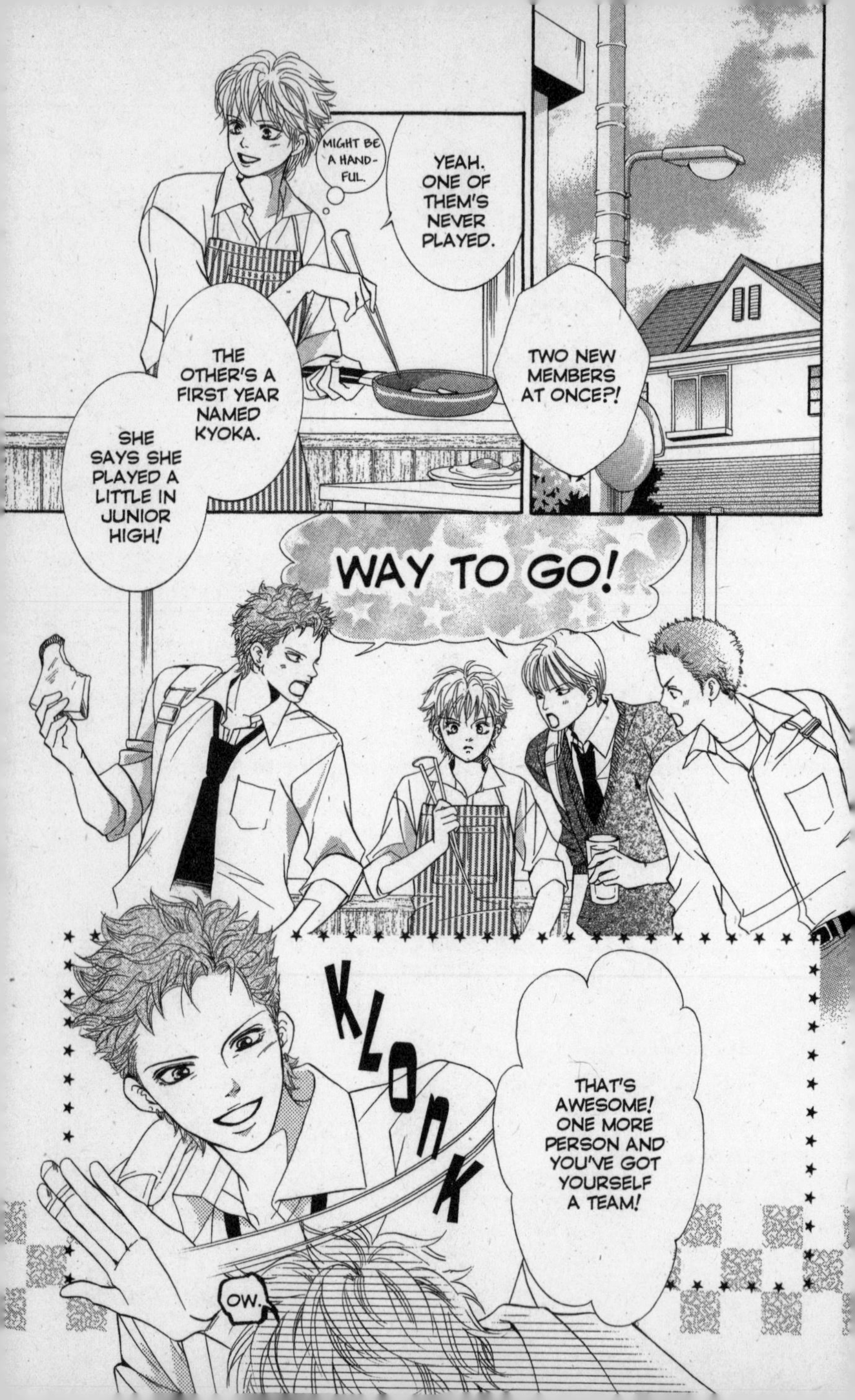
TWO NEW MEMBERS AT ONCE?!
YEAH. ONE OF THEM'S NEVER PLAYED.
MIGHT BE A HAND-FUL.
THE OTHER'S A FIRST YEAR NAMED KYOKA.
SHE SAYS SHE PLAYED A LITTLE IN JUNIOR HIGH!
WAY TO GO!
THAT'S AWESOME! ONE MORE PERSON AND YOU'VE GOT YOURSELF A TEAM!
KLONK
OW.

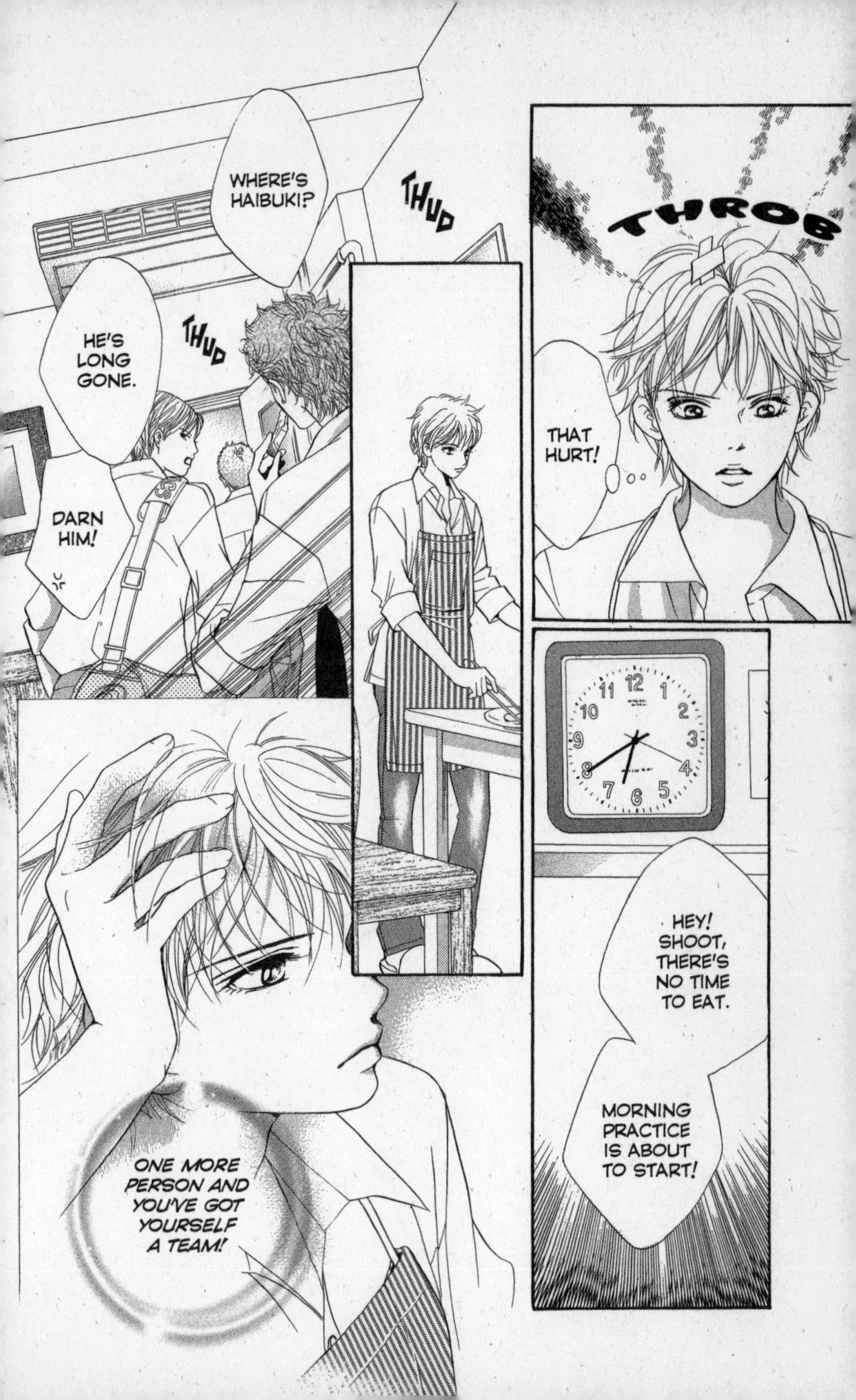
THROB
THAT HURT!
WHERE'S HAIBUKI?
THUD
THUD
HE'S LONG GONE.
DARN HIM!
HEY! SHOOT, THERE'S NO TIME TO EAT.
MORNING PRACTICE IS ABOUT TO START!
ONE MORE PERSON AND YOU'VE GOT YOURSELF A TEAM!

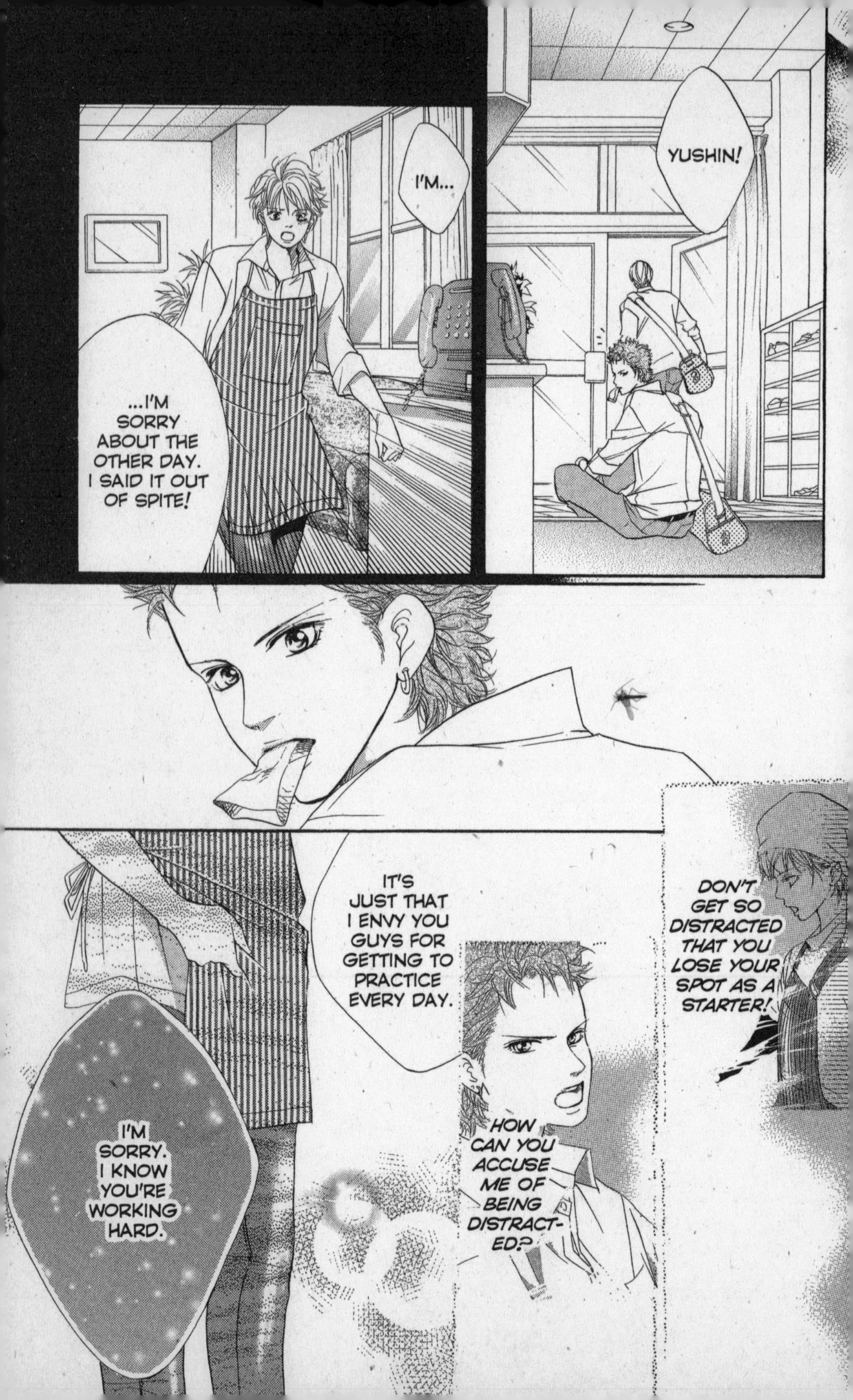
YUSHIN!
I'M...
...I'M SORRY ABOUT THE OTHER DAY. I SAID IT OUT OF SPITE!
IT'S JUST THAT I ENVY YOU GUYS FOR GETTING TO PRACTICE EVERY DAY.
DON'T GET SO DISTRACTED THAT YOU LOSE YOUR SPOT AS A STARTER!
HOW CAN YOU ACCUSE ME OF BEING DISTRACT-ED?
I'M SORRY. I KNOW YOU'RE WORKING HARD.

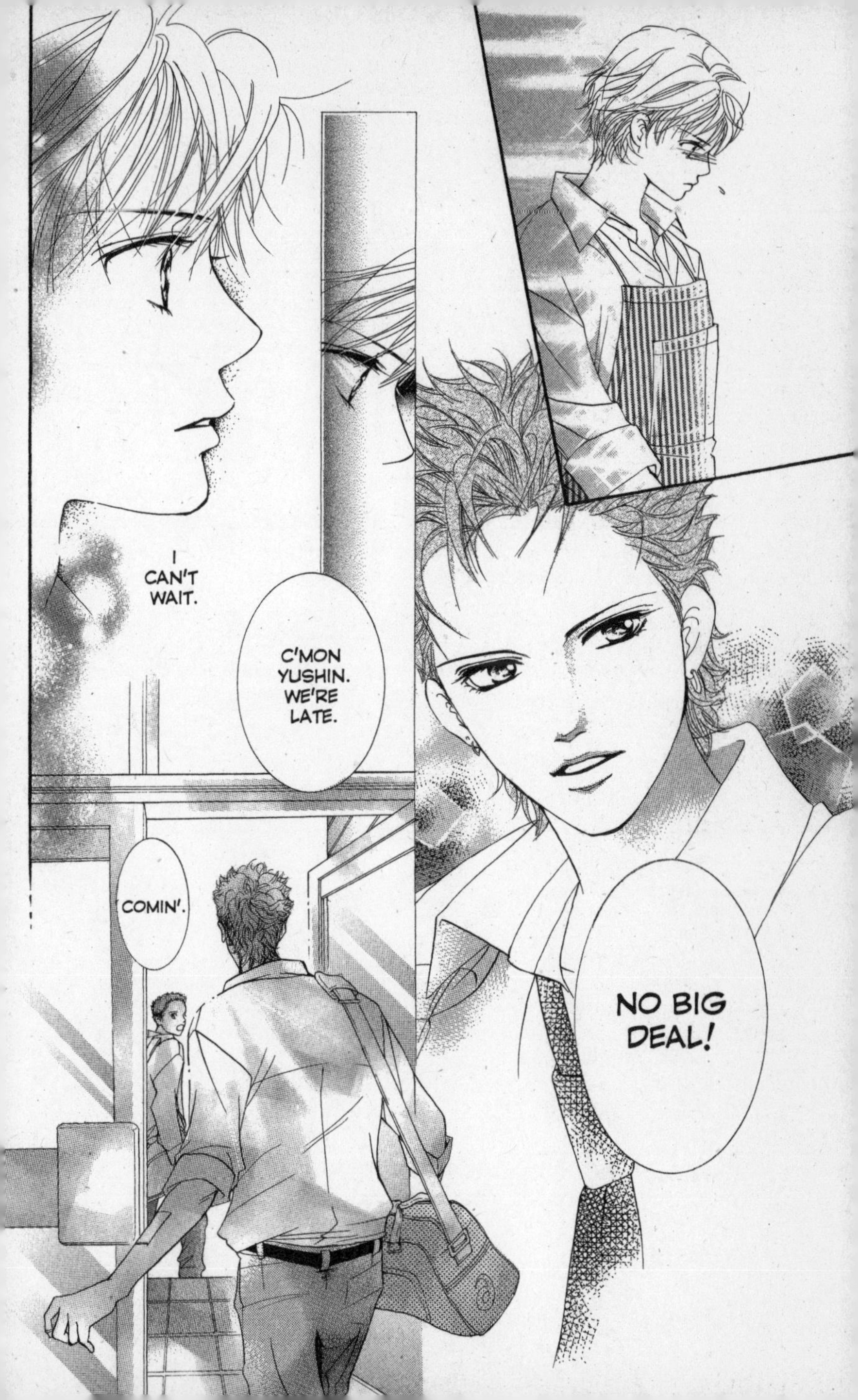
NO BIG DEAL!
I CAN'T WAIT.
C'MON YUSHIN. WE'RE LATE.
COMIN'.

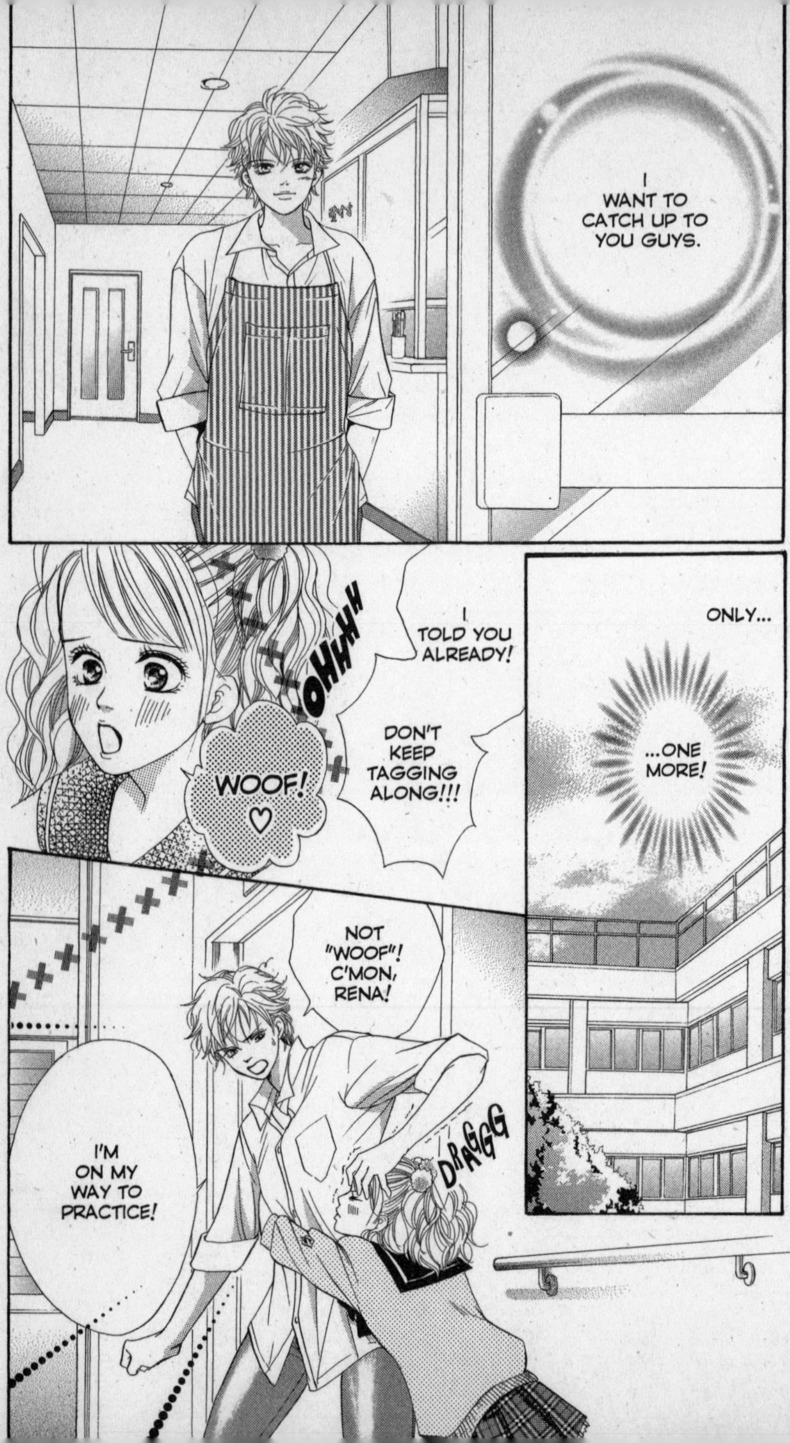
I WANT TO CATCH UP TO YOU GUYS.
ONLY...
...ONE MORE!
I TOLD YOU ALREADY!
DON'T KEEP TAGGING ALONG!!!
OHHHH
WOOF! ♡
NOT "WOOF"! C'MON, RENA!
I'M ON MY WAY TO PRACTICE!
DRAGGG

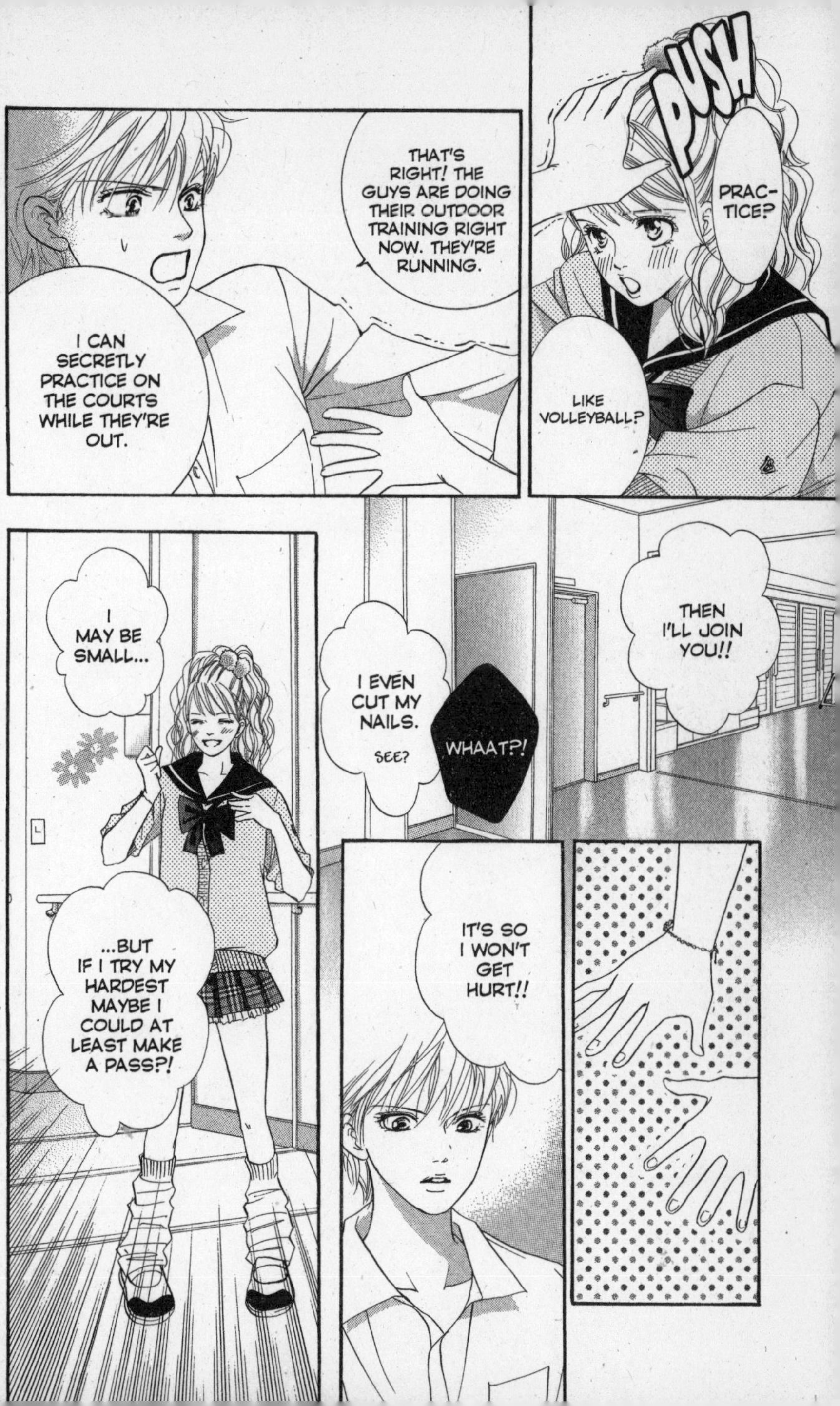
PUSH
PRAC-TICE?
LIKE VOLLEYBALL?
THAT'S RIGHT! THE GUYS ARE DOING THEIR OUTDOOR TRAINING RIGHT NOW. THEY'RE RUNNING.
I CAN SECRETLY PRACTICE ON THE COURTS WHILE THEY'RE OUT.
THEN I'LL JOIN YOU!!
WHAAT?!
I EVEN CUT MY NAILS.
SEE?
IT'S SO I WON'T GET HURT!!
I MAY BE SMALL...
...BUT IF I TRY MY HARDEST MAYBE I COULD AT LEAST MAKE A PASS?!

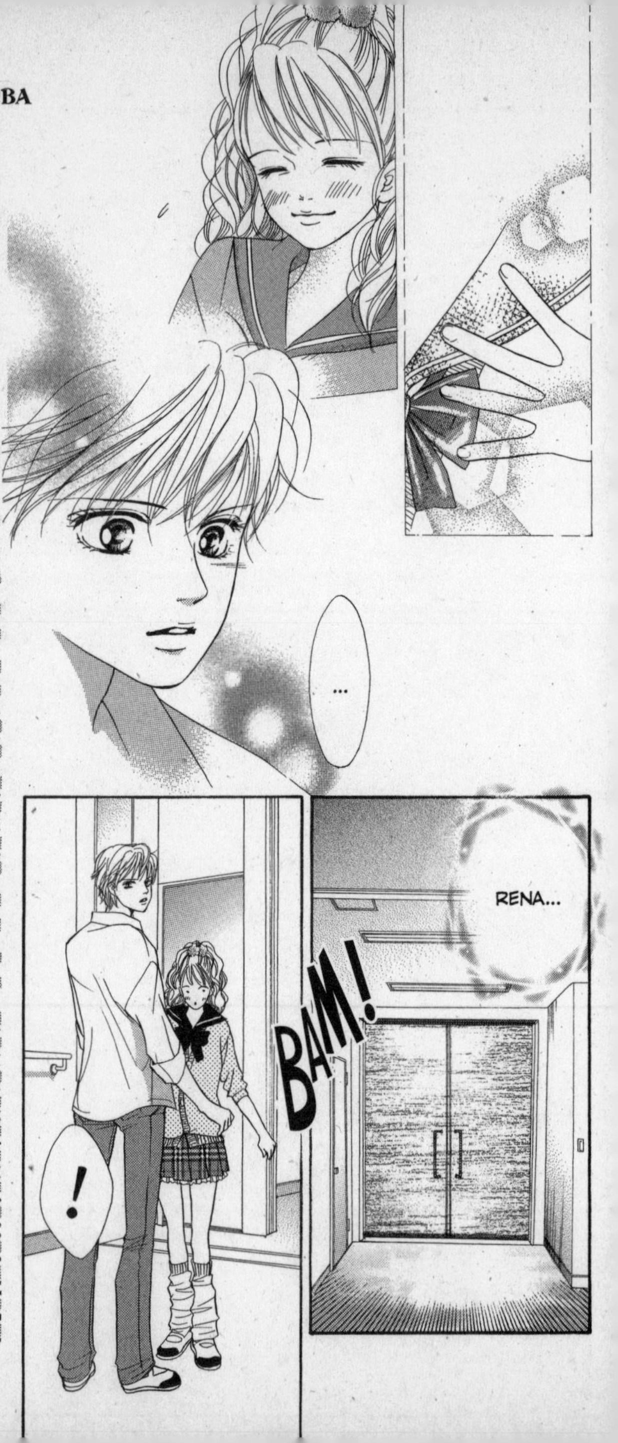
...
RENA...
BAM!
!

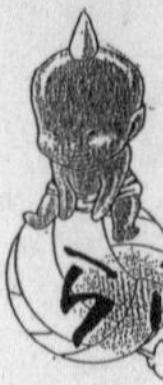

MITSUBA CLUB

Vol. 3

CRIMSON HERO, VOLUMES 1-2. ON SALE NOW...!

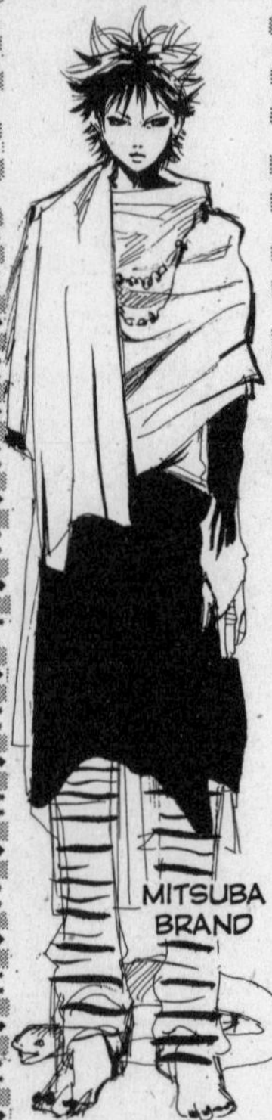
MITSUBA BRAND

ALL ELEVEN VOLUMES OF **THE DEVIL DOES EXIST** ARE ON SALE. I DON'T KNOW IF IT'S INTERESTING OR NOT. READ IT.*

*MITSUBA IS REFERRING TO THE JAPANESE RELEASE OF THE BOOK.

-SHOJO BEAT TEAM

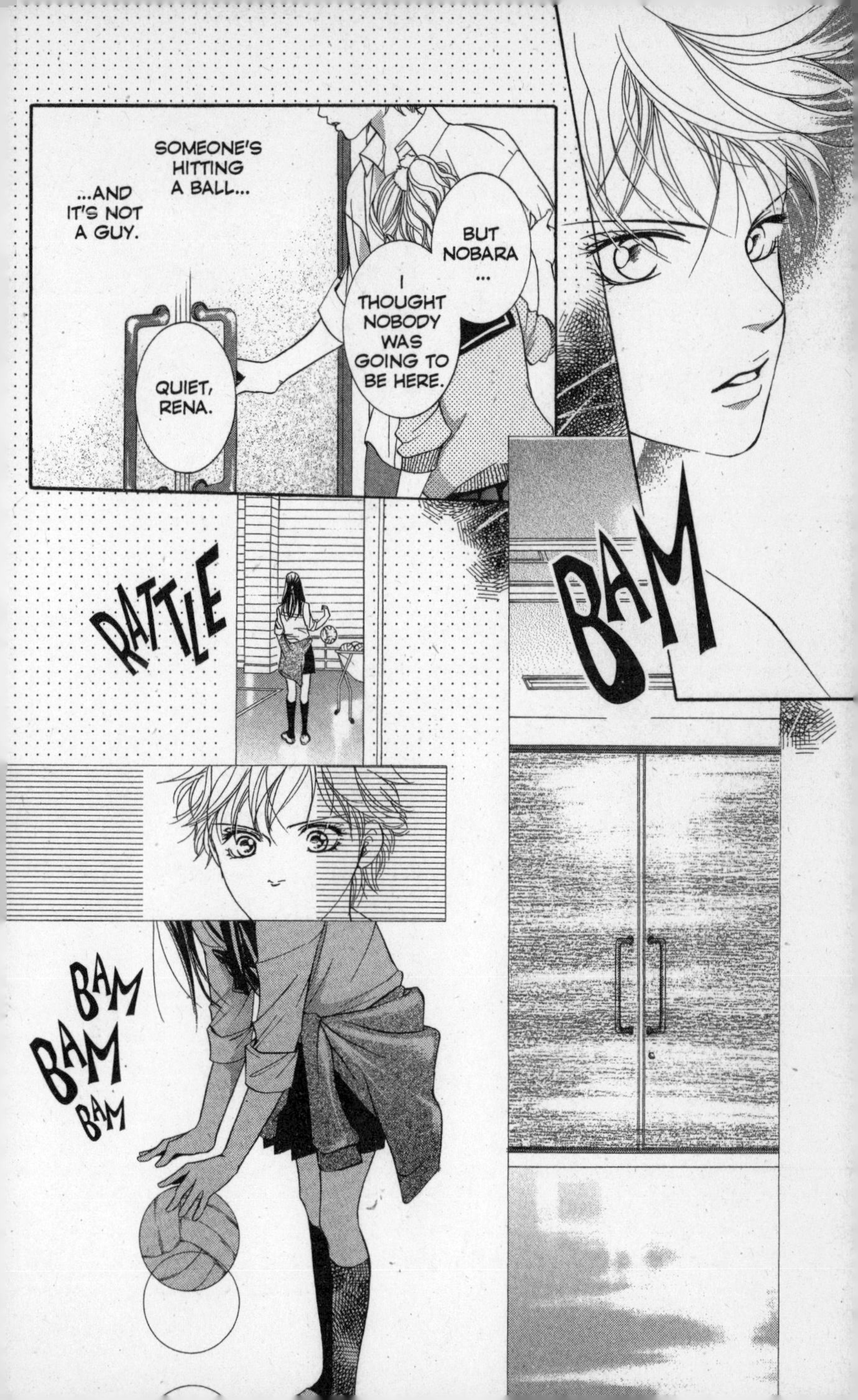
BUT NOBARA ...
I THOUGHT NOBODY WAS GOING TO BE HERE.
SOMEONE'S HITTING A BALL...
...AND IT'S NOT A GUY.
QUIET, RENA.
BAM
RATTLE
BAM BAM BAM

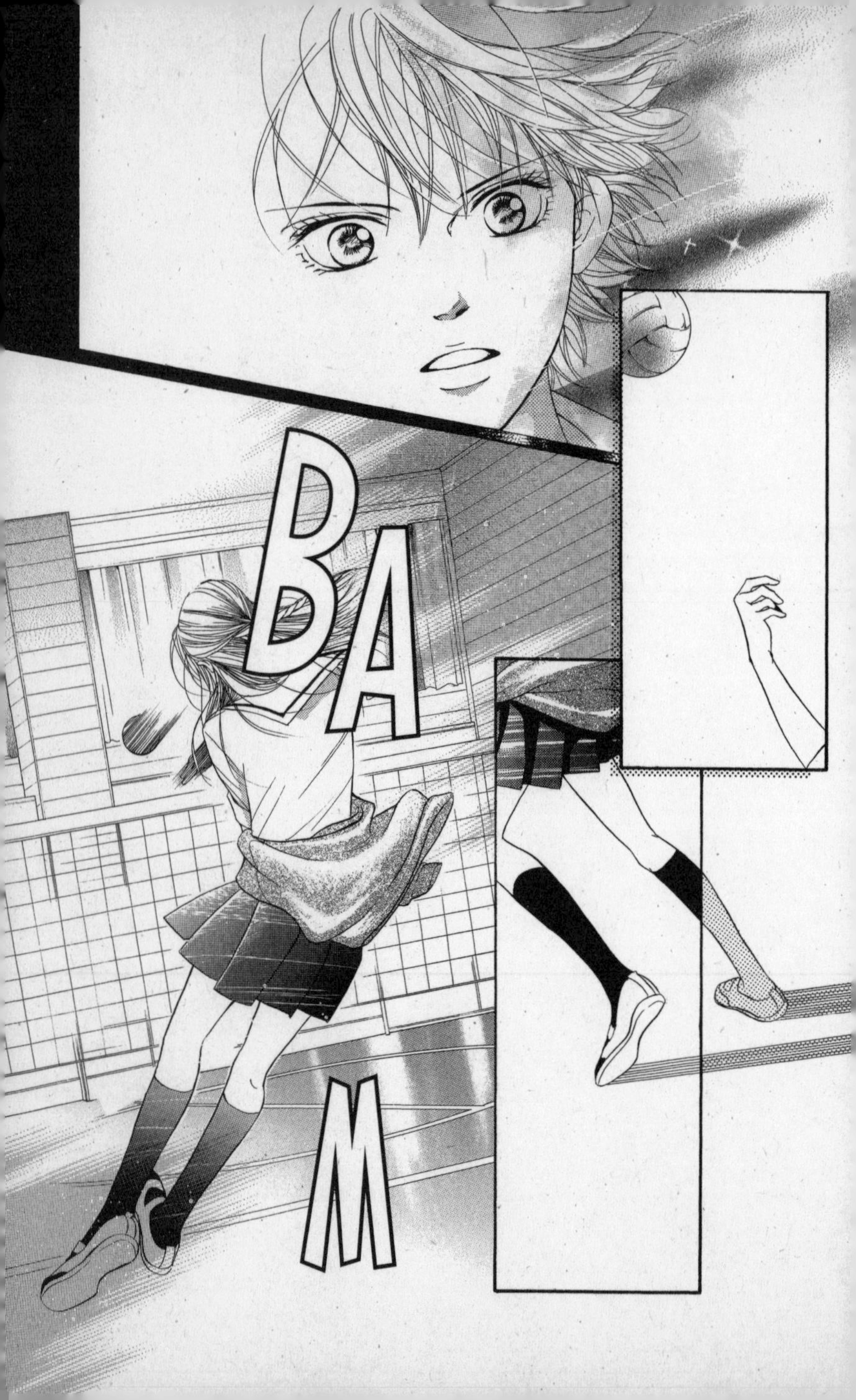
BAM

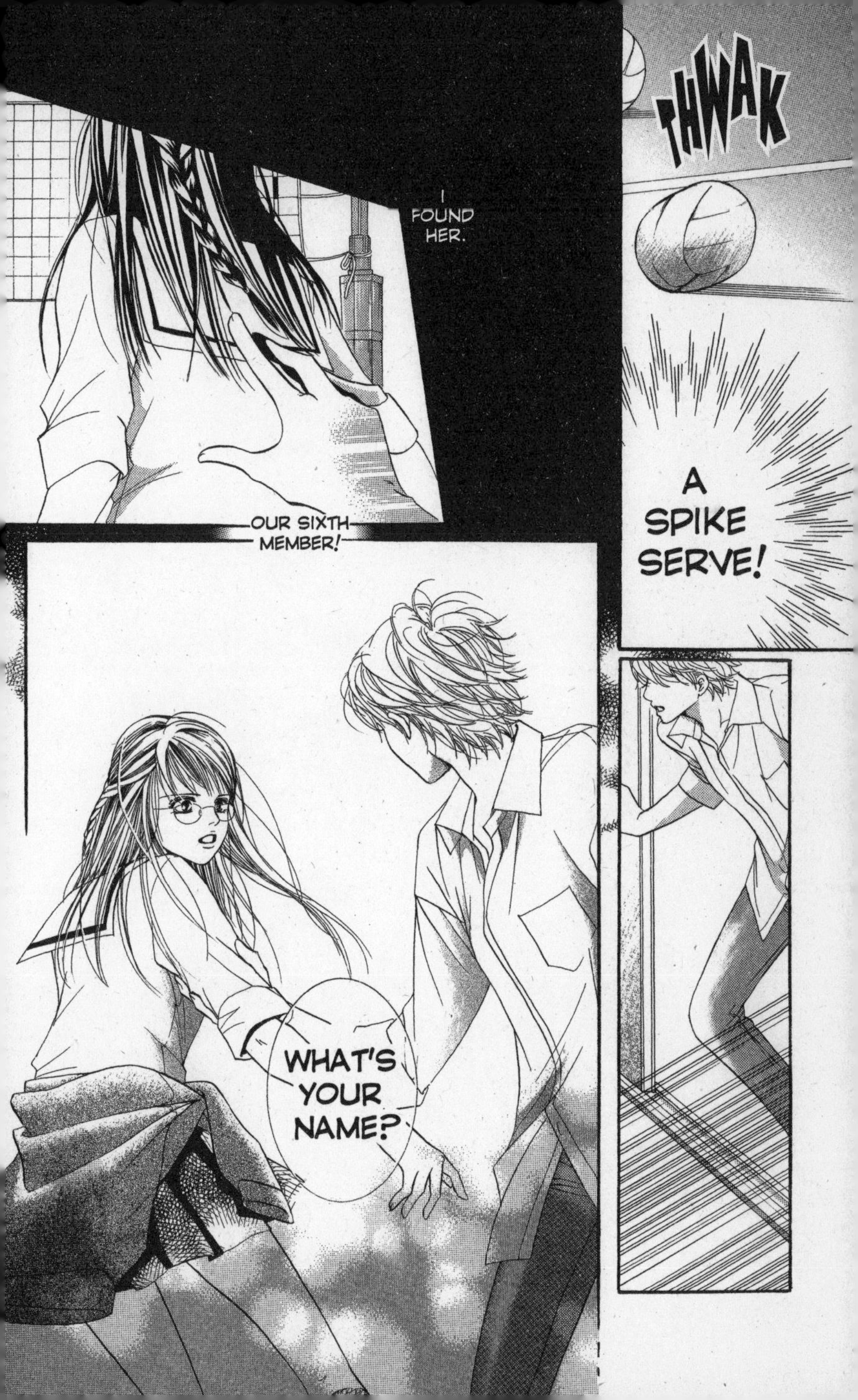
THWAK
A SPIKE SERVE!
I FOUND HER.
OUR SIXTH MEMBER!
WHAT'S YOUR NAME?

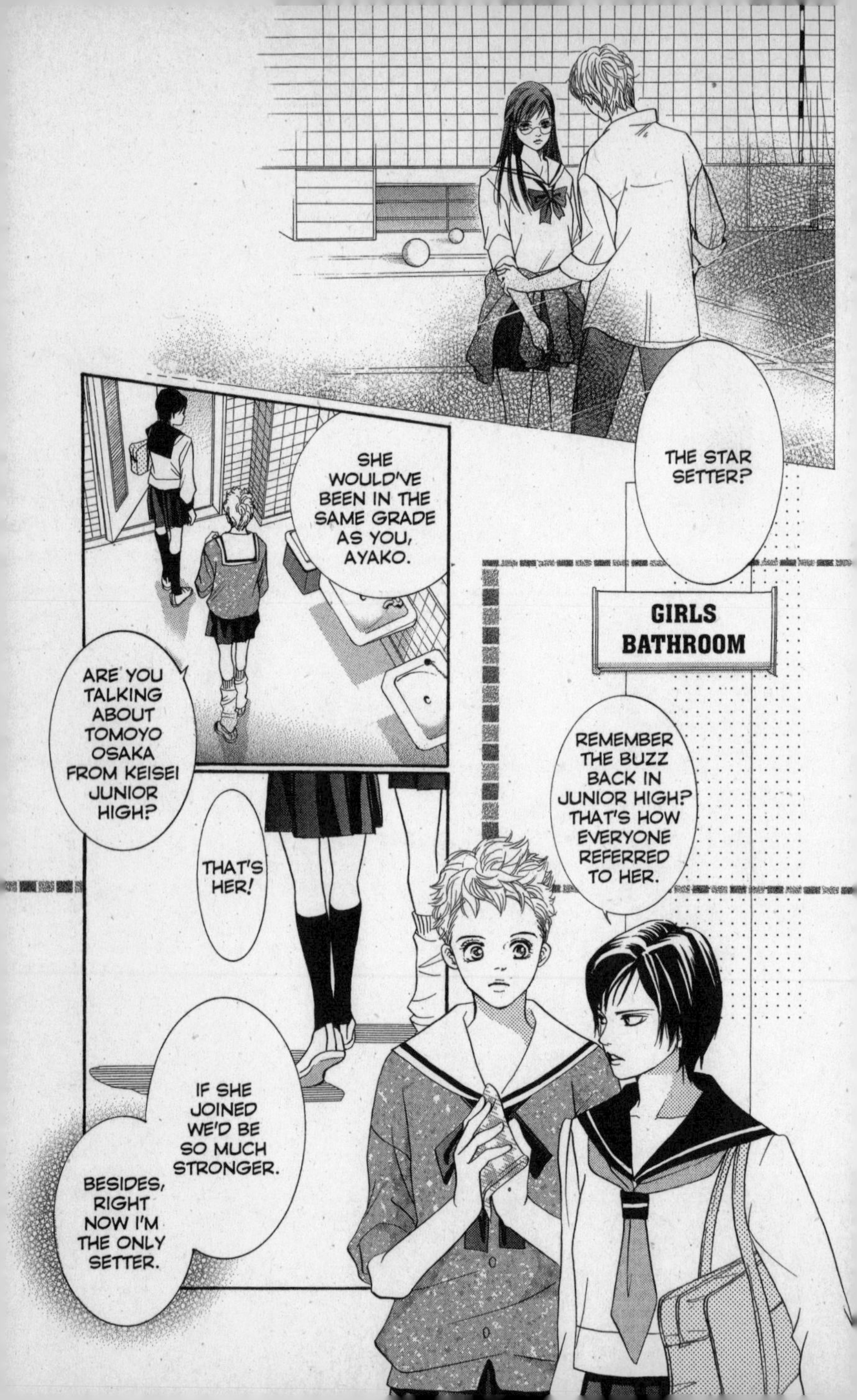
THE STAR SETTER?
GIRLS BATHROOM
REMEMBER THE BUZZ BACK IN JUNIOR HIGH? THAT'S HOW EVERYONE REFERRED TO HER.
SHE WOULD'VE BEEN IN THE SAME GRADE AS YOU, AYAKO.
ARE YOU TALKING ABOUT TOMOYO OSAKA FROM KEISEI JUNIOR HIGH?
THAT'S HER!
IF SHE JOINED WE'D BE SO MUCH STRONGER.
BESIDES, RIGHT NOW I'M THE ONLY SETTER.

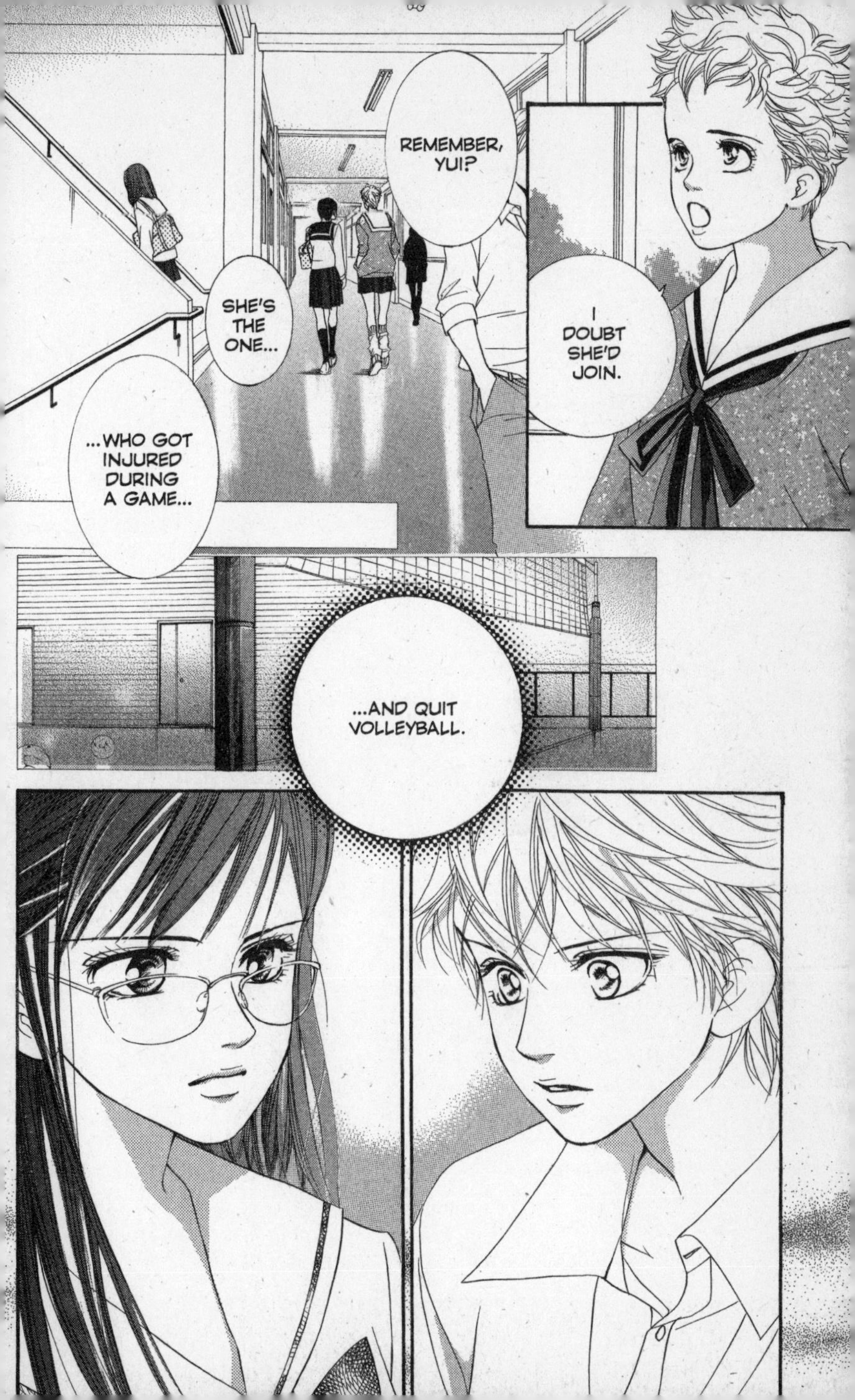
REMEMBER, YUI?
I DOUBT SHE'D JOIN.
SHE'S THE ONE...
...WHO GOT INJURED DURING A GAME...
...AND QUIT VOLLEYBALL.

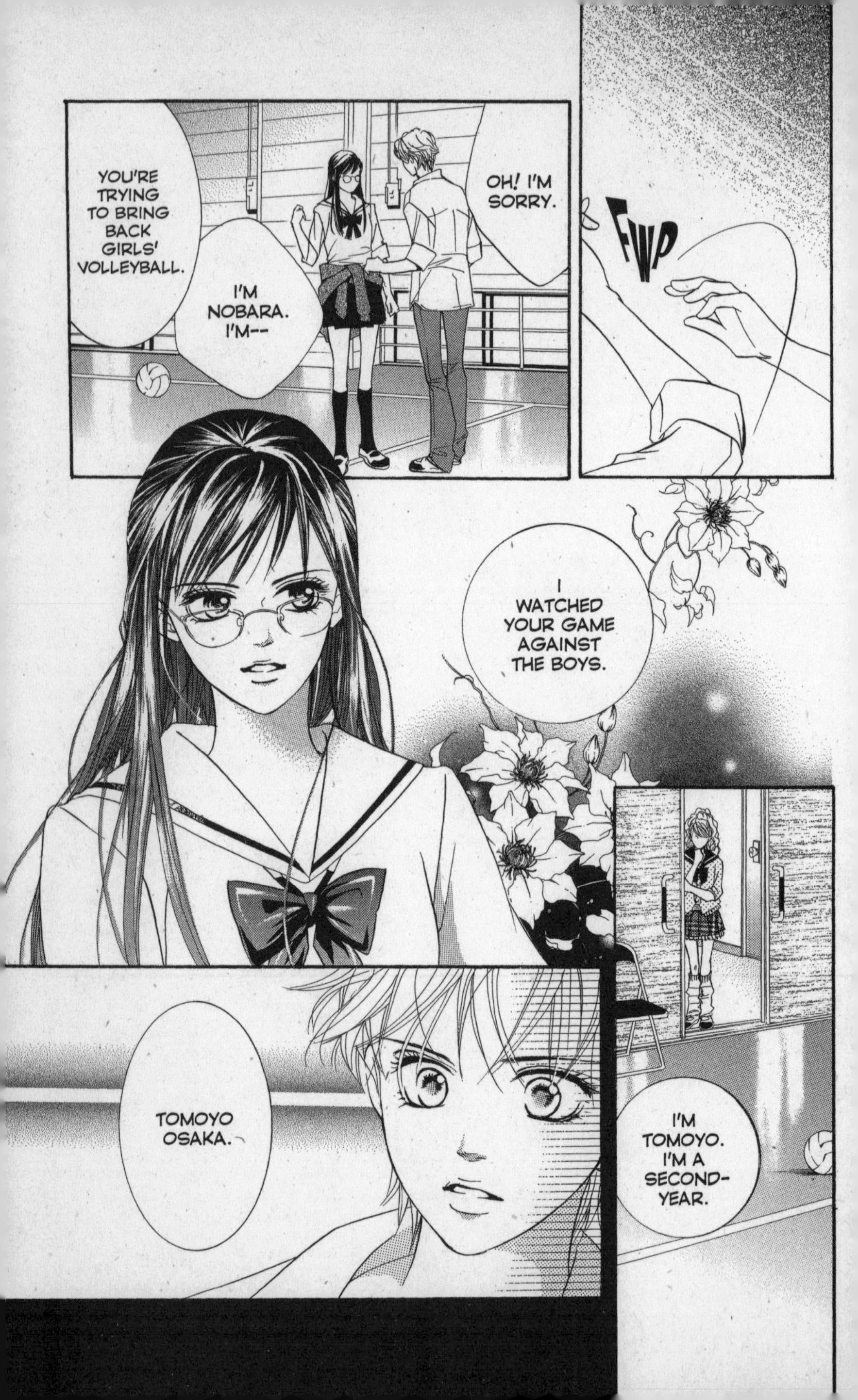
FWP
OH! I'M SORRY.
YOU'RE TRYING TO BRING BACK GIRLS' VOLLEYBALL.
I'M NOBARA. I'M--
I WATCHED YOUR GAME AGAINST THE BOYS.
I'M TOMOYO. I'M A SECOND-YEAR.
TOMOYO OSAKA.

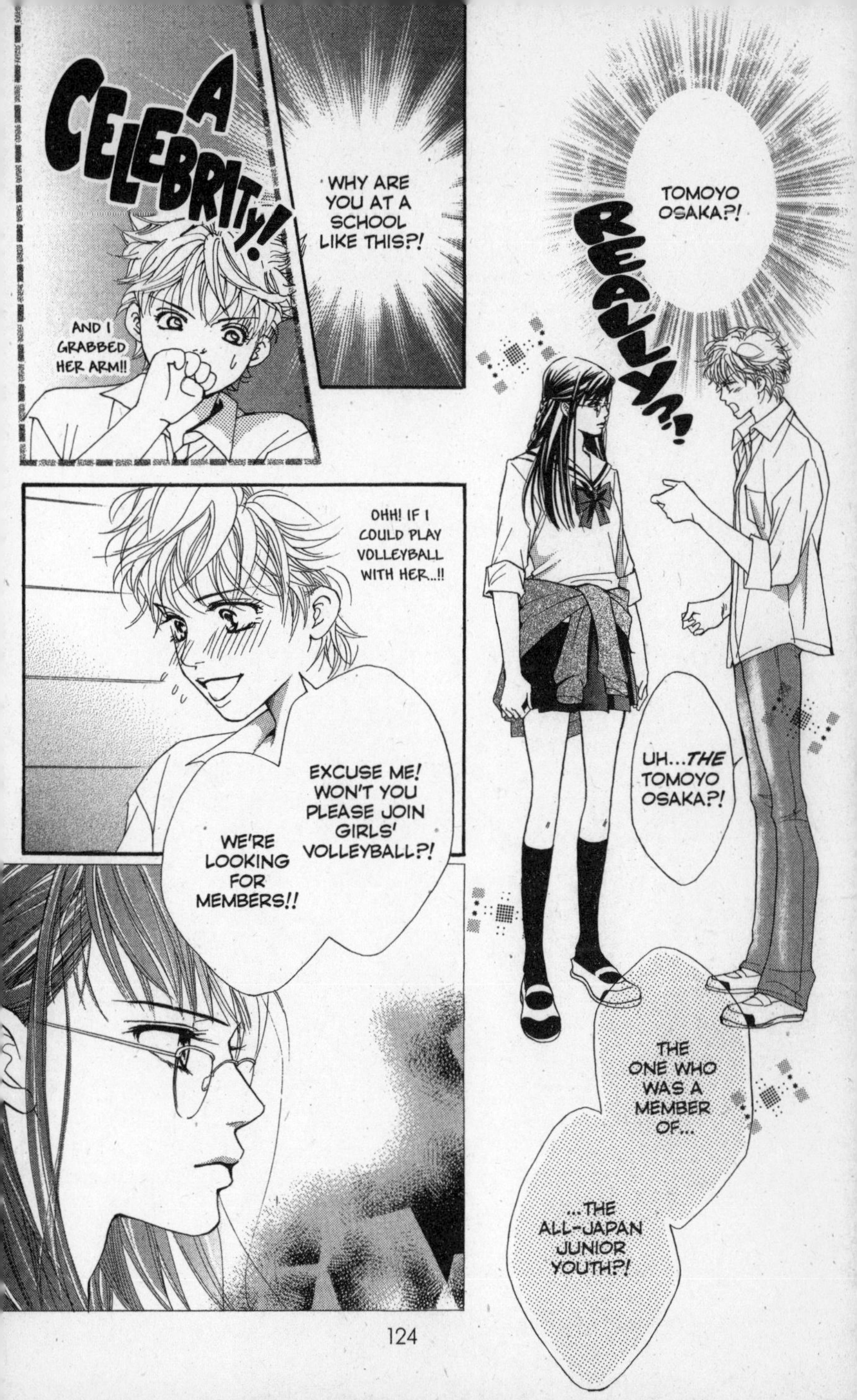
TOMOYO OSAKA?!
REALLY?!?!
UH...THE TOMOYO OSAKA?!
THE ONE WHO WAS A MEMBER OF...
...THE ALL-JAPAN JUNIOR YOUTH?!
WHY ARE YOU AT A SCHOOL LIKE THIS?!
A CELEBRITY!
AND I GRABBED HER ARM!!
OHH! IF I COULD PLAY VOLLEYBALL WITH HER...!!
EXCUSE ME! WON'T YOU PLEASE JOIN GIRLS' VOLLEYBALL?!
WE'RE LOOKING FOR MEMBERS!!

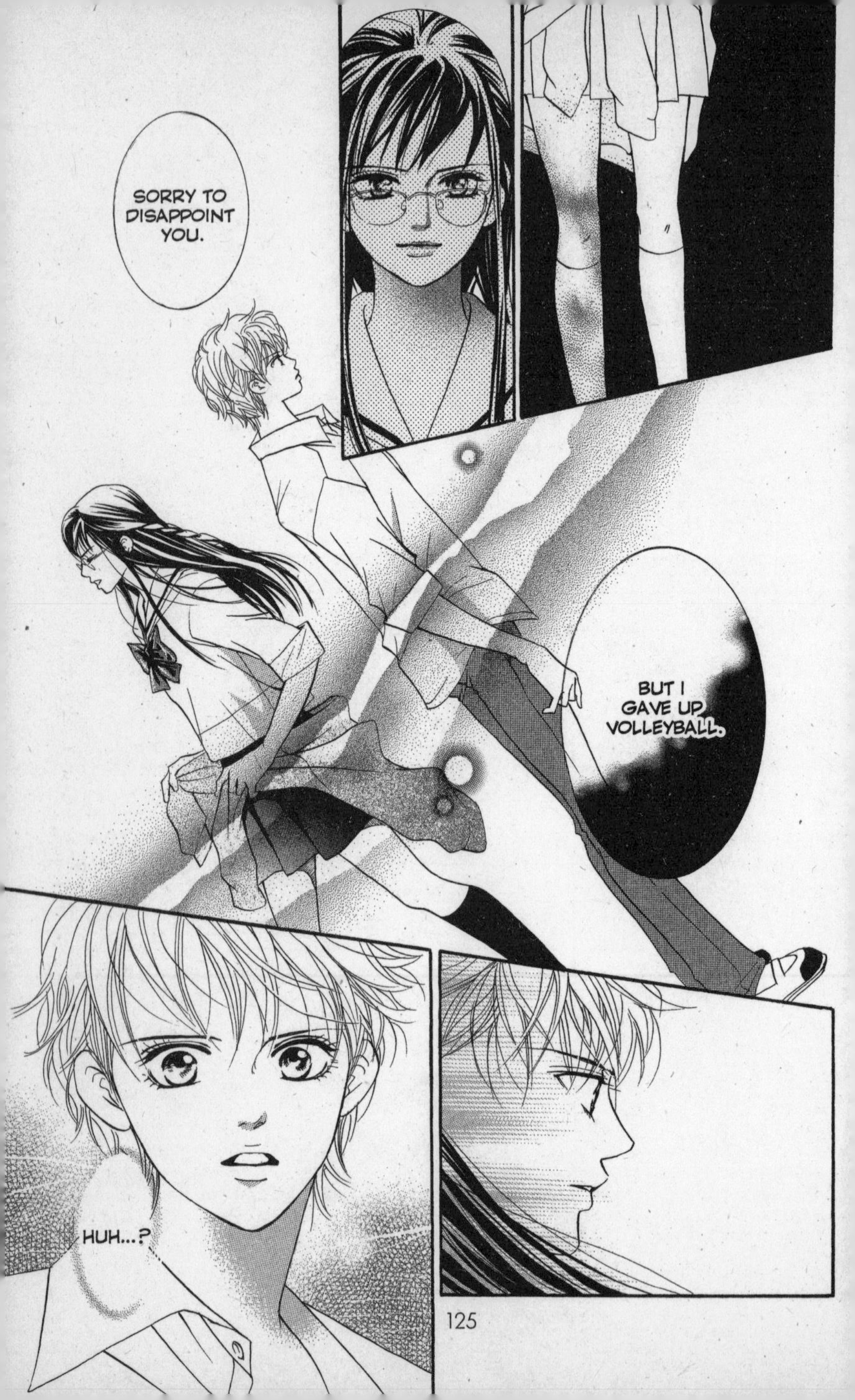
SORRY TO DISAPPOINT YOU.
BUT I GAVE UP VOLLEYBALL.
HUH...?

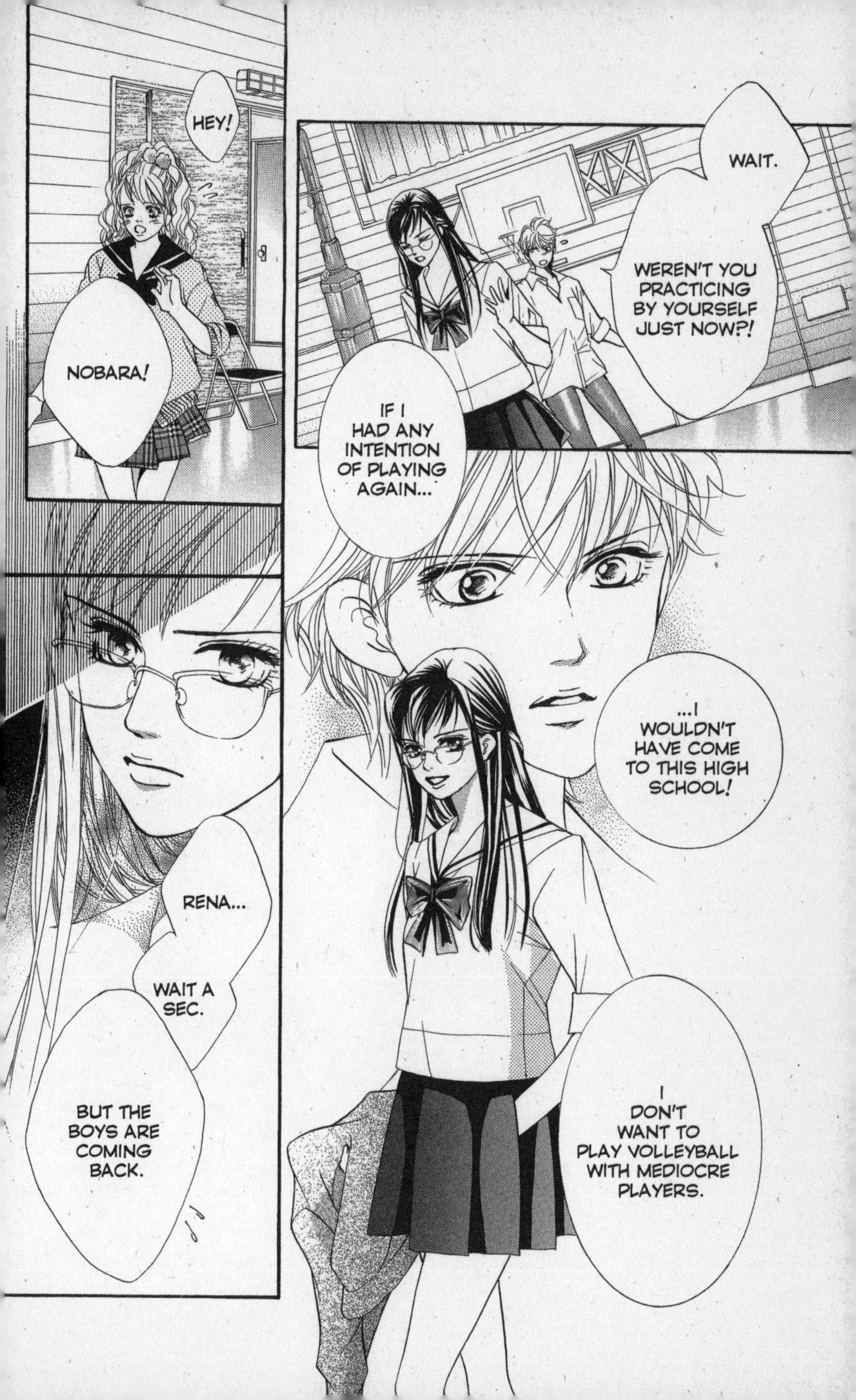
WAIT.
WEREN'T YOU PRACTICING BY YOURSELF JUST NOW?!
HEY!
NOBARA!
IF I HAD ANY INTENTION OF PLAYING AGAIN...
...I WOULDN'T HAVE COME TO THIS HIGH SCHOOL!
I DON'T WANT TO PLAY VOLLEYBALL WITH MEDIOCRE PLAYERS.
RENA...
WAIT A SEC.
BUT THE BOYS ARE COMING BACK.

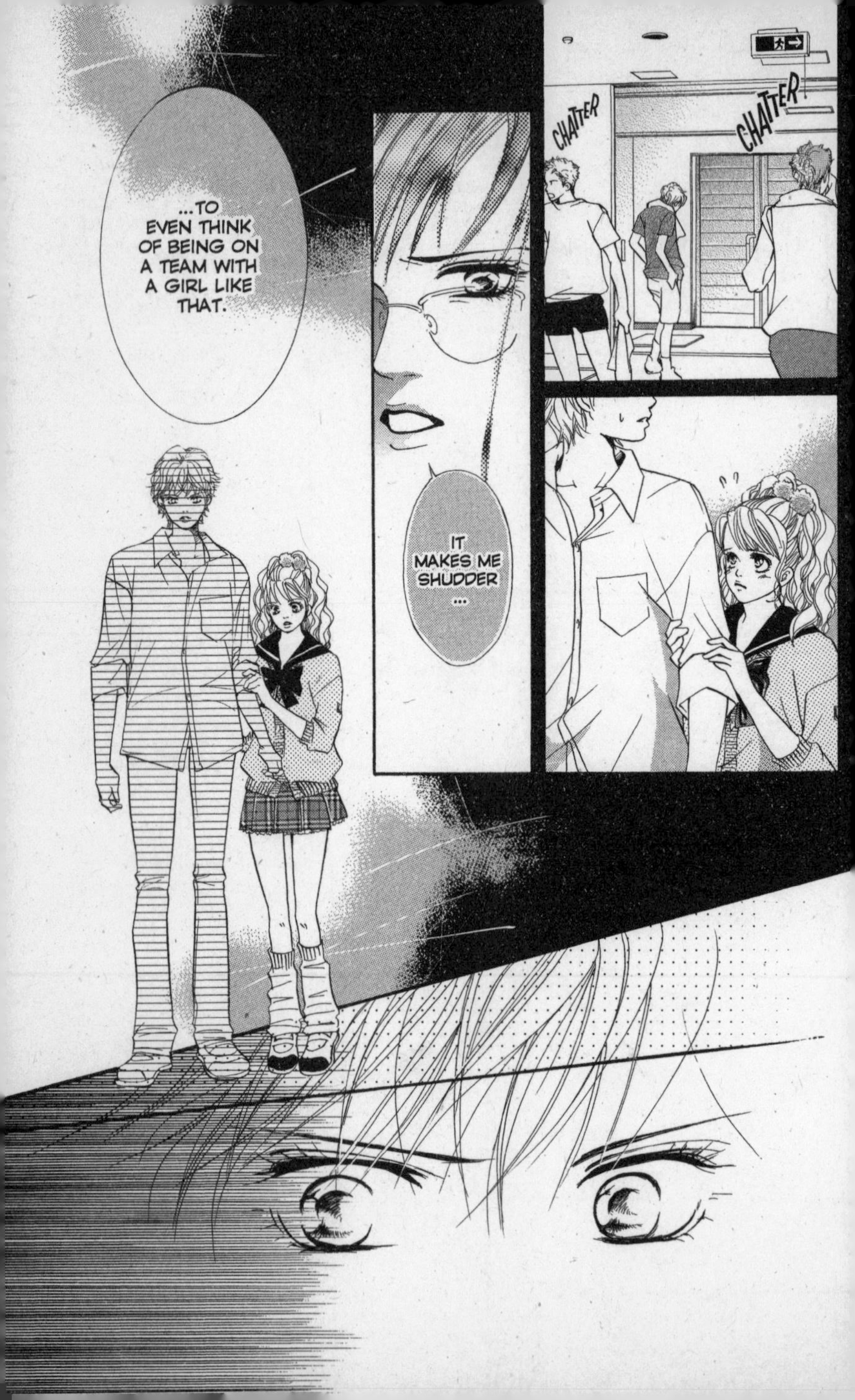
CHATTER
CHATTER
IT MAKES ME SHUDDER ...
...TO EVEN THINK OF BEING ON A TEAM WITH A GIRL LIKE THAT.

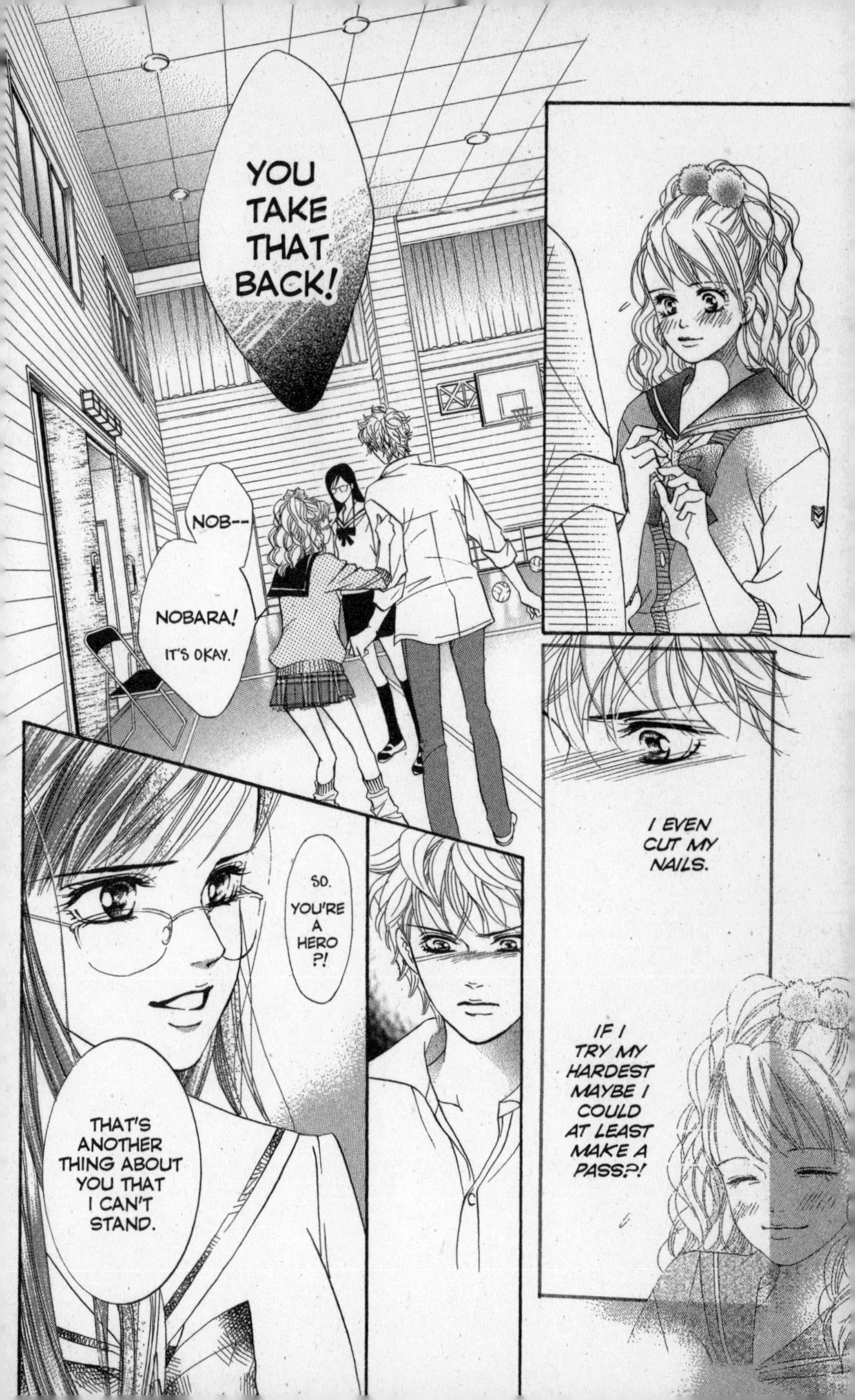
YOU TAKE THAT BACK!
NOB--
NOBARA!
IT'S OKAY.
I EVEN CUT MY NAILS.
SO. YOU'RE A HERO?!
THAT'S ANOTHER THING ABOUT YOU THAT I CAN'T STAND.
IF I TRY MY HARDEST MAYBE I COULD AT LEAST MAKE A PASS?!

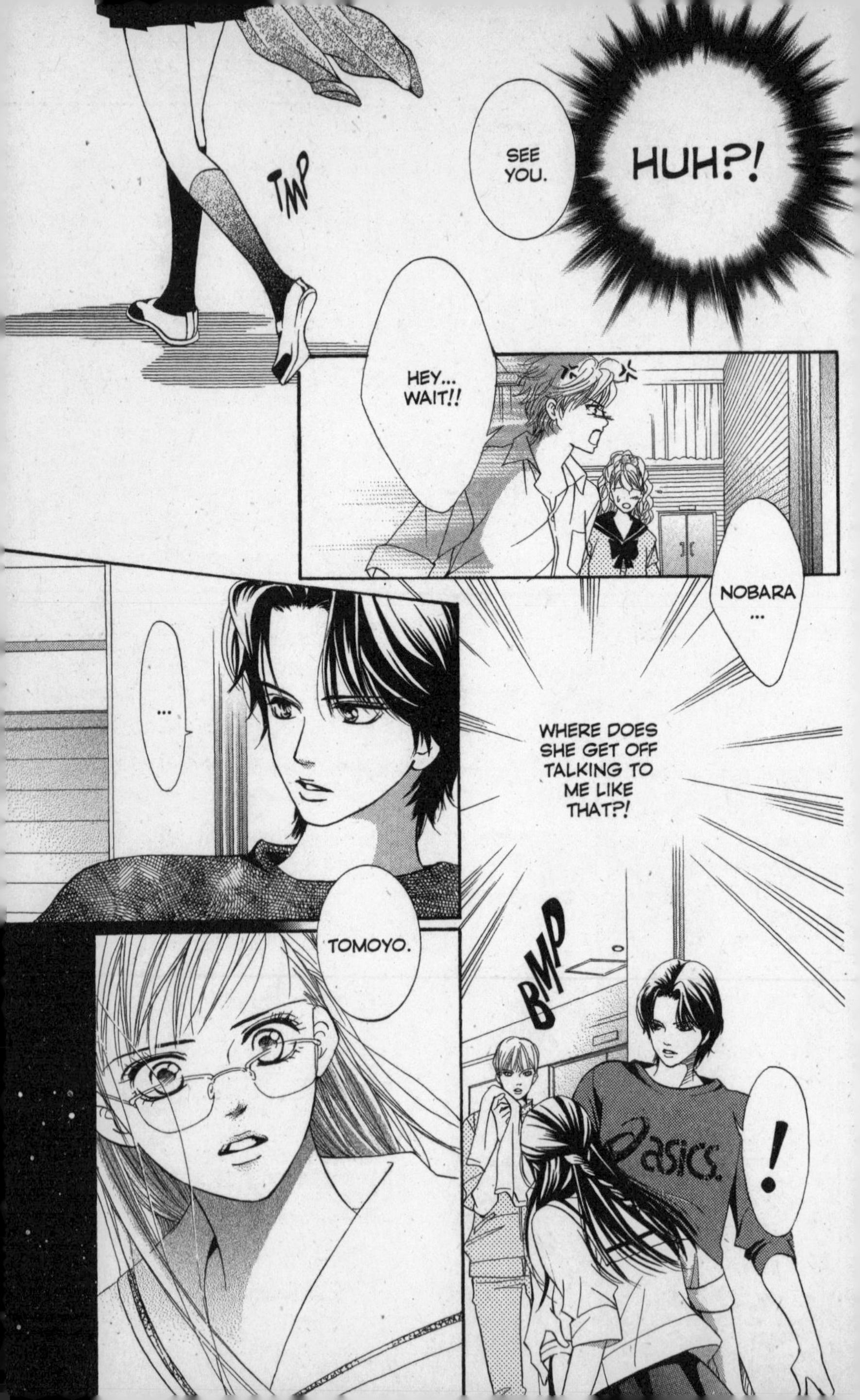
SEE YOU.
TMP
HUH?!
HEY... WAIT!!
NOBARA ...
WHERE DOES SHE GET OFF TALKING TO ME LIKE THAT?!
...
BMP
!
TOMOYO.

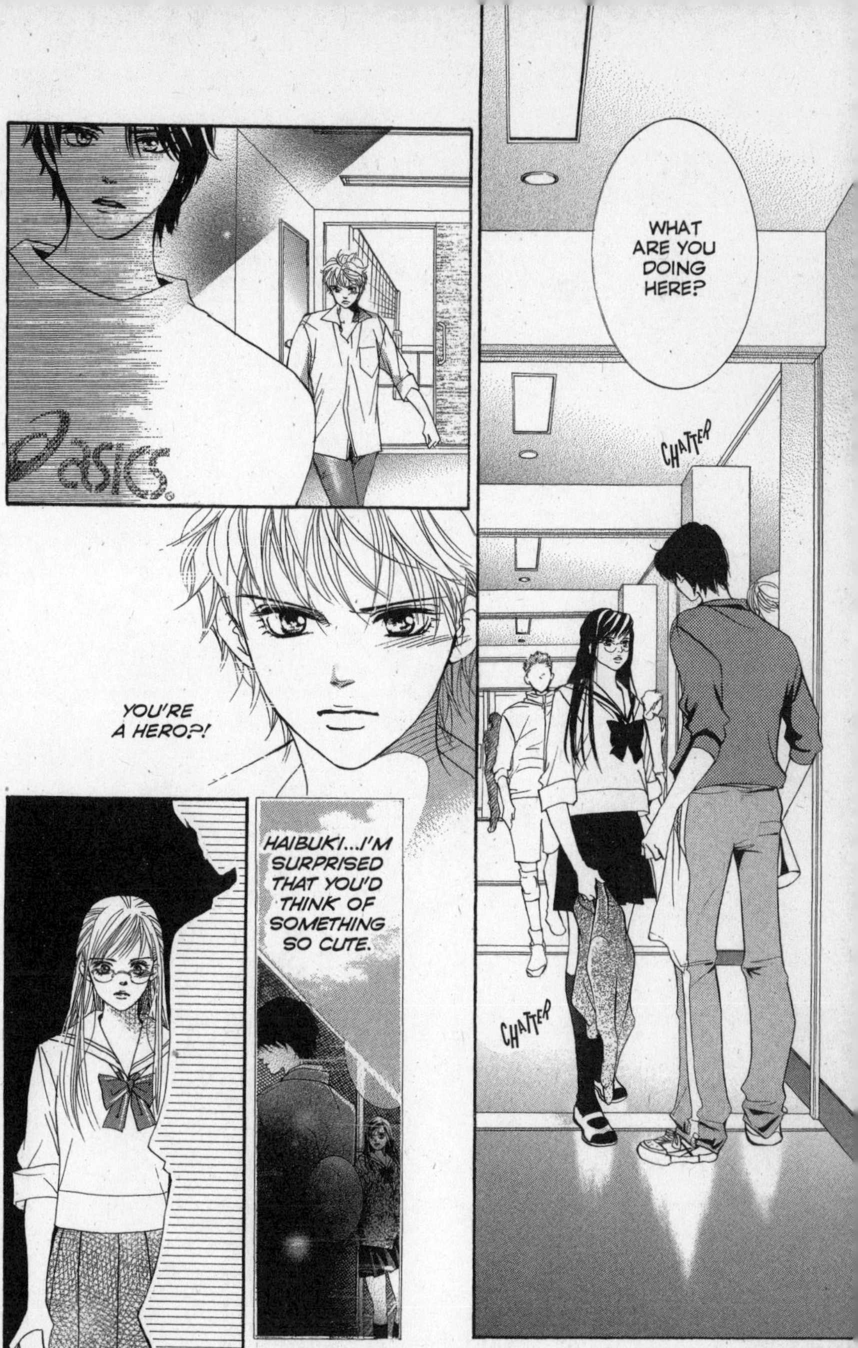
WHAT ARE YOU DOING HERE?
CHATTER
CHATTER
YOU'RE A HERO?!
HAIBUKI...I'M SURPRISED THAT YOU'D THINK OF SOMETHING SO CUTE.

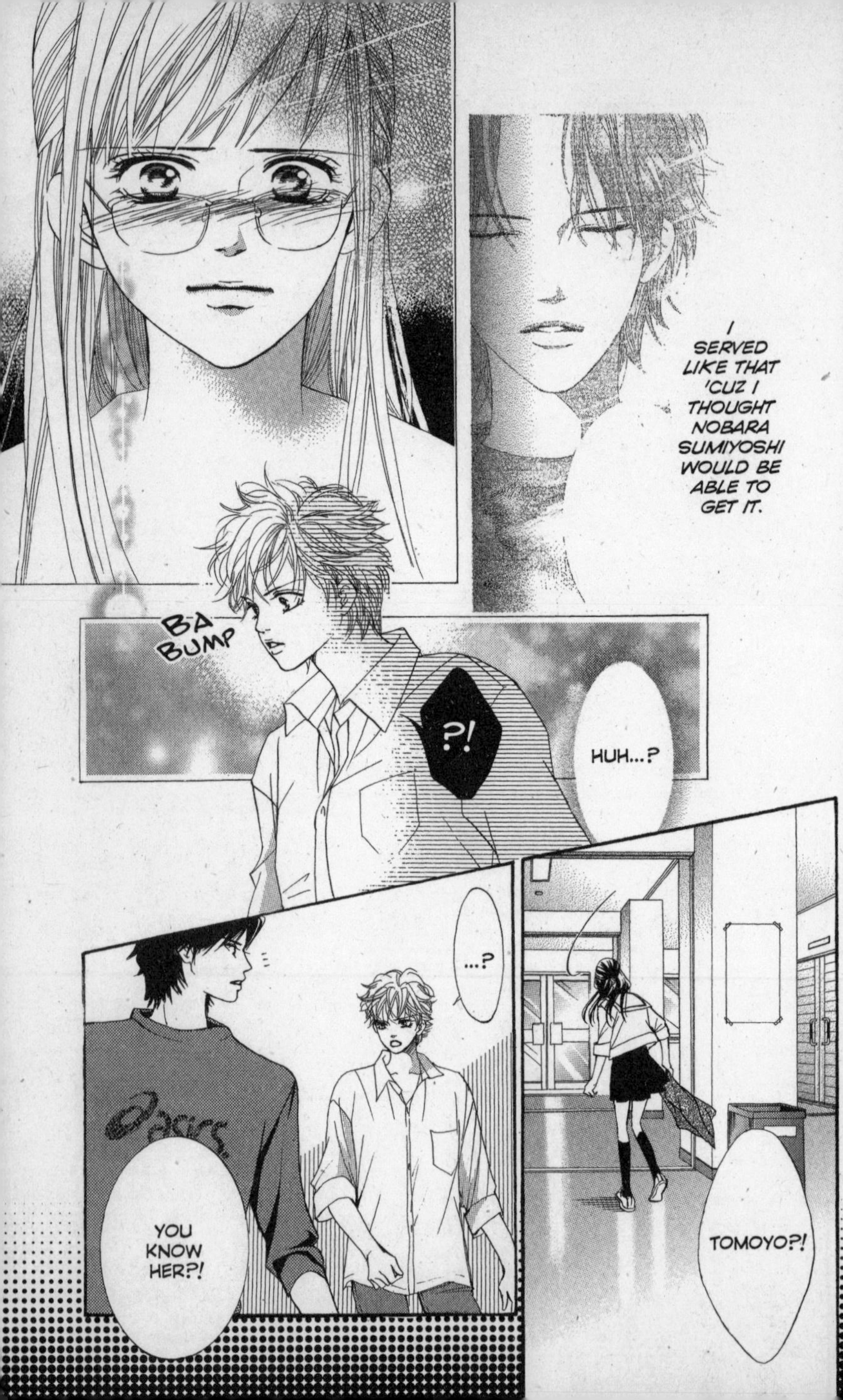
I SERVED LIKE THAT 'CUZ I THOUGHT NOBARA SUMIYOSHI WOULD BE ABLE TO GET IT.
HUH...?
?!
BA BUMP
TOMOYO?!
...?
YOU KNOW HER?!

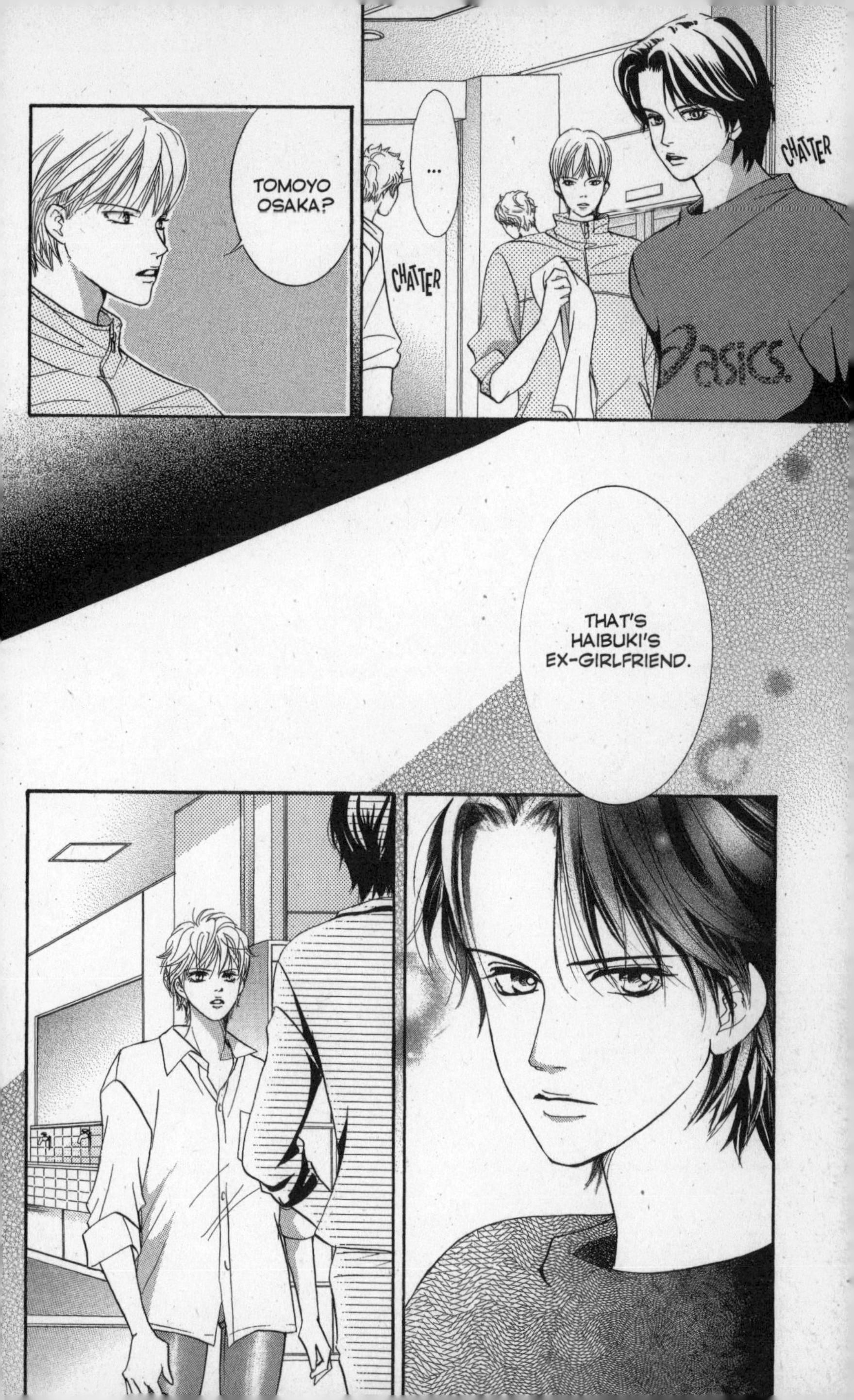
CHATTER
...
CHATTER
TOMOYO OSAKA?
THAT'S HAIBUKI'S EX-GIRLFRIEND.

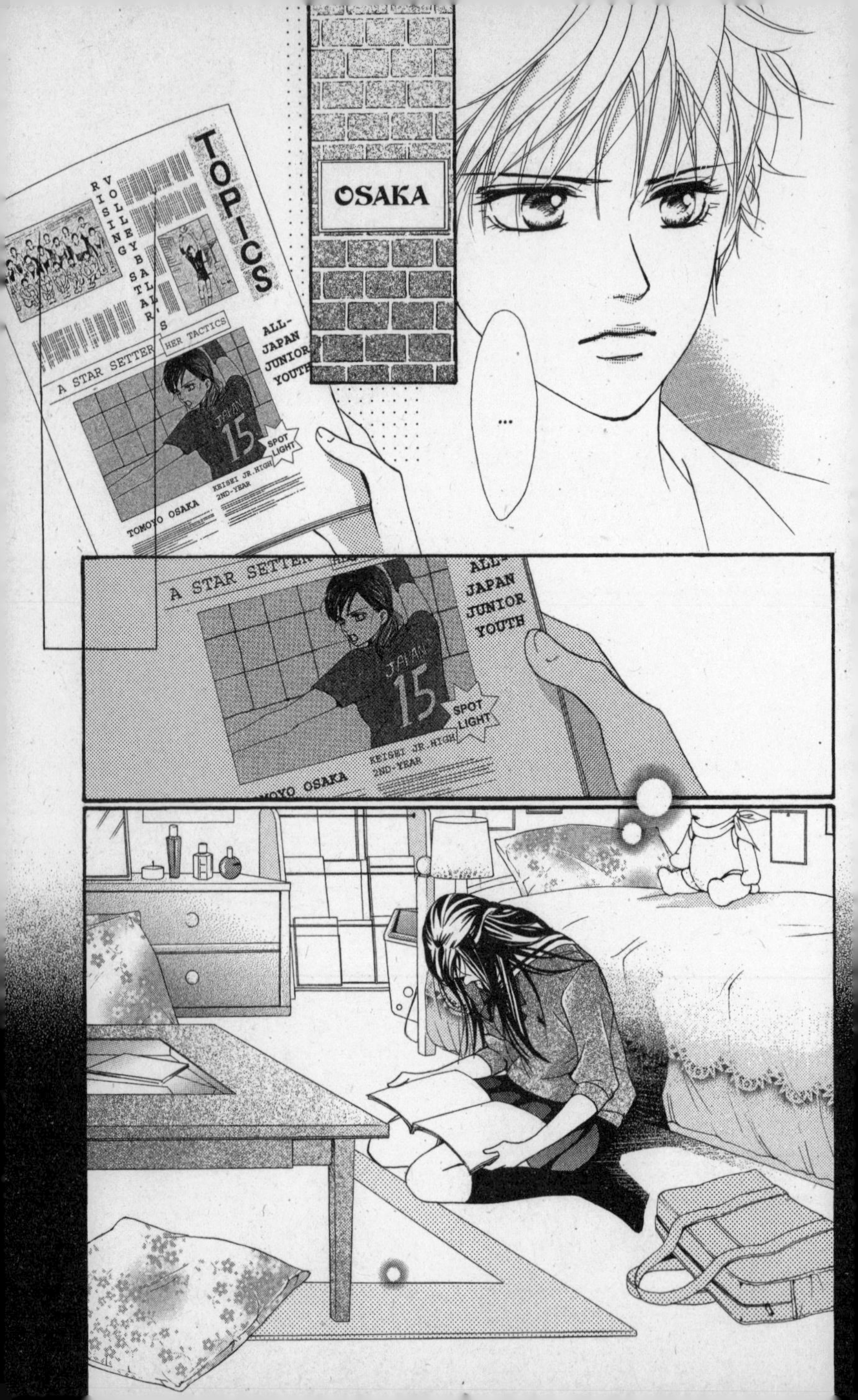
...
OSAKA
TOPICS
RISING VOLLEYBALL STARS
HER TACTICS
A STAR SETTER
ALL-JAPAN JUNIOR YOUTH
JAPAN 15
SPOT LIGHT
KEISEI JR. HIGH 2ND-YEAR
TOMOYO OSAKA
A STAR SETTER
ALL-JAPAN JUNIOR YOUTH
JAPAN 15
SPOT LIGHT
KEISEI JR. HIGH 2ND-YEAR
TOMOYO OSAKA

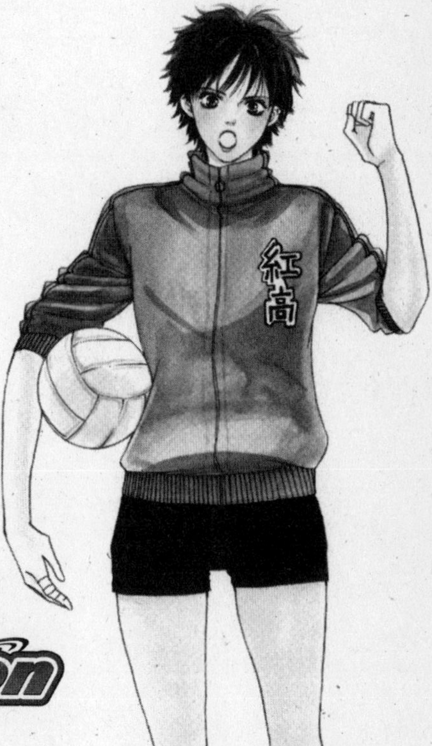
紅高

Crimson Hero

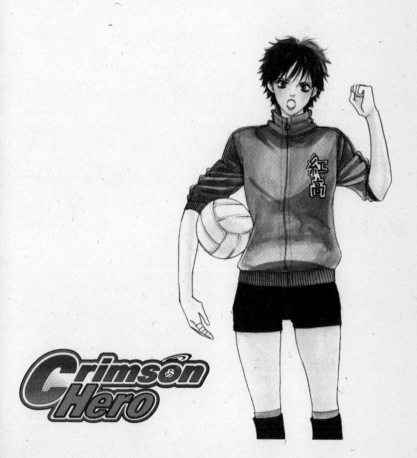

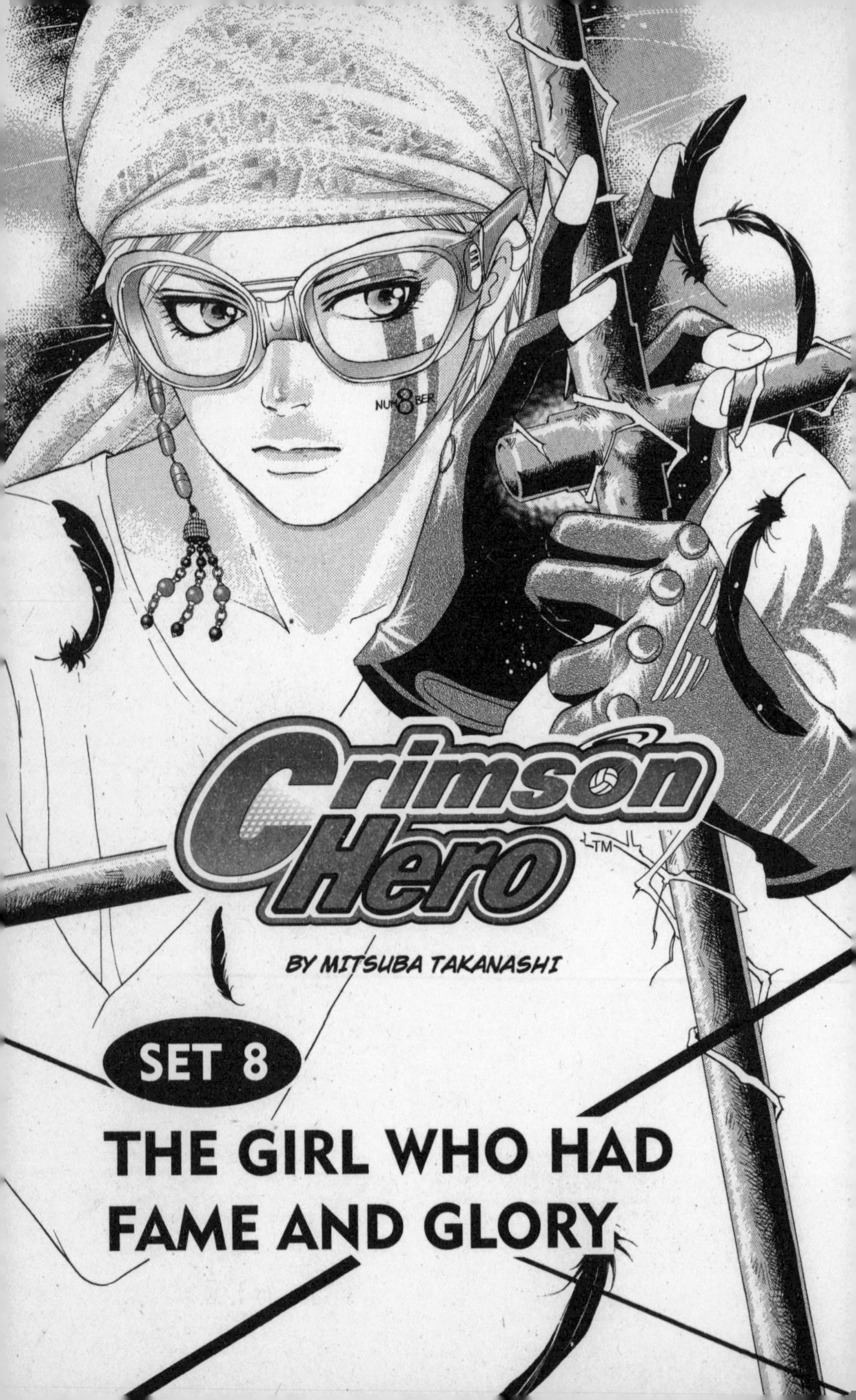
NUMBER
Crimson Hero
TM
BY MITSUBA TAKANASHI
SET 8
THE GIRL WHO HAD FAME AND GLORY

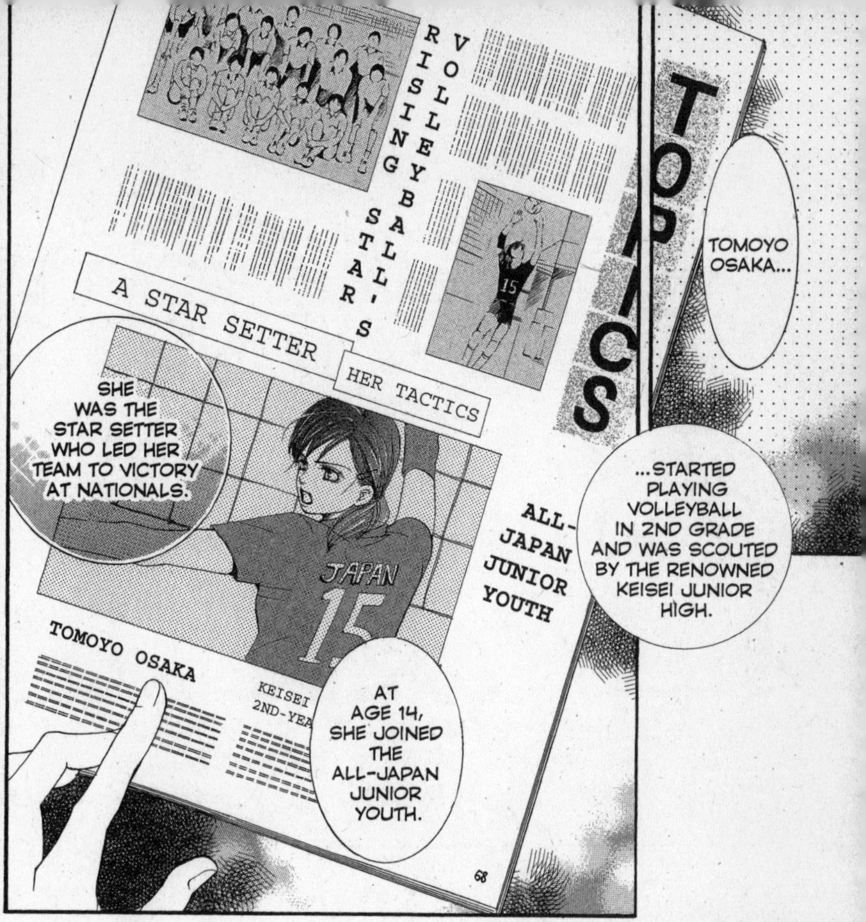
TOPICS
TOMOYO OSAKA...
...STARTED PLAYING VOLLEYBALL IN 2ND GRADE AND WAS SCOUTED BY THE RENOWNED KEISEI JUNIOR HIGH.
VOLLEYBALL'S RISING STARS
A STAR SETTER
HER TACTICS
ALL-JAPAN JUNIOR YOUTH
SHE WAS THE STAR SETTER WHO LED HER TEAM TO VICTORY AT NATIONALS.
JAPAN 15
TOMOYO OSAKA
KEISEI 2ND-YEA
AT AGE 14, SHE JOINED THE ALL-JAPAN JUNIOR YOUTH.
68

THE MAKING OF CRIMSON HERO

Vo4.

—AFTER THE SPRING VOLLEYBALL TOURNAMENT—

I GOT CARRIED AWAY ABOUT MY HERO FROM THE SPRING TOURNAMENT. I TOLD EVERYONE ON STAFF ABOUT HIM AND DELIVERED FERVENT TESTIMONIALS AS I WATCHED HIM ON TV AND VIDEO. (A NUISANCE, I'M SURE.)

IT'S HIM!! HE'S THE ONE!!

YEAH...I CAN SORTA SEE WHY YOU'D LIKE HIM.

I HEARD WHILE WORKING ON MY DRAFT THAT HIS TEAM LOST IN THE THIRD ROUND. I THOUGHT THEN THAT IF IT WAS GOING TO COME TO THAT, I SHOULD'VE ABANDONED MY WORK AND GONE TO CHEER HIM ON INSTEAD. BUT OH WELL. I DECIDED TO BE CONTENT WITH THE FACT THAT I'D MANAGED TO TAKE SOME PHOTOS OF HIM UP CLOSE. BUT ALAS!!!

IT SEEMS MY CAMERA WAS BROKEN. NOT ONE PICTURE IN THREE ROLLS OF FILM. OH NO!

CHILL

PHOTOS. ALL BLACK.

MEANIE!

WAAA WAAA WAAAA...

SHE'S STILL MOANING AWAY?!

WORKING WHILE WEEPING.

SEE HOW HOPELESS I AM? NONETHELESS I'M HEADED FOR MIYASAKI TOMORROW TO RESEARCH THE ALL-JAPAN GIRLS' TRAINING CAMP. I CAN'T WAIT!

I'VE GOT TO BE CAREFUL NOT TO ASK ABSURD QUESTIONS!! BUT FIRST I'VE GOT TO BUY A NEW CAMERA! MY CAMERA'S HEAVY FROM ALL THE REPAIRS, BUT I STILL USE IT.

SO THIS HERE TURNS THE POWER OFF?

HOW MANY TIMES DO I HAVE TO TELL YOU FOR YOU TO REMEMBER?!

ADVERTISEMENT
CELEBRATE VOLLEYBALL ON NOVEMBER 11TH! IT'S THE OPENING OF THE 2003 WORLD CUP!

BABO BABO

THIS IS TOTALLY IRRELEVANT, BUT I'M SCARED OF GACHAPIN.

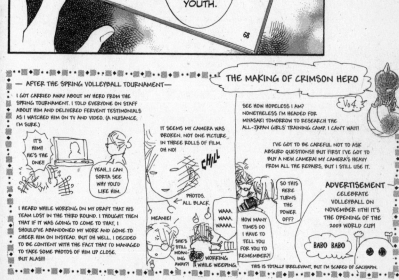

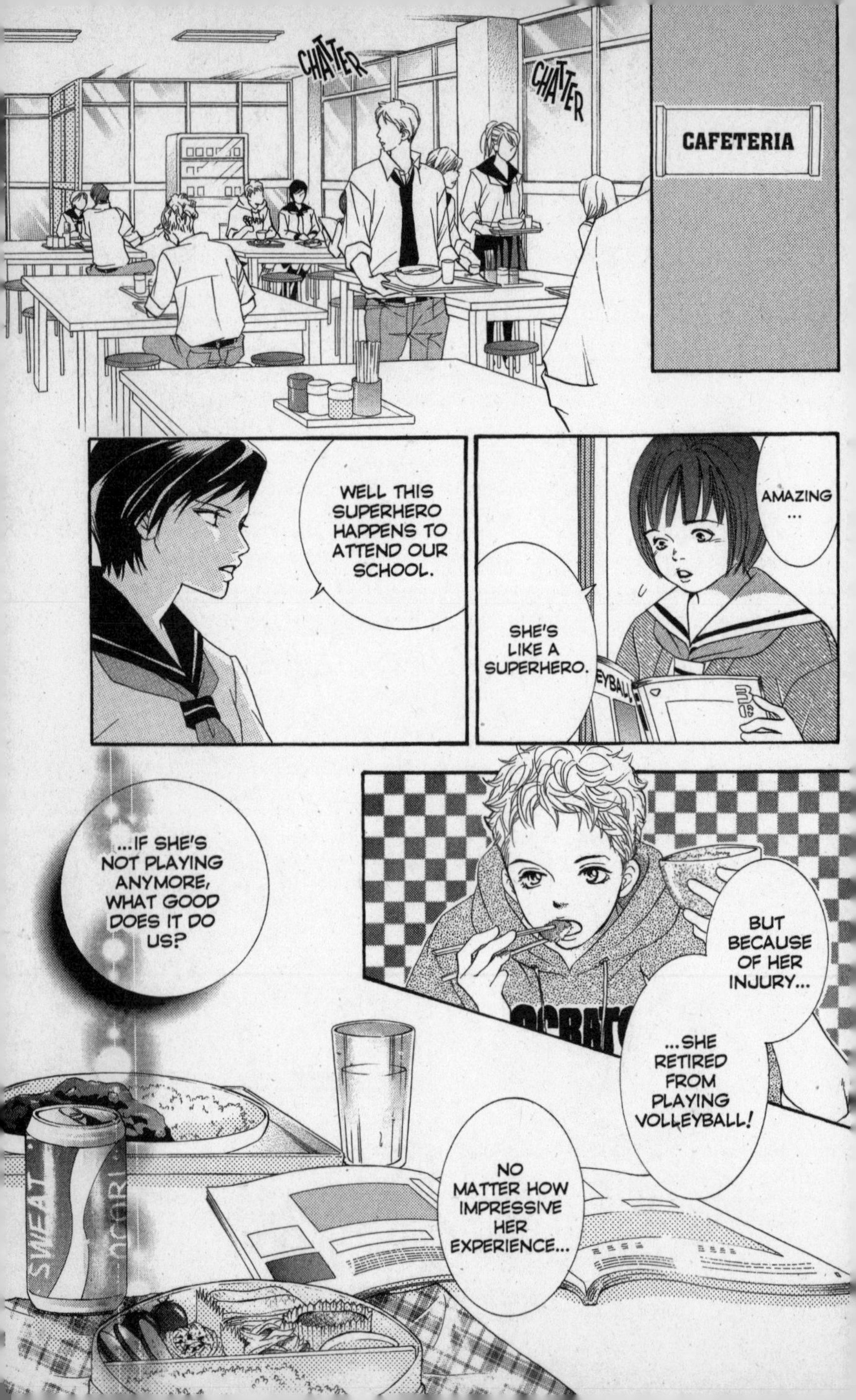
CAFETERIA
CHATTER
CHATTER
AMAZING ...
SHE'S LIKE A SUPERHERO.
WELL THIS SUPERHERO HAPPENS TO ATTEND OUR SCHOOL.
BUT BECAUSE OF HER INJURY...
...SHE RETIRED FROM PLAYING VOLLEYBALL!
NO MATTER HOW IMPRESSIVE HER EXPERIENCE...
...IF SHE'S NOT PLAYING ANYMORE, WHAT GOOD DOES IT DO US?

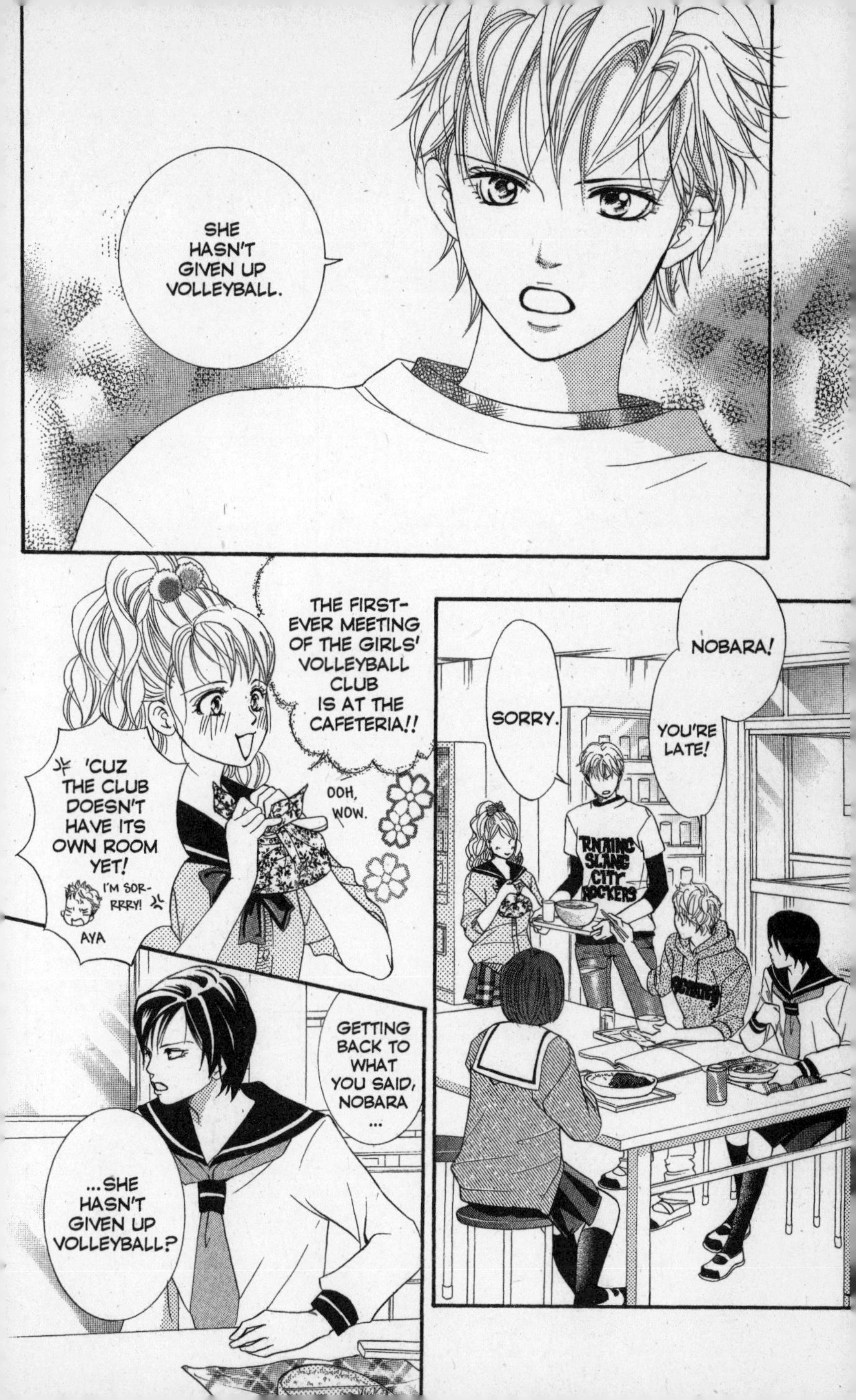
SHE HASN'T GIVEN UP VOLLEYBALL.
NOBARA!
YOU'RE LATE!
SORRY.
THE FIRST-EVER MEETING OF THE GIRLS' VOLLEYBALL CLUB IS AT THE CAFETERIA!!
OOH, WOW.
'CUZ THE CLUB DOESN'T HAVE ITS OWN ROOM YET!
I'M SOR-RRRY!
AYA
GETTING BACK TO WHAT YOU SAID, NOBARA ...
...SHE HASN'T GIVEN UP VOLLEYBALL?

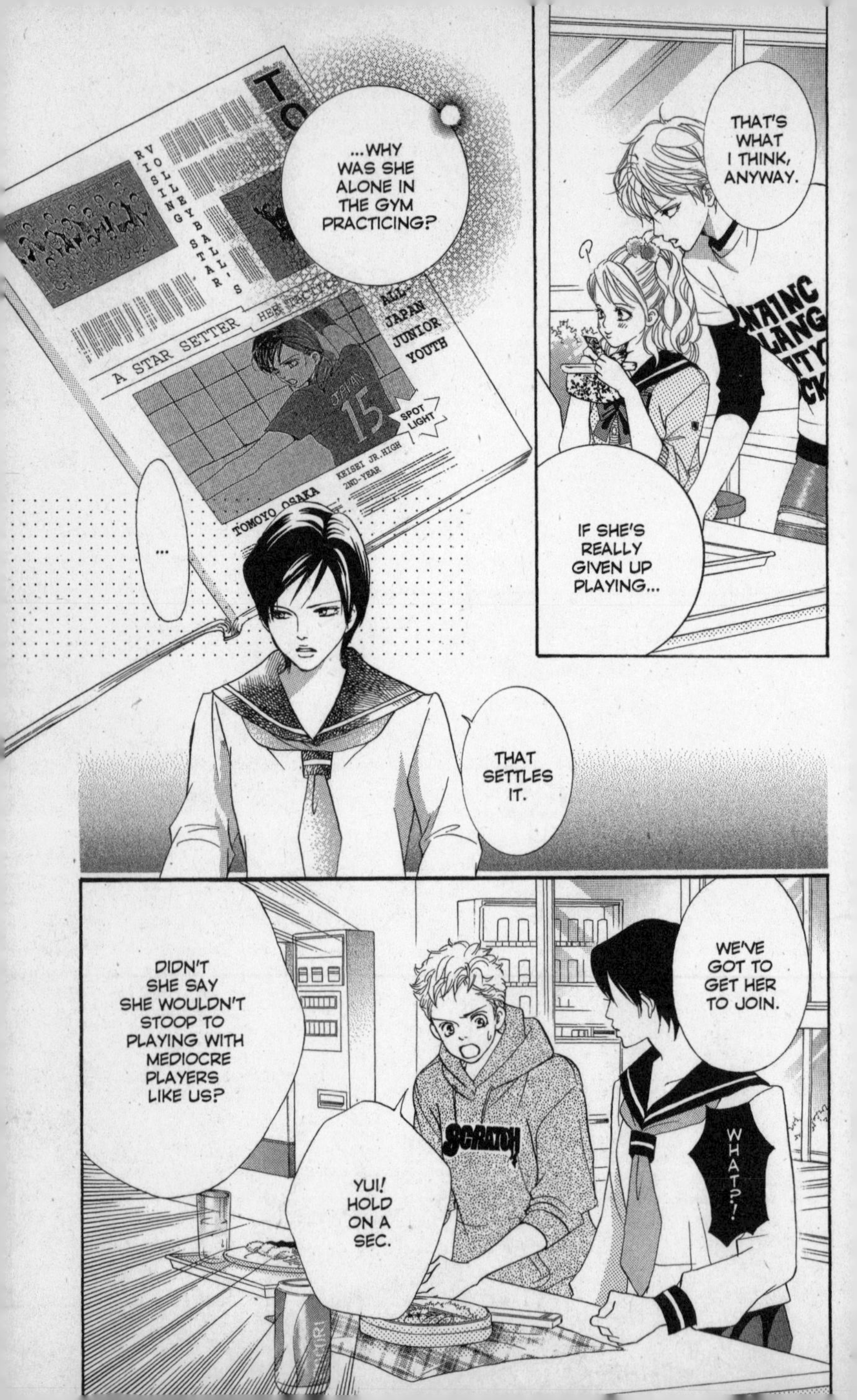
THAT'S WHAT I THINK, ANYWAY.
IF SHE'S REALLY GIVEN UP PLAYING...
...WHY WAS SHE ALONE IN THE GYM PRACTICING?
RISING VOLLEYBALL'S STAR
A STAR SETTER
ALL-JAPAN JUNIOR YOUTH
SPOT LIGHT
KEISEI JR. HIGH 2ND-YEAR
TOMOYO OSAKA
...
THAT SETTLES IT.
WE'VE GOT TO GET HER TO JOIN.
WHAT?!
DIDN'T SHE SAY SHE WOULDN'T STOOP TO PLAYING WITH MEDIOCRE PLAYERS LIKE US?
YUI! HOLD ON A SEC.

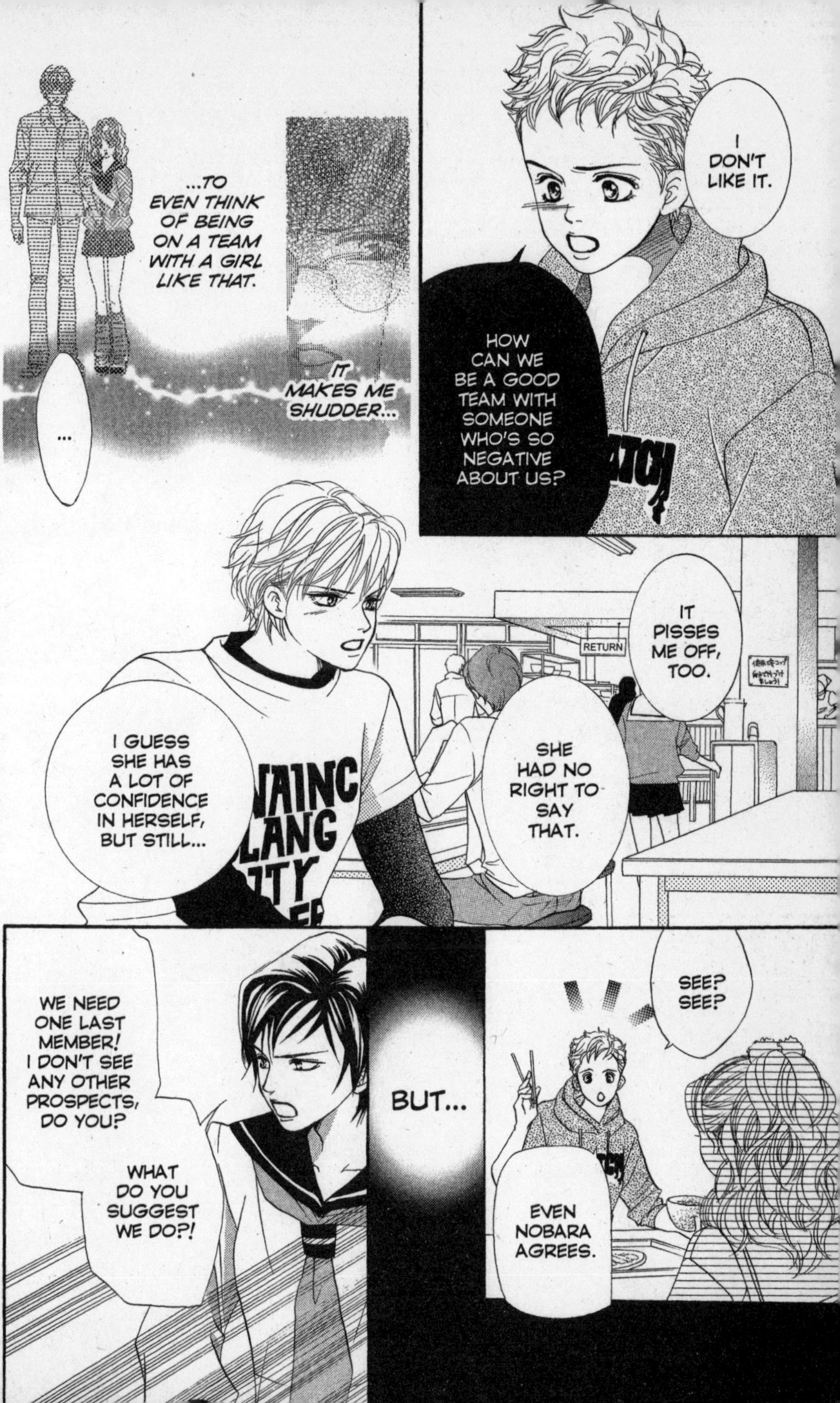
I DON'T LIKE IT.
HOW CAN WE BE A GOOD TEAM WITH SOMEONE WHO'S SO NEGATIVE ABOUT US?
...TO EVEN THINK OF BEING ON A TEAM WITH A GIRL LIKE THAT.
IT MAKES ME SHUDDER...
...
IT PISSES ME OFF, TOO.
RETURN
SHE HAD NO RIGHT TO SAY THAT.
I GUESS SHE HAS A LOT OF CONFIDENCE IN HERSELF, BUT STILL...
SEE? SEE?
EVEN NOBARA AGREES.
BUT...
WE NEED ONE LAST MEMBER! I DON'T SEE ANY OTHER PROSPECTS, DO YOU?
WHAT DO YOU SUGGEST WE DO?!

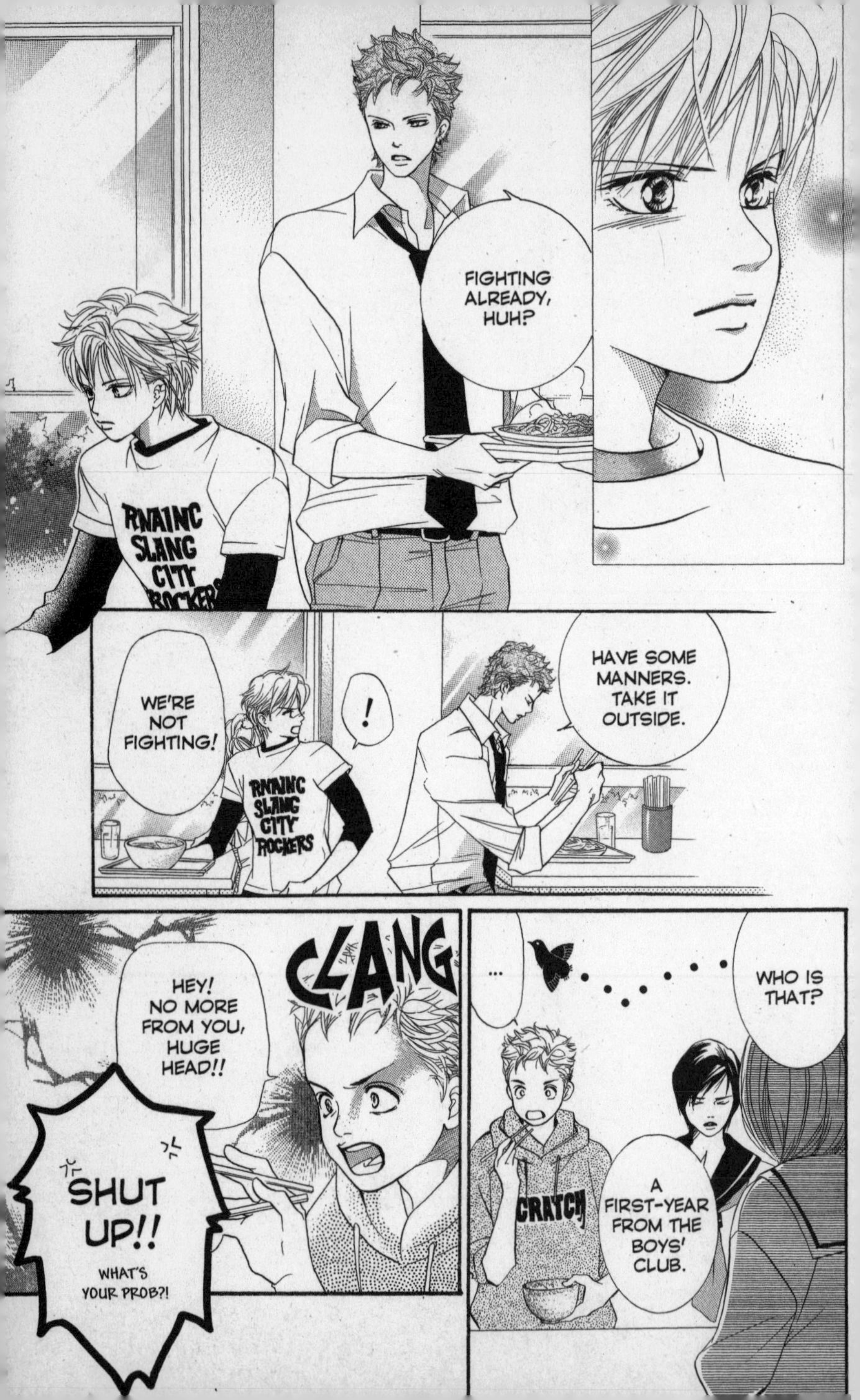
FIGHTING ALREADY, HUH?
RNAINC SLANG CITY ROCKERS
HAVE SOME MANNERS. TAKE IT OUTSIDE.
!
WE'RE NOT FIGHTING!
RNAINC SLANG CITY ROCKERS
WHO IS THAT?
...
A FIRST-YEAR FROM THE BOYS' CLUB.
CRATCH
CLANG
HEY! NO MORE FROM YOU, HUGE HEAD!!
SHUT UP!!
WHAT'S YOUR PROB?!

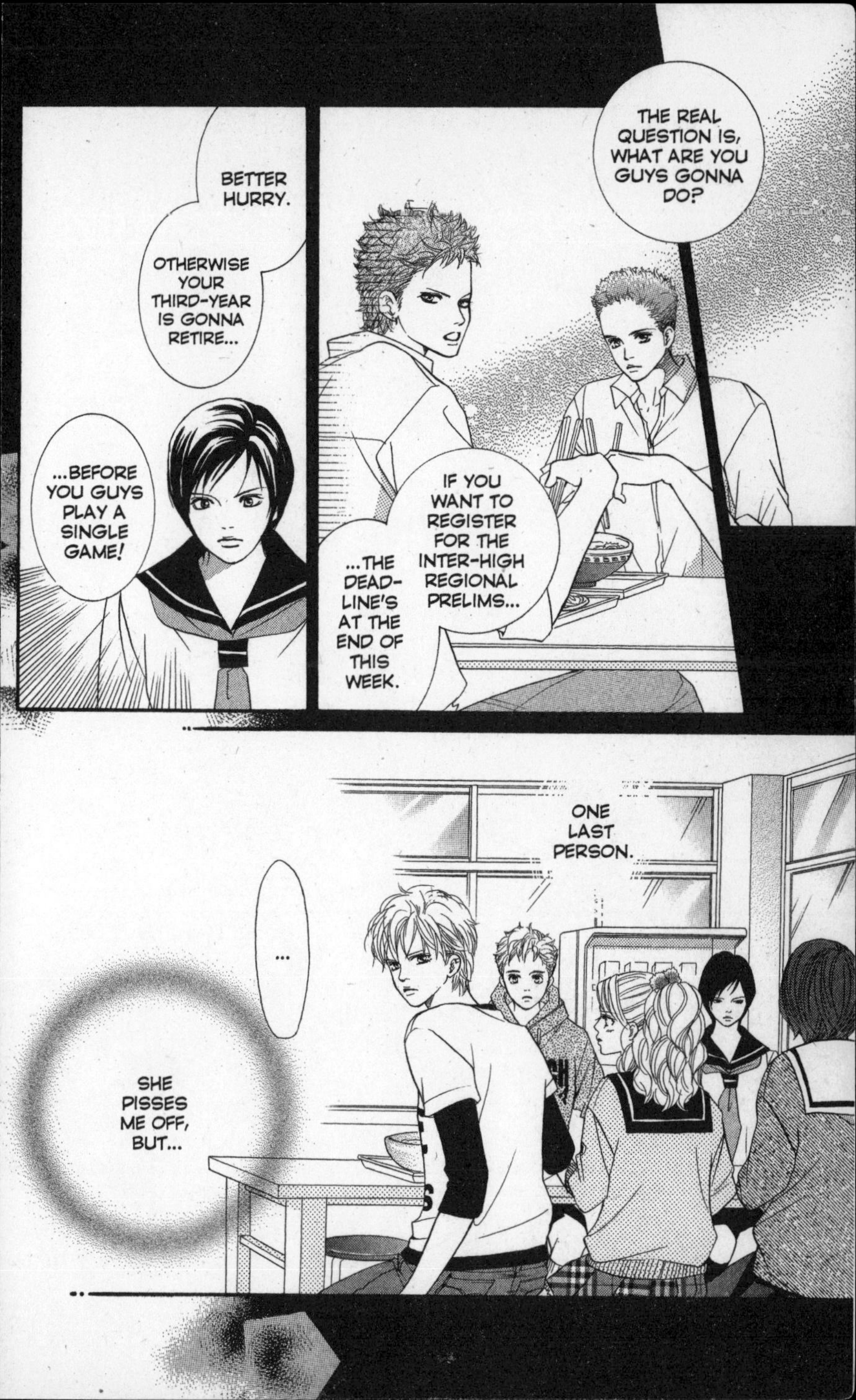
THE REAL QUESTION IS, WHAT ARE YOU GUYS GONNA DO?
IF YOU WANT TO REGISTER FOR THE INTER-HIGH REGIONAL PRELIMS...
...THE DEADLINE'S AT THE END OF THIS WEEK.
BETTER HURRY.
OTHERWISE YOUR THIRD-YEAR IS GONNA RETIRE...
...BEFORE YOU GUYS PLAY A SINGLE GAME!
ONE LAST PERSON.
...
SHE PISSES ME OFF, BUT...

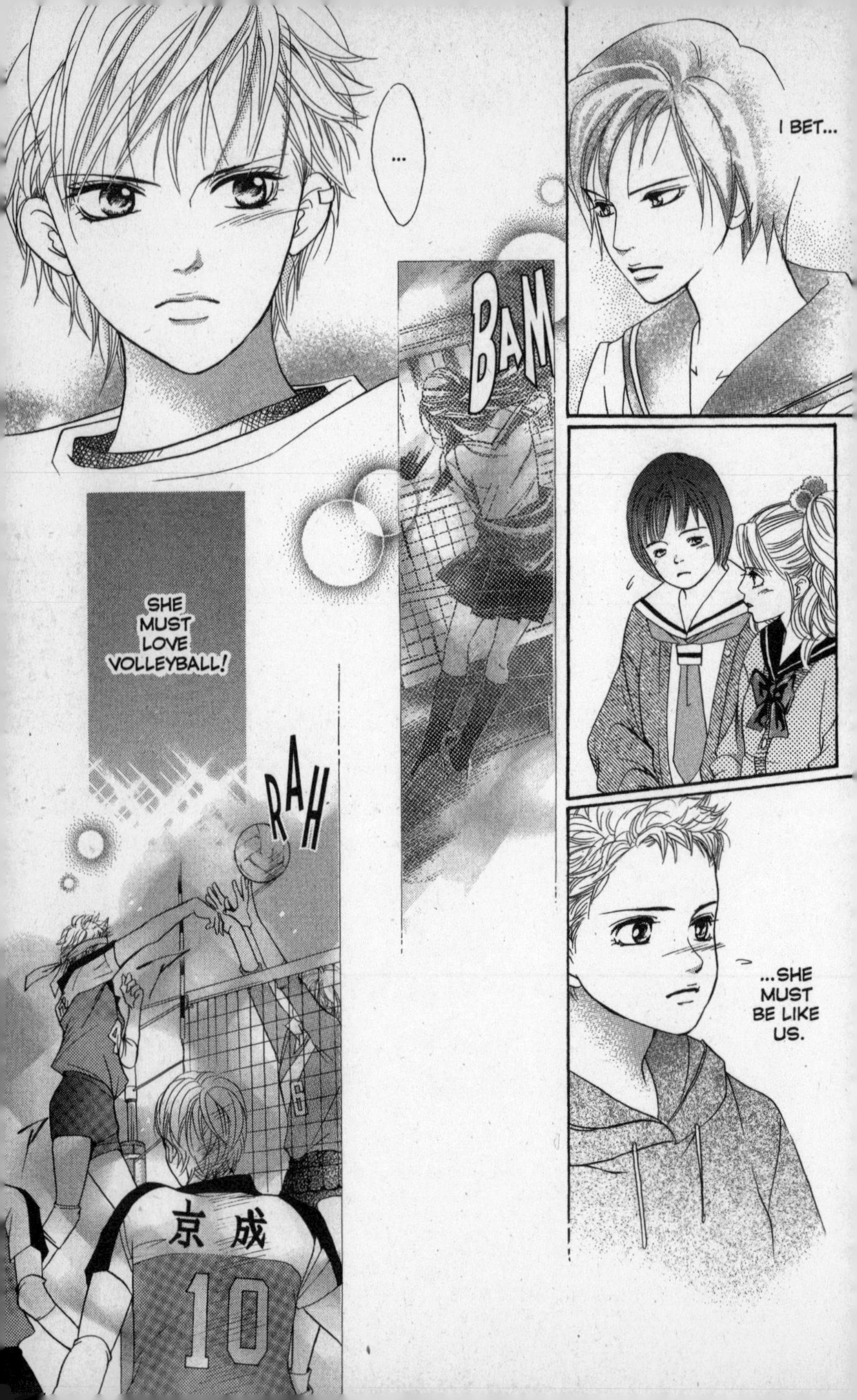

I BET...
...
BAM
SHE MUST LOVE VOLLEYBALL!
RAH
京成
10
...SHE MUST BE LIKE US.

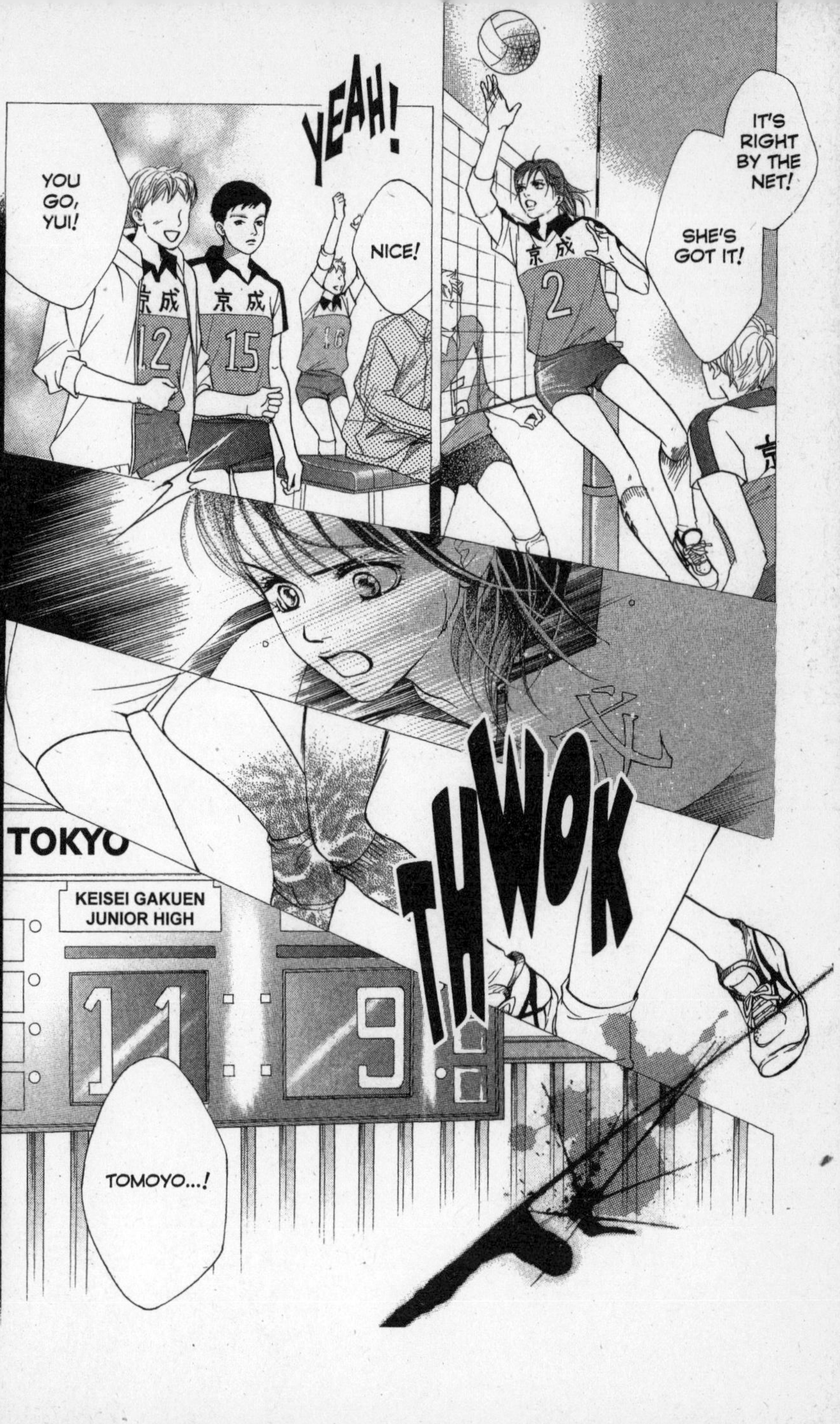
IT'S RIGHT BY THE NET!
SHE'S GOT IT!
YEAH!
NICE!
YOU GO, YUI!
THWOK
TOKYO
KEISEI GAKUEN JUNIOR HIGH
11
9
TOMOYO...!

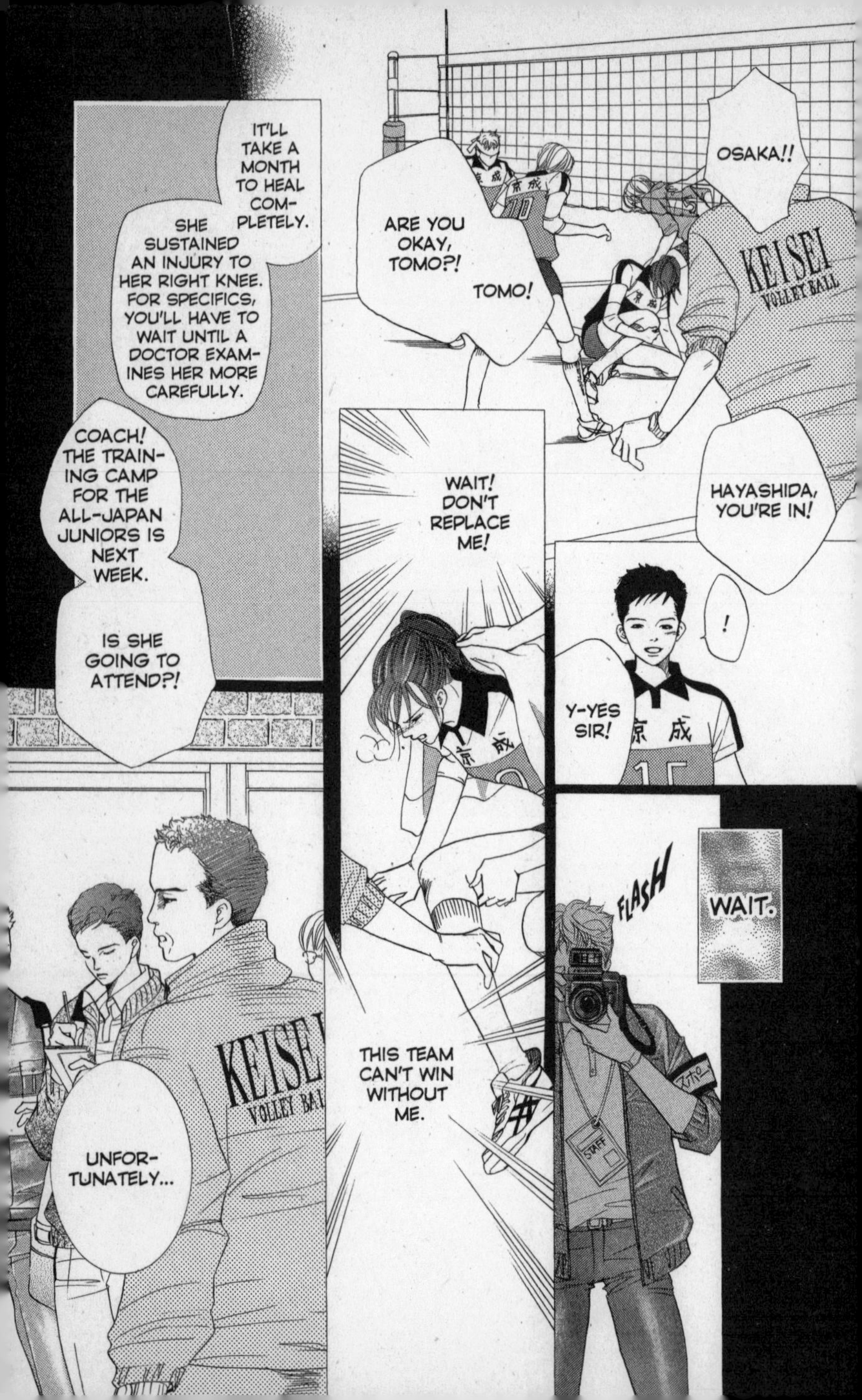
OSAKA!!
ARE YOU OKAY, TOMO?!
TOMO!
HAYASHIDA, YOU'RE IN!
!
Y-YES SIR!
FLASH
WAIT.
WAIT! DON'T REPLACE ME!
THIS TEAM CAN'T WIN WITHOUT ME.
IT'LL TAKE A MONTH TO HEAL COMPLETELY.
SHE SUSTAINED AN INJURY TO HER RIGHT KNEE. FOR SPECIFICS, YOU'LL HAVE TO WAIT UNTIL A DOCTOR EXAMINES HER MORE CAREFULLY.
COACH! THE TRAINING CAMP FOR THE ALL-JAPAN JUNIORS IS NEXT WEEK.
IS SHE GOING TO ATTEND?!
UNFORTUNATELY...

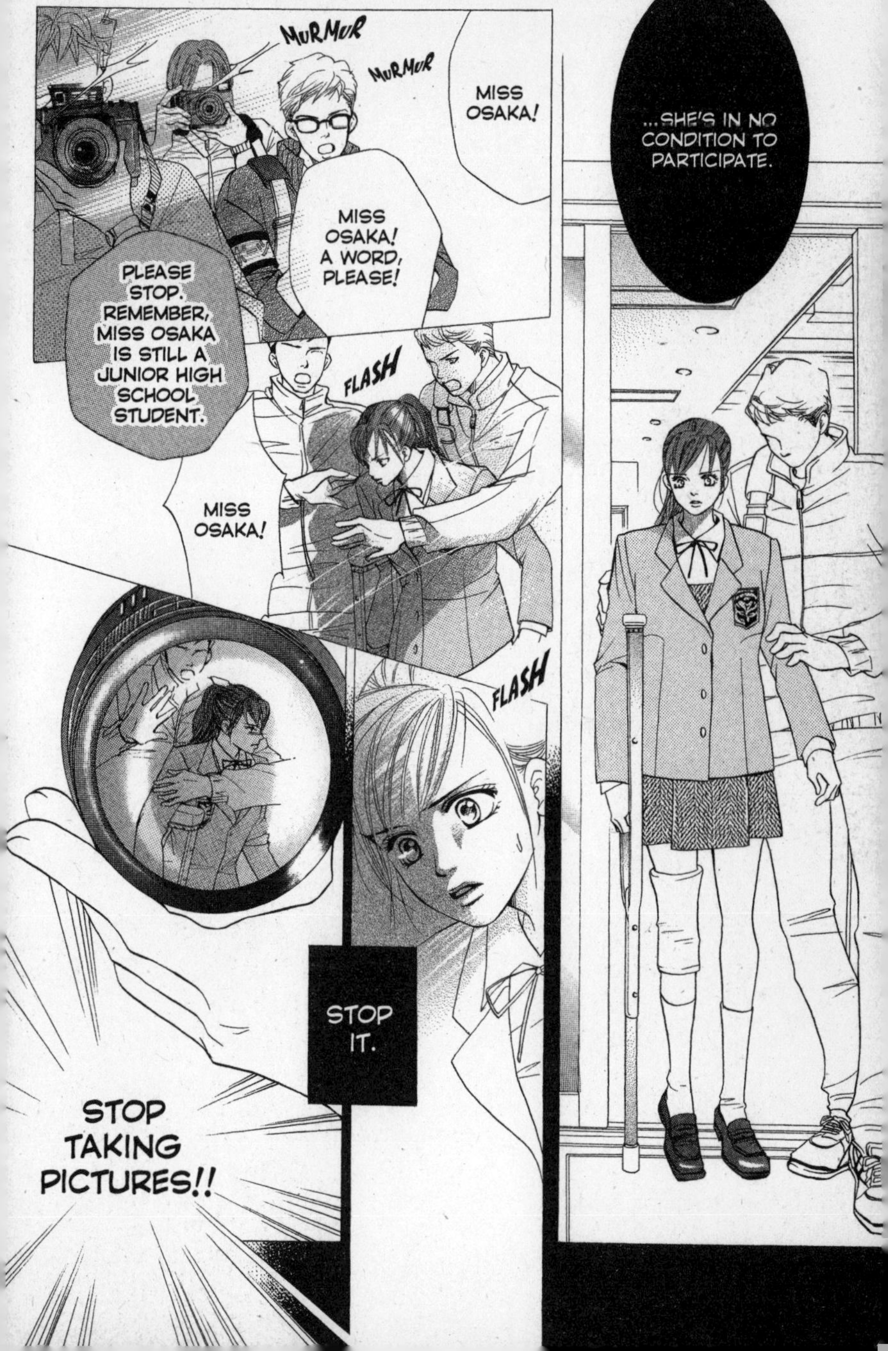
...SHE'S IN NO CONDITION TO PARTICIPATE.
MISS OSAKA!
MURMUR
MURMUR
MISS OSAKA! A WORD, PLEASE!
PLEASE STOP. REMEMBER, MISS OSAKA IS STILL A JUNIOR HIGH SCHOOL STUDENT.
FLASH
MISS OSAKA!
FLASH
STOP IT.
STOP TAKING PICTURES!!

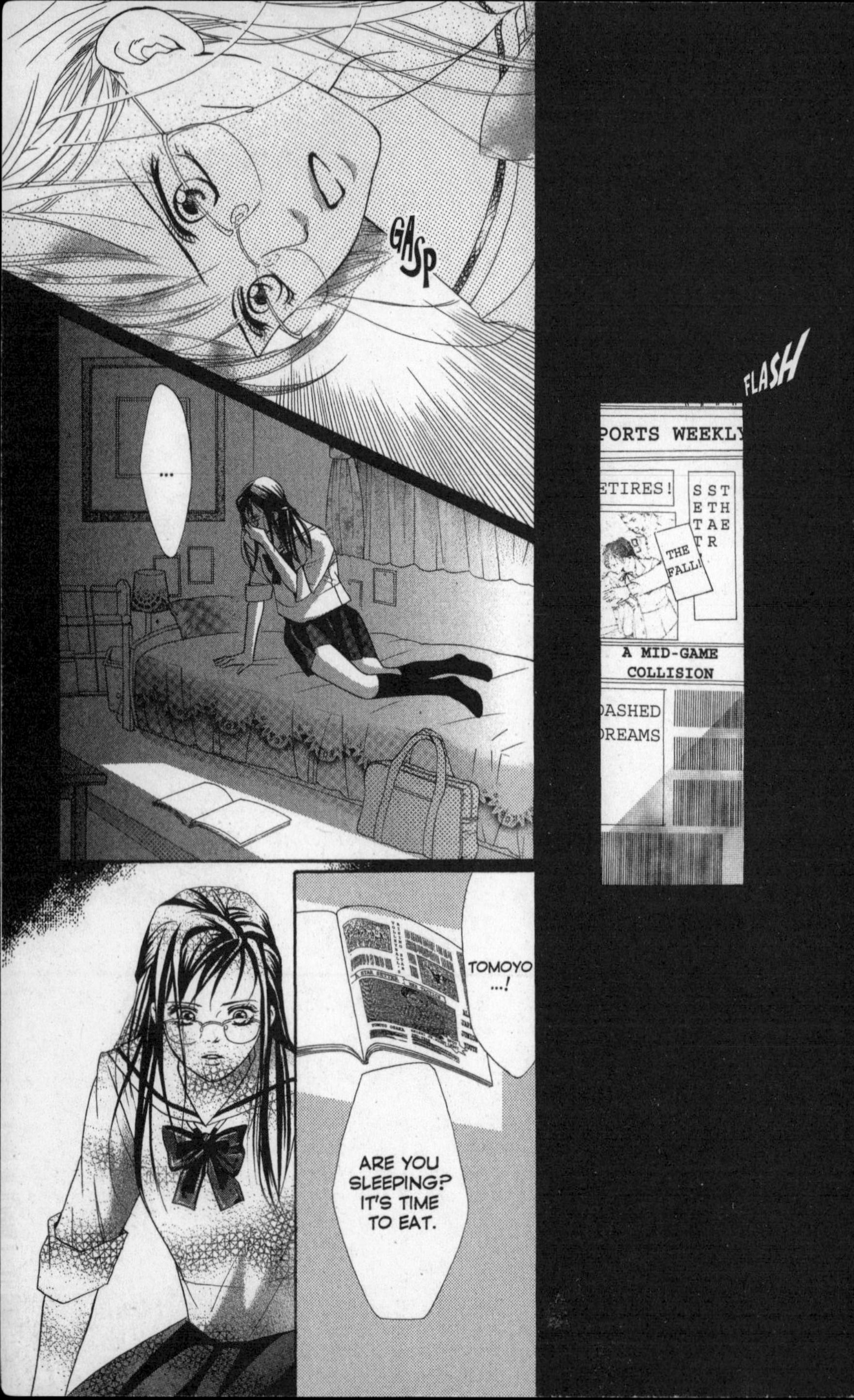
FLASH
PORTS WEEKLY
ETIRES!
THE FALL!
A MID-GAME COLLISION
DASHED
REAMS
GASP
...
TOMOYO ...!
ARE YOU SLEEPING? IT'S TIME TO EAT.

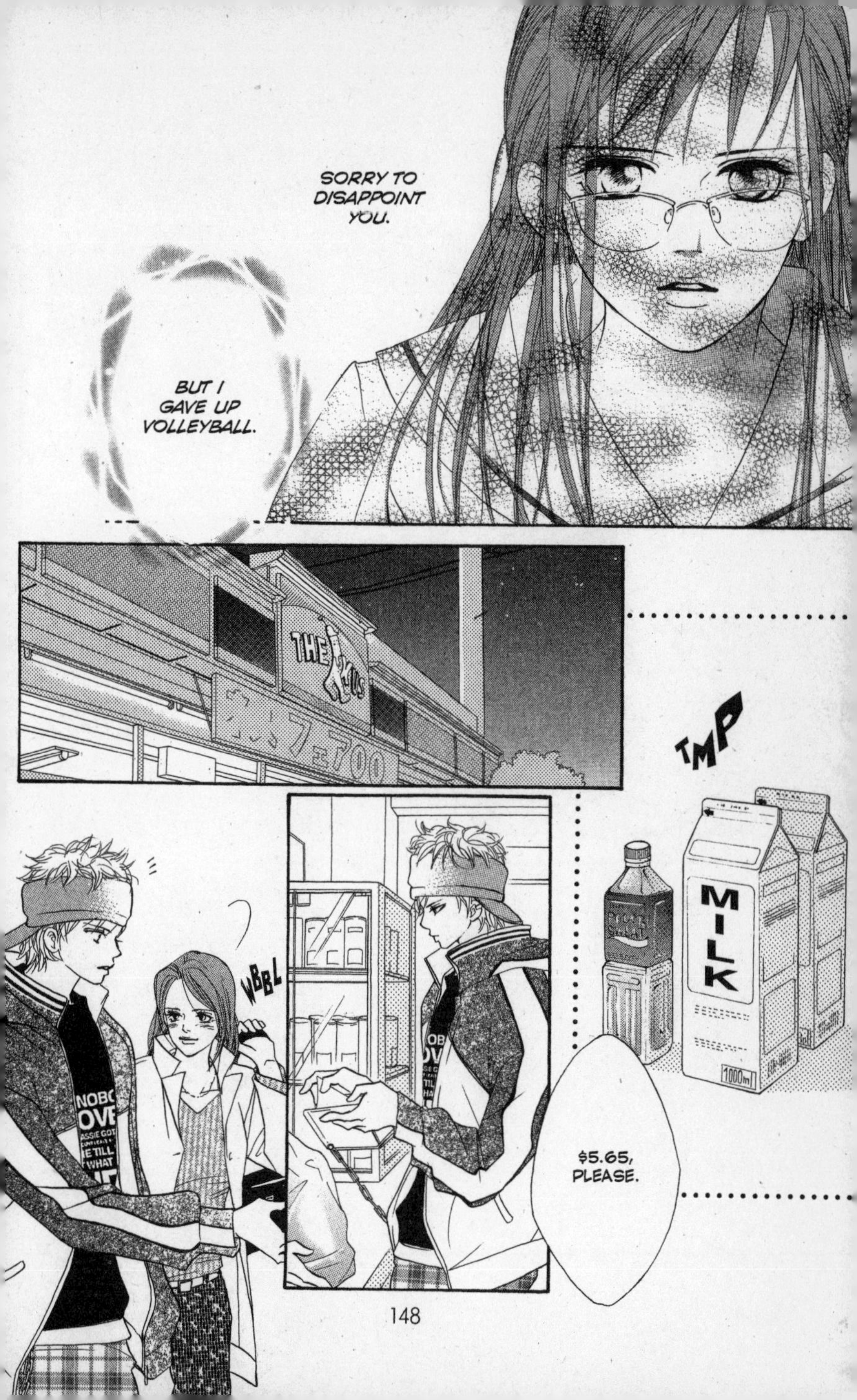
SORRY TO DISAPPOINT YOU.
BUT I GAVE UP VOLLEYBALL.
THE
TMP
MILK
1000ml
$5.65, PLEASE.
WBBL

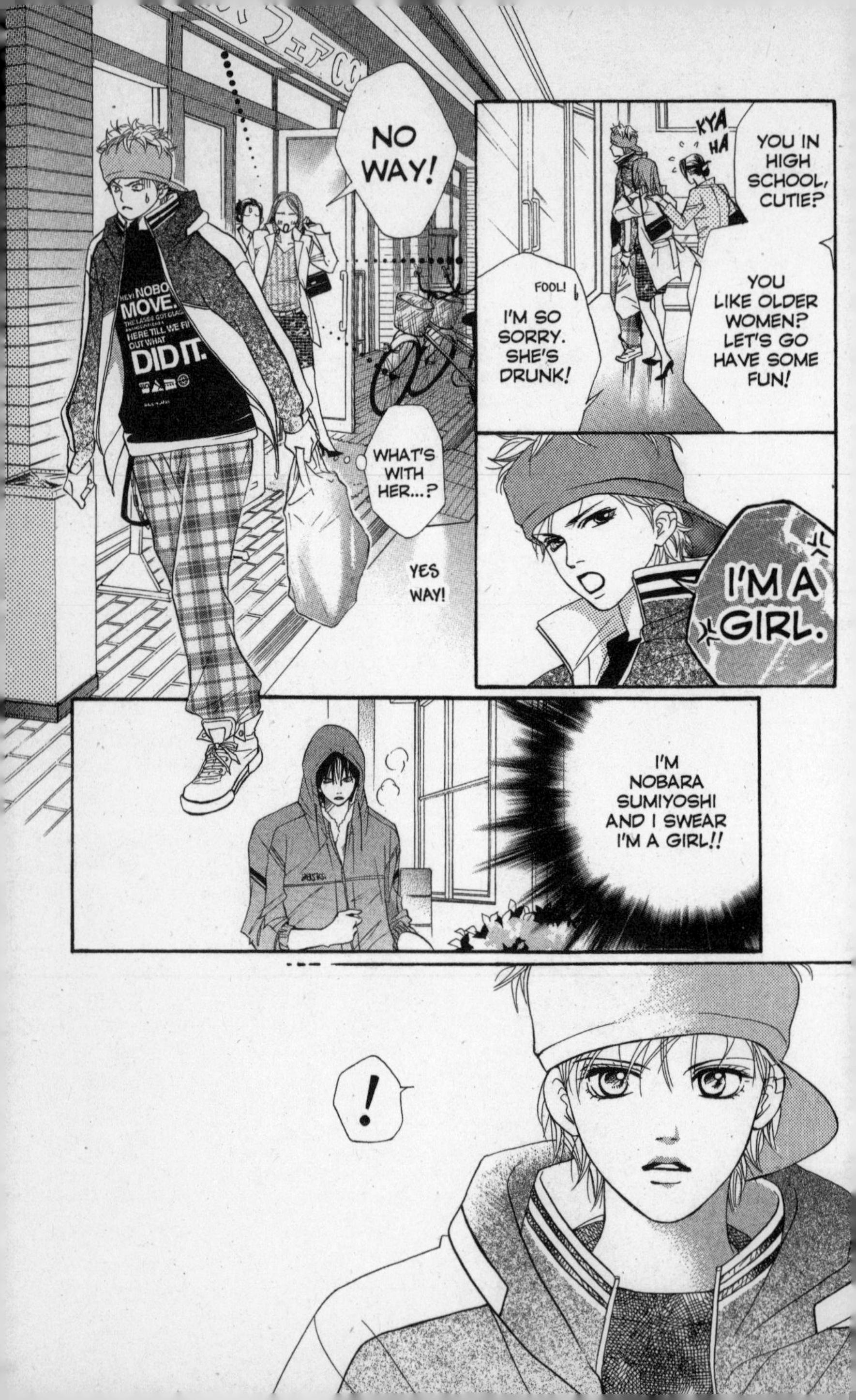
KYA HA
YOU IN HIGH SCHOOL, CUTIE?
YOU LIKE OLDER WOMEN? LET'S GO HAVE SOME FUN!
FOOL!
I'M SO SORRY. SHE'S DRUNK!
I'M A GIRL.
NO WAY!
WHAT'S WITH HER...?
YES WAY!
I'M NOBARA SUMIYOSHI AND I SWEAR I'M A GIRL!!
!

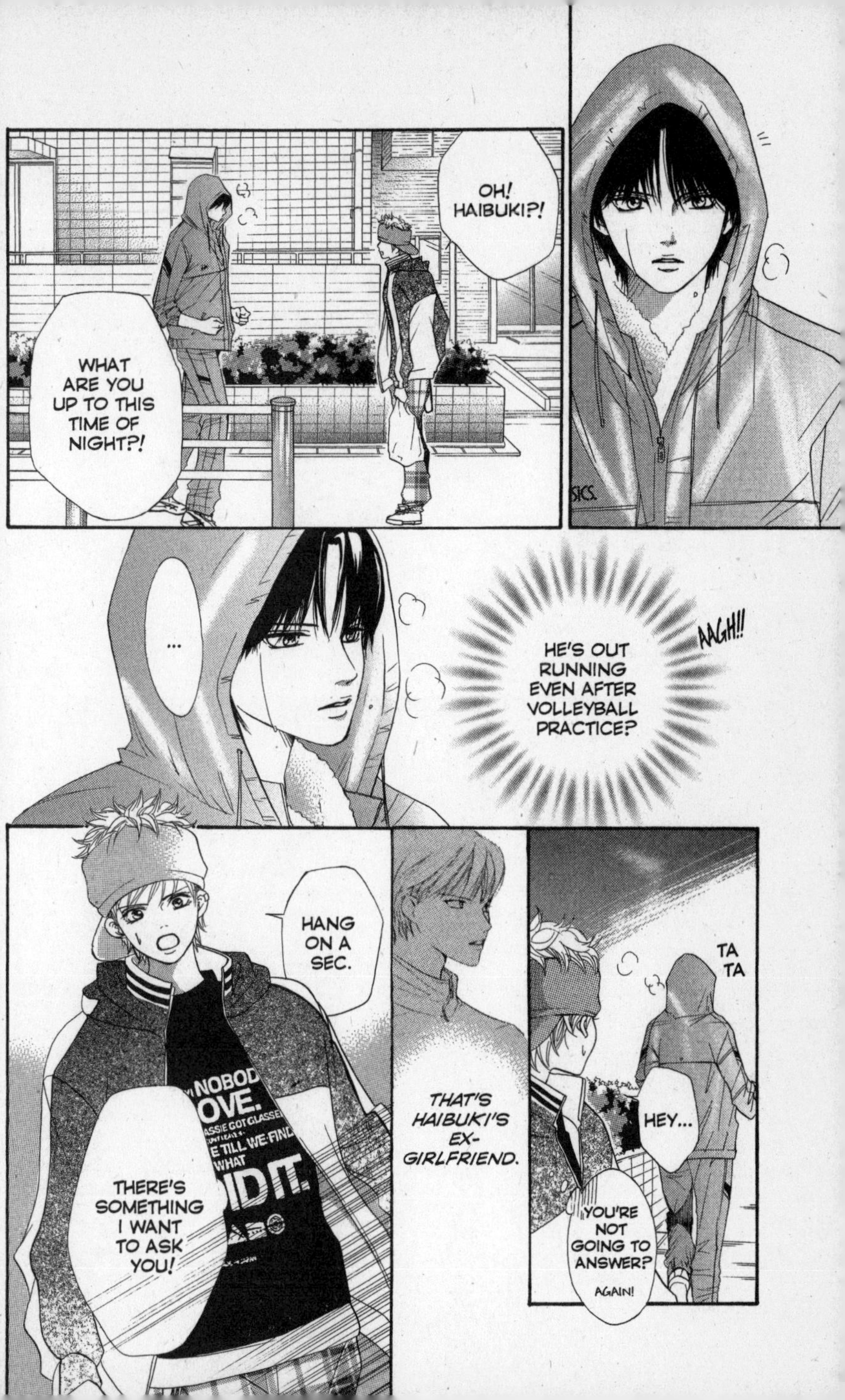
OH! HAIBUKI?!
WHAT ARE YOU UP TO THIS TIME OF NIGHT?!
AAGH!!
HE'S OUT RUNNING EVEN AFTER VOLLEYBALL PRACTICE?
...
TA TA
HEY...
YOU'RE NOT GOING TO ANSWER?
AGAIN!
THAT'S HAIBUKI'S EX-GIRLFRIEND.
HANG ON A SEC.
THERE'S SOMETHING I WANT TO ASK YOU!

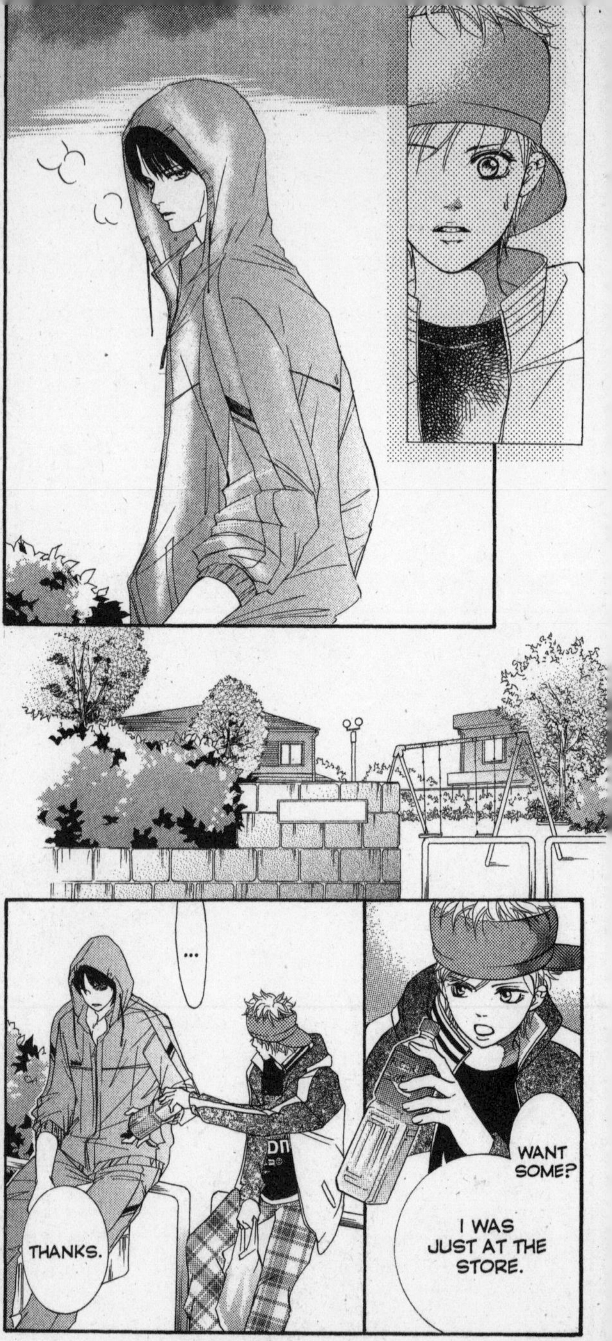
WANT SOME?
I WAS JUST AT THE STORE.
...
THANKS.

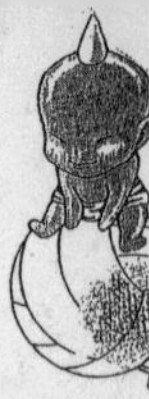

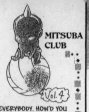

MITSUBA CLUB

Vol. 4

SO, EVERYBODY. HOW'D YOU LIKE IT? THERE WAS THAT SCENE WITH THE GAME (THO IT WAS THREE ON THREE SO IT WASN'T LIKE AN OFFICIAL GAME) AND I HAVE TO SAY, I FELT LIKE I USED PARTS OF MY BRAIN THAT I DON'T NORMALLY USE WORKING ON SHOJO MANGA. IT'S TOUGH TO DO A SPORTS MANGA!! BUT I HAD FUN WORKING ON SCENES WITH MOVEMENT IN THEM. NOW THAT NOBARA HAS BEGUN TO FIND TEAM-MATES, YOU CAN LOOK FORWARD TO SEEING WHAT NEW DRAMA UNFOLDS. SEE YOU AGAIN IN VOLUME THREE. THAT IS TO SAY, PLEASE READ IT! I'LL DO MY BEST!

— Special Thanks —

Nina.
Itsuki. Kitagawa
Chie. Abe
Sayuri. Kawasugi
Kanon. Ozawa
+
Aiji. Yamakawa
Io. Sakisaka
+
S. Imai
+
M. Nakayama
Ryô

and You.

— ADDRESS LETTERS TO: —

CRIMSON HERO
C/O SHOJO BEAT
VIZ MEDIA, LLC
P.O. BOX 77010
SAN FRANCISCO, CA 94107

WHAT ARE YOUR TEAMS AND SCHOOL CLUBS LIKE? WHAT GOES ON IN THEM? IF YOU HAVE A STORY TO SHARE WITH ME, PLEASE WRITE.

WELL THEN. SEE YA.

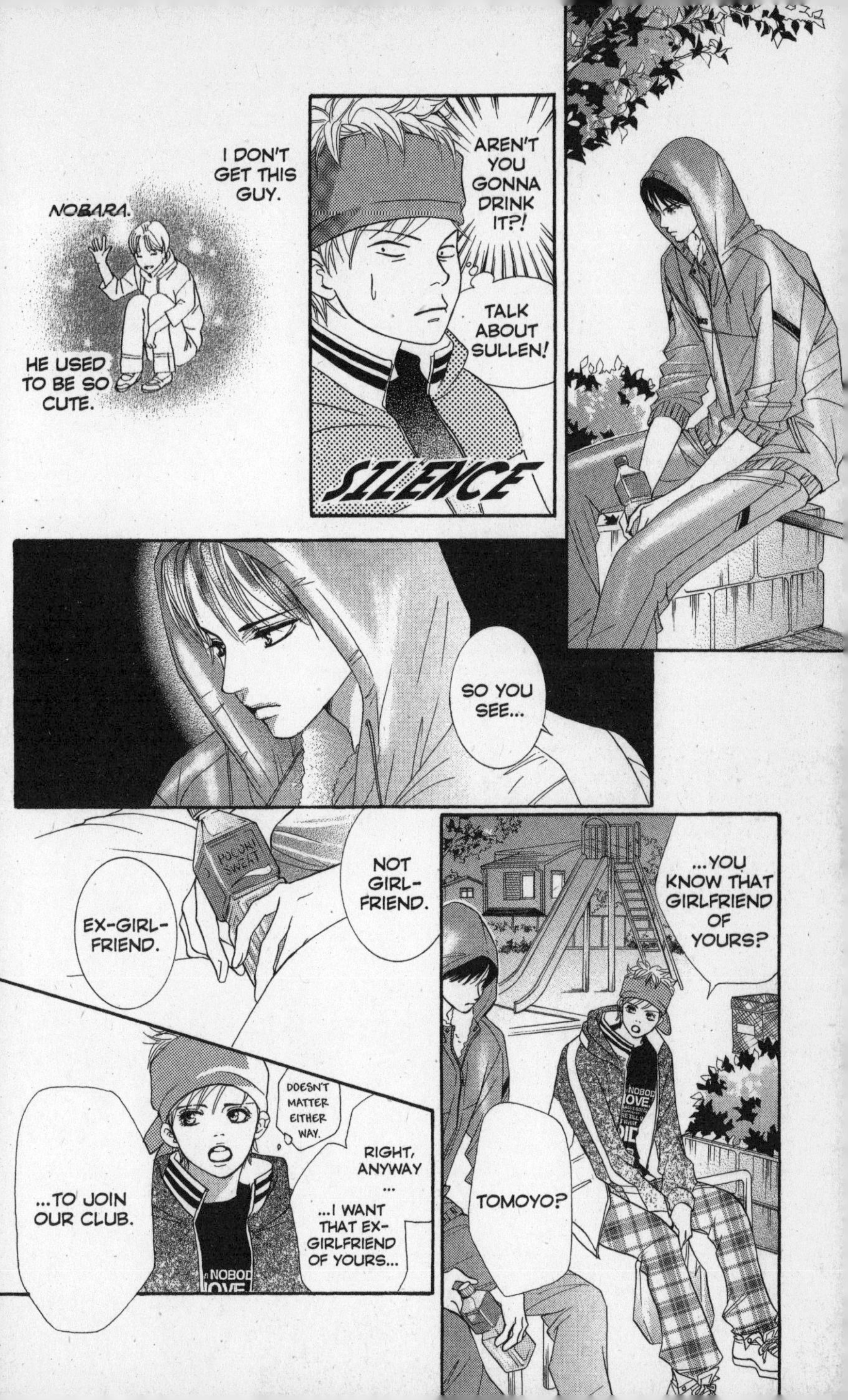
AREN'T YOU GONNA DRINK IT?!
TALK ABOUT SULLEN!
SILENCE
I DON'T GET THIS GUY.
NOBARA.
HE USED TO BE SO CUTE.
SO YOU SEE...
...YOU KNOW THAT GIRLFRIEND OF YOURS?
TOMOYO?
NOT GIRLFRIEND.
EX-GIRLFRIEND.
DOESN'T MATTER EITHER WAY.
RIGHT, ANYWAY...
...I WANT THAT EX-GIRLFRIEND OF YOURS...
...TO JOIN OUR CLUB.

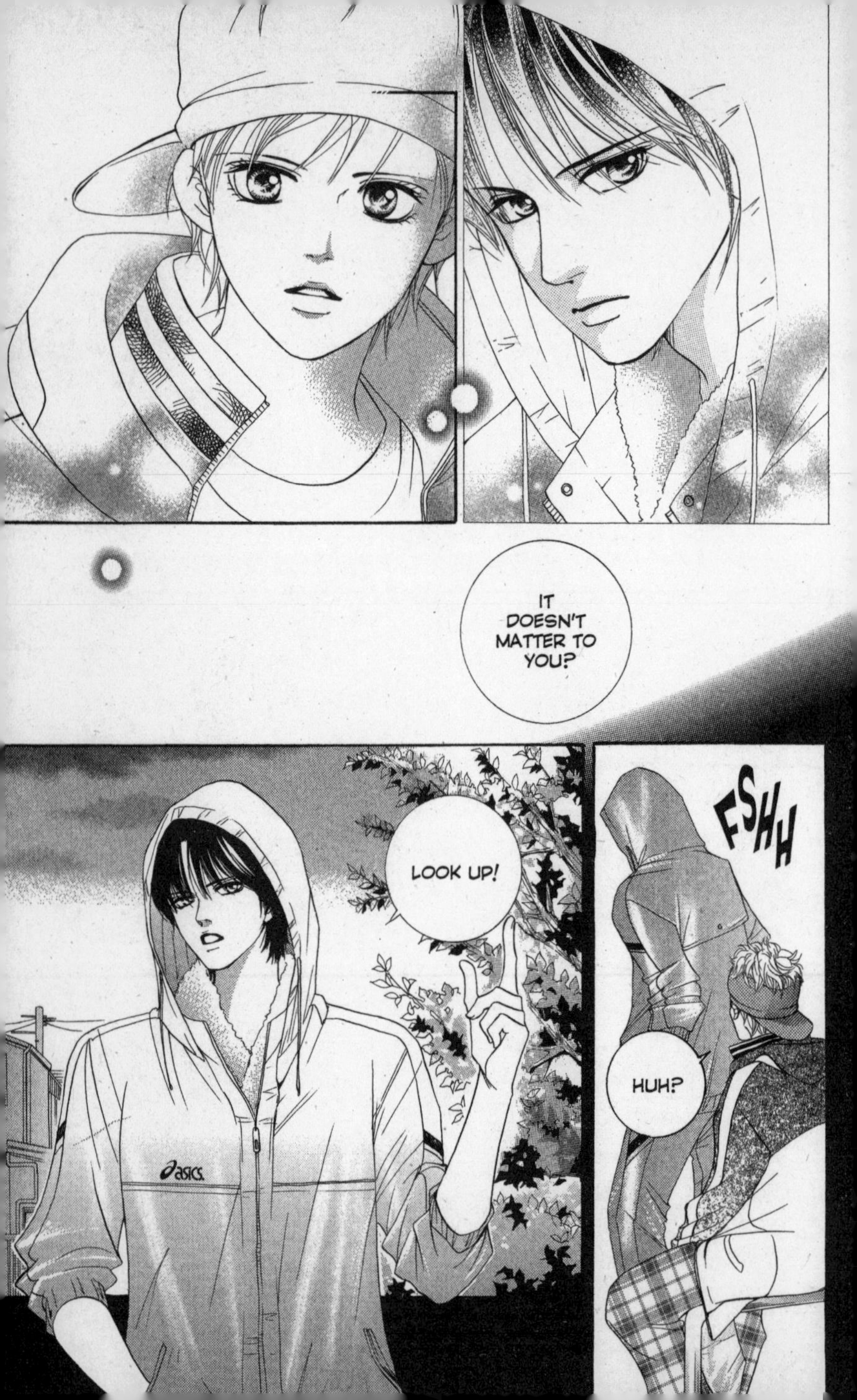
IT DOESN'T MATTER TO YOU?
FSHH
HUH?
LOOK UP!
asics

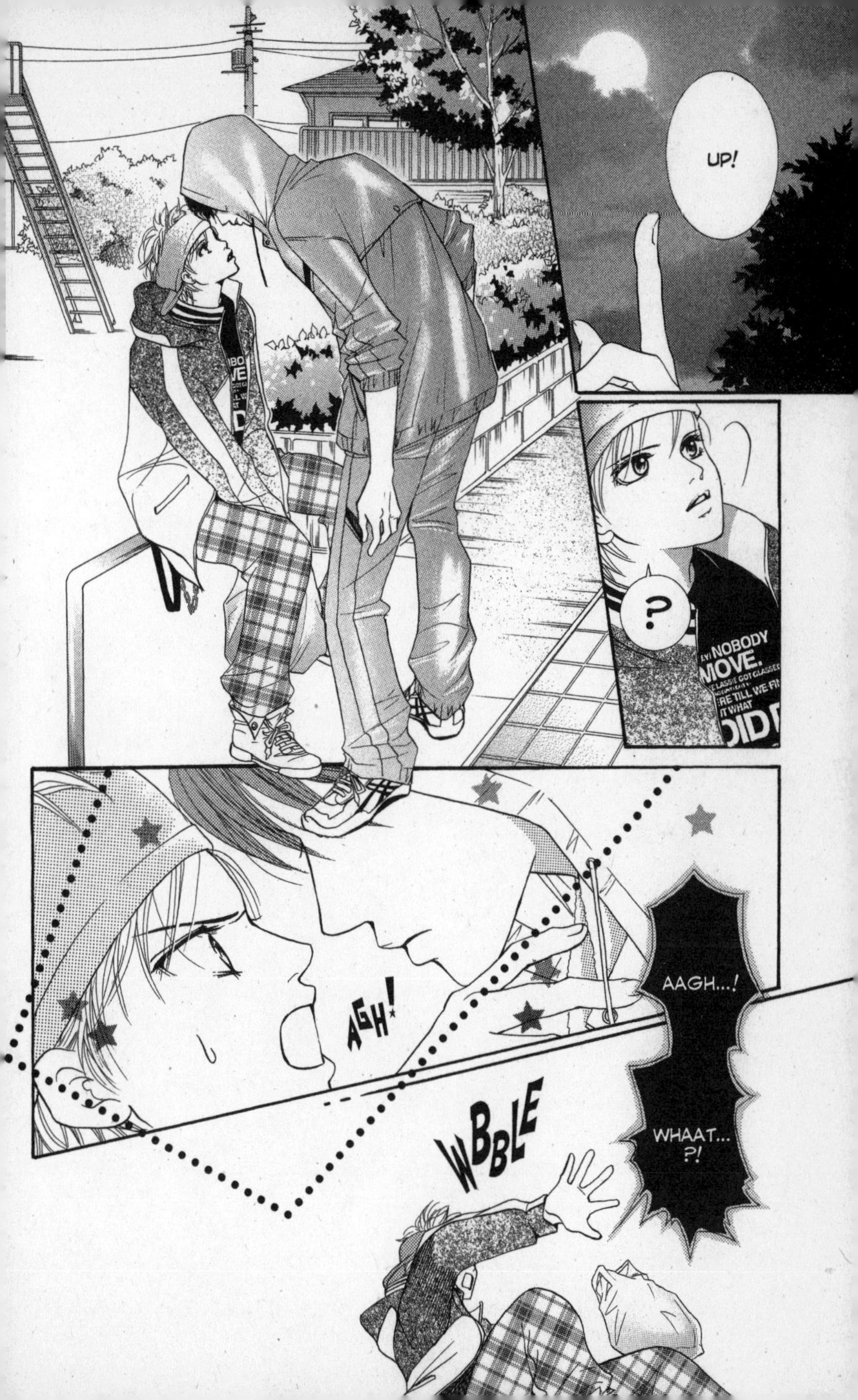
UP!
?
NOBODY
MOVE.
AAGH...!
AGH!
WHAAT...
?!
WBBLE

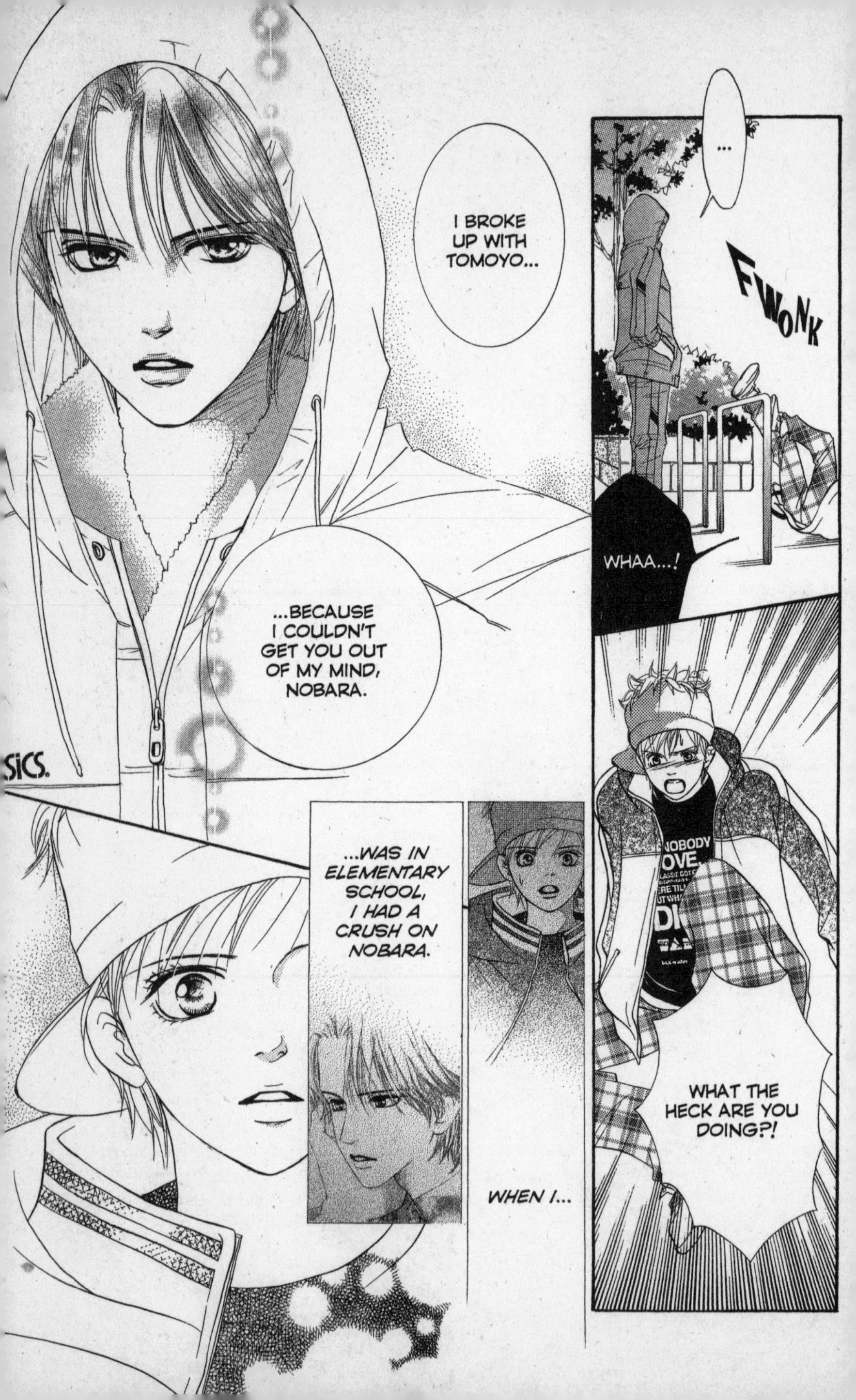
...
FWONK
WHAA...!
WHAT THE HECK ARE YOU DOING?!
I BROKE UP WITH TOMOYO...
...BECAUSE I COULDN'T GET YOU OUT OF MY MIND, NOBARA.
SICS.
WHEN I...
...WAS IN ELEMENTARY SCHOOL, I HAD A CRUSH ON NOBARA.

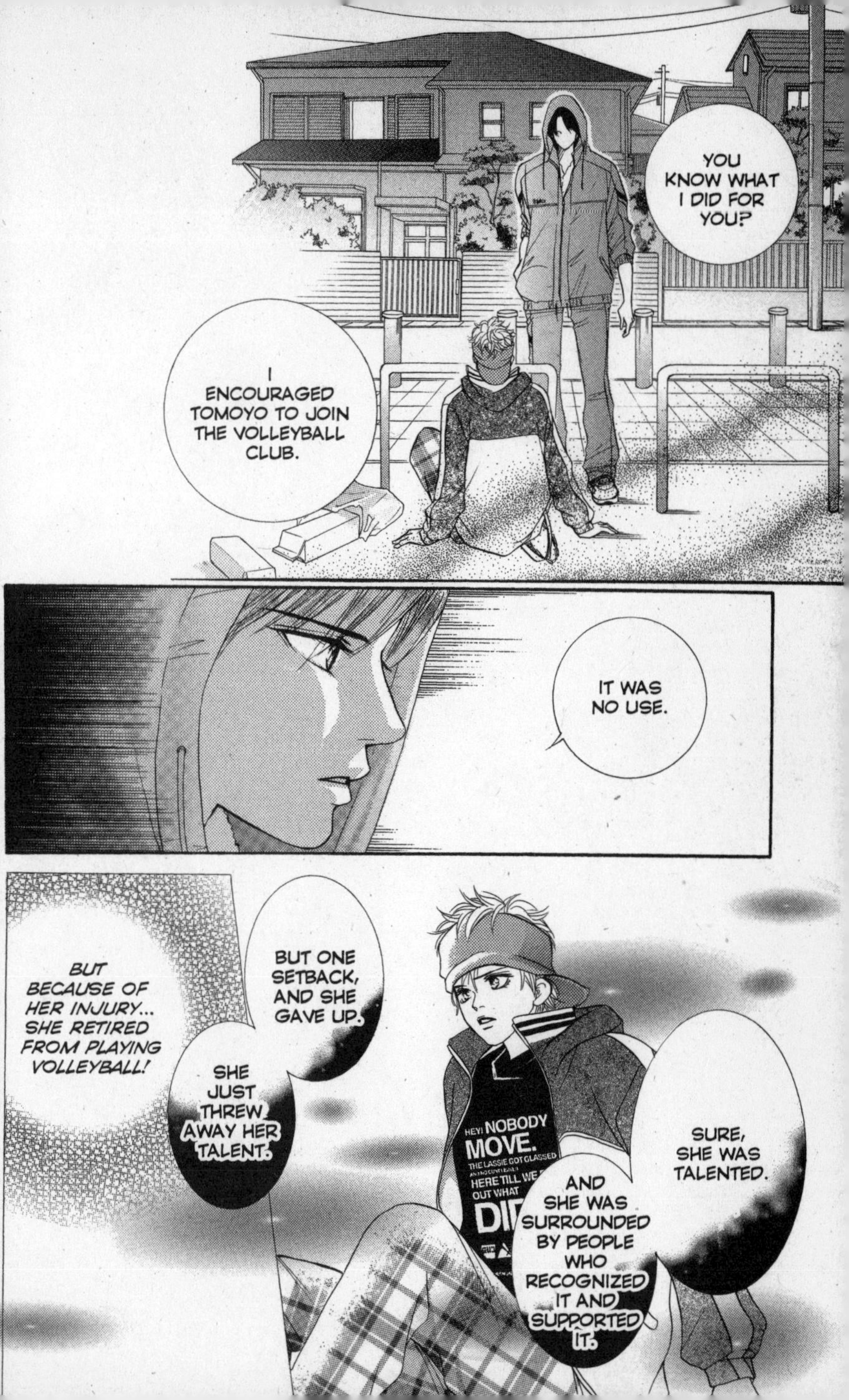
YOU KNOW WHAT I DID FOR YOU?
I ENCOURAGED TOMOYO TO JOIN THE VOLLEYBALL CLUB.
IT WAS NO USE.
SURE, SHE WAS TALENTED.
AND SHE WAS SURROUNDED BY PEOPLE WHO RECOGNIZED IT AND SUPPORTED IT.
HEY! NOBODY MOVE.
BUT ONE SETBACK, AND SHE GAVE UP.
SHE JUST THREW AWAY HER TALENT.
BUT BECAUSE OF HER INJURY... SHE RETIRED FROM PLAYING VOLLEYBALL!

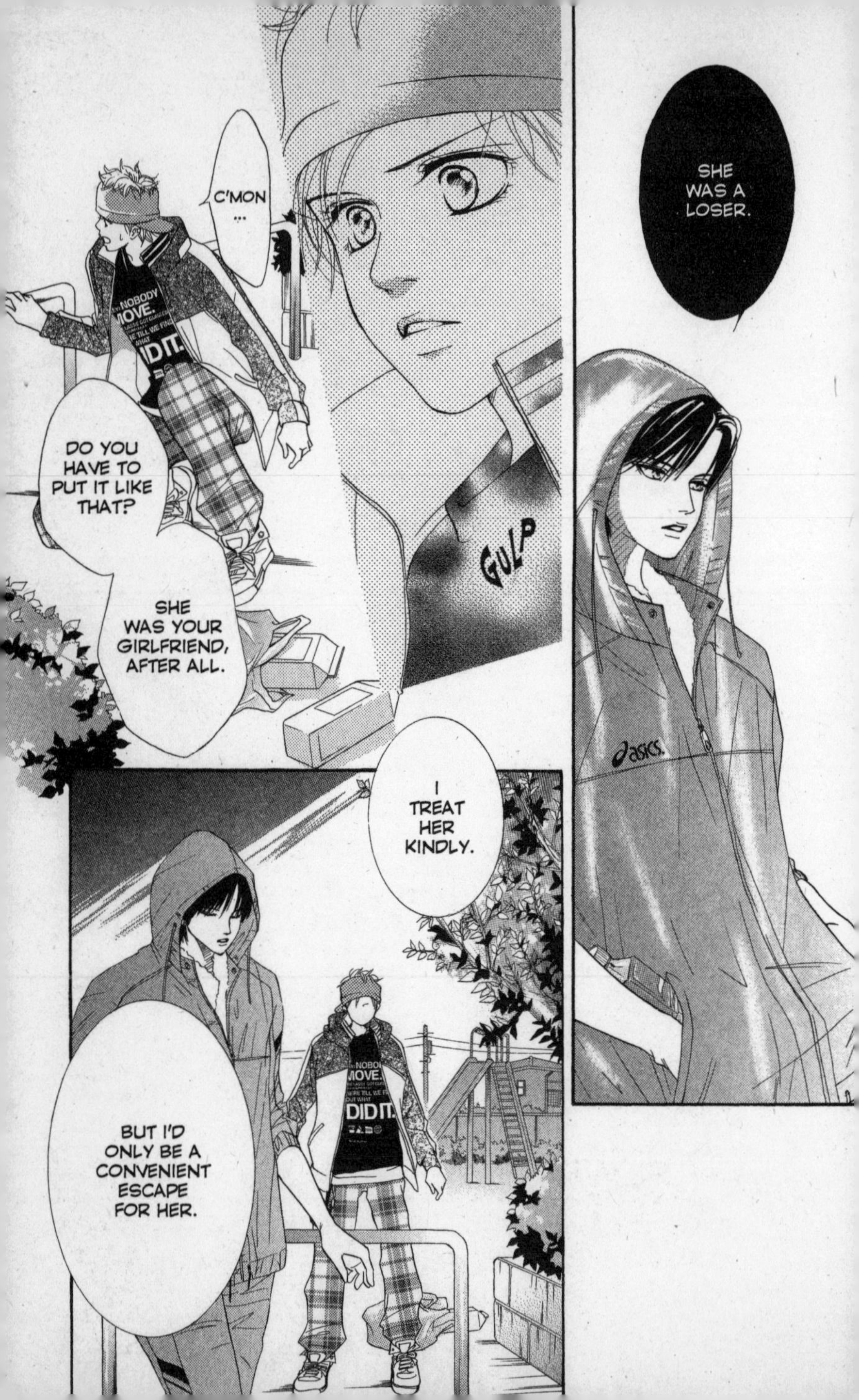
SHE WAS A LOSER.
C'MON ...
GULP
DO YOU HAVE TO PUT IT LIKE THAT?
SHE WAS YOUR GIRLFRIEND, AFTER ALL.
I TREAT HER KINDLY.
BUT I'D ONLY BE A CONVENIENT ESCAPE FOR HER.

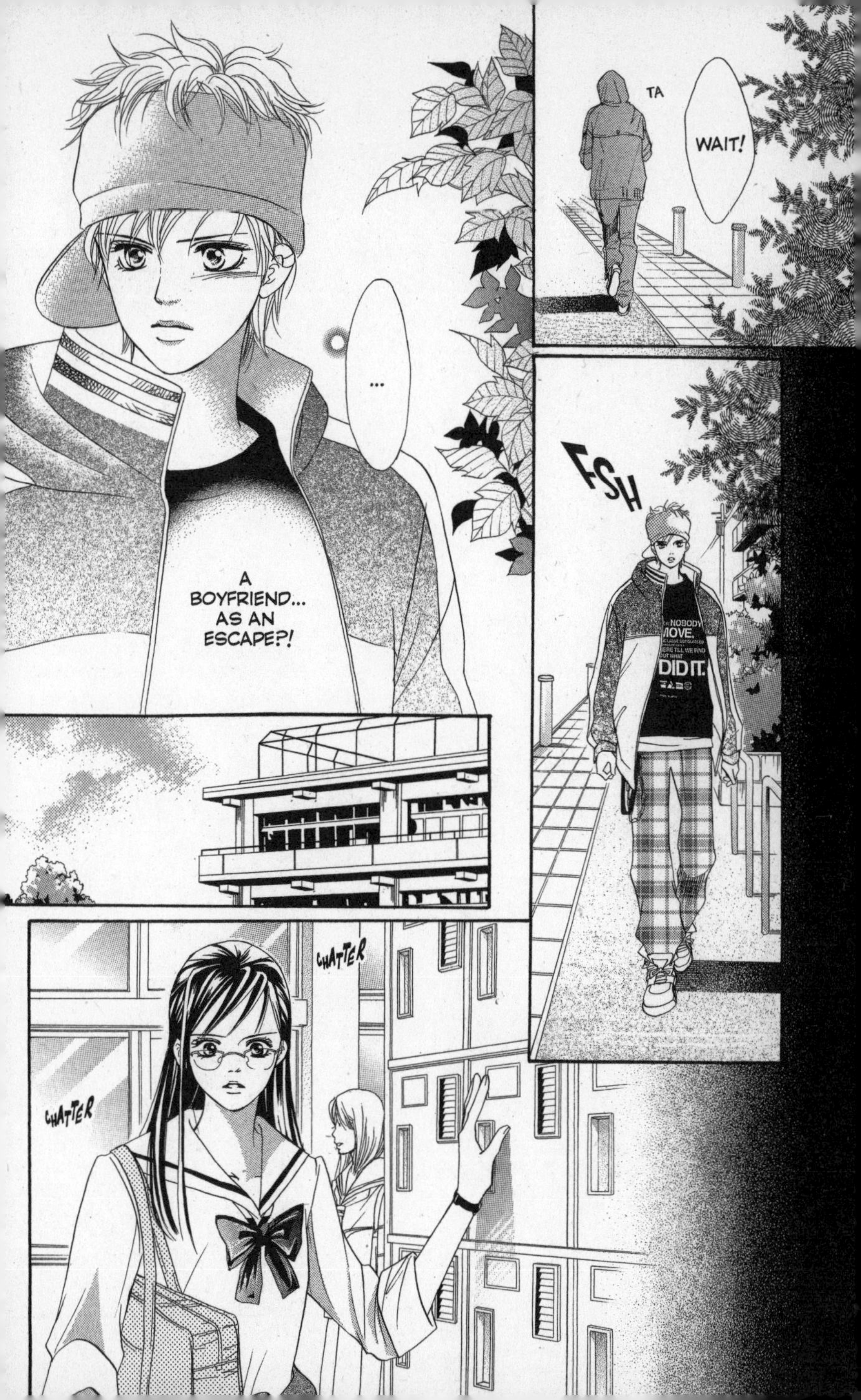
TA
WAIT!
FSH
...
A BOYFRIEND... AS AN ESCAPE?!
CHATTER
CHATTER

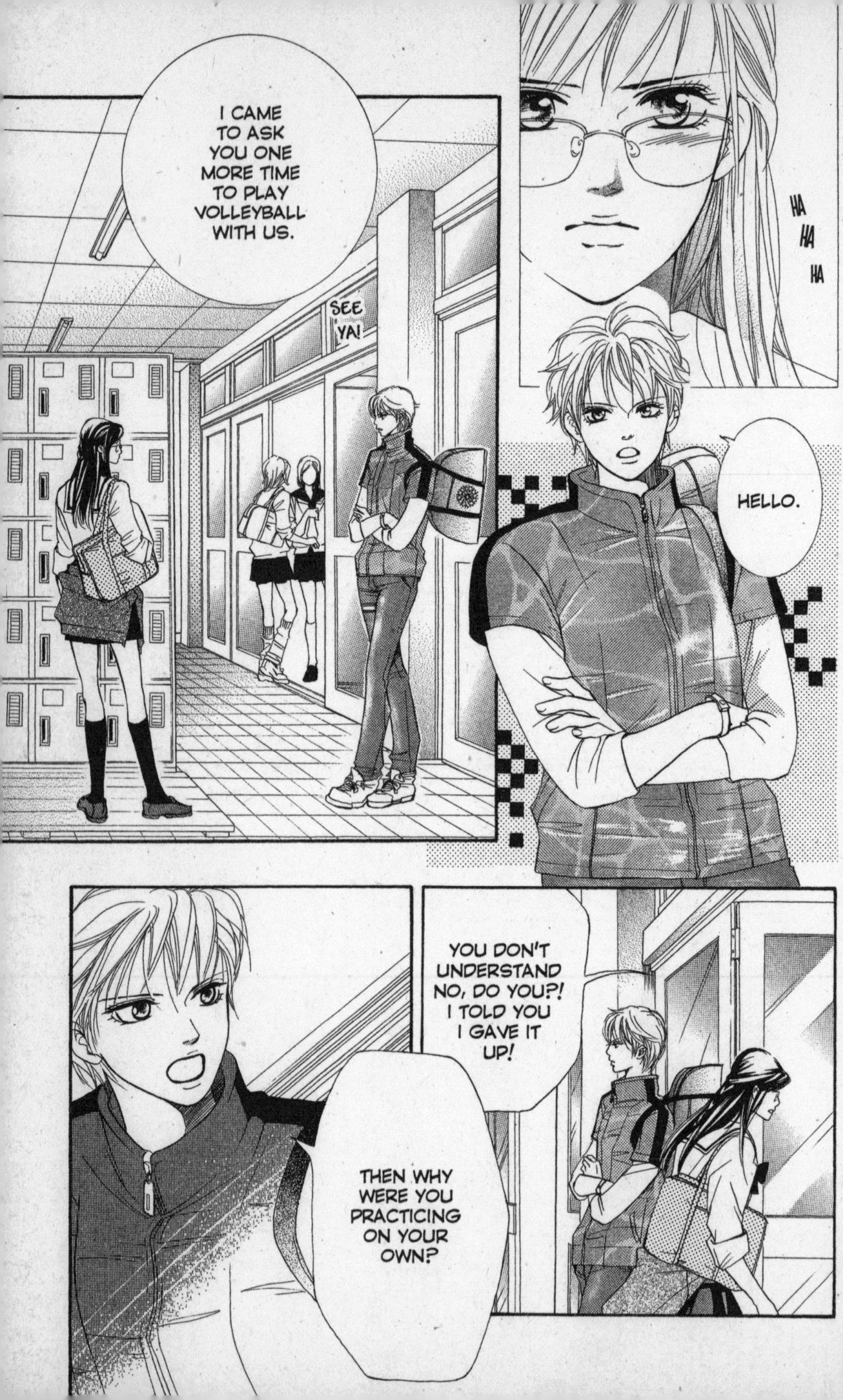
HA
HA
HA
HELLO.
I CAME TO ASK YOU ONE MORE TIME TO PLAY VOLLEYBALL WITH US.
SEE YA!
YOU DON'T UNDERSTAND NO, DO YOU?! I TOLD YOU I GAVE IT UP!
THEN WHY WERE YOU PRACTICING ON YOUR OWN?

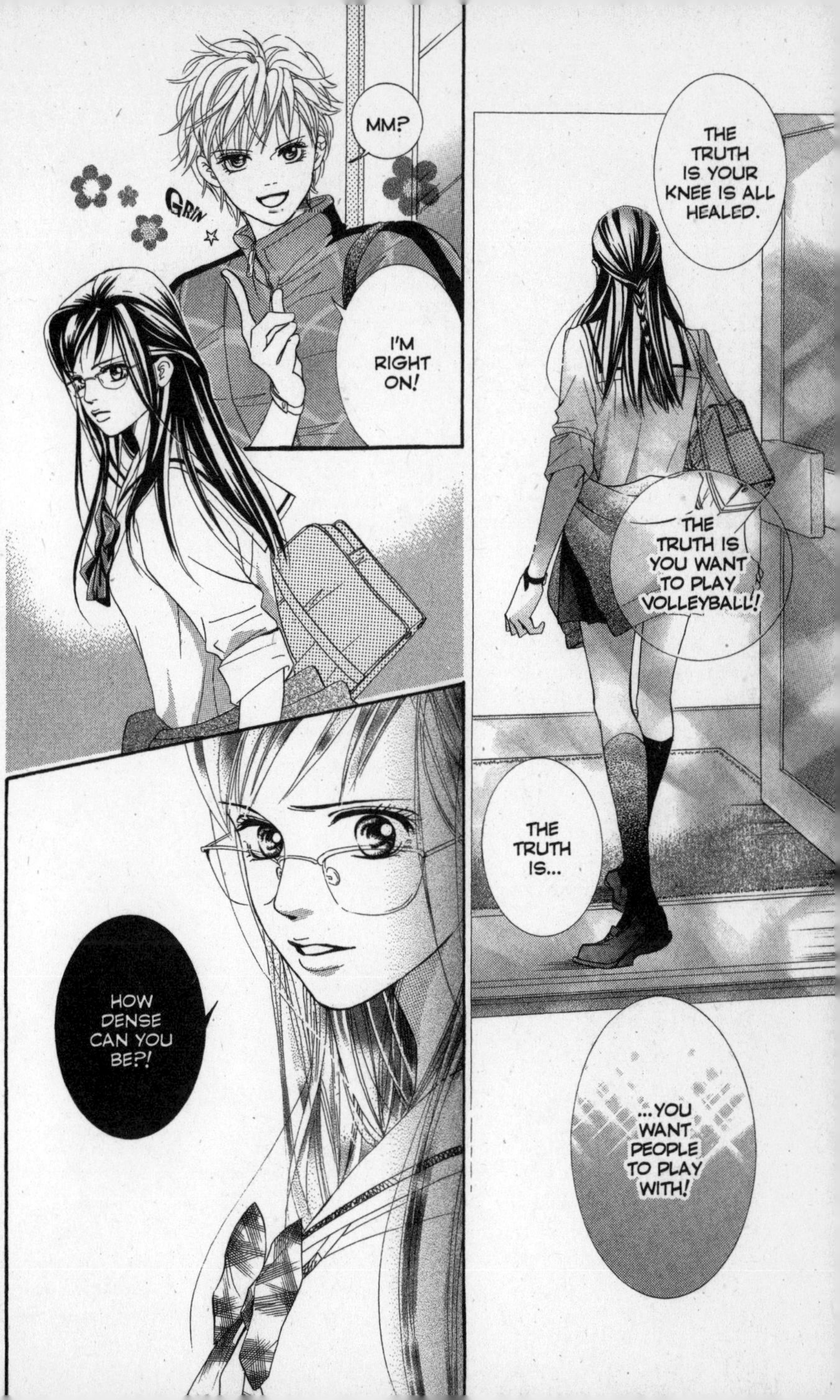
THE TRUTH IS YOUR KNEE IS ALL HEALED.
THE TRUTH IS YOU WANT TO PLAY VOLLEYBALL!
THE TRUTH IS...
...YOU WANT PEOPLE TO PLAY WITH!
MM?
GRIN
I'M RIGHT ON!
HOW DENSE CAN YOU BE?!

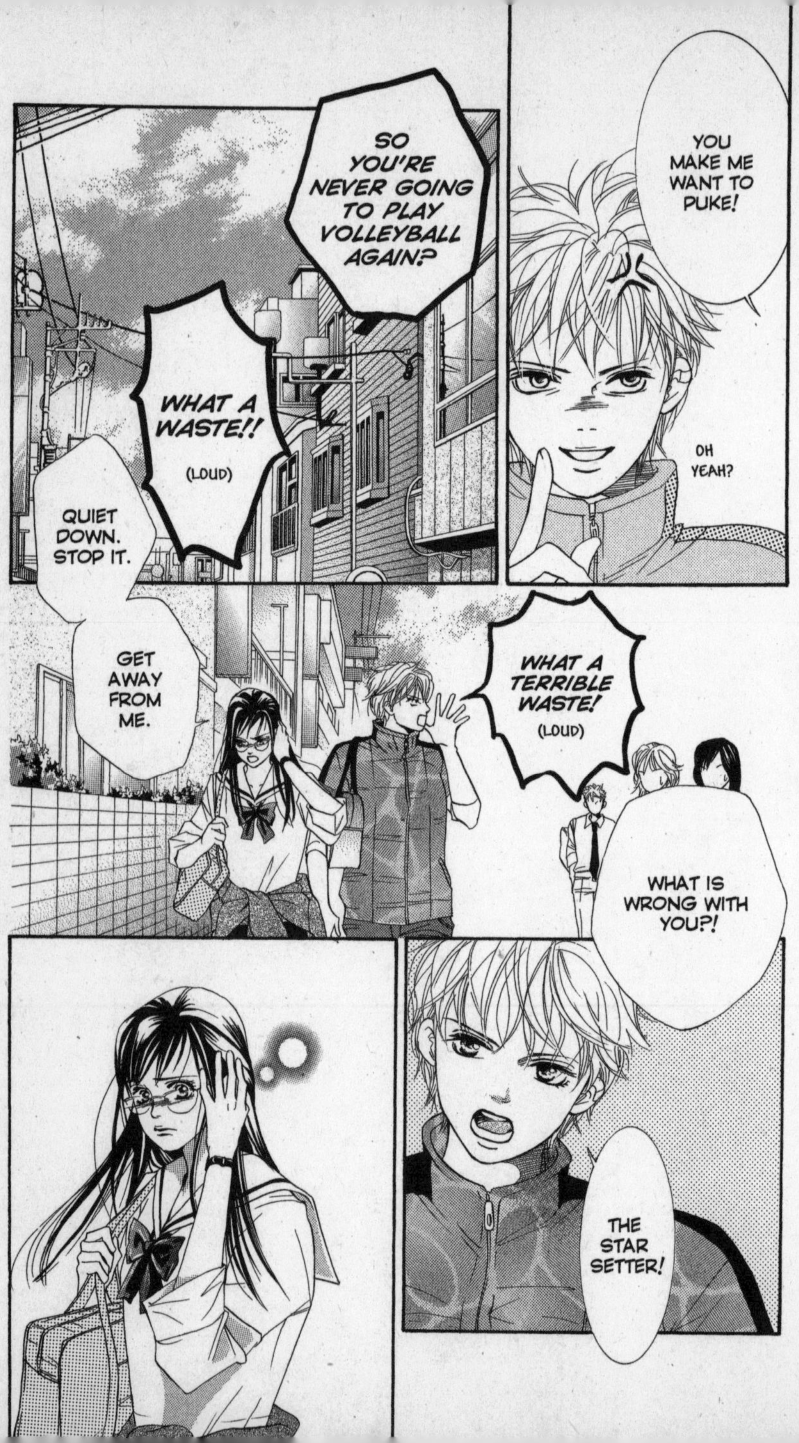
YOU MAKE ME WANT TO PUKE!
OH YEAH?
SO YOU'RE NEVER GOING TO PLAY VOLLEYBALL AGAIN?
WHAT A WASTE!!
(LOUD)
QUIET DOWN. STOP IT.
WHAT A TERRIBLE WASTE!
(LOUD)
GET AWAY FROM ME.
WHAT IS WRONG WITH YOU?!
THE STAR SETTER!

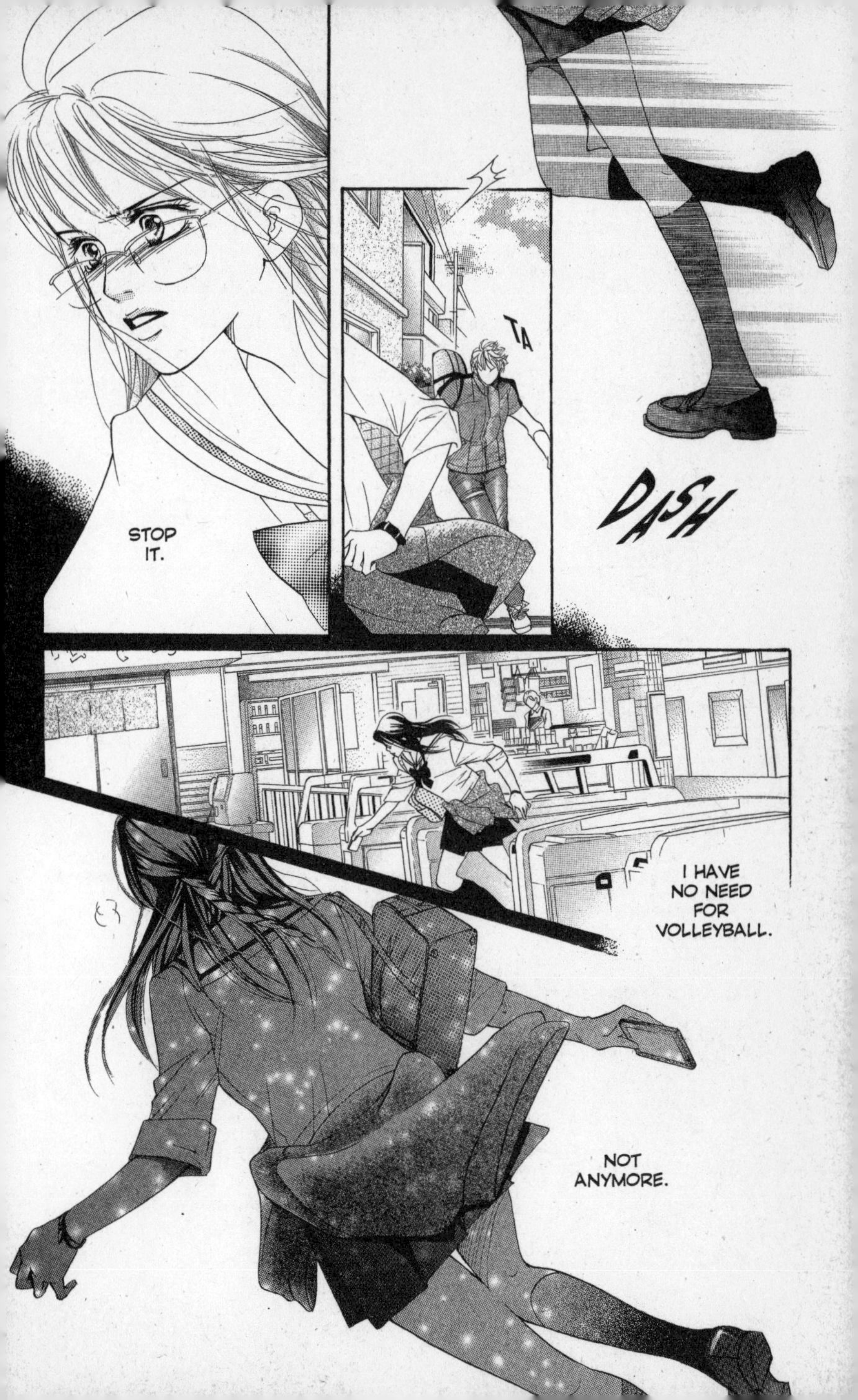
DASH
TA
STOP IT.
I HAVE NO NEED FOR VOLLEYBALL.
NOT ANYMORE.

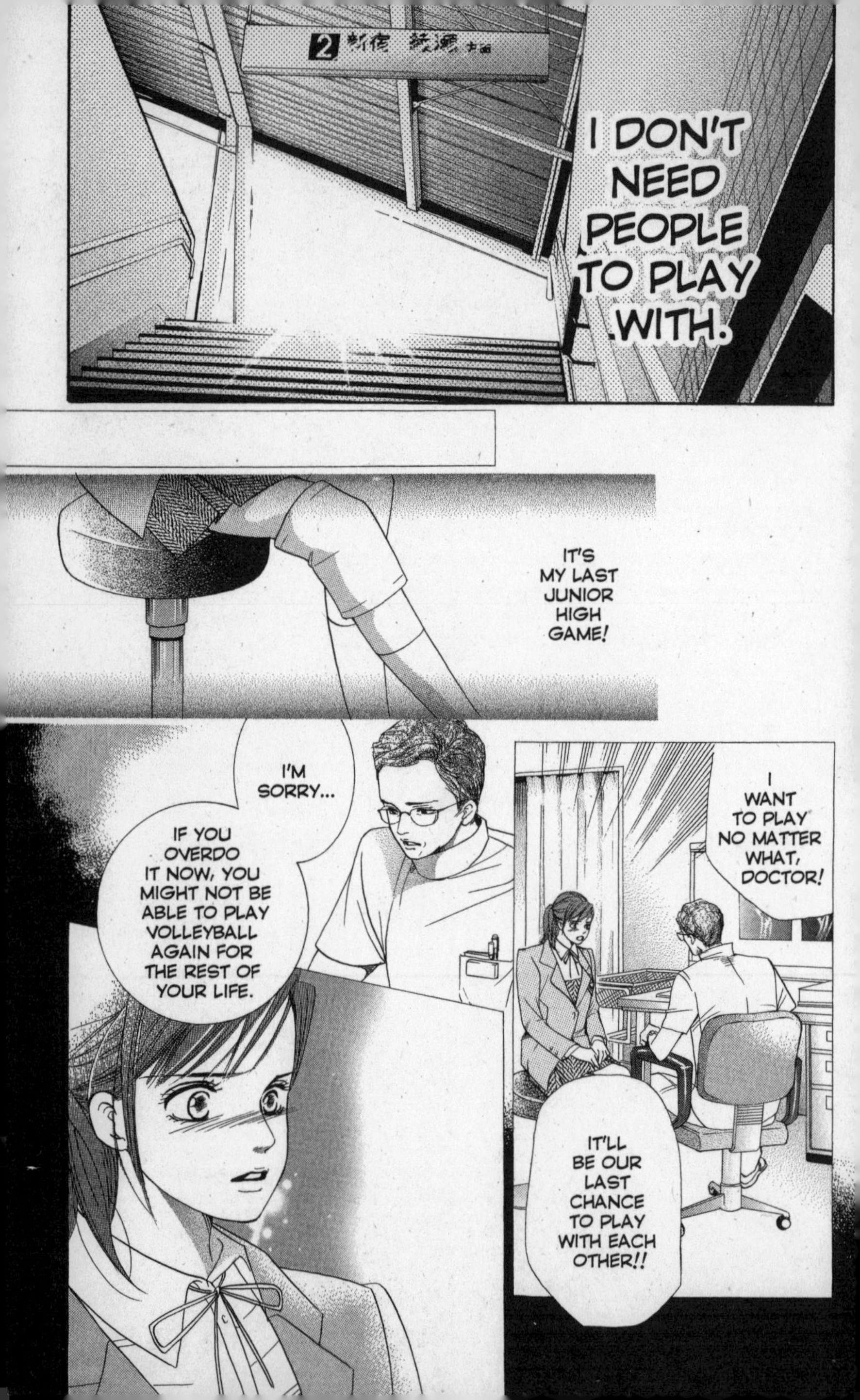
I DON'T NEED PEOPLE TO PLAY WITH.
IT'S MY LAST JUNIOR HIGH GAME!
I WANT TO PLAY NO MATTER WHAT, DOCTOR!
IT'LL BE OUR LAST CHANCE TO PLAY WITH EACH OTHER!!
I'M SORRY...
IF YOU OVERDO IT NOW, YOU MIGHT NOT BE ABLE TO PLAY VOLLEYBALL AGAIN FOR THE REST OF YOUR LIFE.

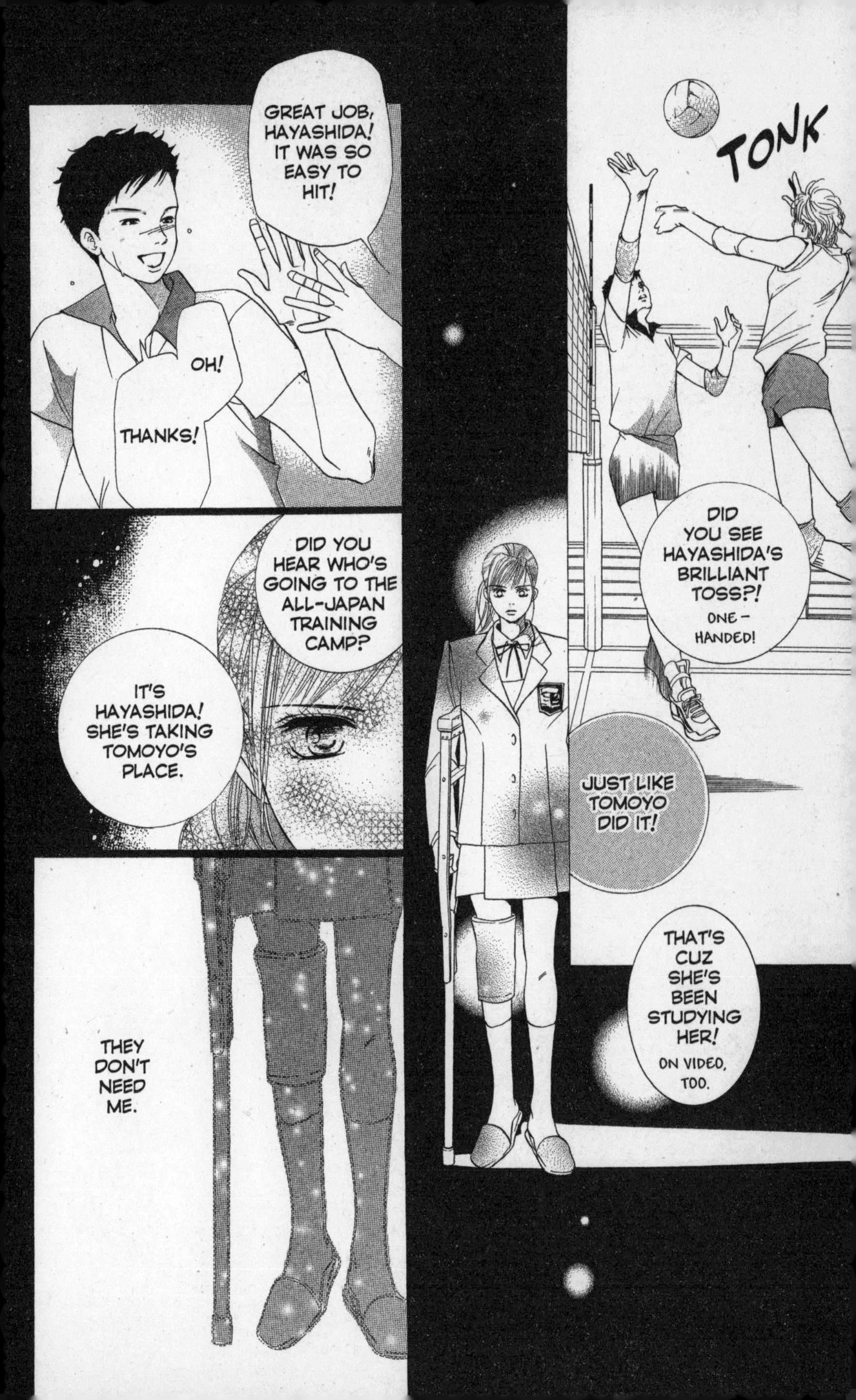

TONK
DID YOU SEE HAYASHIDA'S BRILLIANT TOSS?!
ONE-HANDED!
JUST LIKE TOMOYO DID IT!
THAT'S CUZ SHE'S BEEN STUDYING HER!
ON VIDEO, TOO.
GREAT JOB, HAYASHIDA! IT WAS SO EASY TO HIT!
OH!
THANKS!
DID YOU HEAR WHO'S GOING TO THE ALL-JAPAN TRAINING CAMP?
IT'S HAYASHIDA! SHE'S TAKING TOMOYO'S PLACE.
THEY DON'T NEED ME.

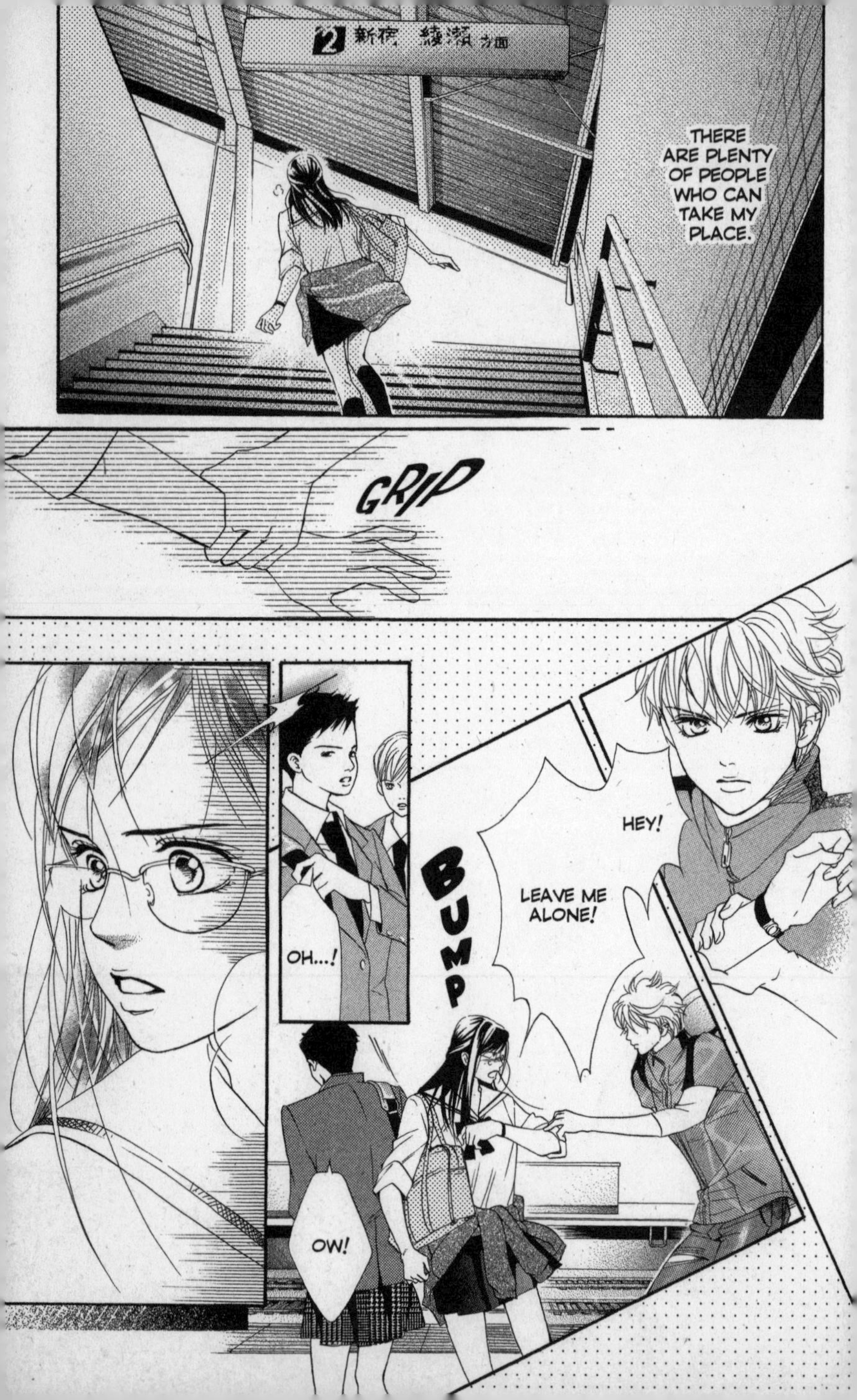
THERE ARE PLENTY OF PEOPLE WHO CAN TAKE MY PLACE.
GRIP
HEY!
LEAVE ME ALONE!
BUMP
OW!
OH...!

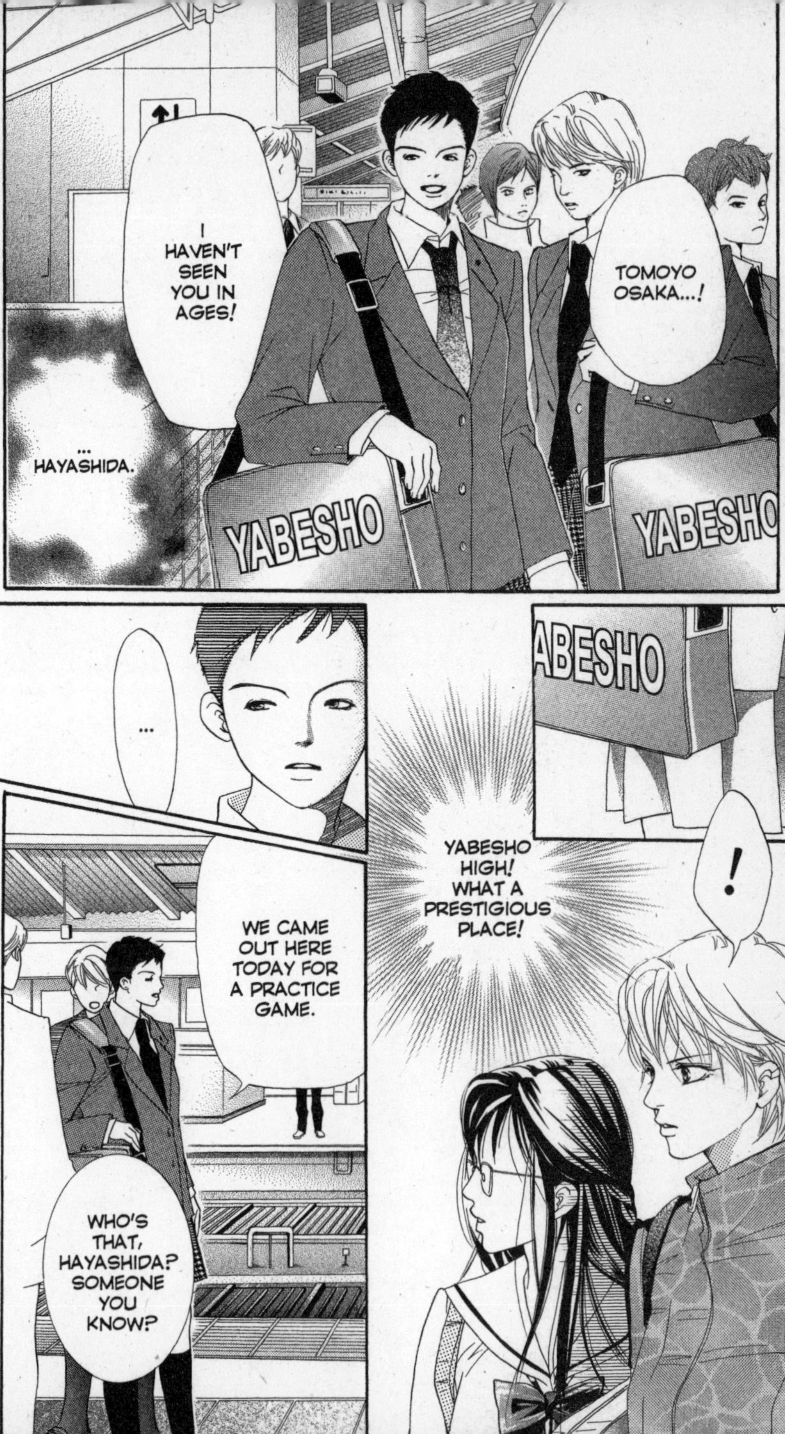
TOMOYO OSAKA...!
I HAVEN'T SEEN YOU IN AGES!
... HAYASHIDA.
YABESHO
YABESHO
ABESHO
...
YABESHO HIGH! WHAT A PRESTIGIOUS PLACE!
!
WE CAME OUT HERE TODAY FOR A PRACTICE GAME.
WHO'S THAT, HAYASHIDA? SOMEONE YOU KNOW?

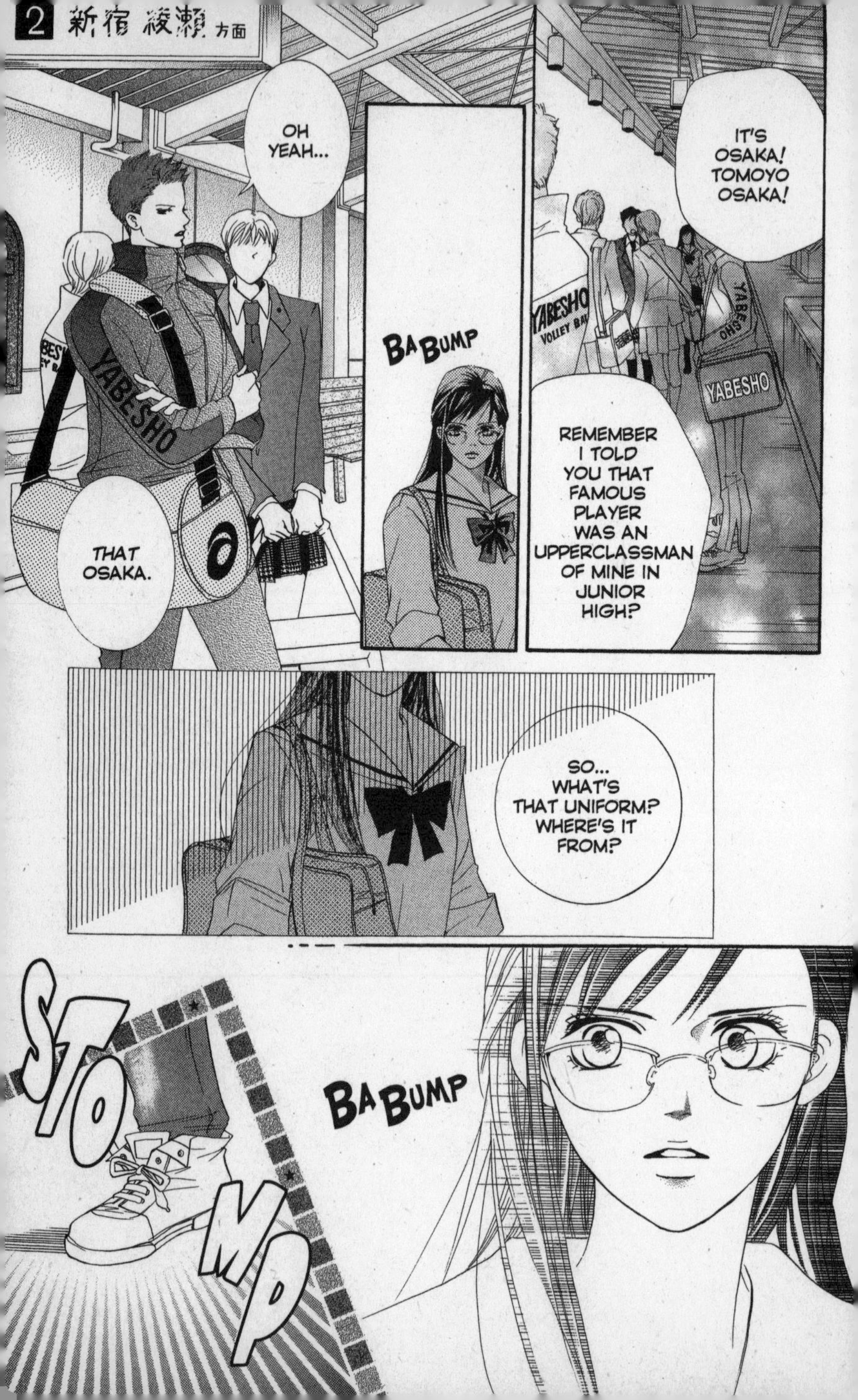
IT'S OSAKA! TOMOYO OSAKA!
REMEMBER I TOLD YOU THAT FAMOUS PLAYER WAS AN UPPERCLASSMAN OF MINE IN JUNIOR HIGH?
YABESHO
BA BUMP
2 新宿 綾瀬 方面
OH YEAH...
THAT OSAKA.
YABESHO
SO... WHAT'S THAT UNIFORM? WHERE'S IT FROM?
BA BUMP
STOMP

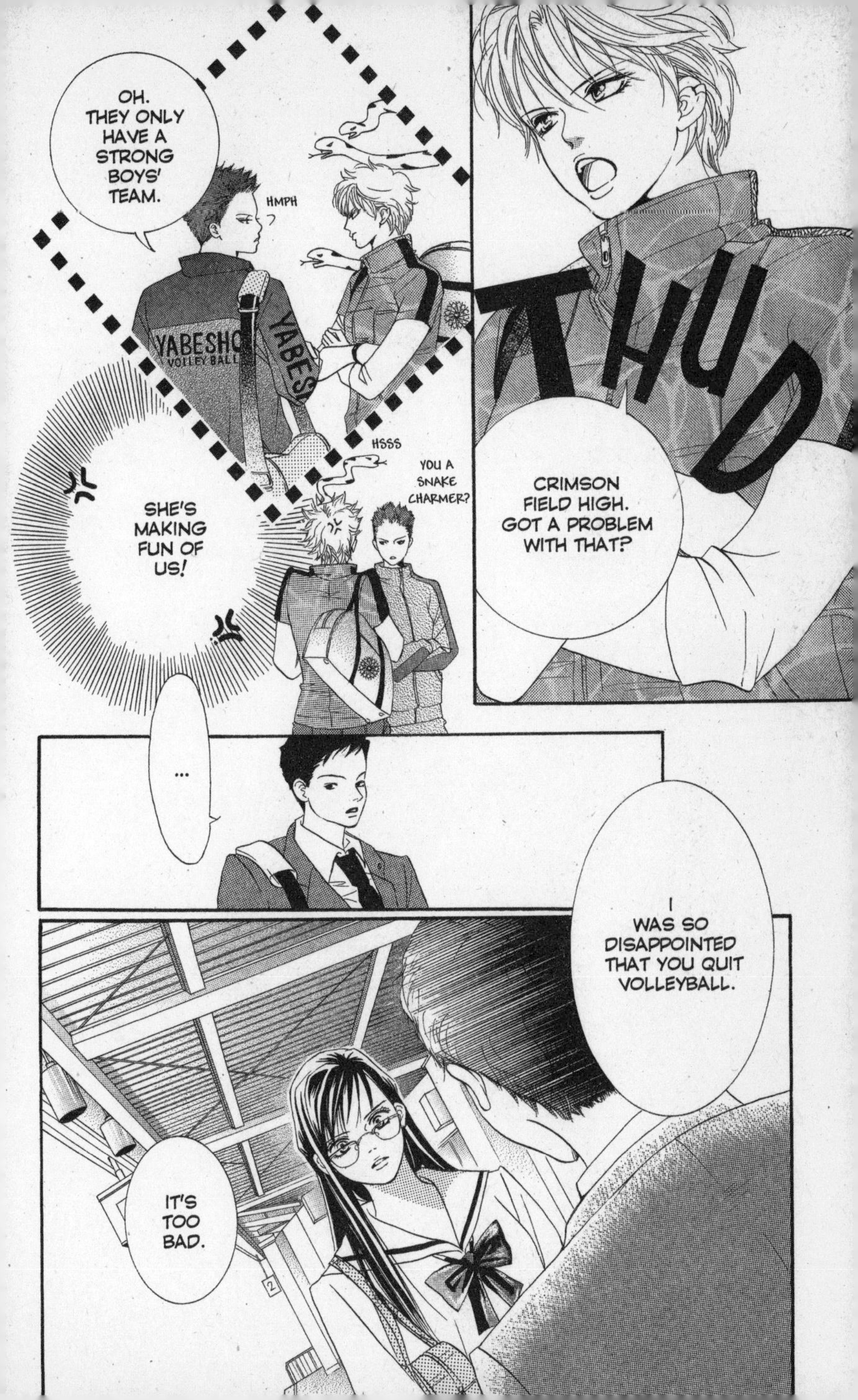
THUD
CRIMSON FIELD HIGH. GOT A PROBLEM WITH THAT?
OH. THEY ONLY HAVE A STRONG BOYS' TEAM.
HMPH
YABESHO VOLLEYBALL
HSSS
YOU A SNAKE CHARMER?
SHE'S MAKING FUN OF US!
...
I WAS SO DISAPPOINTED THAT YOU QUIT VOLLEYBALL.
IT'S TOO BAD.

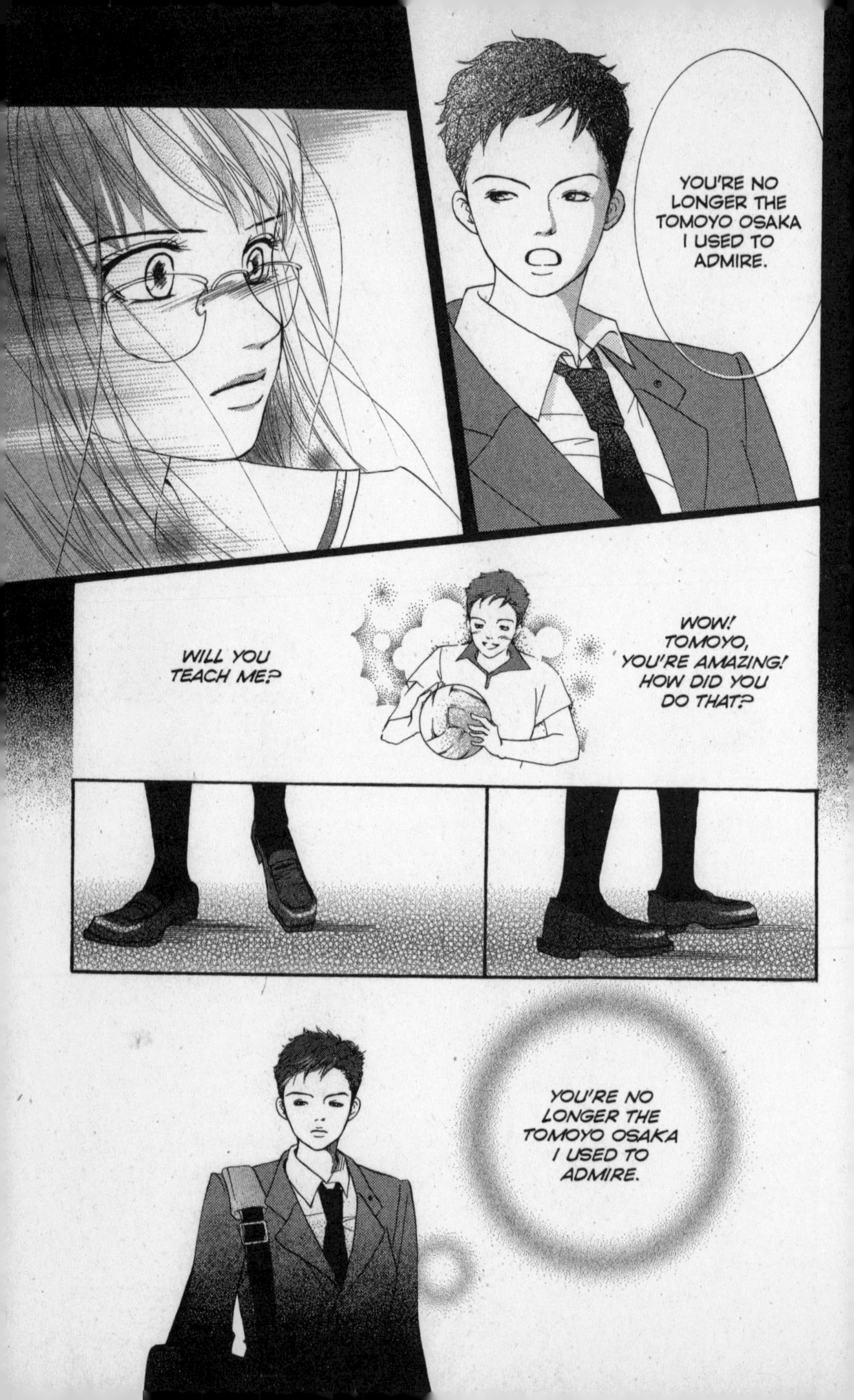
YOU'RE NO LONGER THE TOMOYO OSAKA I USED TO ADMIRE.
WOW! TOMOYO, YOU'RE AMAZING! HOW DID YOU DO THAT?
WILL YOU TEACH ME?
YOU'RE NO LONGER THE TOMOYO OSAKA I USED TO ADMIRE.

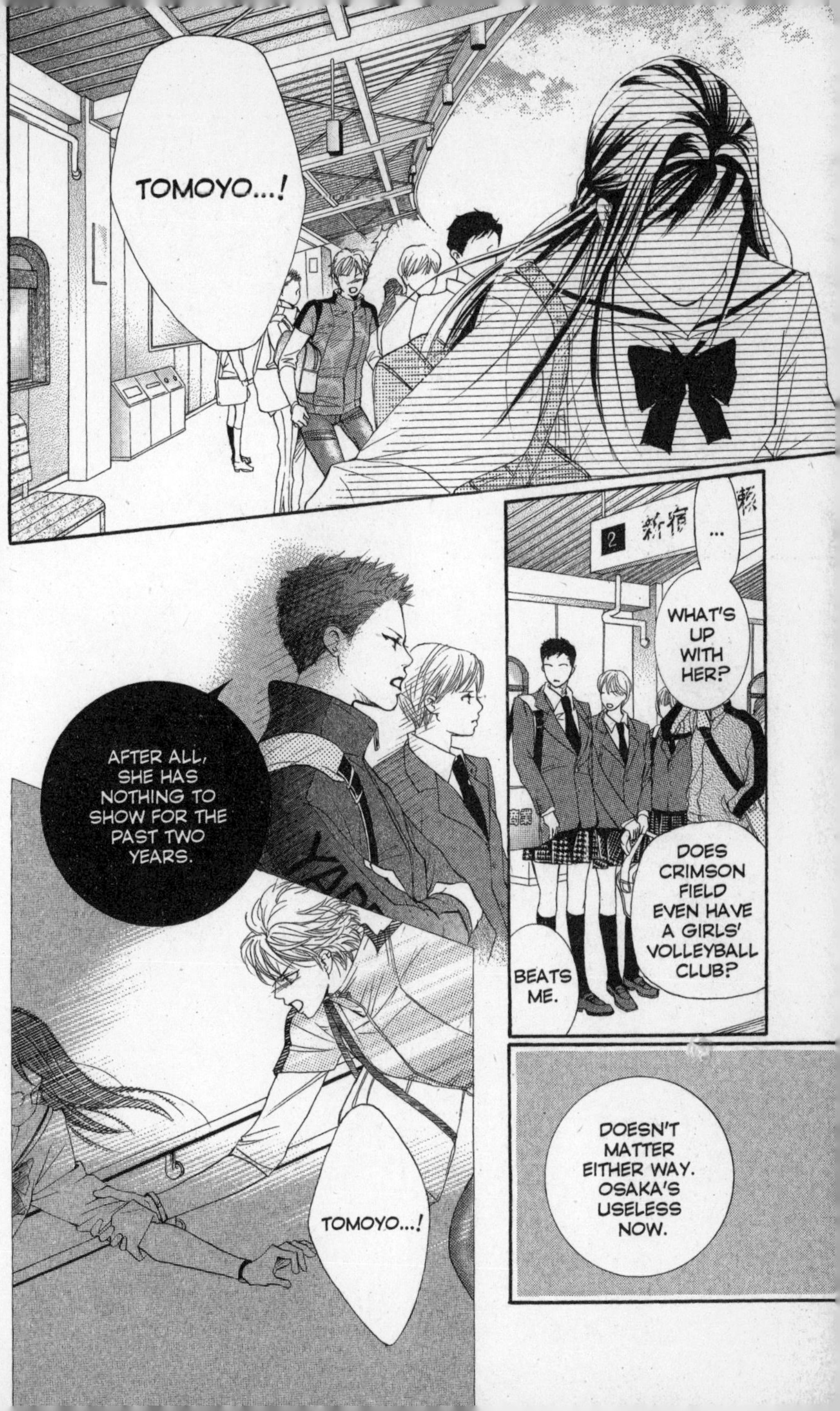
TOMOYO...!
2 新宿
...
WHAT'S UP WITH HER?
DOES CRIMSON FIELD EVEN HAVE A GIRLS' VOLLEYBALL CLUB?
BEATS ME.
DOESN'T MATTER EITHER WAY. OSAKA'S USELESS NOW.
AFTER ALL, SHE HAS NOTHING TO SHOW FOR THE PAST TWO YEARS.
TOMOYO...!

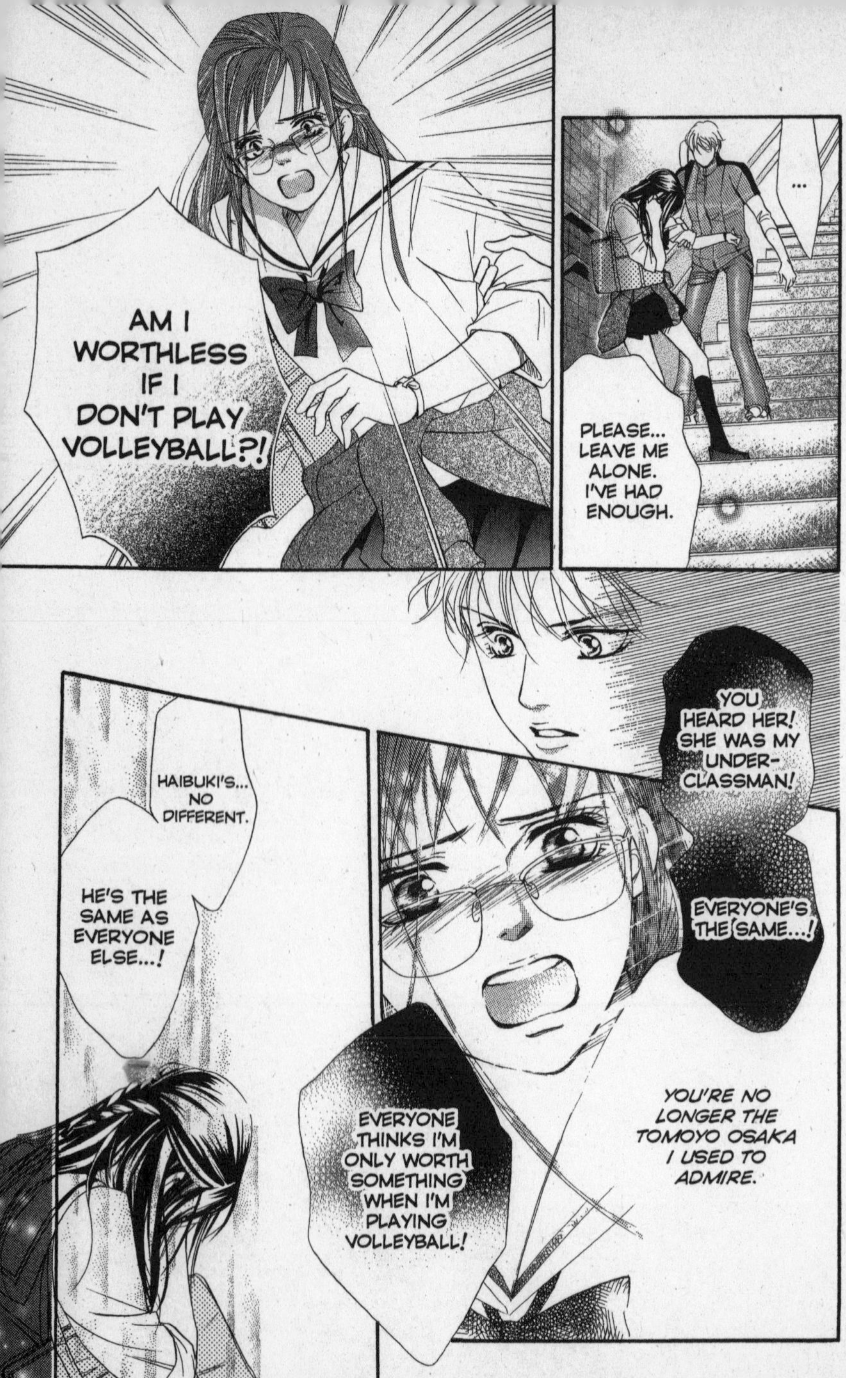
...
PLEASE... LEAVE ME ALONE. I'VE HAD ENOUGH.
AM I WORTHLESS IF I DON'T PLAY VOLLEYBALL?!
YOU HEARD HER! SHE WAS MY UNDER-CLASSMAN!
EVERYONE'S THE SAME...!
YOU'RE NO LONGER THE TOMOYO OSAKA I USED TO ADMIRE.
EVERYONE THINKS I'M ONLY WORTH SOMETHING WHEN I'M PLAYING VOLLEYBALL!
HAIBUKI'S... NO DIFFERENT.
HE'S THE SAME AS EVERYONE ELSE...!

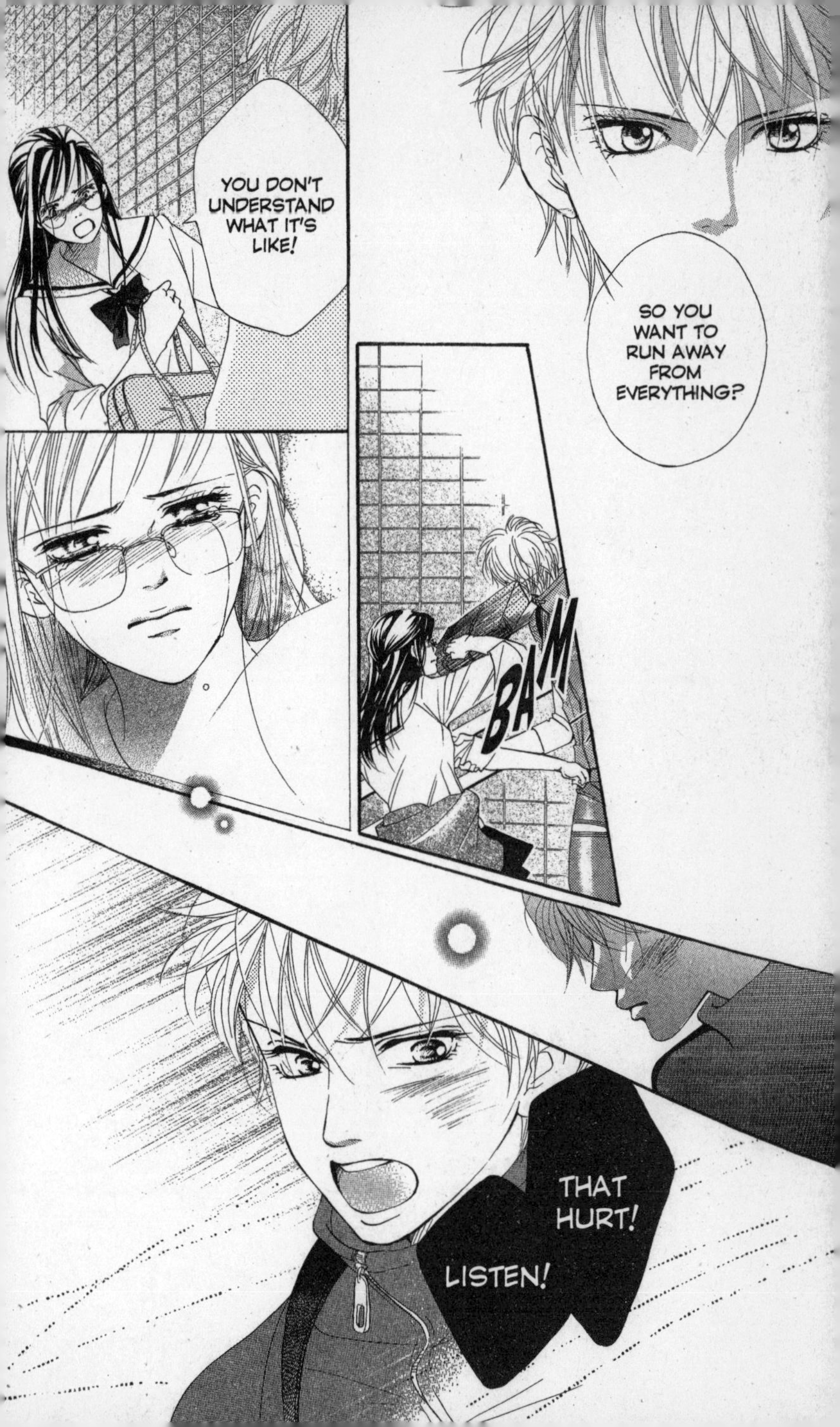
SO YOU WANT TO RUN AWAY FROM EVERYTHING?
YOU DON'T UNDERSTAND WHAT IT'S LIKE!
BAM
THAT HURT!
LISTEN!

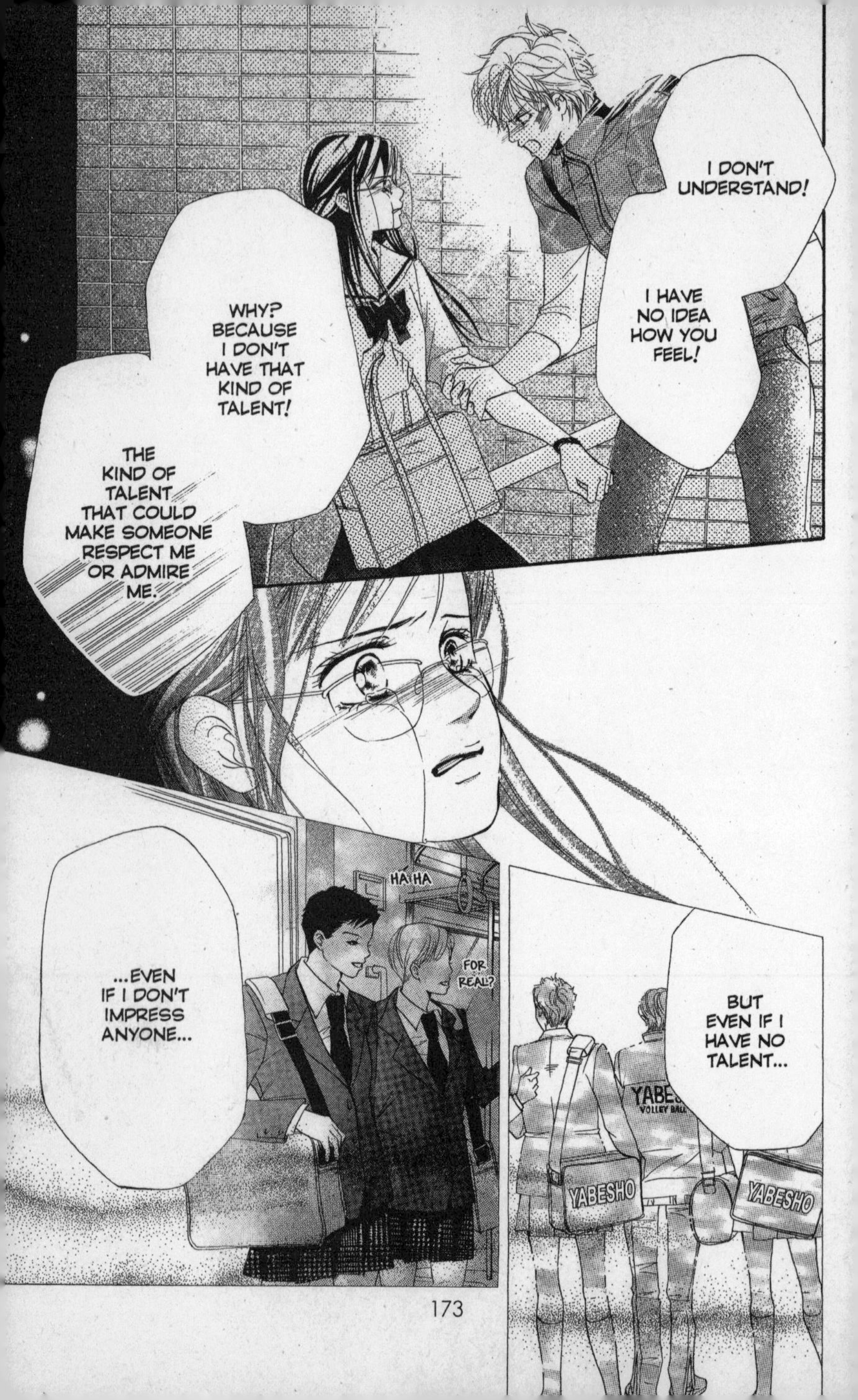
I DON'T UNDERSTAND!
I HAVE NO IDEA HOW YOU FEEL!
WHY? BECAUSE I DON'T HAVE THAT KIND OF TALENT!
THE KIND OF TALENT THAT COULD MAKE SOMEONE RESPECT ME OR ADMIRE ME.
BUT EVEN IF I HAVE NO TALENT...
YABESHO
VOLLEY BALL
YABESHO
YABESHO
HA HA
FOR REAL?
...EVEN IF I DON'T IMPRESS ANYONE...

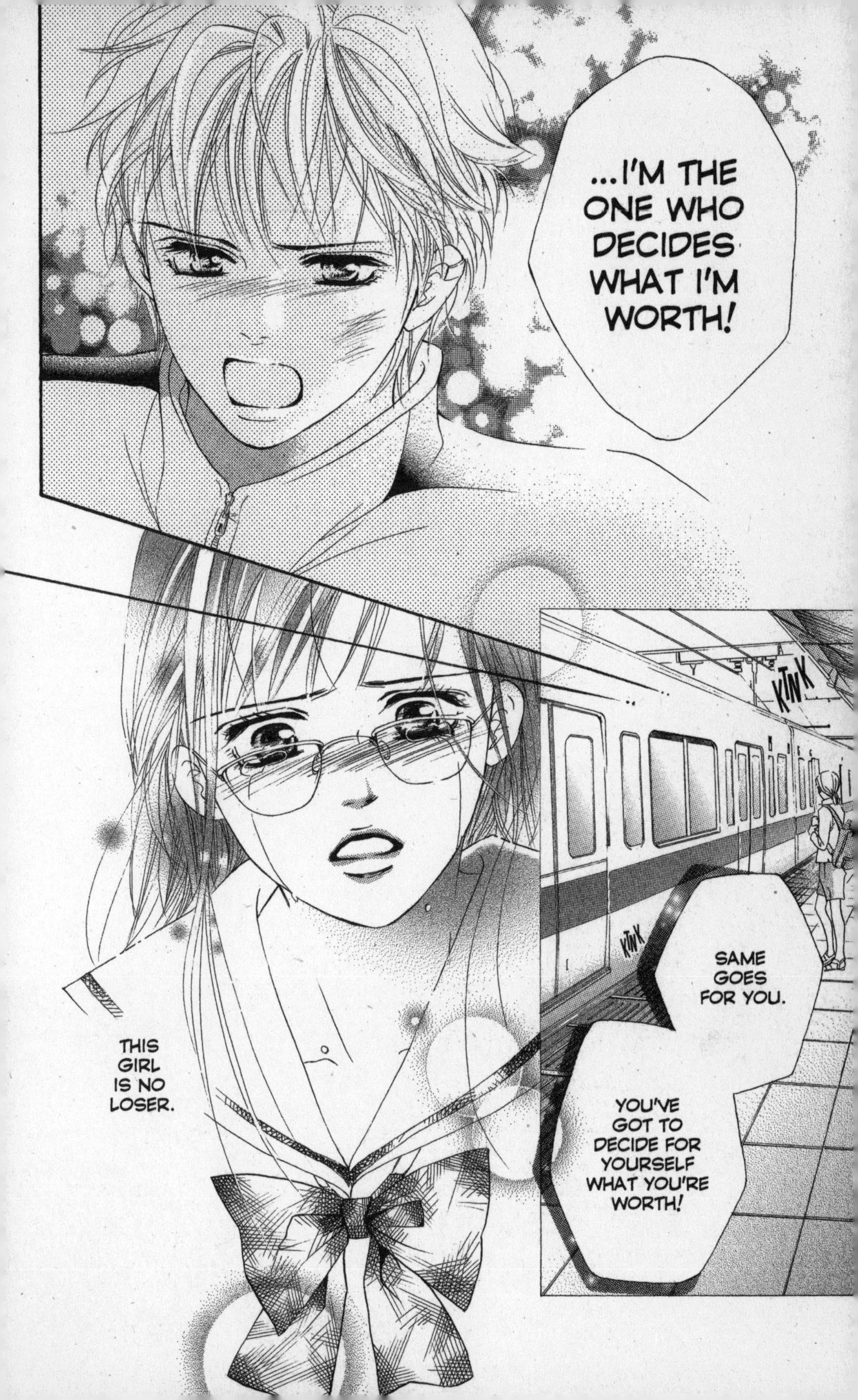
...I'M THE ONE WHO DECIDES WHAT I'M WORTH!
KTINK
SAME GOES FOR YOU.
KTINK
YOU'VE GOT TO DECIDE FOR YOURSELF WHAT YOU'RE WORTH!
THIS GIRL IS NO LOSER.

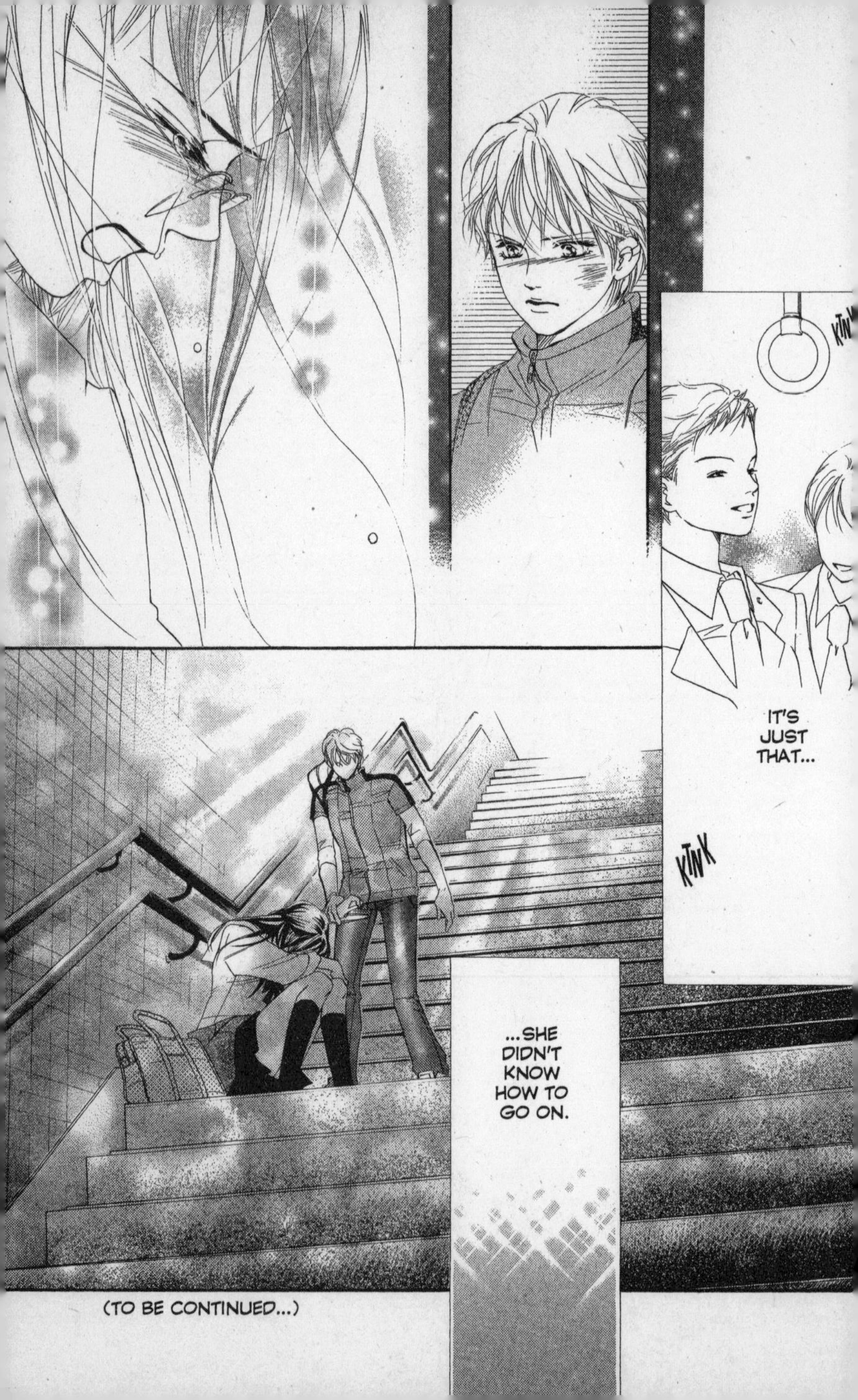
KIN
IT'S JUST THAT...
KINK
...SHE DIDN'T KNOW HOW TO GO ON.
(TO BE CONTINUED...)

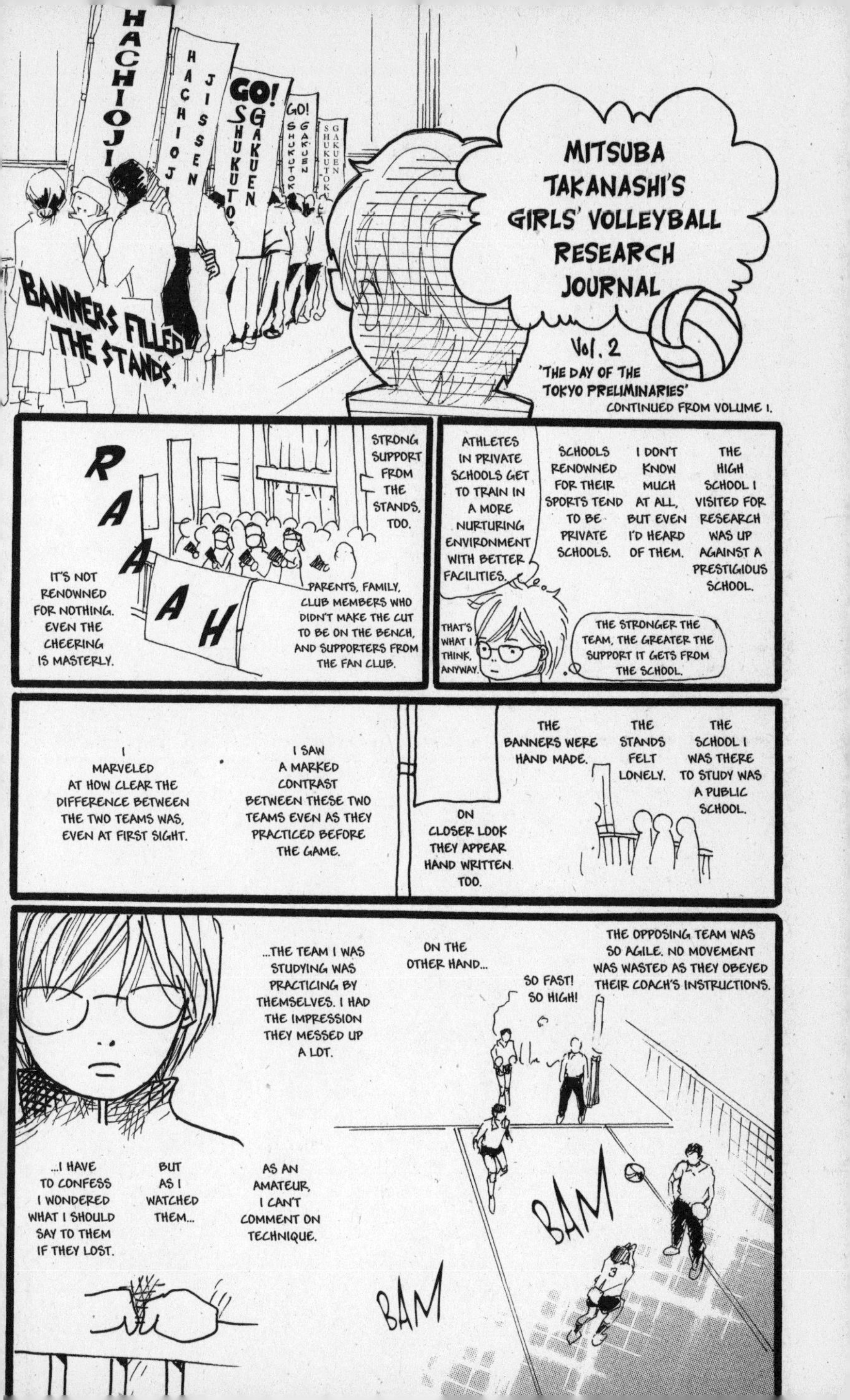
MITSUBA TAKANASHI'S GIRLS' VOLLEYBALL RESEARCH JOURNAL
Vol. 2
'THE DAY OF THE TOKYO PRELIMINARIES'
CONTINUED FROM VOLUME 1.
HACHIOJI
HACHIOJI JISSEN
GO! SHUKUTO GAKUEN
GO! SHUKUTOK GAKUEN
SHUKUTOK GAKUEN
BANNERS FILLED THE STANDS.
THE HIGH SCHOOL I VISITED FOR RESEARCH WAS UP AGAINST A PRESTIGIOUS SCHOOL.
I DON'T KNOW MUCH AT ALL, BUT EVEN I'D HEARD OF THEM.
SCHOOLS RENOWNED FOR THEIR SPORTS TEND TO BE PRIVATE SCHOOLS.
ATHLETES IN PRIVATE SCHOOLS GET TO TRAIN IN A MORE NURTURING ENVIRONMENT WITH BETTER FACILITIES.
THE STRONGER THE TEAM, THE GREATER THE SUPPORT IT GETS FROM THE SCHOOL.
THAT'S WHAT I THINK, ANYWAY.
STRONG SUPPORT FROM THE STANDS, TOO.
RAAAAH
PARENTS, FAMILY, CLUB MEMBERS WHO DIDN'T MAKE THE CUT TO BE ON THE BENCH, AND SUPPORTERS FROM THE FAN CLUB.
IT'S NOT RENOWNED FOR NOTHING. EVEN THE CHEERING IS MASTERLY.
THE SCHOOL I WAS THERE TO STUDY WAS A PUBLIC SCHOOL.
THE STANDS FELT LONELY.
THE BANNERS WERE HAND MADE.
ON CLOSER LOOK THEY APPEAR HAND WRITTEN TOO.
I SAW A MARKED CONTRAST BETWEEN THESE TWO TEAMS EVEN AS THEY PRACTICED BEFORE THE GAME.
I MARVELED AT HOW CLEAR THE DIFFERENCE BETWEEN THE TWO TEAMS WAS, EVEN AT FIRST SIGHT.
THE OPPOSING TEAM WAS SO AGILE. NO MOVEMENT WAS WASTED AS THEY OBEYED THEIR COACH'S INSTRUCTIONS.
SO FAST! SO HIGH!
BAM
ON THE OTHER HAND...
...THE TEAM I WAS STUDYING WAS PRACTICING BY THEMSELVES. I HAD THE IMPRESSION THEY MESSED UP A LOT.
BAM
AS AN AMATEUR, I CAN'T COMMENT ON TECHNIQUE.
BUT AS I WATCHED THEM...
...I HAVE TO CONFESS I WONDERED WHAT I SHOULD SAY TO THEM IF THEY LOST.

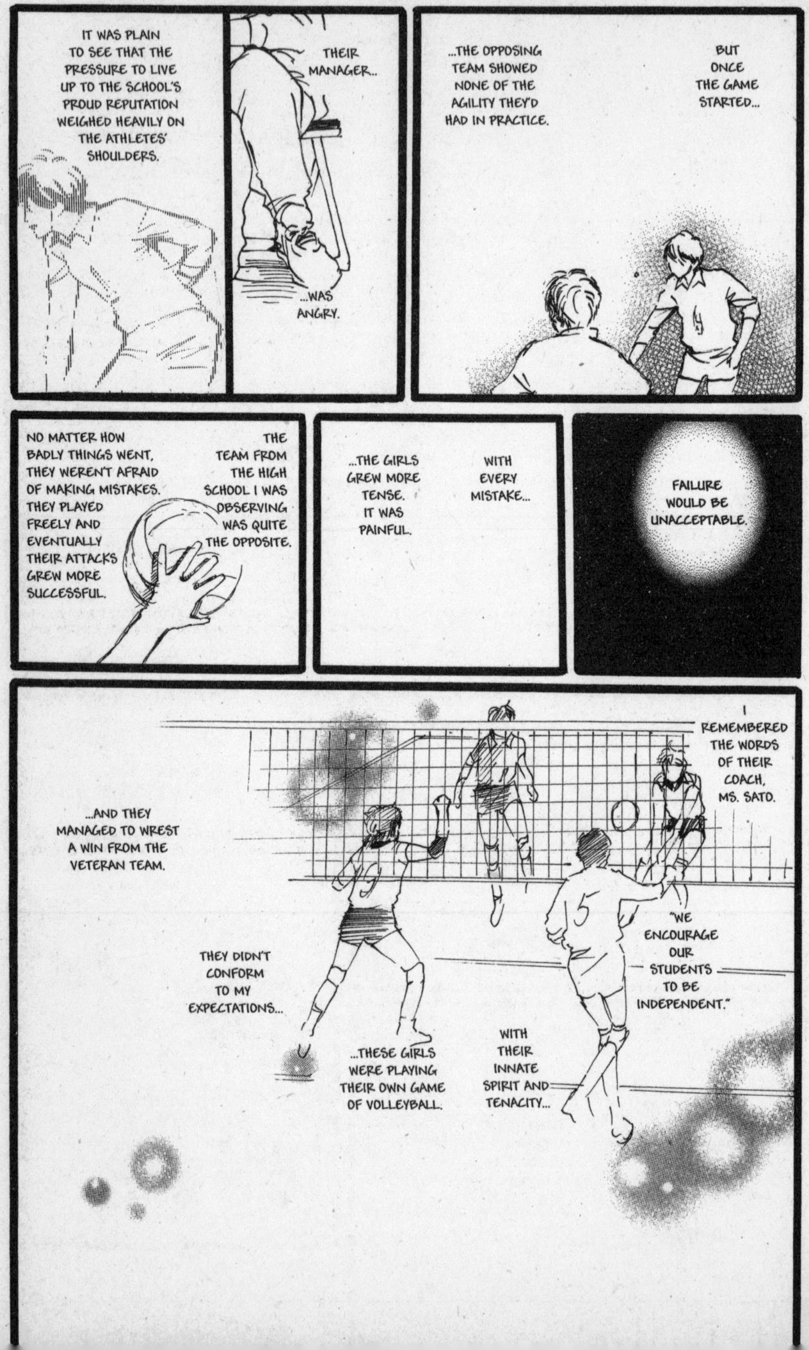
BUT ONCE THE GAME STARTED...
...THE OPPOSING TEAM SHOWED NONE OF THE AGILITY THEY'D HAD IN PRACTICE.
THEIR MANAGER...
...WAS ANGRY.
IT WAS PLAIN TO SEE THAT THE PRESSURE TO LIVE UP TO THE SCHOOL'S PROUD REPUTATION WEIGHED HEAVILY ON THE ATHLETES' SHOULDERS.
FAILURE WOULD BE UNACCEPTABLE.
WITH EVERY MISTAKE...
...THE GIRLS GREW MORE TENSE. IT WAS PAINFUL.
THE TEAM FROM THE HIGH SCHOOL I WAS OBSERVING WAS QUITE THE OPPOSITE.
NO MATTER HOW BADLY THINGS WENT, THEY WEREN'T AFRAID OF MAKING MISTAKES. THEY PLAYED FREELY AND EVENTUALLY THEIR ATTACKS GREW MORE SUCCESSFUL.
I REMEMBERED THE WORDS OF THEIR COACH, MS. SATO.
"WE ENCOURAGE OUR STUDENTS TO BE INDEPENDENT."
THEY DIDN'T CONFORM TO MY EXPECTATIONS...
...THESE GIRLS WERE PLAYING THEIR OWN GAME OF VOLLEYBALL.
WITH THEIR INNATE SPIRIT AND TENACITY...
...AND THEY MANAGED TO WREST A WIN FROM THE VETERAN TEAM.

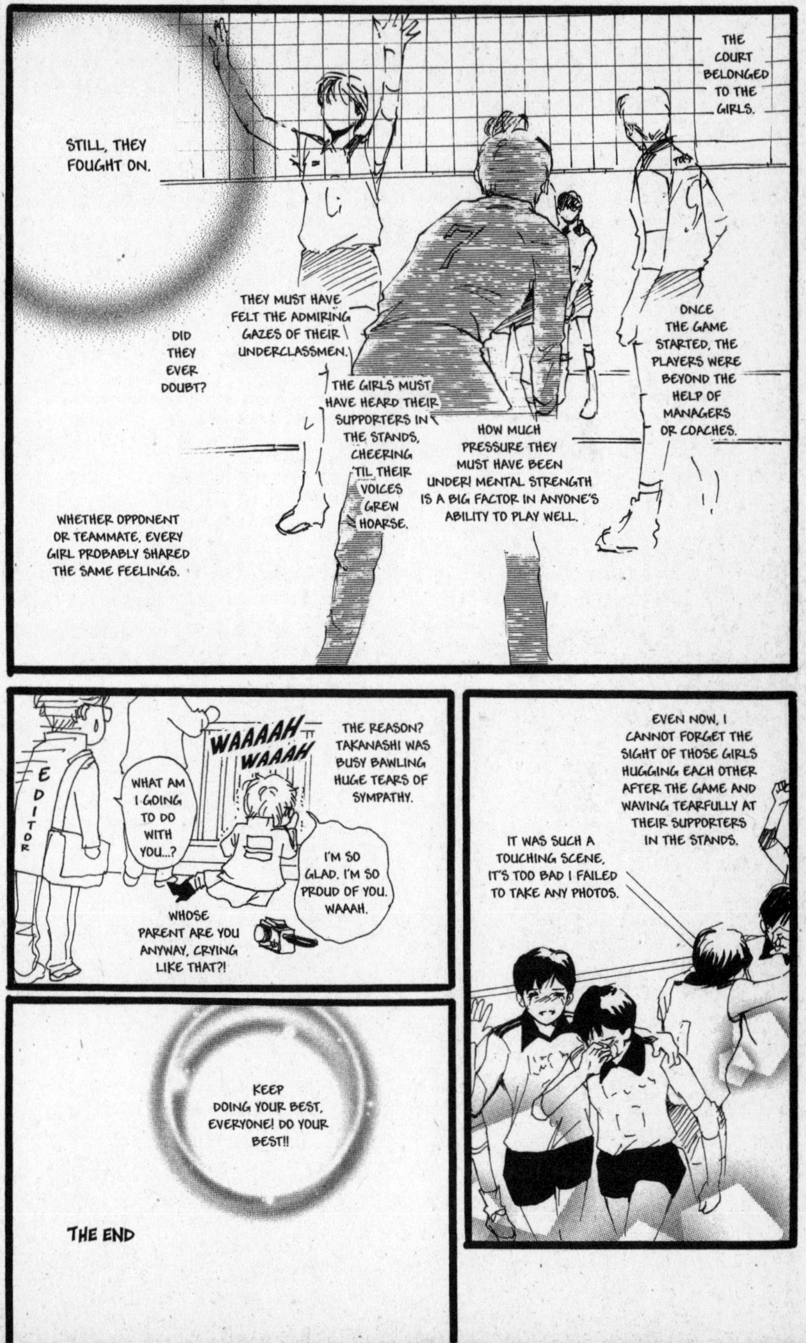
THE COURT BELONGED TO THE GIRLS.
STILL, THEY FOUGHT ON.
ONCE THE GAME STARTED, THE PLAYERS WERE BEYOND THE HELP OF MANAGERS OR COACHES.
THEY MUST HAVE FELT THE ADMIRING GAZES OF THEIR UNDERCLASSMEN.
DID THEY EVER DOUBT?
THE GIRLS MUST HAVE HEARD THEIR SUPPORTERS IN THE STANDS, CHEERING 'TIL THEIR VOICES GREW HOARSE.
HOW MUCH PRESSURE THEY MUST HAVE BEEN UNDER! MENTAL STRENGTH IS A BIG FACTOR IN ANYONE'S ABILITY TO PLAY WELL.
WHETHER OPPONENT OR TEAMMATE, EVERY GIRL PROBABLY SHARED THE SAME FEELINGS.
EVEN NOW, I CANNOT FORGET THE SIGHT OF THOSE GIRLS HUGGING EACH OTHER AFTER THE GAME AND WAVING TEARFULLY AT THEIR SUPPORTERS IN THE STANDS.
IT WAS SUCH A TOUCHING SCENE, IT'S TOO BAD I FAILED TO TAKE ANY PHOTOS.
THE REASON? TAKANASHI WAS BUSY BAWLING HUGE TEARS OF SYMPATHY.
WAAAAH WAAAH
I'M SO GLAD. I'M SO PROUD OF YOU. WAAAH.
WHAT AM I GOING TO DO WITH YOU...?
EDITOR
WHOSE PARENT ARE YOU ANYWAY, CRYING LIKE THAT?!
KEEP DOING YOUR BEST, EVERYONE! DO YOUR BEST!!
THE END